Class, Race, Gender, and Crime

Class, Race, Gender, and Crime

The Social Realities of Justice in America

Third Edition

Gregg Barak, Paul Leighton, and Jeanne Flavin

ROWMAN & LITTLEFIELD PUBLISHERS, INC.
Lanham • Boulder • New York • Toronto • Plymouth, UK

Published by Rowman & Littlefield Publishers, Inc.
A wholly owned subsidary of The Rowman & Littlefield Publishing
Group, Inc.
4501 Forbes Boulevard, Suite 200, Lanham, Maryland 20706
http://www.rowmanlittlefield.com

Estover Road, Plymouth PL6 7PY, United Kingdom

British Library Cataloguing in Publication Information Available

Library of Congress Cataloging-in-Publication Data
Barak, Gregg.
  Class, race, gender, and crime : the social realities of justice in America /
Gregg Barak, Paul Leighton, and Jeanne Flavin.
      p. cm.
  Includes bibliographical references and index.
  ISBN 978-0-7425-9969-7 (cloth : alk. paper) — ISBN 978-0-7425-9970-3
(pbk. : alk. paper) — ISBN 978-0-7425-9971-0 (electronic)
  1. Criminal justice, Administration of—United States. 2. United
States—Social conditions. I. Leighton, Paul, 1964- II. Flavin, Jeanne,
1965- III. Title.
  HV9950.B34 2010
  364.973—dc22   2010008823

∞™ The paper used in this publication meets the minimum requirements of
American National Standard for Information Sciences—Permanence of Paper
for Printed Library Materials, ANSI/NISO Z39.48-1992.

Printed in the United States of America

Contents

List of Tables, Boxes, and Figures

INTRODUCTION

CHAPTER 1

CHAPTER 2

CHAPTER 8

CHAPTER 9

CHAPTER 10

x

List of Figures and Tables

Preface

"Those who won our independence by revolution were not cowards," wrote Supreme Court justice Louis Brandeis. "They did not exalt order at the cost of liberty" (*Whitney v. California*, 274 U.S. 357 [1927]). Not only were the radicals who founded this country brave enough to fight, they were not afraid to articulate their belief in the importance of freedom and argue it through to its logical conclusion: a government dependent on the People, who were free to change it. They wrote in the Declaration of Independence: "We hold these truths to be self-evident, that all men are created equal, that they are endowed by their Creator with certain unalienable Rights, that among these are Life, Liberty and the pursuit of Happiness."

It's a commonly known irony that many of those talking about liberty and equality were slave owners, leading some to wonder exactly how "self-evident" these truths really were. Indeed, the Declaration contains a list of grievances against England to justify violent rebellion, and the original Declaration attacked the king for waging "Cruel war against human nature itself, violating its most sacred rights of life & liberty in the persons of a distant people who never offended him, captivating & carrying them into slavery in another hemisphere, or to incur miserable death in their transportation thither" (Christianson 1998, 66). The passage had to do with the British policy of transportation, whereby convicts—as well as poor people kidnapped for cheap labor—were put on boats bound for Australia or the American colonies. At the request of slave states, this passage was deleted and replaced with the more general "long train of abuses and usurpations."

The Founding Fathers not only had slaves but also prohibited all women and many poor men from voting for a government supposedly "of, by and for, the People." But it is easy to be overly cynical, and Supreme Court justice William O. Douglas reminds us that "the enduring appeal lay in two of its conceptions: First, that revolution can be a righteous cause, that the throwing off of chains by an oppressed people is a noble project; and second, that all men have a common humanity, that there is a oneness in the world which binds all men together" (1954, 3). We hope that a more modern expression of that sentiment would more explicitly include women, but the basic sentiment is correct and shapes the contours of this book. Specifically, we believe in social justice, a concept that will be developed throughout the book, and we strongly value the ideals of freedom and equality. Yet, at the same time, we are all too aware of the numerous current inequalities and ways in which the United States is not living up to its ideals, as well as the intense struggles it took to get the country from the limited notions of equality at its founding to the much more expansive understanding today.

Because freedom and inequality are such large topics, this book focuses on the areas of crime and criminal justice. The criminal justice system has a monopoly on the coercive use of force through the powers of the police to detain, arrest, and use deadly force; the court's power to find guilt and pass sentence; and the prison system's ability to deprive freedom and execute. The law defines what actions are harmful and thus gives direction to the formidable powers of the criminal justice system. "Law and order" can be an oppressive criminal justice protecting privilege in an unequal society, or it can be the call of conscience reminding the country about its promises of equality and liberty. While this book focuses on law and criminal justice, our method is to connect those topics to social structures and inequality. A key to linking these is through the integration of class, race, and gender.

Thus, this book is also about class, race, and gender, which represent some of the most fundamental divisions not only in the United States but also in most other societies. Indeed, Marx argued that all of human history was a class war that involved the struggle between the haves and have-nots—and that law was a tool in this struggle. Feminists point out that Marx's analysis of the workers and owners of the means of production left out women, who were at home doing unpaid housework and reproductive labor; the battle of the sexes is thus also crucial, including issues of sexual access and reproductive control. Finally, race has been a key issue throughout history in terms of conquest and empire, and any honest telling of U.S. history needs to start with whites taking land from Native Americans and building the wealth of the country through black slaves (and other immigrants).

Of course, not only is it important to understand class, race, and gender separately but also how they work in combination. For example, history frequently reports that the Fifteenth Amendment gave the former slaves the right to vote. A more accurate statement is that it gave the former male slaves the right to vote; black women had to wait for the passage of the

Nineteenth Amendment in 1920 before they, or white women, could vote. This book emphasizes the integration of class, race, and gender as a way to get beyond frustrating overgeneralizations about Hispanics or women and to create a more sophisticated or nuanced analysis that can come from looking at multiple aspects of identity. It can also reveal some stark discrepancies, as in chapter 9's analysis of incarceration rates: while 3.4 percent of whites born in 2001 will spend time in prison, 18.6 percent of blacks will; while 1.5 percent of women will spend time in prison, 11.3 percent of men will; while 0.9 percent of white women will spend time in prison, 32.2 percent of black men will.

Some may believe that black men are overinvolved in crime and drugs and thus should have overrepresentation in prison. But the statistics indicate that disparities in street crime do not explain that much of the excess prison population, and whites and blacks use illegal drugs in rough proportion to their size in the population. Further, using street crime as an assessment for how "criminal" a group is leaves out the problem that much harm done by corporations is not criminalized, even though such actions hurt workers, consumers, communities, and the environment. As but one example, a manager's willful violation of safety regulations that results in a worker's death is punishable by a maximum of six months in prison while a few grams of crack cocaine mean a mandatory sentence of five years.

One of the underlying assumptions that drive this study of criminal justice has to do with the fundamental distinction anthropologists, sociologists, and others make between insider and outsider groups. Whether we are talking about matters within nations or between nations, the ages-old interactions and conflicts among social groups have always possessed an element of we/they or us/them. Accordingly, "insiders," or members of one social group, tend to see themselves as possessing virtues not possessed by "outsiders," or members of the other social groups. For example, members of one's own group of origin are typically seen as less violent, aggressive, or criminal and more trustworthy, peace loving, and law-abiding than members of the "other" group.

For many millennia and throughout the world, these ethnocentric beliefs have shaped social relations across lines of what we now think of as class, race/ethnicity, gender, nationality, sexuality, religion, and more. In our own contemporary period, when it is politically incorrect to hold bigoted views about some "others" (i.e., racial and ethnic minorities, women, gays, Jews), it is still politically acceptable to hold such views about "criminals." So when public discourse has dwelled on "welfare cheats" or "violent offenders," what typically comes to mind are racially/ethnically charged subtexts with derogatory images of the "other." In the 1980s, this phenomenon of stereotyping was classically demonstrated when the media and ethnographers alike talked about drug-addicted mothers, perpetuating racial images of African American women trading sex for crack, rather than middle-class white women snorting the more expensive powder cocaine. While pregnant poor and black women became targets of the criminal justice system, middle- and upper-class women escaped scrutiny of criminal justice agents into the confines of private detoxification facilities (Flavin 2009, Humphries 1999). While it is not politically correct to hold overtly sexist views, many still focus on why women stay in an abusive relationship or what a woman was wearing when she was raped rather than asking about why men are violent to women.

In other words, this book treats crime as more than the violation of a legalized social norm and justice as more than the equal application of laws. Similarly, we see the study of crime and crime control as more than analyzing the behavior of criminals and the institutional agents of the criminal justice system. As Visano has emphasized:

> The study of crime is an analysis of being, becoming and experiencing "otherness." Crime is a challenge to a particular socially constructed and historically rooted social order. The study of crime, therefore, is an inquiry into expressions of power, cultural controls and contexts of contests. Accordingly, the designated criminal is set apart and relegated to the margins according to a disciplining discourse about differences (1998, 1).

This book is an attempt to locate the study of crime and crime control in the context of being and becoming persons of "class, race, and gender." And while those terms are typically reserved for the poor, minorities, and women, everyone fits into a class, whites have race, and men have gender. In communicating and experiencing otherness in the social realities of crime and justice, we are interested not only in how class, race, and gender biases become reflected in the administration of everyday criminal justice but also in the roles played by criminology, law, and the mass media to help (re-)create the other. In short, our effort here is to show that "crime" and "criminals" as well as the "criminal justice apparatus" as a whole are socially constructed phenomena, reproduced daily though various discussions in the streets, the media, the home, the governing bodies, the courts, and other cultural bodies; they are a product of moral agents, social movements, political interests, media dissemination, and policymakers (Best 1990; Jenkins 1994; Potter and Kappeler 1998). In the process, crime control becomes the regulation of a relatively small number of acts that have been designated as threatening the social order, and the administration of criminal justice becomes the institutionalized or patterned responses for processing those threats. This way of criminal justice functioning becomes accepted and normalized; ideologies, legal and otherwise, convince people that the patterns are inevitable and just.

For reasons like this, concepts of "equal protection" and "due process" are important, but limited. Although the police might not coerce a suspect into confessing and the defendant might have a lawyer for representation in court, the late Judge David L. Bazelon once noted: "It is simply unjust to place people in dehumanizing social conditions, do nothing about those conditions, and then command those who suffer, 'Behave—or else!'" (Quoted in Leighton and Reiman 2001, 39). Justice Brandeis, in the case noted at the opening of this chapter, would have agreed, because he noted that the Founding Fathers "knew that order cannot be secured merely through fear of punishment for its infraction; that it is hazardous to discourage thought, hope and imagination; that fear breeds repression; that repression breeds hate; [and] that hate menaces stable government" (*Whitney v. California*, 274 U.S. 357 [1927], 375).

The point is that the narrow rational-legalistic conceptions of crime and justice are valid and pragmatic, but they are not sufficient by themselves. Instead, the analysis of criminal justice is strengthened when the broader social, cultural, and historical conceptions of crime and justice are added to the mix, then investigated and evaluated together. This kind of comparative inquiry sheds more light on important (but frequently neglected) questions of "equal justice for all." In the spirit of critical pedagogy, we believe that this type of integrative analysis and its implications can help move the administration of justice closer to the ideals of peace, equality, and human liberation.

ABOUT THE THIRD EDITION

Both the structure (three parts instead of the previous two) and the ordering of the chapters are different from either the second or first editions. The material on criminology and criminal justice now forms Part I to facilitate its use in a larger number of classes and as a complementary read for introductory classes on criminal justice or criminology. After almost ten years of working with and using this text, we believe that we have finally gotten the organization of the material to our satisfaction. This edition provides updated statistics as well as coverage of events (like the financial crisis) and research.

In addition, since the last edition was published nearly four years ago, this version significantly updates the appropriate data across the criminal justice system. We have substantively added and deleted figures and illustrations where needed, incorporated several new content boxes, provided fresher as well as classic examples, and expanded our discussions related to the issues of homeland security, globalization, immigration, privatization, terrorism, torture, the rule of law, and the ebbing and flowing wars on crime. We have likewise fine-tuned and expanded our policy recommendations. Also, sprinkled appropriately throughout this new edition are analyses of the control and regulation of financial crimes involving the likes of Bernard Madoff, AIG, Countrywide, and other banking, insurance, and mortgage companies regarded by some as "too big to fail." We do so within the context of a financial rescue package last reported at the time of this writing as costing the American middle class over decades to come to a whopping $12.8 trillion (Cockburn 2009a). Finally, in light of the ongoing theoretical and empirical developments in the areas of policy inquiry and justice practice, this edition reflects further modification of our evolving analysis of the intersections of class, race, gender, and crime.

Through the changes and updates, we have kept what we believe to be the strengths of the book. It is the only nonedited book in the field to thoroughly address class, race, and gender in relationship to crime and justice. We have kept the chapters that provide substantive introductions to class (chapter 3), race (chapter 4), gender (chapter 5), and intersections (chapter 6). The chapters on victimization (chapter 7), criminal law (chapter 8), policing and prosecution (chapter 9), and punishment (chapter 10) all share a common structure, with headings for class, race, gender, and intersections. As with the previous edition, each chapter starts with an opening narrative of interest that sets the tone for the chapter.

The authors would like to thank Maya Pagni Barak, our research assistant for this edition. Maya collected and delivered many of the updated figures, tables, and other data—and during this process, she provided valuable feedback about the new data that have been incorporated into the discussions in this third edition. Thanks also to Katie Martin, at Eastern Michigan University, for help preparing the manuscript for submission to the publisher. We appreciate the thorough and prompt work of Dana Horton on the index. Gregg Barak would like to thank Eastern Michigan University for a Spring/Summer Fellowship that provided dedicated time for preparing this third edition.

GB, PL, JF, January 2010

Introduction

Crime, Inequality, and Justice

Several bold scholars argue that the criminal justice policies of postindustrial America are the preferred methods for managing the rising inequality and surplus populations of the United States (Michalowski and Carlson 1999; Parenti 1999). *Surplus populations* refer primarily to economically marginal persons and those who are unemployed or unemployable; they are people with little attachment to the conventional labor market and little "stake in conformity" (Anderson 1974). Because of this status, surplus populations are also called "marginal classes" or "dangerous classes." Of course, the war on crime is not publicly discussed as an explicit war on the "down-and-out" or conceptualized as involving the enforcement of inequality and privilege. Usually, it has been described as a war targeting the "bad" and "mad" in the context of law.

But the result of the current war on crime has been to fill an ever-expanding prison system with the poor and a disproportionate number of young minorities. These dynamics are not new, and a historical overview of social control reveals that on the frontier as well as in industrial America, the administration of justice was about regulating and controlling the "dangerous classes." Freed black slaves were subject to harsh Jim Crow laws, and the Chinese were highly criminalized after they finished work on the transcontinental railroad. Still, over time, the criminalizing of behavior has been subject to periods of legal and constitutional reform that have gradually expanded the meanings of "due process" and "equal protection" for a wider and more diverse group of people.

Despite the vaunted democratization of criminal justice during the late nineteenth and twentieth centuries, the effects of crime control have always been to the disadvantage of the nation's most disentitled and marginalized members (Auerbach 1976; Barak 1980; Harring 1983; Walker 1980). When it was a young nation, the political and legal apparatuses of the United States were dominated by the organized power of wealthy, white, and male interests to the detriment of slaves, freedmen, workers, nonworkers, women, people of color, and (ex) convicts. Since our nation's beginnings, then, the various struggles for justice, inside and outside the administration of criminal law, have included the goal of empowering people and granting all access to the same political and legal bodies of rule making and rule enforcing. As the notion of struggle suggests, history is not a linear progression of ever-greater equality. Achievements can result in backlashes, and those who are "more equal" always resist gains of the "less equal." Moreover, new forms of inequality often arise to take the place of old forms, and being granted a right in law does not make it a reality.

The remainder of this chapter provides a series of discussions to help establish the foundation for the rest of the book. The next section provides some brief historical context for understanding class, race, and gender in the United States. Because the book will make numerous mentions of the "criminal justice system," a subsequent section discusses some of the meanings and frames of reference for understanding this system. A third section elaborates on the ideas of social construction and cultural production, as these are tied to both contemporary inequality and the intensification of market society. Finally, we provide an overview of the new and revised third edition.

CLASS, RACE, GENDER, AND JUSTICE: A HISTORICAL OVERVIEW

Class Justice

Throughout most of the nineteenth and well into the twentieth century, a blatant kind of class justice prevailed in the selective enforcement and differential application of the criminal and civil laws to the "haves" and the "have-nots" (Auerbach 1976; Barak 1980). The laws themselves were heavily influenced by a reverence for private property and laissez-faire social relations. In terms of commercial transactions, the philosophy of the day was caveat emptor, "buyer beware." In the area of business, farmers and merchants alike were subject to few regulatory laws of any kind. In other words, both groups were allowed the freedom to expand their particular domains and to compete and acquire both property and capital with little legal interference. By contrast, labor was highly regulated. Unions were an illegal interference with "freedom of contract" and an unlawful conspiracy that interfered with the employer's property rights.

Railroads were crucial to the expansion of the economy at the turn of the century, and companies were amassing large fortunes from this industry. However, they fought attempts at minimum wages for employees and often required employees to live in a company town, rent dwellings from the company, and shop at company stores. The prices charged by the company were usually more than the wage, so families became bound to the company as indentured servants. For industry as a whole, the average workweek was sixty hours. Fatigue, combined with the employers' indifference to workplace safety, created "an appalling record of industrial accidents. An incomplete survey showed that at least half a million workers were killed, crippled, or seriously injured on the job in 1907" (Gilbert 1998, 57).

In other areas, exposes on the meat-packing industry shocked the public and motivated legislators to enact the first Food and Drug Acts. The journalists, called muckrakers, believed that "big business was 'bad business' insofar as it was more concerned with profit than human life" (Lynch and Frank 1992, 13). Lawyers such as Louis Brandeis, who would soon become a U.S. Supreme Court Justice, shared their concerns. He was writing about the "curse of business" and the problems of companies becoming large in the interests of being a monopoly—one that violated public trust rather than worked in its interest. "No country," he wrote, "can afford to have its prosperity originated by a small controlling class" (in Douglas 1954, 187). Justice Douglas (1954) explained, "Brandeis did not want America to become a nation of clerks, all working for some overlord."

The administration of criminal (and civil) justice was chaotic, often corrupt, and subject to the buying of law enforcement and juries (Barak 1980). An independent and decentralized criminal justice system designed for a more homogenized, pioneer, and primarily agricultural society was ill adapted for the needs of an increasingly complex, urban, and industrialized society. A social and cultural environment that was experiencing increasing numbers of immigrants from southern and eastern Europe, a changing means of rapid communication and transportation, and an expanding presence of wage-earning working classes called for a coordinated system of criminal justice.

By the turn of the century, the buying of justice that had prevailed earlier (available to those who could afford representation in the legislatures, in the courts, and in the streets) was threatening the very legitimacy of criminal justice in America (Cantor 1932). The initial laissez-faire emphasis on the right to acquire private property had blossomed into a full-fledged national preoccupation with wealth and power. Political corruption became widespread, and political machines dominated urban areas: "The machines controlled city governments, including the police and the courts. Payrolls were padded and payoffs were collected from contractors" (Edelstein and Wicks 1977, 7). Graft and other forms of bribery contributed not only to the buying of justice by those who could afford it but also to a changing national morality. "Rackets," "pull," and "protection" were common antidotes for stubborn legal nuisances. Prevailing values of wealth and success predominated as guiding principles of right and wrong. "The ability to 'make good' and 'get away with it' offsets the questionable means employed in the business as well as professional world. Disrespect for the law and order is the accompanying product of this scheme of success" (Cantor 1932, 145).

Those who were marginalized, especially the poor, unemployed, women, and people of color, were rarely, if ever, in a position to buy justice. As the marginalized groups of immigrants and others grew in urban cities across America, and as the miscarriages of justice flourished, the need to reform the institutions of criminal justice grew because the country was beginning to experience bitter class wars. The working classes aggressively resisted exploitation through on-the-job actions and wide social movements. To combat challenges to the emerging monopoly or corporate order of industrial capitalism, the wealthy and ruling classes initially employed illegal violence, such as the hiring of thugs and private armies. Later, they retained the services of private security companies, such as the Pinkertons, to infiltrate and break up worker organizations. However, as the number of violent incidents increased, as the contradictions of American democracy became more apparent, other methods for regulating and controlling the masses were needed—methods reflective of a modern, rational system of crime control and a criminal justice system based on a more equal-appearing application of the rule of law (Barak 1980).

During the Progressive Era of the early twentieth century, the plight of the poor gained the attention of some industrialists and political leaders. The discontent of those who were not benefiting from the expanding economy threatened the growing prosperity of those who were. As a response to the growing resentment of the lower and working classes and to the middle-class Progressives who believed in the "perfectible society," the ruling strata sought to stabilize the social order in general and to reform the administration of criminal justice in particular. There emerged a number of reforms, some "hard" and some "soft" (Center for Research on Criminal Justice 1975).

Examples of the harder or technical reforms included the formation of systems of state policing, the initiation of truancy laws, and the forced sterilization of some "mentally defective" persons, poor people, and sex offenders. Examples of the softer or humane reforms included the development of the juvenile justice system, the public defender system, and a bit later, systems of treatment and rehabilitation. Each of these soft reforms aimed at a fairer, more objective, scientific, and humane administration of criminal justice. In combination, these reforms helped secure and legitimate the needs of an emerging corporate capitalism as they contributed to more rational, bureaucratic, and efficient systems of criminal justice. At the same time, these legalistic reforms not only improved the practices and the images of due process and equal protection under the law, they also legitimated greater state intervention into the lives of those marginally defined and segregated on the basis of their class, race, and gender. The practice of forced sterilization, for example, continued until as recently as the 1970s and provided the foundation for chemical castration as well as policies aimed at getting women on welfare to agree to be implanted with the contraceptive Norplant.

Racial Justice

The consistencies in the practice of racial justice in the Americas date as far back as Christopher Columbus and his ill treatment of the indigenous peoples and subsequently to the early colonists' treatment of Native Americans and the institutionalized enslavement of Africans by slave codes. This intense and sustained history of mistreatment has raised questions about genocide in the United States with respect to both Native Americans (Weyler 1992) and African Americans (Johnson and Leighton 1999; Patterson 1970, 1971). Katheryn Russell has shown that one constant remained as the slave codes became the black codes and the black codes became the Jim Crow segregation statutes:

> Blackness itself was a crime. The codes permitted Blacks to be punished for a wide range of social actions. They could be punished for walking down the street if they did not move out of the way quickly enough to accommodate White passersby, for talking to friends on a street corner, for speaking to someone White, or for making eye contact with someone White (1998, 22).

Each of these "systems of racial justice" operated in racially oppressive and discriminatory ways. Some were blatantly racist, and some were subtly so, as in the "separate but equal" ruling in *Plessy v. Ferguson* in 1896 (see chapter 4). In either situation, these forms of racial (in)justice, until midway into the twentieth century, were ruled to be both "moral" and "rational-legal" by the highest court in the land.

Slave codes, from 1619 to 1865, constituted the criminal law and procedure applied against enslaved Africans (Gorman 1997; Oshinsky 1996). The codes regulated slave life from cradle to grave and were virtually uniform across the states in upholding the institutions of chattel slavery. "Under the codes, the hardest criminal penalties were reserved for those acts that threatened the institution of slavery (e.g., the murder of someone White or a slave insurrection). The slave codes also penalized Whites who actively opposed slavery" (Russell 1998, 15). But their primary purposes were to enumerate applicable laws and to prescribe the social boundaries for slaves:

where they could go, what types of activity they could engage in, and what type of contracts that they could enter into. Slaves were subject not only to the administration of separate, special tribunals, but also to procedural practices that did not accord them the same rights as free white men, such as the rights to a jury trial, to be convicted by a unanimous verdict, to be presumed innocent, and to appeal a conviction. Nor were slaves permitted to serve as jurors or to act as witnesses against whites. In short,

> the codes create a caste system under which Whites, Blacks, and mulattoes were accorded separate legal statuses and sanctions. This meant that in addition to the blatant double standards of the slave codes, Blacks were further marginalized by laws that assessed punishment by "degree of Blackness" (Russell 1998, 15).

Under such a caste system, the slave codes of most states allowed whites to beat, slap, and whip slaves with impunity. When it came to sex crimes, especially ones involving interracial relations, racial double standards of enforcement and punishment prevailed. For example: "a Black man who had sex with a White woman faced the most severe penalty, while a White man who had sex with a Black slave woman faced the least severe penalty" (Russell 1998, 16). In fact, more black men were executed for raping white women than for killing white persons. Similarly, under Virginia law, the only law carrying the punishment of castration was the rape of a white woman by a black man. According to most slave codes, however, the rape of a black woman by a white man or by a black slave was not a crime. Under the slave codes, the prevailing modes of enforcing slavery were not only through separate but unequal laws and tribunals but also by the notorious slave patrols, or the precursors to the first American forms of policing. Slave patrollers, working in conjunction with the militia, were allowed to stop, search, and beat slaves who did not have proper permission to be away from their plantations. Slave laws also sanctioned extrajudicial forms of justice, such as "plantation justice," which permitted slave owners to impose sanctions, including lashes, castration, and hanging, and to hire bounty hunters to catch runaway slaves (Russell 1998).

After the Civil War and emancipation, newly freed black men and women were given the right to enter into contracts and to marry. At the same time, the first Black Codes adopted in 1865 created a new system of involuntary servitude, expressly prohibited by the recently adopted Thirteenth Amendment. For example, the adoption of vagrancy laws allowed blacks to be arrested for the "crime" of being unemployed, and licensing requirements were imposed to bar blacks from all but the most menial of jobs in the South. Finally the newly granted rights for blacks served to mobilize white vigilantes, including the likes of the Ku Klux Klan. The harsh nature of racial justice also can be seen by the institutionalization of the "lynching ritual," an extreme form of vigilante racial justice that between 1892 and 1964 claimed the lives of 3,000 to 10,000 black Americans (Tolnay and Beck 1995).

Jim Crow laws began to take hold in the early 1900s following the *Plessy v. Ferguson* decision. These laws mandated separate public facilities for blacks and whites and applied to just about any type of social interaction, including cemeteries, hospital wards, water fountains, public restrooms, church bibles, swimming pools, hotels, movie theaters, trains, phone booths, lunch counters, prisons, courthouses, buses, orphanages, school textbooks, parks, and prostitution (Myrdal 1944). In effect, the segregation statutes and covenants in the South as well as in the North in terms of where "Whites, Coloreds, and Negroes" could rent or buy property, for example, spoke to the way in which these laws sought to effectively regulate both the private and public lives of blacks. Both before and after *Brown v. Topeka, Kansas, Board of Education* in 1954, outlawing "separate but equal," the world of social etiquette made no pretense regarding social equality. Russell offers this explanation:

> Rules of racial etiquette were an integral part of Jim Crow. These unwritten rules required that Black men refer to White men as "Mister" or "Sir." At the same time, however, Whites would commonly refer to a Black man as "boy." The rules governing racial manners also required Blacks to step aside and bow their heads in the presence of Whites. This system of verbal and physical deference reflected the White belief that no matter how much racial equality the Constitution promised, Whites would never view Blacks as their social equals (1998, 22).

African Americans are not the only nonwhite groups who have experienced racial injustice, imposed separation, and cultural imperialism. The thefts of land from Native Americans and the government's subsequent breaking of treaties have left many of them on small, isolated reservations (Lazarus 1991). Similarly, there were the thefts of personal property and land as well as the internment of Japanese Americans in "relocation camps" during World War II. Many Latinos today live in rural and inner-city barrios, not unlike the proliferation of Chinatowns and black and brown ghettos that grew up all across America in the past century.

Patterns of residential segregation have remained the rule, even though "separate but equal" was struck down (Massey and Denton 1993). The social isolation experienced by these racial others has created "many deleterious effects, both structural (e.g., systematic differences in opportunities to acquire disposable income and to generate wealth) and psychological (e.g., being unable to understand what life is like for members of other groups)" (Mann and Zatz 1998, 5).

Gendered Justice

Historically, the differential treatment of men and women—and later of boys and girls—has reflected gendered notions of public and private space. The expression or legacy of a gendered double standard dates back to the chauvinistic sexual customs and conceptions of private property first articulated in ancient Greek and Roman laws (Posner 1992). Until recently these customs explicitly prevailed in U.S. law. Women were considered chattel or possessions of their fathers and husbands, forbidden from holding property in their own names or from entering into business deals or contracts. Women were treated as different or as "second-class" citizens, and they were subject to the patriarchal rules of family, usually under the guise of protecting them and controlling them "for their own good." Whether in the public or private sphere, gendered justice denied women equal protection under the law. In fact, it was not until the 1980s that husbands could be charged with the crime of raping their wives. Moreover, the burdens of legal proof involved in extramarital rape cases before then were always hard to meet, making rape the single most difficult crime to successfully prosecute on behalf of women victims seeking justice from the criminal law.

Early European feminists worked to raise awareness of women's oppression, a tradition that continued in spite of social revolutions in Europe and passionate discourses about equality and brotherhood. Indeed, in the late 1700s, Mary Wollstonecraft, in the name of "sisterhood," observed "the inconsistency of radical males who fought for the freedom of individuals to determine their own happiness and yet continued to subjugate women, leaving them to 'procreate and rot'" (Kandal 1988, 12).

In the United States, few advocates of abolishing slavery saw any connection with women's suffrage. For example, the Grimké sisters used their status as part of a prominent southern family to argue that female slaves "are our sisters" and have a "right to look for sympathy with their sorrows and effort and prayer for their rescue." But the New England abolition society chastised them for forgetting "the great and dreadful wrongs of the slave in a selfish crusade against some paltry grievance . . . some trifling oppression" of their own (Kandal 1988, 214).

With the arrival of the Progressive Era, social reformers sought to address the widespread prostitution and venereal diseases that resulted from the temporary shortage of women that accompanied the great waves of immigration in the late nineteenth and early twentieth centuries. Laws were passed that tried to suppress abortion, pornography, contraception, and prostitution. Federal laws such as the Mann Act of 1910 outlawed the importation of contraceptives, the mailing of obscene books and other materials, and the interstate traffic in prostitutes. The selective enforcement of those laws against the female sellers and the male purchasers of sex remains to this day a de facto component of the social relations of gendered justice and social control.

To be sure, persons handled formally by the criminal justice system and who ended up in prisons through the nineteenth and twentieth centuries were 95 percent male and 5 percent female (Rafter 1990). However, at least since the nineteenth century, the social control of girls and women has also included the patriarchal institutions of marriage and family, the associated treatment of females for their recalcitrance and waywardness, and the medicalization and the hospitalization of their problems (Foucault 1980; Platt 1969).

Women also experienced gendered justice in other ways besides the chivalry that has been shown primarily to white women but denied to other women. For instance, when the first wave of organized imprisonment of women occurred between 1870 and 1900, many reformatories were opened as alternatives for white women. These women were regarded as in need of moral reform and protection. Women's case files in the American West in the late 1880s "rarely expressed an official opinion that an incarcerated female offender represented a threat to society. Instead, parole boards denied a woman freedom because she 'had not been sufficiently punished,' or she 'traveled with bad companions in the past,' or she 'broke the hearts of her respected parents'" (Butler 1997, 226).

While the reformatory movement "resulted in the incarceration of large numbers of white working-class girls and women for largely noncriminal or deportment offenses," such offenses did not extend to women of color (Chesney-Lind 1996, 132). Rather, African American women, for example, continued to be warehoused in prisons where they were treated much like male inmates (Butler 1997). In the South, black women often ended up on chain gangs and were expected to keep up with the men in order to avoid beatings (Rafter 1990).

Gendered justice has also socially constructed the "normal" criminal as male and the "abnormal" criminal as female. In other words, men were seen as rational creatures of culture and women as governed by their nature. Thus, criminology constructed crimes by men as being bad choices that reflected a normal weighing of gain and loss, but crimes by women were seen as "unnatural" because they went against the allegedly docile and submissive "nature" of women (Hart 1994; Rafter 1990). Links have also been made between the "unnaturalness" of female criminality and lesbianism (Faith 1993; Hart 1994).

STUDYING THE "SYSTEM" AND "APPARATUS" OF CRIMINAL JUSTICE

People who think about criminal justice studies do so from a variety of perspectives or orientations. Each of these orientations or approaches to criminal justice study emphasize slightly different "motive forces," or ways of thinking about the evolution and development of law and order. So it follows that the study of the administration of criminal justice in the United States should not be a simple enterprise, even when it is confined to legal-political explanations of criminal justice and not, in addition, to social and economic explanations of justice as well. Complicating the matter further, the administration of criminal justice may be viewed as both a "system" and a "nonsystem" (Bohm and Haley 2004); it may also be viewed as an "apparatus" involving both public and private or state and nonstate sectors (Duffee 1980; Kraska 2004). Hence, when scholars of crime and justice speculate about "criminal justice" in this or any other country, they do so as a means of orienting themselves to various symbolic and cognitive frameworks for understanding the causation of crime and crime control as well as the underpinning of norms, values, and beliefs surrounding the social interactions of the administration of criminal law.

When it comes to the symbolic and cognitive frameworks or motive forces behind the development and expansion of criminal justice over the past half century, Peter Kraska (2004) has identified eight essential orientations or theoretical metaphors to the study of criminal justice. He also notes that four of these orientations are primarily concerned with the formal criminal justice system and that four are concerned with criminal justice as a broader apparatus.

The first group views criminal justice as *formal models of the administration of criminal justice as a system*. These include: rational/legalism; system; crime control versus due process; and politics. The second group views criminal justice as *informal models of a criminal justice apparatus as a nonsystem*. These include: socially constructed reality; growth complex; oppression; and late modernity.

The *rational/legal* theoretical orientation "does not constitute a well-defined area of scholarship. It exists, instead, as a way of thinking dispersed throughout various literatures in criminology/criminal justice" (Kraska 2004, 19). This model argues that criminal justice operations are the product of rational, impartial decision making, based on the rule of law, at least in the ideal, if not the practice. The systems *theoretical* orientation has been considered the dominant paradigm in criminal justice studies for more than fifty years. As a biological metaphor, criminal justice is viewed as larger than the sum of its parts or subsystems—police, courts, and corrections. As a way of thinking, it was also a social movement in organizational behavior, with various stakeholders within the criminal justice system stepping forward to research and study criminal justice primarily as a means to make it operate more efficiently and effectively (Barak 1980; Walker 1992).

Both the rational/legal and systems models view the recent expansion and growth in size and power of the criminal justice system as a "forced reaction" to a worsening, real or imaginary, crime problem rather than a policy choice. The next two orientations, crime control versus due process and politics, require different explanations. These move from a condition of the criminal justice system being forced to act to one where it chooses to act, in a particular fashion, based on the criminal justice system's (or the government's) value preferences.

In terms of the *crime control versus due process* orientations, Herbert Packer (1964) discussed how the criminal justice pendulum swings back and forth, conservatively and liberally, favoring crime control at certain times and favoring due process ("rule of law") at other times. He also made it clear that crime was a sociopolitical artifact, not a natural phenomenon, subject to and dependent upon what we choose to count as criminal, and then, to the ways in which we process (i.e., order versus liberty; efficiency versus equity) those that we define as criminal. The *politics* orientation to criminal justice is inclusive of Packer's two political models, but it expands the political metaphor by assuming that politics "is at play at all levels of the criminal justice apparatus—from the everyday actions of the corrections or police practitioner, to the political influence of local communities, to agencies involved in criminal justice policy formation and implementation, and to law-making at the national and state levels" (Kraska 2004, 206). In short, these two orientations view all criminal justice activity and thinking as interest-based, involving inherent conflicts, power struggles, influence building, and hardened ideological positions.

The next four models, with their focus on the criminal justice apparatus, broaden the object of criminal justice study to include the activities of numerous state and nonstate responses to the crime problem, including: "1) crime control practices carried out by state and non-state entities; 2) the formal creation and administration of criminal law carried out by legislators, the police, courts, corrections, and juvenile subcomponents; and 3) others involved in the criminal justice enterprise, such as the media, academic researchers, and political interest groups" (Kraska 2004, 7–8.) In the context of the larger culture and society, these apparatus-oriented models view the police, courts, and corrections agencies as engaging in ritualistic ceremonies and in promoting various myths of crime and crime control for the purposes of establishing and maintaining their legitimacy in relationship to the prevailing hierarchical order.

For example, the *socially constructed reality* orientations, such as "symbolic interactionism," "dramaturgical analysis," or "moral panic," adopt interpretative approaches to criminal justice that do not assume that reality is predetermined or given (much as the previous four orientations do). In other words, reality, criminal justice or otherwise, is not taken for granted, but rather, it's a human accomplishment. Social realities of criminal justice do not simply exist; they are the result of an intricate process of learning and constructing meanings and definitions of situations through language, symbols, and interactions with other people, crime-fighters and non-crime-fighters alike. They are the products, in short, of believable stories about crime and justice.

Similarly, the *growth complex* orientations to criminal justice are about believable stories of "crime-fighting" and the legitimacy of the criminal justice bureaucracy's survival and growth as a social industry. The arguments for the ideals of equal justice for all, or of administering justice and controlling crime, become subordinate to the divergent and competing interests of the various subsystems of criminal justice, on the one hand, and to the common and mutual interests of the criminal justice system as a whole, on the other hand.

The *oppression* orientations to criminal justice have varied from those that take a more "instrumental" approach to those that take a more "structural" approach; the former arguing that the criminal justice apparatus is simply a tool of the economically powerful to control the behavior of the poor, the disadvantaged, and the threatening classes, the latter arguing that in addition to the instability issues of "class," there are also the instability issues of "race" and "gender." This orientation especially focuses its thinking on the class, race, gender, and other biases that operate in the construction and administration of criminal law prohibitions that help to reproduce the political and social status quo.

Finally, the *late modernity* orientations to criminal justice explain changes in crime and punishment as adaptations to late modern social conditions or risks, such as the rise in economic globalization, telecommunications, privatization, and the decline of state sovereignty. These orientations to recent criminal justice trends locate crime and crime control within the macroshifts of a rapidly changing world, and they attempt to explain how the various responses to crime and injustice over time occurred. According to Kraska, these are potentially the most theoretical of the eight essential orientations because they offer a perspective capable of fusing or integrating the other orientations.

THE SOCIAL RELATIONS OF CLASS, RACE, GENDER, AND CRIME

Examining class, race, and gender in relationship to law, order, and crime control provides an appreciation for the unique histories of the individual social groupings and interrelated axes of privilege and inequality. At any given moment, class, race, or gender may "feel more salient or meaningful in a given person's life, but they are overlapping and cumulative in their effect on people's experience" (Andersen and Hill Collins 1998, 3). For example, Roberts (1993), in her examination of the intersections of crime, race, and reproduction, discusses the convergence between the racial construction of crime and the use of reproduction as an instrument of punishment. She links crime, race, and reproduction to show how racism and patriarchy function as mutually reinforcing systems of domination that help determine "who the criminals are, what constitutes a crime, and which crimes society treats most seriously" (Roberts 1993, 1945). More specifically, in terms of abortion, birth control, and social control, Roberts discusses how this domination is meted out through the control of black women's bodies that discourages procreation, subordinates groups, and regulates fertility. As part of our integrative analysis of class, race, and gender, we also attempt to explore how each of these hierarchies helps sustain the others and how they reinforce the types of crime and justice in our society.

Our study of class, race, gender, and crime reveals that while class, race, or gender may feel more important at a specific point, one is not obviously more important than the others over time or situations. Only by studying their combinations and integrating them can one come to fully appreciate how bias undergirds the construction of what will and will not become criminal, as well as the affects of implementation and administration of those biased rules. This bias also shapes the construction of individual experience and identity, including experience of crime and the criminal justice system.

More specifically, we bring several assumptions to the study of the social relations of class, race, gender, and crime control:

- First, these categories of social difference all share similarities in that they convey privilege on some groups and marginalize others, so they relate to power resources in society. Ideology works to naturalize privilege, so those who have privilege do not see themselves as having it and are much more likely to believe there is a "level playing field."
- Second, systems of privilege and inequality derived from the social statuses of class, race, and gender are overlapping and have interacting effects that can be more than the sum of their parts. Here, 1 + 1 is more than 2, or gendered racism is much more powerful than simply adding gender and race.
- Third, while class, race, and gender privilege all tend to be similarly invisible because of ideology, the experience of marginalization will vary

considerably depending on the specific nature of the prejudice and stereotypes. Understanding marginalization also requires appreciating the diversity within categories—Native Americans represent hundreds of different tribes, Hispanics and Asians represent dozens of different countries and cultures.

- Fourth, there are connections between these systems of class, race, and gender. Few people are pure oppressors or victims, so it is a complex matrix in which everyone is more aware of their victimization than privilege.

As subsequent chapters examine the workers involved in the crime control enterprise in the United States as well as the victims and victimizers/perpetrators/offenders, the analysis incorporates data from quantitative, ethnographic, and social constructionist studies as well as studies related to time and place. While using this array of material, we strive to unravel the complexities of class, race, and gender as they interact with the cultural and social production of crime, justice, and inequality. Our mass-mediated analysis of crime and justice further assumes that the inequalities in crime control and the administration of criminal justice are part and parcel of popular culture, market society, and the social constructions of class, race, and gender differences as these are experienced in relation to one's place, order, conflict, and perception.

Perceptions, public and private, of what constitute unacceptable social injuries and acceptable social controls are shaped by the underlying elements of social organization, including the production and distribution of economic, political, and human services (Michalowski 1985). We are not talking about conspiracies of elites and decision makers here, but rather about crime and crime control institutions that both reflect and re-create the changing nature of capitalist social relations. So "serious crime," defined from above or below, from the suite or the street, and from official reports of the Federal Bureau of Investigation or by the unofficial cultural media, becomes a statistically mediated and socially constructed artifact.

In popularly organized numbers, narratives, and images alike, a distorted view and limited perception of harmful behavior emerges. Crime and criminals are restricted primarily to the tabulations and representations of the conventional criminal code violations: murder, rape, burglary, robbery, assault, and face-to-face larceny-theft. Almost all crimes in the suites, if not ignored, are typically downplayed rather than focusing on human decisions and harms done to society. There are no databases or publications for corporate crime like the FBI has for street crime, so many white-collar corporate frauds and offenses against the environment, workplace, and consumer are not captured in FBI press releases about "Crime in America." Reporters and authors, including academics, analyze data that are more readily available, and those findings get reported in textbooks on criminal justice that focus on street crime.

Culturally produced images of crime and criminals reinforce one-dimensional notions that criminality and harmful behavior are predominantly the responsibility of the poor and marginal members of society. As mass consumers, we all share mediated facsimiles of lawbreakers and crime fighters. Common stories of crime and criminal justice appear and reappear over and over in the news, in films, on television, and in literature, helping to reproduce or reconstruct in the imagination of the American psyche similar renderings of crime, criminals, law enforcement, adjudication, and punishment. It is no wonder that when most people try to picture the typical American crime, the common image that emerges is one of young male victimizers. There are also the numerous police action reenactments that can be viewed regularly on such television programs as *Top Cops* or *America's Most Wanted* that similarly recycle images of these young men as dangerous drug dealers whose dwellings must be invaded during the early hours of dawn by "storm troopers" and other law enforcement personnel in order to pursue, secure, and repress the dangerous faces in the "war on crime." (USA network does have a program, *White Collar*, which focuses on art theft, counterfeiting, and smuggling—not corporate crime or ways in which elites victimize employees, consumers, and the environment. [Leighton 2010])

In like fashion, the images of crime control that are constructed of the criminal justice system as one moves from law enforcement to adjudication and from sentencing to incarceration again serve to reinforce fairly limited and often distorted realities of criminal justice in action. For example, images of a criminal courtroom come to mind from relatively long and involved trials exposed in feature-length films or from *Court TV*'s gavel-to-gavel coverage of celebrated trials, or from other cable network television outlets on the trials and acquittals of Robert Blake for the killing of his wife and of Michael Jackson for molesting teenage boys or the two-time tried and finally convicted record producer Phillip Spector in 2009 of murdering actress Lana Clarkson at the defendant's Alhambra mansion in 2003. The public is also led to believe, based on artist sketches or succinct and curt shots of highly charged courtroom scenes from various television series such as *The Practice* and *Law and Order: Special Victims Unit*, that attorneys for each side, engaged in vigorous battle, always do their legal best to secure justice for all. However, in these dramatizations, whether fictional or "reality-based television" (with editing), the images that do not come to mind are the overwhelming majority of criminal cases (90 percent) that are plea-bargained every day in courthouses throughout America. These negotiated deals in lieu of trials usually take less than a few minutes for judges and courts to process and uphold. The coercion to "go along" is hidden, and they virtually eliminate the possibility of appeal (see Kipnis in Leighton and Reiman 2001).

With punishment, popular images of dangerously violent offenders who need to be locked up indefinitely are prevalent in the media. For more than thirty-five years, politicians have appeared before the media talking about a "get tougher" platform that criticizes the current "leniency" of the previous election cycles. Admittedly, the 2004 and 2008 elections were exceptions; with a virtual crime wave on Wall Street from Enron in 2001 to the global financial crisis in 2007, and the simultaneous decline of street crime, the political candidates were virtually silent on the subject of crime and punishment, as most folks were paying attention to the Middle East wars on terror and to a slumping economy. Nevertheless, such previous campaigns had generally influenced draconian penal policies and made unimaginable even the possibility of ever reuniting the offender, the victim, and the community in some of kind of restorative form of justice. As part of the inherited politics of a war on crime and of the political economy of incarceration and the privatization of penal services, the languages and images of dangerousness and retribution continue to contribute to the United States' more than $100 billion-a-year criminal justice–industrial complex (Dyer 2000; Shelden 1999).

Representations of dangerous offenders convey the images of feuding convicts divided into racial and religious cliques doing "scared time"; not of inmates engaged in school or the learning of a vocation or of former offenders reintegrating or fitting back into society. The recently discontinued and award-winning HBO dramatic series of life in a maximum-security prison, *Oz*, portrayed a based-on-facts fictional account of the complexity of one of those "hell on earth" archipelagos. On the one hand, its representation ignored the social realities of some 1,500 other state and federal prisons of lesser pain. On the other hand, *Oz* did not actually do justice to the still-growing apartheidlike conditions of crime and punishment that disproportionately affect marginally black and brown Americans.

Meanwhile, commercially successful prison films such as *Lock Up* (1989), *The Shawshank Redemption* (1994), and *The Green Mile* (1999) tend to present images of ethnic and cultural diversity in prison as they tell stories of mostly white inmate protagonists in conflict with mostly white correctional antagonists, against a background of "out of control" systems of criminal justice (Horton 1996). In terms of mass culture and the relations of class, race, and gender, box I.1 discusses the celebrated "trial of the century" of O. J. Simpson.

Box I.1. Murder, Criminal Justice, and Mass Culture: A Case Study in Class, Race, Gender, and Crime

One of the most celebrated courtroom dramas of all time was the televised trial of O. J. Simpson for the cold-blooded murder of his ex-wife and her male friend. For more than eighteen solid months, the Simpson case was both a media circus and a public obsession, not to mention a small cottage industry of consumer goods, legal pundits, and television coverage—the latter was still going on in 2004, commemorating the tenth anniversary of the murders. And, legal commentators to this day still make reference to criminal trials in light of the "dynamics" caught up in the Simpson phenomenon that had garnered worldwide attention for eighteen months, from June 1994 to November 1995. The interest, appeal, attraction, disgust, or whatever with this case had much to do with its converging issues of class, race, and gender as it did to the celebrity antagonist of this legal tragedy.

One can also safely say that the Simpson trial, both inside and outside the courtroom, represented the criminal civics lesson of the 1990s, as it socially constructed and reconstructed, over and over again, the general workings of the American systems of law enforcement and criminal justice. The trial became a "crash course" for the masses in constitutional and criminal law and in articulating the rights of the individual versus the rights of the state. Beyond the social realities and legal realisms of whether the criminal justice system was "fixed" or "broken" were the historical experiences and perceptions that whole groups of people, based on the complexities of their class, race, and gender backgrounds, brought to their evaluations of the systems of law and justice in the United States. These real (and imagined) differences in experience of the legal system undoubtedly shape and influence people's views of the administration of justice. The evidence is clear that people's social experiences based on class, race, and gender were more important than the actual facts of the case.

In other words, for the most part, people's views of the criminal justice system and of Simpson's guilt or innocence remained the same from beginning to end. In short, beliefs and attitudes were consistent before, during, and after the criminal trial. Some commentators have claimed that the case was an exercise in the reification of whatever people believed in the first place. Other commentators claimed that the Simpson case represented a Rorschach test of sorts. Thus, people could make anything they liked out of it. We believe that the first of these two claims is much closer to the truth. After all, in reality there were many more "spinners of" than there were "spins on" the Simpson phenomenon (see Barak 1996). For us, however, the interesting question has less to do with the fact that people's views of criminal justice and Simpson remained fairly constant throughout the debacle and more to do with the ways in which class, race, and gender shaped those views.

(continued)

Box I.1. (*continued*)

Take the question of guilt or innocence. Generally, persons from higher socioeconomic groups thought that Simpson committed the murders, and it appears that race and gender made no significant difference. Among blacks, 70 percent thought Simpson was innocent; more African American males than females thought he was guilty. Among whites, 70 percent thought that Simpson was guilty, with slightly more affirmative women than men. How did the jury compare to the public at large? The jury officially voted 12–0 not guilty on the second round of "polling" themselves. On the first round it was different, as one Hispanic, eight black women, and one black man voted not guilty, while the two white women voted guilty. So the breakdowns of the first jury responses appear similar to those of the general public.

As meaningful as some of these differences appear, such black-and-white distinctions were incomplete and misleading to the extent that they failed to poll the reactions of Asians, Hispanics, and other societal groupings. More important, these polls in black-and-white, unlike the more complex and sophisticated polling of the body politic or electorate, failed to break down the interpretations by age, occupation, class, gender, ethnicity, sexuality, religion, and other demographics. Such data would have helped shed light on the background similarities and differences, for instance, between the 30 percent of whites who agreed with 70 percent of blacks that he was not guilty. In future public discussions of crime and punishment, for example, expanded data of other ethnic groups in relation to their socioeconomic and gender positions would help the body politic move beyond simple black-and-white distinctions and move closer to the more complex relations of class, race, and gender diversification.

What were particularly interesting to observe during the Simpson saga were the mass-mediated reconstructions to "normalize" this case within the context of everyday practices of criminal justice in America. In other words, the Simpson case was an aberration in the administration of criminal justice as it departed from the more traditional images and stereotypes of criminal defendants, trial attorneys, expert witnesses, and juries of one's peers. For example, criminal prosecutors and criminal defense attorneys are much more often than not white and male, the bailiffs are usually men and more often than not of color, court reporters are invariably women, and juries, as infrequent as they are, are rarely constituted of one's peers. Typically, juries are from higher socioeconomic classes than criminal defendants. Ordinarily, both the behavior of the police and the credibility of expert witnesses are beyond reproach. That is, they are generally treated with decorum of deference and respect.

In the circumstances of defendant Simpson, the status quo was ripped apart. After all, Simpson was a wealthy African American male accused of murdering his formerly dependent—psychologically and economically—

white wife and her white, working-class male friend in a "sexual triangle" of sorts. Of course, Simpson was also a media celebrity from television and films and a former all-pro running back for the Buffalo Bills, who was able to retain a million-dollar "dream team" of well-known criminal attorneys, eventually led by the once indefatigable, now recently deceased, Johnnie Cochran. In fact, unlike 99.9 percent and higher of criminal defendants, Simpson had "deeper pockets" than the prosecution did. As for the prosecuting team, they were led by the unusual combination of a white woman and an African American man. As for the jury, they were composed of eleven women and one man: nine African Americans, one Hispanic, and two whites, all members of the working classes. Finally, presiding over this trial was an Asian rather than the typical Anglo or Euro-American judge.

These and other differences from the normal relations of class, race, and gender that usually surround a murder trial accounted for the differential applications of the law, or for the special privileges, that Simpson received during his incarceration period, prior to and pending the outcome of his trial. For example, even before the trial began, Simpson reached an unheard-of deal in the annals of American criminal justice history. He was able, through his attorneys, to successfully negotiate a deal with the prosecution that should he be convicted of the double murder, the state would not execute him. Generally, if such deals are reached, the accused has to, in exchange, plead guilty to some crime or another, saving the state the expense of a costly and uncertain trial while eliminating any chances of a nonconviction. Simpson traded nothing except for his incredible popularity.

Similarly, because of the high-powered nature of the defense team, Simpson's attorneys were able to effectively put the motives and competencies of the Los Angeles Police Department and District Attorney's Office on trial. In the process, they raised what appears to have been the "reasonable doubt" in this jury's mind—the key to his acquittal in the criminal trial. In sum, the differences in the management of crime and justice between the Simpson case and the normal-typical case were informed by a novel combination of class, race, gender, and celebrity circumstance.

At the same time, the public reactions to this criminal event were also shaped and influenced by class-based, racial, and gendered experiences with law enforcement and crime control. More specifically, differences in social group experiences with the criminal justice system determine one's trust or lack of trust in justice, or whether one views, for example, the police as professional and competent or as biased and discriminatory. In terms of analyzing the relations of class, race, gender, and justice, ultimately, it is important to account for the diversity of views and experiences.

Barak, Gregg (ed.). 1996. *Representing O. J.: Murder, Criminal Justice, and Mass Culture.* Albany, NY: Harrow and Heston

OVERVIEW OF THE THIRD EDITION

Most studies of crime and justice take a narrow approach and treat crime as simply a violation of a formalized social norm that carries a penal sanction. Justice is equated with the fulfillment of legally guaranteed "due process," "equal protection," or the "rule of law." With the first edition, we expanded on the narrower legalistic meanings of crime control by examining the historical and contemporary practices of criminal justice as they have been shaped and experienced by the rich and poor, by racial and ethnic majorities and minorities, by men and women. We also provided rich contexts for understanding the numerous social realities of justice in America. Our analysis revealed many "social realities" of crime, crime control, and criminal justice, encouraging the reader to see crime and justice from multiple orientations rather than from the more typical one-dimensional orientation of rational-legal thought.

Part of the strength in the first edition was in providing background discussions on class, race, gender, and their intersections, and in the second edition with a more developed, consistent, and systematic examination of these key dynamics examined in twelve rather than six chapters. In the third edition, the chapters from the two parts of the second edition have now been reordered and divided into three parts. We believe that "three times is a charm" and that we have also finally got it right with three parts.

Following this introduction, Part I provides an overview of the history of criminology and the contemporary organization of criminal justice. It is divided into two chapters—"Criminology and the Study of Class, Race, Gender," and "Crime and Criminal Justice Work and the Crime Control Enterprise." Part II provides important general background information, definitions, and discussions of class, race, and gender necessary for understanding the processes of criminalization as well as the administration of criminal justice examined in the third part of the book. The middle section is divided into four chapters—Understanding Class and Economic Privilege, Understanding Race and White Privilege, Understanding Gender and Male Privilege, and Understanding Privilege and the Intersections of Class, Race, and Gender. Part III turns to the criminal justice system, with parallel subheadings for class, race, gender, and intersections in each of the four chapters—Victimology and Patterns of Victimization, Lawmaking and the Administration of Criminal Law, Law Enforcement and Criminal Prosecution, and Punishment, Sentencing, and Imprisonment. Finally, the conclusion provides a summary and overview of criminal, restorative, and social justice as well as an updated set of recommendations and policy considerations for reducing crime and promoting justice.

Part I

1

Criminology and the Study of Class, Race, Gender, and Crime

The story of criminology is the story of three revolutions: the revolution of reason, the revolution of science, and the revolution of reflexivity. These classical, positivist, and critical revolutions, respectively, are spaced roughly one hundred years apart, at 1764, 1876, and 1976. Each of these schools of criminology still has its adherents and is expanding its ideas, methods, and research, and each of these schools still has its relevance to the varied practices of, respectively, equal, restorative, and social justice.

These revolutions in criminological thinking or theory may also be thought of as moving from supernatural to naturalistic to scientific to deconstructive (or critical) explanations of crime and justice. For most of early Western history the dominant theory of crime was the "demonic perspective" (Pfohl 1985) that saw crime as sinful behavior or an offense against God (or the gods). People engaged in crime because evil forces either possessed them or they had succumbed to the temptations of evil forces, such as Satan or demons. Crime was thought to be the result of supernatural forces and brutal methods, including torture, were used to discover and to punish those who were possessed or who had surrendered to the devil.

Up until the middle of the eighteenth century, the demonic perspective was dominant and focused on the supernatural. Then it was challenged by a group of individuals who would become known as classical criminologists. Characteristic of the Age of Enlightenment, classical theory argued that crime was the result of natural, observable, or "worldly" forces, such as the absence of swift, certain, and effective punishments. According to the classical perspective, all people were more or less equal, rational, and free-willed; they had self-control and chose to engage or not engage in crime because they were rationally pursuing their own interests, trying to maximize their pleasure and to minimize their pain. The response to the pursuit of self-interested criminal behavior, therefore, became the rational employment of "swift, certain, and appropriate" punishment to deter potential offenders who calculated the pleasure of crime versus the pain of punishment. This criminology was developed in reaction to the harsh, corrupt, and often arbitrary nature of criminal justice in the 1700s and was inspired by a desire to bring about rational legal reforms. This classical perspective dominated criminology from the late 1700s until the late 1800s, when it was challenged by a more modern and scientific approach, influenced to varying degrees by the introduction of Darwin's theory of evolution.

The positivist school, with its divergent and yet related biological, psychological, and sociological orientations to the study of criminal behavior, argues that criminals are not in fact normal, rational human beings who choose to engage in crime to maximize their pleasure and minimize their pain. Instead, criminals are viewed as different than noncriminals—and it is their differences that compel them to engage in crime. Such "criminogenic properties" call for intervention, reform, treatment, and reconstruction to environmentally control crime and to socially engineer individual criminals away from deviance.

While still the dominant model or paradigm in criminology today, positivism has been successfully challenged by the emergence of the critical school of criminology in the 1970s, which was part of a larger philosophical critique of "value-free, objective, and neutral" social and behavioral science. Rooted in the sixties and in the crisis in American institutions, critical criminology (at least in the United States) reflected the reality that with racism, sexism, imperialism, and other types of inequality, social justice remained an American dream. This "newest" of criminologies stressed the fact that the traditional older criminologies, classical and positivist alike, both ignored and thus left unchallenged the powerful interests that benefit from both the attention paid to crime in streets rather than crime in the suites and the lack of concern about inequality. In contrast, critical criminologies—feminist, peacemaking, constitutive, etc.—turn their focuses not only to the social relations of crime and punishment but also to the very structural forces that sustain them. They examine, for example, the mean streets of American inner cities, complete with drive-by shootings, as well as the cutthroat operations of a deregulated Wall Street where the infamous boys of Enron, Arthur Andersen, and AIG were busy robbing people with very sophisticated Ponzi schemes and other financial manipulations.

Finally, the critical school of criminology focuses its attention on social, political, and economic justice rather than on retributive and therapeutic justice per se. The institutional and structural emphases of critical criminologists move away from policies and practices of adversarialism and toward those of mutualism. In general, critical criminology focuses on the "justice" part of criminal justice by striving to bring about more equitable and peaceful societies, locally and globally.

This chapter provides a foundation for criminology and the study of class, race, gender, and crime. It begins by elaborating on the opening narrative and reviewing the three main orientations to the discipline: classical, positivist, and critical. Following the overview of these perspectives are four sections: Class and Criminology; Race and Criminology; Gender and Criminology; and Intersectionality and Criminology. While there are many other types of inequality present, class, race, and gender are the main forms of oppression today. Subsequent chapters explore these variables in greater detail, and these first three sections help orient the reader to how each variable is important for the study of criminology. The fourth section addresses the field of criminology and the interactions (intersections) of class *and* race *and* gender, because in the real world all of these variables (and more) operate simultaneously. This chapter finishes with a brief discussion of some of the implications of criminology and its relations to class, race, and gender on the greater theory and practice of crime and justice.

CLASSICAL CRIMINOLOGY

Classical criminology emerged and developed during the second half of the eighteenth and first half of the nineteenth centuries in the midst of the Enlightenment period in Europe, especially in France and England because of their strong emphasis on rationalism and humanitarianism. As part of a reaction to the turmoil and disorder in many countries across Europe—to the harsh and barbaric punishments administered by a highly arbitrary state and to the many rebellions and fewer revolutions—the classical school of criminology set out to study the relationship of citizens to the state's legal structure. The emphasis was on reforming the state's antiquated, ineffective, and cruel systems of administering crime and punishment, which would result in increased legitimacy for the state and its rule of law. Influenced by a part of the related logic of two new doctrines, the *social contract* and *free will*, classical criminologists adopted the view that "reason and experience, rather than faith and superstition, must replace the excesses and corruption of feudal societies" (Beirne and Messerschmidt 1991, 286).

Classical criminology builds on the idea of the social contract, Thomas Hobbes's (1588–1679) notion that people create government and civil society rather than pursue their own narrow self-interests in a perpetual, unproductive "war of all against all." Other philosophers explored the idea of a social contract, not as a historic event but as a theory that citizens submit to government in exchange for social order, represented by the idea of an agreement that specified the rights and duties of both people and the government. For example, in the bargain that was struck, citizens were to "surrender some measure of their individuality so that government [could] enact and enforce laws in the interests of the common good; the government, in return, [was to] agree to protect the common good but not to invade the natural, inviolable liberties and rights of individual citizens" (Beirne and Messerschmidt 1991, 287).

As part of the Enlightenment agenda, the doctrine of free will asserted that men, at least those who were free and who possessed property, rationally and voluntarily chose to participate in the social contract. Further, "those who challenged the social contract, those who decided to break its rules, and those who pursued harmful pleasures and wickedness were liable to be punished for their misdeeds" (Beirne and Messerschmidt 1991, 287). The two principal classical theorists were Cesare Beccaria (1738–1794) and Jeremy Bentham (1748–1832), both of whom applied the doctrines of free will and rational, pleasure-maximizing choices to the study of crime and punishment.

Reacting against the cruel and inhumane legal practices of the time, these two leading classical criminologists objected to the inequities in the administration of the criminal law. They proposed substantive and procedural reforms of penal justice consistent with their conceptions of human life that sought to balance the good of society with the rights of the individual. Human beings were to be viewed as responsible for their own actions because they were rational and free to engage in rightful or wrongful behavior. Accordingly, punishment was to fit the social harm caused by the crime, with the formal and institutionalized reactions to crime more important than the informal and individualized efforts to control crime. Throughout the twentieth century and into the present, classical theory has been an integral part of legal and economic thought, and it has influenced the nature of punishment and sentencing in this society, moving it toward and then away from treatment as a rationale for punishment. Recent related approaches would include "crime as rational choice" and "routine activity theory" developed in the 1980s and later (see Cullen and Agnew 1999, chapters 26 and 27).

POSITIVIST CRIMINOLOGY

In the late nineteenth century, the theoretical movement of positivism, which began to study crime as a social phenomenon, buttressed the emergence of a scientifically based criminology. Relying on the point of view of the natural sciences and borrowing from their methodology, positivists sought to analyze crime not by speculation and observation alone but also by the collection of scientific "facts" through systematic data collection and analysis. The positivist analyses of crime, following such disciplines as physics, chemistry, and biology, began a process that still continues of uncovering, explaining, and predicting the ways in which observable facts occurred in regular patterns.

Positivist criminology turned its focus away from law and crime and toward behavior as a reaction to the failures of classical criminology to stem the rising tides of criminality through moral reformation (e.g., religious teachings) and humanitarian reform (e.g., incarceration rather than corporal or capital punishment), and to differentiate between delinquent and pathological inmates (who included the likes of syphilitics, alcoholics, idiots, vagabonds, immigrants, prostitutes, and petty as well as professional thieves). Based on a variety of determining forces or causal factors, positivist criminologists also began to assert that the "treatment should fit the criminal" rather than the "punishment should fit the crime." In effect, the positivist criminology maintained that criminal actions were not the product of free wills, but, rather, they arose as a result of biological, psychological, economic, and social forces that propelled individuals into engaging in them.

One of the most influential early positivists was the Belgian astronomer Adolphe Quetelet (1796–1874). Using scientific methods and social statistics, he set out to develop a "social mechanics" of crime in which he attempted to demonstrate that the same lawlike regularity existing in the world of nature also existed in society. Quetelet argued that there were many causes of crime that could be divided up into three categories: *accidental* (wars, famines, tsunamis), *variable* (personality), and *constant* (age, gender, occupation). Society, too, was a cause of crime, but he ultimately concluded that crime had biological causes.

Other influential theorists came from the fields of anthropology, medicine, and psychiatry in the early and middle nineteenth century, such as Francis Gall's work on phrenology (head shape), Gregor Mendel's work on genetics, Charles Darwin's work on the origins of species, and Benjamin Rush's work on the diseases of the mind. Biology found its criminological proponent in the father of modern criminology, Cesare Lombroso (1835–1909). Rounding out the Italian school of positivism was two of Lombroso's students, Enrico Ferri (1856–1929) and Raffaele Garofalo (1852–1934). The former argued for a sociopolitical criminality that emphasized the interrelatedness of social, economic, and political factors that contribute to crime; the latter argued for a doctrine of "natural crimes," a Social Darwinist approach that viewed crimes as offenses "against the law of nature."

Throughout the rest of the nineteenth and into the twentieth centuries, positivist criminologists debated the relative importance for crime of *nature* versus *nurture*, or heredity versus social environment. By the turn of the twentieth century, there had already been the rise and fall of biological determinism as exemplified by the discrediting of Herbert Spencer's "bioevolutionary" model of society and Lombroso's "born criminal" who was an "atavistic throwback" to an earlier evolutionary stage. Rising to replace biology in popularity was the psychogenesis school of criminal causation, influenced by the psychiatrist Sigmund Freud (1856–1939), followed by the rise of sociology and the related influence of sociologist-criminologist Edwin Sutherland and his theory of "differential association" first presented in 1939.

During the twentieth century and into the early twenty-first century, the powers of positivism and the methods of quantitative science have dominated much of criminology. At the same time, each of the theoretical orientations or schools and disciplines of positivist criminology have continued to evolve and develop, including: individual traits and crime; social disorganization and crime; learning and crime; anomie/strain and crime; control and crime; and labeling and crime. The past several decades also witnessed the rise of integrated theories within (and without) positivist criminology. Among the shortcomings of positivism is its overemphasis on individual as compared to social or organizational analyses of criminality and on the belief that changes in behavior of offenders can occur without changes in social conditions, including political and economic structures.

CRITICAL CRIMINOLOGY

The newest school of criminology is the critical school. About thirty-five years old, this school first emerged as radical criminology, and now encompasses feminist criminology, left-realist criminology, peacemaking criminology, constitutive criminology, news-making criminology, integrated criminology, cultural criminology, postmodern criminology, and anarchist criminology. Despite the diversity of critical criminologies, what they have in common is agreement on the limitations of criminological knowledge and justice policy inherent in the classical and positivist criminologies.

For example, critical criminologists are skeptical of the rational and positivist belief that an orderly universe can be necessarily organized by knowledge and the manipulation of the external world. Critical criminologists are skeptical about objectivity and point out that there are no "value-free" standpoints—everyone has certain assumptions and values. Certain assumptions and points of view may seem "natural" or objective because they are widely shared by the dominant groups. Critical criminologists therefore acknowledge their subjectivity, that they are part of a moral and political endeavor. Finally, with their rejection of mechanistic conceptions about how facts are related and gathered, critical criminologists typically do not present causal models of crime; explanations and arguments about crime and justice revolve around both social and cultural interactions as well as the structural relations of the political economy as these intersect with the everyday activities of people (Barak 2009).

The emergence of a critical criminology in part represents a departure from the traditional practices of criminology that have focused attention on changing the behavior of the lawbreakers either through punishment (classical criminology) or treatment (positivist criminology). Not that critical criminology is unconcerned with punishment and treatment or with reforming the administration of criminal justice. On the contrary, it is, but it prefers to locate these changes within the contexts of social, political, and economic justice. Critical criminology is thus concerned not so much with "law and order," but "whose law?" and "what order?" (Chambliss and Mankoff 1976)—that is, with the power relations involved in the law, the fairness of social order that law is protecting, and solutions that promote justice rather than simply repress criminals.

In sum, unlike classical and positivist criminologists, critical criminologists are also reflexive criminologists, meaning they question the privilege that goes with having one's viewpoint be seen as "objective" and how such privileged standpoints and "knowledge" contribute to inequality. They have turned the activity of explanation back upon itself: in the process of reflection and introspection, critical criminology asks about "first principles," like the basic assumptions and thought processes of criminological inquiry that generate our "knowledge" about crime. Morally and politically, critical criminology questions the status quo, official versions of reality, and prevailing ideologies about the "solutions" to crime control. Critical criminology represents alternative modes of analysis and better pathways to human liberation and crime reduction in all its forms, but it also remains committed to empirically supporting its scholarship and interventions into policy formation.

CLASS AND CRIMINOLOGY

Social and economic class are generally discussed less than race or gender. Indeed, the ideas that the United States is a classless society and "anyone can make it if they try hard enough" drown out analysis of the distribution of income and wealth. Unfortunately, both are unequally distributed and class mobility is more limited than most people would like to believe. These assertions are developed in chapter 3, and this section reviews some of the important ways that understanding class and economic power relate to criminology. For example, criminological theory is frequently based on an unquestioning acceptance of how the criminal law defines crime. But class is related to political power and lawmaking, so it is also deeply implicated in understanding what has been defined as crime and why almost forty years of being "tough on crime" has hardly applied to white-collar crime. Economic resources also play a role in the working of a justice system to process those defined as criminal. The first part of this section provides an overview of these issues, followed by a discussion of the link between inequality and crime and the relative neglect of white-collar, corporate, and governmental crime.

Crime theory frequently assumes that criminal law is a direct reflection of consensus, or of folkways hardening into custom and finally law rather than the contingent outcome of a political process that includes class conflict and class biases. As Reiman notes, "criminology is in the unusual position of being a mode of social inquiry whose central concept is defined officially, by governments" so "politics openly, necessarily, insinuates itself into the heart of criminology. Political systems hand criminology a ready-made research agenda" (in Reiman and Leighton 2010a, 238). In other words, criminologists' focus on street crime, and thus the crimes of the marginally poor, become seen as a "natural state of affairs" rather than as an expression of inequality and privilege, so criminology develops theories about the criminality of the poor rather than examining harms of the rich. In turn, the criminal law's controlling of the offenses of the poor rather than the offenses of the rich appears to reflect the legitimacy of an agreed-upon definition of "dangerous" crime.

When crime theory unreflectively takes the criminal law as a given, the fiction of crime as neutral law sets in (Platt 1974). Working within the confines of "crime" as defined by the law cedes control of criminology to lawmakers and the political process that produces law. Thus, many social harms—from tobacco smoke to environmental pollution, from workplace injuries to defective products, and from neocolonialism to extraordinary crimes against humanity—are excluded from study even though they present more of a threat to people's well-being and security than much of what is officially designated as a crime (Barak 1991a; Robinson 1998; Reiman and Leighton 2010). If criminology makes

> no moral judgment independent of criminal statutes, it becomes sterile and inhuman—the work of moral eunuchs or legal technicians. If moral judgments above and beyond criminal law were not made, the laws of Nazi Germany would be indistinguishable from the laws of other nations (in Simon 1999, 37).

Among the main theorists in exposing the myth of the neutral criminal law were the nineteenth-century philosophers and political economists Karl Marx and Friedrich Engels, who noted that the law, along with the order it upholds, is one based on very unequal distribution of property and resources. Marx and Engels thus "insisted that the institutions of the state and law, and the doctrines that emerge from them, serve the interests of the dominant economic class" (Beirne and Messerschmidt 2000, 110). For them, crime was not about the defects of morality or biology, but rather about the defects of society and the product of the demoralization and alienation caused by the horrible conditions of industrial capitalism.

Subsequent Marxian analyses of crime and crime control in the United States can be subdivided into "instrumental" and "structural" models of crime and criminal control. Some of the earlier work, for example, of Richard Quinney (1977), is representative of the instrumental model. He argued that within the overall conditions of the capitalist political economy, two kinds of crimes emerge: *crimes of domination* and *crimes of accommodation*. Crimes of domination include "crimes of control" (i.e., acts by the police and the FBI in violation of civil liberties), "crimes of government" (i.e., political acts such as Watergate, Iran-Contragate, or torturing suspected terrorists), "crimes of economic domination" (i.e., corporate acts involving price-fixing, pollution, planned obsolescence), and "crimes" of "social injury" (i.e., acts that may not be illegal but deny basic human rights, such as racism, sexism, and economic exploitation). The crimes of domination, according to the instrumentalist view, are necessary for the reproduction of the capitalist system itself.

In contrast, relatively powerless people of the lower and working classes commit crimes of accommodation. Quinney identified three crimes of accommodation, or of adaptation to the oppressive conditions of capitalism and to the domination of the capitalist class: "predatory crimes" (i.e., burglary, robbery, drug dealing), "personal crimes" (i.e., murder, assault, rape), and "crimes of resistance" (i.e., protests, sabotage). For Quinney, the real (greater) danger to society comes from the crimes of domination rather than the crimes of accommodation. However, the former acts are not criminalized (or minimally so) because they serve the interests of the ruling classes; the latter acts are criminalized and punished as they threaten the political and economic status quo. Hence, crime control becomes class control.

As an example, consider the following quote taken from one of the founding fathers of the classical school, Beccaria, in his book, *Essay on Crimes and Punishments*, first published some two hundred years ago and still in print today. In trying to reason through the appropriate punishment for an offender, he takes the imagined voice of the criminal:

> What are these laws that I am supposed to respect, that place such a great distance between me and the rich man? He refuses me the penny I ask of him and, as an excuse, tells me to seat at work he knows nothing about. Who made these laws? Rich and powerful men who have never deigned to visit the squalid huts of the poor, who have never had to share a crust of moldy bread amid

the innocent cries of hungry children and the tears of a wife. Let us break these bonds, fatal to the majority and only useful to a few indolent tyrants; let us attack justice at its source. I will return to my natural state of independence; I shall at least for a little time live free and happy with the fruits of my courage and industry. The day will perhaps come for my sorrow and repentance, but it will be brief, and for a single day of suffering I shall have many years of liberty and of pleasures (quoted in Vold and Bernard 1986, 29).

The speaker points out the social injuries that are part of the crimes of domination that help secure the unequal distribution of resources. At the same time, the speaker advocates unspecified crimes of accommodation in response to oppression. Vold and Bernard (1986) note that the revolutionary implication behind the passage is obvious and that crimes of need could be better prevented by a more equal distribution of money than by the severity of the penal law. Instead, Beccaria argued that the death penalty is an ineffective deterrent that should be replaced by the more protracted suffering of life imprisonment.

William Chambliss (1988) articulated a structural-contradictions theory of crime and class control, in which recognition is given to the resistance and pressures from other classes besides the ruling classes. In his model, Chambliss identifies certain contradictions inherent within capitalism, such as those between profits, wages, and consumption—or between wages and the supply of labor. These contradictions ultimately culminate in crime as underclasses are formed that cannot consume the goods that they were socialized to want as necessary for being happy. One solution for these underclasses is to resort to criminal or illegitimate behavior. The state then responds to these acts in the name of crime control.

Although research on the link between social disadvantage and crime is no longer a priority as it once was for a brief period during President Lyndon Johnson's Great Society of the 1960s, criminologists have continued to explore it. An important finding is that poverty itself is not the key, because "if that was the case, then graduate students would be very dangerous people indeed" (Currie 1998, 134). The important theoretical concepts relate to inequality, relative deprivation, and blocked opportunities. As Currie (1998, 34) points out, the important contribution to crime and violence is "the experience of life year in, year out at the bottom of a harsh, depriving, and excluding social system [that] wears away at the psychological and communal conditions that sustain healthy human development."

Further, high levels of inequality mean that there are more poor and destitute than would exist under a more even or equal distribution. Thus, "there are criminals motivated by the need for a decent standard of living, where 'decent' can mean what they perceive most people in their community enjoy, what whites but not blacks enjoy, what they used to enjoy before they lost their jobs, or what they were led to expect to enjoy by advertising and dramatization of bourgeois lifestyles on television" (Braithwaite 1992, 82). Inequality also produces more structural degradation, which Braithwaite argues is important because of the links among humiliation, rage, and violence. Ultimately, the "propensity to feel powerless and exploited among the poor and the propensity of the rich to see exploiting as legitimate . . . enable crime" (94).

Because most of criminology tends to be guided by the criminal law, the focus of crime theory is almost exclusively on the behavior of the poor. Notably, one of the first important mentions for criminology of "crime" in relation to the behaviors of the upper classes was in 1908 when E. A. Ross promoted the notion of a "criminaloid." Friedrichs (1996, 2) notes that Ross used this term to discuss "the businessman who committed exploitative (if not necessarily illegal) acts out of an uninhibited desire to maximize profit." Ross's discussion, however, did not immediately inspire sociologists to explore the topic, party because criminology was attempting to establish itself as a "science," which meant distancing itself from the passionate outrage that characterized many of the journalists who were busy condemning robber-baron industrialists and pointing to the excesses of the capitalist system.

But this work did get the attention of Sutherland, who was interested in the criminality of the rich because of his attempt to develop a general theory of crime. He believed that a major deficiency of criminological theory was that it could not explain crime by the rich, which made for not only class-biased criminological theory but also for a practice and policy of criminal and juvenile justice steeped in class biases as well (Platt 1969). In 1939, Sutherland introduced the term *white-collar crime* in his presidential address to what is now the American Sociological Association. The key elements included that the perpetrator be an upper-class or white-collar person, the crime be committed in the course of one's occupation, the crime be a violation of trust, and the crime be processed through civil or administrative proceedings rather than a criminal court.

Once again, criminology was slow to follow up on Sutherland's research, and its primary focus still remains with street crime, although crimes by the upper class exact a far heavier toil in terms of dollars and lives (Clinard 1990; Reiman and Leighton 2010a; Simon 1999). Box 1.1 reviews many of the different types of white-collar crime, but much of the literature on this topic is devoted to explaining shoplifting or employee theft rather than the wrongdoing and violence by corporations. The most frequently discussed white-collar crimes are employee pilfering and credit card fraud, in which businesses, corporations, and financial institutions are the victims. The least frequently discussed are corporate and government crime, in which the powerful are the perpetrators who are victimizing employees, consumers, taxpayers, and/or the environment.

Box 1.1.   The Diverse Types of White-collar Crime

Terms like *economic crime, financial crime, business crime,* and even categories like *technocrime* and *computer crime* should cover the range of possible victimizations, but they are frequently limited to acts against financial institutions or businesses. Criminologists and tough-on-crime politicians, however, rarely highlight the executive who harms employees by cutting corners on workplace safety, who knowingly markets unsafe products, or who causes environmental damage in order to help boost corporate profits. (The corporate scandals involving Enron and others are a special case that we discuss in chapter 8. Because the magnitude of the wrongdoing was so large that it threatened the integrity of the financial system, so the state was forced to get tough on this corporate crime.)

More specifically, *occupational crime* is done to benefit the perpetrator personally rather than the business. At times, the victim will be the business, although at others it may be consumers. In each case, the crime is linked to the perpetrator's occupational position. Examples include auto mechanics charging for unnecessary work, bank managers embezzling the institution's funds, or doctors fraudulently billing insurance companies.

Individuals in a corporation who act in its interests in violation of the law and benefit themselves individually through bonuses and promotions perpetrate *corporate crime.* The victims include workers, consumers, taxpayers, communities, the government, and the environment (Winslow 1999). Acts may include fraud against the government, taxpayers, or consumers, and anticompetitive practices that cause higher prices. *Corporate violence* refers to acts that inflict physical and emotional suffering rather than simply monetary losses, as in the case of dangerous or defective products, unsafe working conditions, and medical conditions caused by pollution or toxic exposure.

Public officials who are trying to perpetuate a specific administration, exercise general government power, or accomplish undue influence on behalf of large campaign contributors perpetrate *state crime.* The victims can be as widespread as all taxpayers who are forced to pay for corruption and fraud; victims can also be a specific political group—or even its leaders—who are denied basic political rights through surveillance and harassment (Barak 1991a).

Thus, even when criminology does engage the topic of white-collar crime, much of the time it does so with a blindness to important power dynamics. Indeed, also neglected within the sphere of the crimes of the powerful are state crime, including the denial of human rights, torture, surveillance, and other crimes of state domination. Or, in the terms of the class biases operating in the social construction of "perpetrators" and "victims," serial killers are a trendy topic of study for criminologists, but criminology devotes little attention to trafficking in human beings or to mass murders involving genocide. Indeed, criminologist Margaret Vandiver noted that "if we had as much research and theory on genocide as we do on shoplifting, we would be far ahead of where we are now" in reducing human suffering (1999, personal communication).

RACE AND CRIMINOLOGY

Race is socially defined by a constellation of traits that include physical characteristics, national origin, language, culture, and religion. That is, while people have real differences, racial and ethnic categories are made up based on prevailing beliefs, political pressures, and a host of nonobjective reasons. Consider that the racial categories used in the United States have changed over time and that no other country uses them. "Hispanic" is an ethnicity rather than a race because of lobbying by the Mexican government, which did not want Mexicans categorized as nonwhite. These issues are further explored in chapter 4, and this section reviews some of the connections between criminology and the racial hierarchies that privilege some and disadvantage others.

Historically, research on crime has consciously and unconsciously reproduced the racism of prevailing social attitudes, while it has also been a site for resistance. For example, Lombroso wrote, "The white races represented the triumph of the human species, its hitherto most perfect advancement" (Quoted in Miller 1996, 185). This belief influenced his criminal anthropology and its implications that criminality was related to atavistic or evolutionary throwbacks. In contrast, Bonger's 1943 study, *Race and Crime*, was written as a critique against the growing fascist movement in Europe and arguments about the superiority of Nordic peoples (Hawkins 1995, 23). Today, many criminology texts do not mention Lombroso's early racism or his repudiation of such ideas as *Criminal Man* (1870) over the course of his career. Most texts without an interest in race and/or ethnicity ignore altogether the critical work of Bonger on race and crime, though they almost always mention his work on economics and crime.

American criminology and social science has generally been characterized by a "liberal political tone and assumptions" that document, for example, black disadvantage and attribute it to white prejudice rather than biological notions of inferiority (Hawkins 1995). Hawkins starts his analysis with some of the work of W. E. B. Du Bois (1868–1963), a prominent black intellectual and writer who is typically omitted from criminology texts. He is an important figure because "many of the most virulently racist, social Darwinist critiques of black life were published during the period he wrote [and] Du Bois was among the first to provide a retort to their argument"

(Hawkins 1995, 13). Du Bois seemed to accept the higher rates of black (street) criminality; he ascribed them to the social disruption and urban migration that occurred after the end of slavery as well as to the degradation and legacies of slavery.

Criminologists such as Sutherland and Thorsten Sellin shared some of Du Bois's analysis of crime, although they both urged much more caution in concluding, based on official statistics, that blacks had a higher rate of crime than whites. At the same time, Sellin (1928, 64) recognized that black crime rates might still be higher than whites, but he argued this was not a condemnation of blacks because "it would be extraordinary, indeed if this group were to prove more law-abiding than the white, which enjoys more fully the advantages of a civilization the Negro has helped to create." Sutherland and Sellin did recognize the salience of *culture* as relevant to criminality but argued that culture is somewhat different from nationality (based on political boundaries) and race. Important data for them included the observation that immigrants from the same culture would have different rates of criminality depending on the age at which they arrived in the United States and the number of generations their family had been here— data that cannot be explained by reference to biology or genetics.

Clifford Shaw and Henry McKay's study of social ecology in Chicago neighborhoods also raised questions about the importance of biology and genetics because "no racial, national or nativity group exhibits a uniform, characteristic rate of delinquents in all parts of Chicago" (Shaw and McKay 1942, 153). The key factor for them in explaining delinquency was social disorganization and community attributes rather than the racial traits of those who lived in certain areas. Marvin Wolfgang and Bernard Cohen (1970) later elaborated on the persistence of high rates of criminality among blacks while other immigrant groups had moved out of socially disorganized communities and zones of transition. In particular, they noted that blacks faced more blocked opportunities because of racism than white immigrants and that the legacy of racial oppression might make blacks less ambitious than immigrants, who would be more optimistic about achieving the American dream.

Wolfgang and Cohen's *Crime and Race* (1970) also critiqued biological determinism by noting that there could not be a genetic predetermination to general criminality because neither crime nor the definition of crime is stable in time and place. They noted that most criminals obey most of the laws and generally break laws carefully as to avoid drawing attention from the police. Like Bonger, they argued that criminality is not a specific trait like eye color:

> According to Mendel's rule of inheritance of specific traits, if criminality were genetically determined, we should inherit specific tendencies for embezzle-

ment, burglary, forgery, etc. And if we inherited specific *criminal* forms of behavior, and some us were genetically destined to be burglars or stock embezzlers, rapists or check forgers, we would also have to inherit specific *noncriminal* occupations, which would mean some of us would be genetically destined to become police officers or truck drivers or school teachers, as to have red hair (Wolfgang and Cohen 1970, 92, emphasis original).

The critique in the preceding paragraphs does not mean criminology should exclude the disciplines of biology, physiology, and genetics from a comprehensive and integrated approach (Barak 1998). Indeed, the emphasis here is that there are no genetic bases for race, which makes the link between race and crime problematic. The physical and other characteristics that are often used to create racial categories are socially constructed; they do not correlate with criminality but can mean that minority groups are subjected to greater social control because they are more involved with the criminal justice system.

Hawkins concludes his thoughtful overview of literature on race and crime by noting that the liberal tradition tries to balance a recognition that racial bias inflates the officially counted criminality of minorities with an awareness that minorities frequently live in criminogenic conditions. He is skeptical of efforts to find the "real" rate of crime and of attempts to get more accurate counts of real misconduct. Instead, he argues for the development of a conflict perspective, which examines official records of minority crime as an index of social control and an understanding of "how the criminal justice system is used by the dominant ethnic and racial groups to maintain their status" (Hawkins 1995, 34). This perspective is developed in chapter 7 and contends that contact with the criminal justice system has as much, or more, to do with social standing rather than with criminal conduct.

More recently, criminologists associated with the Racial Democracy, Crime, and Justice Network produced a volume for the Annals of the American Academy of Political and Social Science. This special edition of *The Annals* empirically examined (1) the structured *patterns*, (2) the socially constructed *processes*, and (3) the societal *consequences* of racial-ethnic inequality in crime and justice (Krivo and Peterson 2009). Although the specific findings from these studies will be incorporated in subsequent chapters where applicable, an important point is that it is well past time that social scientists, the mass media, and the public at large move beyond the traditional black-and-white dichotomies of American life. The range of consequences included how experiences with "injustice at the hands of criminal justice officials support existing societal inequalities" and the ways in which "ethnoracial inequalities in the United States in education, employment, and health are exacerbated by the disproportionate imprisonment of groups of color" (Krivo and Peterson 2009, 9–10).

GENDER AND CRIMINOLOGY

Sex generally refers to the biological components that characterize males and females. Gender typically refers to femininity and masculinity, or about the roles and behaviors dominant society encourages for males and females. Gender thus refers to the social expectations for how males should be masculine and how females should be feminine. While sex is a relatively fixed biological anchor, gender involves the social processes through which people learn and are socialized into acting according to the ever-changing notions of what is appropriate for men and women in our society. Women are a majority of the American population, but men are the dominant gender. These issues are further explored in chapter 5, and this section reviews some of the connections among criminology, gender roles, and male domination.

A wide variety of people (family, friends, coworkers) and institutions (schools, advertising, mass media) help create expectations about appropriate gender behavior and apply pressure for conformity. Further, "as an official agent of social control, the criminal justice system responds not only to crime but also transgressions against gender norms" (Flavin 2009, 4). One important way the criminal justice system achieves this end is by becoming involved in matters of reproductive choice. As Flavin explains in *Our Bodies, Our Crimes* (2009, 4):

> By restricting some women's access to abortion and obstetric and gynecological care, by telling some women not to procreate and pressuring them to be sterilized, by prosecuting some women who use drugs and become pregnant, and by failing to support the efforts of incarcerated women and battered women to rear their children, the law and the criminal justice system establish what a "good woman" or "fit mother" should look like and how conception, pregnancy, birth and child care and socialization are regulated.

(Generally, the women prosecuted and subject to this type of control are poor and/or minority women, which highlights the importance of looking at intersections.)

Until recently, gender has not been important to criminology because men have been the vast majority of criminal offenders and have dominated the criminal justice system from lawmaking to parole officer. Women have made up a small percentage of offenders and have tended to commit less serious crimes than men. Until the mid-1970s, these and other factors (discussed more in chapter 5) contributed to a lack of interest in female criminals and their experience within the criminal justice system. However, over the past forty years, there has been an increasing interest in the study of women, gender, and crime. During this sustained period of criminological interest, the areas of both gender and women's studies have evolved in their analyses and sophistication. A five-stage framework developed by McIntosh (1984) and others (Andersen 1988; Daly 1995; Goodstein 1992) provides an overview of the ongoing process by which the fields of criminology and criminal justice have considered, do consider, and could consider women (Flavin 2001; Daly 2006).

Stage One: The Intellectual Falklands

The Falklands are a series of islands whose total area is smaller than Connecticut and are located between South America and the Antarctic. Up to the nineteenth century, most researchers ignored women's criminality, and the study of female criminality was considered "an intellectual Falklands"; that is, "remote, unvisited, and embarrassing" (Heidensohn 1995, 124). Theorists who did consider women saw them as being particularly determined by their biology. Lombroso, for example, studied female offenders to support his theory that criminals were physically anomalous. His methodology involved extensive measurements of criminals to isolate the "born criminal." He found that female criminals were not significantly different from other women, a fact that he attributed to a lack of external differentiation in women generally. At the same time, Lombroso concluded that the born female offender was closer to a normal man than a normal woman. However, he also seemed to distinguish between female criminals, as Hart (1994, 23) explains:

> unlike the "semi-masculine, tyrannical and selfish" born criminal who wants only to satisfy her own passions, the occasional [female] offender puts trust in her male protectors and regains confidence in men—especially her lawyer, and in some cases that Lombroso is fond of relating, her executioner.

Other positivist theorists, especially those with a psychological or psychoanalytic approach, perceived women's deviance as peculiarly sexual. For example, Otto Pollak (1950) argued that women's tendency toward deceit stemmed from their physiological ability to hide their true sexual feelings and the social expectation that they will conceal menstruation and menopause.

Stage Two: "Add Women and Stir"

In the twentieth century, criminologists moved away from viewing deviant behavior as inherently abnormal and pathological and toward seeing deviance as normal. Thus, models that examined external sources of crime, such as poverty, social structure, and racial discrimination, gradually replaced those older models that examined internal sources such as biology and psychology. Once again, before the 1970s, most studies of crime continued to look exclusively at men and boys. In the mid-1970s, however, women insisted they be included in criminological research and analysis about crime and the criminal justice system. Unfortunately, the result was simply to "add women and stir" them into existing research rather than reconsider and challenge what was or is "known" about crime.

Eileen Leonard's work (1982, 1995) provides perhaps the most comprehensive attempt at using traditional positivist theories of crime such as anomie/strain, differential association, subcultural, labeling, and Marxism to explain women's low involvement in crime. Because these theories excluded consideration of women's criminality, Leonard developed hypotheses that the theorists might have constructed had they been so inclined or informed. For example, Merton's anomie theory holds that when people lack legitimate means (e.g., a job, a savings account) to achieve socially accepted goals (e.g., material and monetary success), they are more likely to innovate (e.g., steal, write bad checks) to achieve these cultural ends. Leonard points out that although women are overrepresented among the poor and thus arguably are subjected to more strain than men, women are less likely to deviate. Leonard also challenged whether monetary success is as salient a goal for women as it is for men. She further critiqued Merton for assuming that women's goals (and men's too) are shared across class, race, and ethnicity. Following her systematic review and analysis of traditional theories, Leonard concluded that these theories are unsuited for explaining female patterns of crime. She called upon scholars not to develop a separate "criminology of women" but to reconsider the understanding of women *and* men's criminal behavior.

Stage Three: Enter Feminism

The first of the feminist stages reflects some scholars' realization that women have been excluded from crime theories or that when women *are* discussed their behavior is distorted. This stage focuses more attention on crimes that adversely affect women more than they affect men, such as domestic violence. Also, increasing attention is paid to the ways in which women's experiences differ not just from men's but also from each other's based on characteristics such as race, ethnicity, class, age, and sexual orientation.

While this stage is a marked improvement over ignoring women altogether or "adding and stirring," it still has its shortcomings. Most notably, this stage reflects a tendency to treat men as the normative and women as the anomalies. Labeling one sex the "anomalies"—relegating them to a marginalized status—is incompatible with aims to achieve more equal opportunities for men and women on the professional golf circuits as well as in a court of law. It reflects male privilege (discussed in chapter 5), and the implications of androcentric or male-centered thinking for the criminal justice apparatus are significant. For example, the historically male-centered legal system meant delays in recognizing marital rape and stalking as crimes, providing vocational programs for women prisoners, and addressing sexual harassment in the workplace.

The development of feminism has helped raise consciousness about the male biases reflected in criminology, and it has re-created its theoretical understandings and practice. While feminist theories of crime and justice do try to correct the exclusion or silences about women's beliefs, experiences, and achievements, most acknowledge that the understanding of women's lives also requires consideration of masculinity and male sex-role expectation. When neither males nor females are the hidden or invisible norm of criminological analysis, then the discipline is in a better position to understand the fact that men also have a gender, whites also have a race, the wealthy have a class, and straight people have a sexual orientation. These types of feminist insights help move criminology in the direction of describing gendered oppression in all of its forms, of identifying and explaining its causes and consequences, and of prescribing strategies for the political, economic, and social equality of the sexes (Rice 1990; Tong 1989).

Stages Four and Five: "An Emerging Whole New Pie"

The fourth and fifth stages are still at conceptual or imaginary levels because women and minority men do not currently form enough of our basis of knowledge, although that too has begun to change over the past decade or so. The current literature does reflect a growing willingness to reconsider what is "known" about women and crime and to examine racial and ethnic differences among women and men. In the fourth stage, scholars have begun not only to locate women with men at the center of research but they are also studying women on their own terms without reference to male norms. As an established body of feminist theory and research grows, it is becoming possible to build on feminist knowledge itself rather than merely dedicating time and attention to critiquing and evaluating traditionally male-dominated criminological theories and research.

During the fourth stage, rather than addressing how the study of crime and criminal justice contributes to our understanding of women's criminality, research has begun to emphasize how feminist insights contribute to our understanding of crime and men's high incidence of criminality. At this point, the research goes beyond a sociology or criminology of women. The work of such scholars as Jody Miller (2001, 2002, 2008) and James Messerschmidt (1993, 1995, 2004), for example, does in fact suggest that we have crossed into the fourth stage where we are increasingly integrating our knowledge of masculinities and femininities.

In the fifth stage, our knowledge base will be fully transformed and feminist, and it will include a theoretical and analytical focus on multiple relations of class, race, and gender. Kathleen Daly (1995) has identified a number of challenges to be met in the process of reaching this stage (which will be taken up later in Part III of this book). Among these challenges is the fact that our inherited ways of thinking obstruct our ability to imagine alternative ways of viewing crime and punishment. In other words, the existing biases built into our knowledge bases make it difficult to imagine what a fully inclusive and transformed body of knowledge, gendered and otherwise, will be like.

INTERSECTIONALITY AND CRIMINOLOGY

Discussions of intersections and intersectionality refer to efforts to combine the analysis of class *and* race *and* gender. While each is important in its own right, by themselves they provide an incomplete description of a person's life experiences and "social location." A person may be white, but multibillionaires are different from those considered "white trash"; rich and poor white women will have some different experiences than their male counterparts. While it may seem obvious to use class and race and gender and get a "fix" on a person's social location, it is also easier said than done. One of those dimensions may be more important than the others in a specific situation, but that factor will not always be most important—and theorists have not created good models to understand whether class or race or gender will be most important (and why). Further, the combination of factors does not work in a simple additive way like one plus one. Combining devaluation because of gender with devaluation because of race creates gendered racism, which can be far more powerful because of the interacting dynamics.

Intersectionality is further explored in chapter 6, and this section provides an overview of criminology's limited efforts to explore how class and race and gender all apply at the same time. Too frequently, researchers focus on one of these three social relations to the near exclusion of others. For example, the short-lived *radical* perspective in criminology that emerged in the late 1960s and early 1970s drew heavily from Marx's ideas about capitalism and the social relations of production, so it emphasized how class conflict was at the root of most crime. Subsequently, variations in this approach to class would incorporate race and gender but still treat them as subordinate to class relations of production.

Eventually, the almost exclusive focus on class would broaden to give greater and increasing importance to race and gender because they are independent structuring forces that affect, shape, and influence areas of criminological concern: how people act, how others respond to and define those actions, how certain actions are viewed as more or less serious or as more or less "criminal" and deviant, and how the law and legal systems are organized to control behavior in highly stratified and unequal societies (Lynch 1996). By the 1990s, race and gender had surpassed class in being viewed as key concepts of society, prompting Bohm (1998, 18) and others to call for a reemphasis of "class and class struggle in an understanding of crime and social control in market societies." Currently, *The Rich Get Richer and the Poor Get Prison* (Reiman and Leighton 2010a) is one of the few book-length treatments of class and criminal justice.

Today, there are a variety of race, gender, and hybrid analyses of crime and justice, such as those involving feminist perspectives, critical race theory, or critical legal studies. For example, building on critical sociology, neo-Marxism, and postmodern approaches, *critical race theory* assumes that racism is an ordinary ingrained aspect of American society that cannot be readily remedied by law. Developed in the late 1970s through the efforts of such scholars as Derrick Bell and Alan Freeman, who were discontent with the slow pace of achieving racial justice (Delgado 1995a), critical race theorists argue that the racism that permeates society is part of a socially constructed reality that exists to promote the interests of men and women in elite groups. Hence, not only do they expose the ways in which existing arrangements support racism but also they pursue alternatively constructed social realities.

Similarly, *critical race feminism* emerged from critical race theory to address the essentialism that had pervaded earlier feminist and critical race theories (Wing 1997). Specifically, critical race feminists have objected both to feminist approaches that presume white middle-class women's experiences are representative of all women's experiences and to critical race scholarship that presumes minority women's experiences are all the same and can be represented by the experiences of their minority male counterparts. The effect of essentialist perspectives has been to "reduce the lives of people who experience multiple forms of oppression to addition problems: 'racism + sexism = straight black women's experience'" (Harris 1997, 11). In other words, racial and ethnic minority women—as victims, offenders, and workers—are not simply subjected to quantitatively "more" disadvantage than white women; their oppression is of a qualitatively different kind.

Critical legal scholarship in the form of narrative or storytelling is used as one means of analyzing, challenging, and resisting the dominant myths, presuppositions, and "truths" that make up the mainstream culture's views of race, gender, and law. Too often, the scholarly accounts of dominant groups have suppressed, devalued, and marginalized the experiences and perspectives of women and minority men. Narratives are used to break the silence and convey complex issues in a readily accessible form designed to promote understanding. For example, law professor and critical race theorist Richard Delgado (1995b [1993]) explains the debate surrounding essentialism with his fictional alter ego, Rodrigo Crenshaw. In one of his chronicles, Rodrigo has gotten "caught in the crossfire" at a Women's Law Caucus meeting:

> The "debate about essentialism has both a political and a theoretical component," Rodrigo began. . . . "In its political guise . . . members of different groups argue about the appropriate unit of analysis—about whether the Black community, for example, is one community or many, whether gays and lesbians have anything in common with straight activists, and so on. At the Law Women's Caucus, they were debating one aspect of this—namely, whether there is one, essential sisterhood, as opposed to many. The women of color were arguing that to think of the women's movement as singular and unitary disempowers them. They said that this view disenfranchises anyone—say, lesbian mothers, disabled women, or working-class women—whose experience and status differ from what they term 'the norm.'"
>
> "And the others, of course, were saying the opposite?"
>
> "Not exactly," Rodrigo replied. "They were saying that vis-à-vis men, all women stood on similar footing. All are oppressed by a common enemy, namely patriarchy, and ought to stand together to confront this evil . . . [Black feminists' focusing] on their own unique experience contributes to a 'disunity' within the broader feminist movement . . . [it is troubling] because it weakens the group's voice, the sum total of power it wields. Emphasizing minor differences between young and old, gay straight, and Black and white women is divisive, verging on self-indulgence. It contributes to the false idea that the individual is the unit of social change, not the group. It results in tokenism and plays into the hands of male power" (Delgado 1995b [1993], 243–46).

In a similar fashion, *critical white studies* (Delgado and Stefancic 1997) is the most recent body of scholarship that considers what it means to be white in the United States. Far from being a safe haven for white supremacists, critical white studies prompt whites and nonwhites alike to consider the legacy of whiteness and to ask such questions as: How do whites as members of the dominant race benefit (or not) depending on their place in the social order of stratification? What does white privilege mean to the poorest whites—sometimes called "white trash"—and to the poorest white women especially? What part does the law play in defining who is white? How has our culture constructed "whiteness" and "blackness" such that they are not neutral descriptors but laden with meaning, value, and status?

Several more specific examples of analysis close out this section on intersections and criminology. As noted in the previous section, privilege may present itself in terms of the preferred masculinities or femininities. The form of femininity most valued and supported in U.S. culture, for example, emphasizes marriage, housework, child care, fragility, and sociability (Connell 1987; Martin and Jurik 1996). More generally, this idealized femininity is based on white, middle-class, and heterosexual norms. In this respect, Lynda Hart's work (1994) on depictions of lesbianism and female killers suggests that the category "woman" is reserved for white, upper-class, heterosexual females. This categorization serves a disciplinary function, patrolling the boundaries of "normal" femininity by creating an "othered" (not woman) category onto which women's deviance can be displaced. Thus, "the ultimate violation of the social instinct, murder, and the perversion of the sexual instinct, same-sex desire, was linked as limits that marked the boundaries of femininity" (Hart 1994, 30). Lesbians and killers (and women of color) reside together in the "not woman" category.

Three noteworthy studies of crime that have captured various nuances in the interactions between class, race, and gender are Esther Madriz's (1997) examination of women's fear of crime, Mark Totten's (2000) investigation into adolescent girlfriend abuse, and Jody Miller's (2008) detailed excavation of the multiple dimensions of violence experienced by black, inner-city girls. In these ethnographies, the authors are able to encapsulate the qualitative differences in the life experiences of men and women, boys and girls, majorities and minorities, in relation to class, crime, and the administration of justice. They demonstrate that there is no standardized "class" experience, "race" experience, or "gender" experience, but rather there is a repertoire of interacting class, race, and gender identities. Figure 1.1 illustrates the social location of the intersection of these forming identities.

In *Nothing Bad Happens to Good Girls* (1997), Madriz explored the fear of crime among young and old, African American, Latina, and white upper-, middle-, and working-class women. In the process, she is able to demonstrate how fear of crime perpetuates gender inequalities and contributes to the differential social control of women by class and race/ethnicity. For

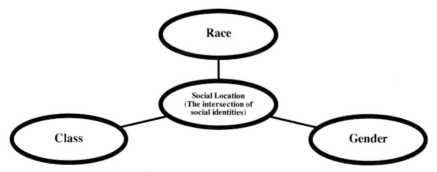

Figure 1.1. An Integrated Illustration of Class, Race, and Gender as It Shapes Crime and Experiences with the Criminal Justice System.

example, Madriz was able to capture the differential responses of informal social control that were in play where women of lower socioeconomic class or of color were more inclined to restrict their movement and activities in the public sector than middle-class white women.

In *Guys, Gangs, and Girlfriend Abuse* (2000), Totten explored the relations between early childhood abuse, family and gender ideologies, and the construction of masculinity on the one hand and the marginal male so-cialization experiences of straight, gay, white, black, and Asian teenagers on the other hand. In his integrated analysis, Totten is not only able to make sense out of the patterned differences of girlfriend abuse with respect to the physical, sexual, and emotional violence meted out by boyfriends but he is also able to explain how the reproduction of violence and social control in these young people's lives is related to the abuse of gays and racial minori-ties. Adolescent males' bashing of girlfriends and gay people is related to feelings of powerlessness, despair, and humility regarding their economic future prospects and living up to the masculine ideal of "breadwinner" as well as their anxieties about and fears surrounding their heterosexuality.

Finally, in *Getting Played: African American Girls, Urban Inequality, and Gendered Violence* (2008), Miller captures the ways in which gender, class, and race inequality exposes many disadvantaged African American girls to sexual harassment, sexual assault, dating violence, and even gang rape. Miller points out that "urban violence" is exclusively about African Ameri-can men, and women's victimization in that context tends to be invisible. She explains how gendered victimization, racial discrimination, and the perpetuation of violence toward these adolescent females, by boys and men alike, are linked to structural inequality. Miller's analysis also significantly demonstrates how young African American women struggle to navigate this dangerous terrain where those who do not stand up for themselves against the daily "testing" of men can become targets for assault, but deflecting male attention in the wrong way can get them labeled as a "bitch" deserv-ing of assault.

IMPLICATIONS

The criminal law furnishes the basis for much of criminology and criminal justice, but it is created by people who have conscious and subconscious in-terests in maintaining privilege and who are responsive to the needs of large campaign donors (like corporations). Reiman asserts that criminology needs philosophical reflection on the nature of crime "to establish its intellectual independence of the state" and thus declare "its status as a social science rather than an agency of social control, as critical rather than servile, as illu-mination rather than propaganda" (in Reiman and Leighton 2010a, 238).

Similarly, criminology also needs reflection on and independence from class, race, and gender constructs if it is not to become simply another tool of social control and propaganda for the status quo in these areas, too.

This reflection on the nature of crime and crime control—which is related to critical criminology and explored throughout this book—is especially important because the definition of crime drives the resources of policing and the rest of the criminal justice system. It also becomes the basis for theorizing about crime as well as the collection of official data that is used for research about crime and presented in criminology books to explain crime. Without critical reflection, the criminal law appears neutral and above question because its values seem reinforced by police activity that is focused on street crime rather than white-collar crime and by criminological theory, data, and books that also have the same emphasis or focus as the criminal law.

Class, race/ethnicity, and gender are each important in understanding the production and social construction of crime and the administration of justice. Understanding that some groups are privileged because of their class, race/ethnicity, and gender is also important because privilege is the unifying concept underlying these three variables. In the United States, each of these variables has been involved in many of the laws that are selectively made (or not made) or that are differentially applied to offenders. These variables are both implicit and explicit in the theories used to explain behavior and provide direction for criminological investigation. In the processes of crime and crime control, however, separating these variables out from each other is as difficult as separating the ingredients out from a person's identity. For example, when minorities are disproportionately poor, separating class from race can be problematic.

However, it is relatively easy to identify the class, race, and gender biases at work in the study of crime and crime control. For example, for a brief period in the 1960s, the President's Commission on Crime and Law Enforcement identified the roles of inequality and discrimination as contributing to the "breakdown" in law and order. Some thirty years later, at a retrospective sponsored by the U.S. Department of Justice, criminologist Todd Clear was one of the few speakers that mentioned the issue of inequality and crime and crime control. Clear also discussed the backlash to President Johnson's Great Society ideas that had been the backdrop for the Commission's report, *The Challenge of Crime in a Free Society*. The commission advocated government taking a lead in crime prevention through social programs and opportunities for disadvantaged citizens. The subsequent rise of the law-and-order mentality and the bipartisan war on crime policies led to a different and more limited "get tough" proincarceration role for the government because crime was seen more as the result of individual failings rather than of discrimination and structural inequality and privilege.

It is also relatively easy to see how privilege is reflected differently in the two prevailing legal interpretations—the *jurisprudential model* and the *sociological model*—of class, race, and gender on "justice" outcomes. The jurisprudential model of criminal justice is an ideal, not a reality per se. It is based on "rationality, equality before the law, and treating of like cases alike" (Agozino 1997, 17). To consider such factors as class, race, and gender, then, is to violate the due process rights of the involved individuals. Because social characteristics are not *supposed* to influence the handling of a case, the jurisprudential model assumes that they do not; it regards law as constant and universal, with the same facts resulting in the same decisions. Consequently, when class, race, or sex discrimination occurs, it is considered the exception, not the rule.

In contrast to the jurisprudential model of justice, the sociological model assumes that political, economic, and social characteristics influence the administration of justice. Far from being constant from one case to another, law is assumed to be variable, changing with the social relations of the parties. Whereas the jurisprudential model is concerned with how the system *should* work, the sociological model examines how it actually *does* work. Sociological models, then, are interactive models of the administration of justice as they incorporate both the ideal and real representations of law and order, involving a variety of extralegal characteristics, including class, race, and gender.

REVIEW AND DISCUSSION QUESTIONS

1. What are the key points of the classical, positivist, and critical revolutions of criminology? How are all three still relevant to contemporary discussions on crime and justice?
2. What are the strengths and weaknesses of classical, positivist, and critical criminologies?
3. Why do the authors believe that reflection and critique of the criminal law is so important for criminology and criminal justice?
4. Briefly explain how the authors define class, race, and gender. What is one example of how each is important for criminology?
5. What is the basic idea of intersectionality? Why is intersectionality difficult to apply, and why would criminology benefit from the effort?

2

Criminal Justice Work and the Crime Control Enterprise

Federal laws barring workplace discrimination do not cover the U.S. Supreme Court. The lack of diversity among law clerks reflects this omission in the law as it raises the question of "supreme hypocrisy." For example, between his appointment to the Supreme Court in 1972 and the beginning of 1999, former Chief Justice William Rehnquist had eighty-two law clerks. During that time, he had only one Hispanic clerk and only eleven women clerks. Not once did he hire a black clerk. Overall, only 1.2 percent of his clerks had been members of minority groups.

The track record of his colleagues had not been much better. Of the 428 law clerks hired during the respective terms of the current justices, only seven were black, five were Hispanic, eighteen were Asian, and not a single one was Native American. Despite the fact that over 40 percent of law school graduates in the 1990s were women, they made up only one quarter of all clerks hired by current justices.

These figures prompted Rep. Gregory Meeks (D-NY) to conclude: "If the court were a Fortune 500 company, the statistics alone would demonstrate illegal discrimination." In an article, "Does the Supreme Court Need Affirmative Action for its Own Staff?" Meeks (1999, 24) criticized the Supreme Court's hiring practices. He reasoned that becoming a clerk is a stepping-stone to other legal positions, including that of a Supreme Court justice. Thus, the hiring practices of the highest court in the land create a structural barrier to obtaining those positions. Moreover, Supreme Court law clerks wield considerable power, playing an extremely influential role in the Court's functioning.

As Meeks wrote: "Clerks have the ear of the justices they serve. They have input on which cases the justices choose to consider. They write the initial drafts of most decisions. *The Supreme Court's decisions are the law of the land and thus affect lives, determine how government resources are allocated, [and] force legislatures to reformulate public policy choices."* In other words, the influence clerks have on both the cases heard and the opinions the court renders should not be underestimated.

For example, recent Supreme Court decisions have narrowed opportunities for people of color as a result of limiting or ruling unconstitutional critical affirmative action programs or by diluting the application of the Voting Rights Act. The fact that clerks preview and review these cases means that they have had an impact on rulings involving civil rights, access to education, workplace discrimination, religious freedom, voting, welfare reform, immigrant rights, school desegregation, sexual harassment, police brutality, and death penalty appeals. Many of these cases have a disproportionate impact on minorities or women. Diversity in the back-ground and experience of clerks can help sensitize the justice to difference.

Court observers note that virtually all the Supreme Court clerks are chosen from clerks for the United States Courts of Appeals. Thus, the lack of diversity of judges on the Court of Appeals influence the pool of clerks for the Supreme Court. Table 2.1 breaks down the race, ethnicity, and sex of Court of Appeals judges appointed between 1981 and 2007 (with lifetime appointments, some of the appointees of President Reagan are still serving). While the data do not allow for the analysis of intersections, the clear implication is that judgeships are very much male and white. To the extent judges seek clerks they are comfortable with because the clerks are "like themselves," judges re-create the pattern set by the white, male presidents who appointed them.

With the election of Barak Obama, the first biracial president, some of these patterns will start to change. His first appointment to the Supreme Court was Sonia Sotomayor, the Court's third woman and first Hispanic woman. But more generally, "Whites still comprise a full 84 percent of the federal judiciary. Women constitute only one in five federal judges. African Americans make up only 8 per-cent of the bench" and less than 1 percent are Asian Americans (Tobias 2009). As of August 30, 2009, there were 876 federal judgeships, of which ninety were vacant; President Obama has appointed sixteen people—not all of who are minor-ity and/or female—and none have yet been confirmed (uscourts.gov 2009). The pace of change for federal judgeships will be slow, and thus clerks will be important for helping give the justices a broader, more rounded, and varied perspective on critical issues. In sum, only by setting a proactive example of inclusion can the Supreme Court fulfill the ideal of justice that it purports to protect. Indeed, the same argument, more or less, can be applied to virtually all careers associated with the administration of justice in America.

∞

The opening narrative discussed the two highest federal courts, which are important but make up a small part of the criminal justice system.

Table 2.1.   Sex, Race, and Ethnicity of Presidential Appointees to the U.S. Court of Appeals

	Reagan 1981–1988	Bush 1989–1992	Clinton 1993–2000	Bush 2001–2007
Sex				
Male	95%	81%	67%	75%
Female	5	19	33	25
Race, Ethnicity				
White	97%	89%	74%	85%
Black	1	5	13	10
Hispanic	1	5	12	5
Asian	0	0	2	0
Number of Appointees	78	37	61	59

Totals may not add to 100 percent because of rounding. *Sourcebook of Criminal Justice Statistics*, table 1.81.2008.

Indeed, the system employs almost 2.5 million people and spends about $20 billion in payroll (see table 2.2). That figure does not include people in private security, private detectives, or other related work not funded by government. Thus, jobs within the criminal justice enterprise are diverse (see box 2.1), and different occupations have unique dynamics with respect to the diversity of class, race, and gender. The first part of this chapter describes the roles and functions of the principal occupations in the three primary areas of criminal justice practice—law enforcement, courts, and corrections—and provides an overview of the relevant breakdowns according to race, gender, and class. In addition, for each of the subsystems of the administration of criminal law, other characteristics such as the number of workers, working conditions, educational requirements, and salaries are provided. The second part of this chapter briefly examines how globalization, privatization, homeland security, and militarization are changing the nature of the criminal justice enterprise—and the jobs and careers within it.

Table 2.2.   Criminal Justice Expenditures, Payroll and Employees, 2006

	Total Expenditures	Employee Payroll	Total Employees
CJ System Total	$214.5 billion	$10.2 billion	2,427,452
Police	$98.9	$5.1	1,154,193
Judicial and Legal	$46.9	$2.3	507,793
Corrections	$68.7	$2.8	756,466

Detail may not add to total because of rounding. Payroll as of March 2006. Source: BJS, *Justice Expenditure and Employment in the United States, 2006*. NCJ224394, tables 1 and 2.

Box 2.1 Careers in Criminal Justice

Law Enforcement/ Security	Courts/Legal	Corrections/ Rehabilitation
BATF Agent	Arbitrator	Activity Therapist
Border Patrol Agent	Attorney General	Business Manager
Campus Police Officer	Bailiff	Case Manager
Crime Prevention Specialist	Clerk of Court	Chaplain
Criminal Investigator	Court Reporter	Chemical Dependency Worker
Criminal Profiler	Jury Coordinator	Child Care Worker
Customs Officer	Juvenile Magistrate	Classification Officer
Deputy Sheriff	Law Clerk	Clinical Social Worker
Deputy U.S. Investigator	Law Librarian	Community Liaison Officer
Drug Enforcement Officer	Legal Researcher	Correctional Officer
Environmental Protection Agent	Mediator	Dietary Officer
FBI Special Agent	Paralegal	Drug Court Coordinator
Fingerprint Technician	Public Defender	Fugitive Apprehension Officer
Forensic Scientist	Public Information Officer	Home Detention Supervisor
Highway Patrol Officer	Trial Court Administrator	Job Placement Officer
INS Officer	Victim Advocate	Juvenile Detention Officer
Insurance Fraud Investigator		Juvenile Probation Officer
Laboratory Technician		Medical Doctor
Loss Prevention Officer		Mental Health Clinician
Military Police Officer		Nurse
Park Ranger		Parole/Probation Officer
Police Administrator		Postal Inspector
Police Dispatcher		Presentence Inspector

Law Enforcement/ Security	Courts/Legal	Corrections/ Rehabilitation
Police Officer		Prison Industries Supervisor
Polygraph Examiner		Programmer/Analyst
Private Investigator		Psychologist
Private Security Officer		Rehabilitation Counselor
Recreation Coordinator		Residence Supervisor
Researcher		Secret Service Agent
State Trooper		Sex Offender Therapist
		Social Worker
		Teacher
		Vocational Instructor
		Warden/ Superintendent
		Youth Service Worker
		Youth Supervisor

CRIMINAL JUSTICE WORKERS

Law Enforcement Workers

In 2006, the United States had almost 18,000 public law enforcement agencies and about 1.2 million sworn law enforcement officers at the municipal, county, state, and federal levels of government (Bureau of Labor Statistics 2008–2009). A breakdown of occupational police types and the employment data for 2006 and projected for 2016 are presented in table 2.3. While this section does try to paint a general picture, Bohm and Haley (2005, 160) point out that virtually no two police agencies in America are

> structured alike or function in the same way. Police officers themselves are young and old; well-trained and ill-prepared; rural, urban, suburban; generalists and specialists; paid and volunteer; and public and private. These

differences lead to [at least three] generalizations about law enforcement in the United States:

1. The quality of police services varies greatly across the nation.
2. There is no consensus on professional standards for police personnel, equipment, and practices.
3. Expenditures for police services vary greatly among communities.

Starting salaries and median annual earnings for nonsupervisory sworn personnel in 2002 and 2003 across local, state, and federal law enforcement agencies were in the low to high $40,000 range. However, supervisory salaries for the federal law enforcement workers topped out at between $85,000 to $106,000 compared to a range of $50,000 to $85,000 for local and state supervisory law enforcement workers (Bureau of Labor Statistics 2004–2005). In 2006, police and sheriff's patrol officers had median annual earnings of $47,460, up from $42,270 in 2002 (Bureau of Labor Statistics 2004–2005; 2008–2009). Minimum to maximum annual salary bases (not including overtime) for police supervisors for 2002 and 2006 are listed in table 2.4.

Educationally, just 1 percent of municipal police departments required new recruits to have a four-year college degree and only 9 percent required at least a two-year degree in 2003. A high school diploma or higher edu-

Table 2.3.   Police Types and Employment, 2006 with Projections for 2016

Projections Data from the National Employment Matrix

Occupational Title	Employment 2006	Percent Employment, 2016	Change, 2006–2016	
			Number	Percent
Police and Detectives	861,000	959,000	97,000	11
First-line Supervisors/ Managers of Police and Detectives	93,000	102,000	8,500	9
Detectives and Criminal Investigators	106,000	125,000	18,000	17
Fish and Game Wardens	8,000	8,000	0	0
Police Officers	654,000	724,000	70,000	11
Police and Sheriff's Patrol Officers	648,000	719,000	70,000	11
Transit and Railroad Police	5,600	5,900	400	6

Note: Data in this table are rounded. *Occupational Outlook Handbook, 2008–2009.* U.S. Bureau of Labor Statistics, 2008–2009. Retrieved from www.bls.gov/oco/ocos160.htm#earnings.

Table 2.4.   Minimum to Maximum Annual Salary Bases (Not Including Overtime) for Police Supervisors for 2002 and 2006

Title	2002	2006
Police corporals	$39,899 to $49,299	$44,160 to $55,183
Police sergeants	$46,899 to $55,661	$53,734 to $63,564
Police lieutenants	$52,446 to $63,059	$59,940 to $72,454
Police captains	$56,499 to $70,177	$65,408 to $81,466
Deputy chiefs	$59,790 to $75,266	$68,797 to $87,564
Police chiefs	$68,337 to $87,037	$78,547 to $99,698

Source: Bureau of Labor Statistics 2004–2005; 2008–2009.

cational achievement was required by 81 percent of local police agencies across the nation (Bureau of Justice Statistics 2006c, 9).

At the federal level, in 2004 there were about sixty-five law enforcement agencies employing about 105,000 full-time personnel authorized to make arrests and carry firearms (BJS 2006b). Agencies include the Federal Bureau of Investigation, the Drug Enforcement Administration, the U.S. Secret Service, and the Bureau of Immigration and Customs Enforcement (formed in 2003 as a part of the Department of Homeland Security). In these and other federal law enforcement agencies, women and minorities are underrepresented, but they fare better than at the local levels of law enforcement. For example, in 2004, women accounted for 16 percent of federal officers; almost 18 percent were Hispanic, 11 percent were African American, 3 percent were Asian, and 1 percent were Native American (BJS 2006b, 1, 6). Total minority representation at the federal level was thus about 33 percent, compared to almost 24 percent at the state and local level. The Bureau of Justice Statistics does not publish data broken down by race and gender, which would reveal the number of minority women employed as federal officers.

Local law enforcement activities constitute the bulk of police work and are carried out primarily by municipal (i.e., city, township) police departments that typically (94 percent) employ fewer than fifty sworn officers. The larger the police agency, the more likely it is to employ women and minority officers. While white males are still highly overrepresented, the overrepresentation has been declining. For example, in 2000, "70.9 percent of full-time sworn officers were white men, down from 78.4 percent in 1997" (Bohm and Haley 2005, 162). From the early 1900s until 1972, when the Equal Employment Opportunity Commission (EEOC) began to assist women police officers in obtaining equal employment status with male officers, policewomen were responsible for protection and crime prevention work with women and juveniles, particularly girls. Today, women engage in virtually all of the duties that men do, but according to the National Center for Women in Policing (2002, 6), the number of women within large police agencies declined from 14.3 percent in 1999 to 12.7 percent in 2001—a trend they attribute to a reduced number of consent decrees in effect because of lawsuits. (Representation in top positions is less in smaller police agencies.) They also note women hold only 7.3 percent of top command positions (chiefs, deputy chiefs, and captains) and 9.6 percent of supervisory positions (lieutenants and sergeants); women of color hold 1.6 percent of top command positions and 3.1 percent of supervisory positions (2002, 4, 7).

Like most municipal police departments, most sheriffs' departments are small. In addition to enforcing the criminal and traffic laws of the state, sworn and not sworn personnel of sheriffs' departments perform functions that range from investigating crimes to supervision of jailed inmates. Unlike municipal police departments, sheriffs are directly elected, so they operate in the context of partisan politics and have the authority to appoint special deputies and to award patronage jobs. Generally, they have a freer hand in running their agencies than police chiefs who usually serve as mayoral appointees, but they are also subject more to local politics than they are to attributes of police professionalism. The first year a woman was elected sheriff was in 1992, when two women were elected—one in Georgia and the other in Arkansas.

In making sense of the statistics and the overall environment, a number of points are important. First, all women and racial minorities interested in working in most areas of criminal justice share the challenge of entering overwhelmingly white male work environments, with women of color being doubly disadvantaged. For example, Susan Martin (1992) concluded that white patrolmen tended to be protective of white women but not black women. Moreover, black men could not be counted on to support and assist black women, and some (as with some white men) were opposed to women on patrol. Further, white female officers tended to view gaining acceptance by male officers as more important and valuable than being accepted by other women, leading one black female supervisor to conclude that "getting unity is like pulling teeth."

Second, sexual and racial discrimination acts to preserve some criminal justice professions, especially law enforcement, as disproportionately white male domains. These forms of harassment can be separate and unrelated or combined, for example, in the form of "racialized sexual harassment" that serves to keep some women of color from entering, advancing, or remaining in a predominantly white male occupation. In general, women of any color and minority males must try to fit into the world of the white male cop. Both of these groups may also lack access to the "old boy" networks in law enforcement, a situation that can be conducive to a catch-22 state of affairs, especially for women. On the one hand, if men of color or women in general do not socialize (either by choice or exclusion), they risk not learning information related to their job or promotion opportunities and may be labeled as aloof or "cold." On the other hand, if women in particular socialize with male colleagues, they may be perceived to be sexually available, which reflects negatively on women's professionalism (Belknap 1995; Fletcher 1995; Martin and Jurik 1996). Gay and lesbian officers, white or of color, have another set of issues to be addressed by law enforcement (see box 2.2). (The situation is still better for them than in the military, where "don't ask, don't tell" denies their equal civil rights and discriminates against them for their sexual identities.)

Third, The National Center for Women in Policing (2002, 3) notes that "once on the job, women often face discrimination, harassment, intimidation, and are maliciously thwarted, especially as they move up the ranks." When such behavior is on the basis of gender discrimination alone, women may encounter sexual harassment in a variety of forms. Such harassment may contribute to a hostile working environment in which submission to unwelcome sexual advances and comments becomes a condition of employment. Women who complain may be ostracized by their colleagues (see chapters 5 and 9).

Fourth, women of color have additional barriers even though some people believe that they receive a double benefit because of their underrepresentation as both women and people of color. In reality, cases like the *United States v. City of Chicago* are more typical (Martin 1992). There, the judge imposed quotas for promotion to encourage the hiring of more racial and ethnic minority officers and women. Initially, black women were called from the promotion list as blacks. When the white women officers realized the black women officers were being promoted ahead of them, the white women filed a claim asserting that all women should be treated as one single minority group—as women. The judge ruled that black women could not be given double benefits and that they had to be judged against other women and not men, with the approval of the lawyer from the African American league (which was representing all black officers) who failed to consult the black women involved in the case. This decision advantaged the black males and disadvantaged the black females, as black women had to compete with white women whose test scores were better than theirs rather than with the black men, whose test scores were not. Of course, the ruling could have placed black women in the minority category of black rather than that of female, wherein the result would have been that black women would have been promoted over black men. Interestingly, when the black female officers filed a lawsuit protesting the decision, the judge agreed that they had a valid complaint but deemed their concerns "not timely."

Fifth, racial/ethnic minorities, blacks and Hispanics in particular, not only have to deal with fitting in and being accepted by their white male counterpart majorities but they often, especially in impoverished ethnic

Box 2.2. Gay and Lesbian Police Officers

The presence of women and gay men on the police force challenges the traditional heterosexually masculine definition of the occupation. Just as being a competent female officer challenges assumptions that policing is a masculine occupation suited only for masculine men, so too does being a competent gay male officer. Many straight male police officers are against anything feminine, be it a female police officer or a male police officer they perceive to be effeminate.

Homophobic attitudes in society and with law enforcement in particular create problems for the gay or lesbian officer. In most states an employer is perfectly within its right to fire (or refuse to hire, or refuse to promote) an employee solely because of his or her sexual orientation. Thus, the gay or lesbian officer who is being mistreated on the job lacks legal protection to confront the problem, much the same as a homosexual has no rights in the armed services (they are prohibited from service, and thousands have been discharged).

Unlike race or sex, officers can choose to try to conceal their sexual orientation. Thus, some officers may experience the stress of staying closeted. Gay officers may try to present a heterosexual image by playing along with the macho sexual bravado. A lesbian officer may tolerate flirtations from male officers in order to protect her sexual identity or dispel rumors that she is a lesbian. Some lesbian officers report harassment on the basis of their gender or their sexual orientation, or a combination of both. Male officers are expected to be masculine or risk being labeled a "faggot." Women officers are expected to be feminine—or at least not masculine—or risk being labeled a "bulldagger" or a "dyke."

Beyond the verbal insults is offensive and harassing conduct by fellow officers, including being assaulted, forced into lockers, and handcuffed (King 1998). Some gay and lesbian officers fear for their safety. A lesbian officer observed, "If I were a gay man, I don't know if I'd be out. . . . I can see where a gay man would really be in fear for his life every single day from his fellow officers" (quoted in Buhrke 1996, 110). For some officers, the torment and ridicule may be severe enough to cause them to seek early retirement or psychiatric treatment.

Recognizing the need of gay and lesbian police officers and other criminal justice professionals to have an arena to discuss their concerns in an atmosphere free of job-related reprisals, the Gay Officers Action League (GOAL) was established in 1981. GOAL continues to provide a safe environment for people who have been, and continue to be, victims of harassment and discrimination in the workplace, while at the same time attempting to change homophobic attitudes in the workplace and in the community at large. Other organizations, such as Law Enforcement Gays and Lesbians (LEGAL), also offer support for gay, lesbian, bisexual, and transgender workers in criminal justice.

communities, find that their community identities or loyalties are subject to questioning. In cases of police brutality or when excessive force is used by black police officers against those in the black community, some see it as evidence that the incident was about brutality and excessive force, not race. But people should not jump to that conclusion without considering that black officers are capable of holding prejudices about black offenders. Ronald Hampton of the National Black Police Association observed, "Success [in a department] is defined in white male terms. So these guys internalize the racist, oppressive culture of the police department in order to succeed" (Ripley 2000). Finally, undercover work requires the involvement of detectives whose dark skin permits them to blend into certain neighborhoods, but they sometimes fear that a white officer will accidentally shoot them (Winerip 2000).

For all the problems, there are some who say that sexism and racism in the workplace is declining. However, affirmative action myths, such as that police or corrections departments must meet quotas in hiring women and minority men, regardless of whether or not they are qualified, seems to be unevenly fading away. In reality, affirmative action programs were designed to determine the percentage of qualified women and minorities available to an organization (such as a police department) and to set flexible goals to be reached in good faith. The courts, in short, imposed quotas only in the case of blatant discrimination against clearly qualified minorities, and this system disappeared after the Supreme Court decided quotas were unconstitutional when used in college admission in *University of California v. Bakke* (438 U.S. 265 [1978]).

In conclusion, there are significant limitations on essentializing gender relations or police-race relations in an occupational setting. Statements such as "all white officers engage in racial profiling" or generalizations about the behavior of female officers are too simplistic. The social reality is that people are influenced not only by their personal attitudes and experiences but also by the context in which they live and work. Whites are capable of recognizing the problems of racial profiling and brutality, and racial and ethnic minority officers are capable of succumbing to them. Women must both adapt to the masculine values in policing even as they also resist and seek to change some aspects of the organization. To suggest otherwise is to diminish everyone by treating people as if their actions are solely dictated by their racial categorization rather than by a variety of individual, occupational, organizational, situational, and other contexts. However, this should not mask some underlying dynamics of privilege, because when it comes to harassment based on gender, sexual orientation, or race/ethnicity in law enforcement, women, gays and lesbians, and people of color each experience the status of "outsider." They are all subjects of police subordination in an occupation that punishes them for entering male only or white male only domains (Martin and Jurik 1996).

Judicial Workers

The number of judicial workers involved in criminal tribunals, from the charging to the sentencing stages, is considerably smaller than the number of workers involved in law enforcement. Further, law enforcement workers are essentially working class and middle class (except those involved in *contract security* as private security officers or "guards" whose average full-time annual salary in 2000 was $17,570 [Bohm and Haley 2005, 180] and those managers either in charge of private security officers or employed in *proprietary security*, with annual salary ranges from the middle $50s to the low six-figure incomes). But judicial workers can be divided by profession and class into two distinctive categories of workers.

First, there are the members of the legal bar—attorneys and judges—who have overwhelming graduated from a four-year college or university as well as a three-year law school, passed a state bar examination, and been certified to practice law. The *Sourcebook of Criminal Justice Statistics* indicates that in 2005, the median salary of prosecutors was $85,000, although this figure includes part-time offices. Full-time prosecutors had a median salary of $95,000 to $149,000 depending on the size of the jurisdiction (*Sourcebook Online*, table 1.87.2005). For states, the median salary for judges in 2009 was about $130,000 for a general trial court up to a median of $145,000 for the highest court (*Sourcebook Online*, table 1.90.2009). However, salaries varied widely by state, so that general-level judges in Montana made about $99,000 while their counterparts in California made almost $179,000. The *Sourcebook* does not provide any data on public defender salaries.

Second, there are the nonlawyers, primarily bailiffs and stenographers but also including the much less frequent occupations of victim-witness or domestic violence advocates. With the exception of bailiffs, the other nonlawyers (especially stenographers) are primarily women and white. The educational backgrounds of these nonlawyers vary greatly, from those with a high school diploma or GED to those with undergraduate and postgraduate degrees. These judicial workers' annual incomes place them in the working and middle classes. For example, the average annual 2006 salary for paralegals and legal assistants was $43,040; court reporters was $45,610; and law clerks in 2008 were earning $40,580 (Bureau of Labor Statistics 2008–2009).

The rest of this discussion on judicial workers focuses on the three key actors in the criminal court process: the prosecutor, the defense attorney, and the judge. These positions influence some of the direct actions taken by police and correctional personnel in the name of crime control, and they also indirectly influence some behavior of general citizens as they conform to the "rule of law." Despite the relative power of these legal actors, they are still captives of a legal order and rigid judicial processes that are, for the most part, well beyond their control.

Prosecutors

Violations of federal law are prosecuted by the U.S. Justice Department, headed by the U.S. Attorney General, and staffed by ninety-three U.S. attorneys (one assigned to each of the federal district court jurisdictions), all nominated by the president and confirmed by the Senate. Within states, district attorneys are generally employed by a county to prosecute violations of state laws. Most chief prosecutors for each county are elected, and they select their assistant or deputy prosecutors who carry out the day-to-day work of the prosecutor's office in all but the small and rural offices. Since most crimes violate state law, these offices receive most of the attention in this section.

In 2005, according to a national survey of prosecutors, there were 2,344 prosecutors' offices in the United States, employing more than 78,000 attorneys, investigators, victim advocates, and support staff (Bureau of Justice Statistics 2006a, table 1). The combined annual budgets in 2005 for state ($4.9 billion) and federal ($3.2 billion) prosecutors came to $8.1 billion (Perry 2006, 1, 4). State prosecutors' offices closed more than 2.4 million felony cases and nearly 7.5 million misdemeanor cases in 2005. This amounted to about ninety felony cases per assistant prosecutor. The median number of felony jury trial verdicts per office was only six, and these represented approximately 3 percent of the total felony cases. The Bureau of Justice Statistics notes "felony trial verdicts were relatively rare" (2006a, 6), underscoring the importance of the plea-bargaining system (DeFrances 2002). The real life of prosecutors and defense attorneys is that of private negotiations rather than the emotionally charged trial that is featured prominently on many television dramas.

Depending on the state, the prosecutor may be called the district attorney, the county attorney, the state's attorney, or several other variations. Whatever the name,

> the prosecutor is the most powerful actor in the administration of justice. Not only do prosecutors conduct the final screening of each person arrested for a criminal offense, deciding whether there is enough evidence to support a conviction, but in most jurisdictions they also have unreviewable discretion in deciding whether to charge a person with a crime and whether to prosecute the case. In other words, regardless of the amount (or lack) of

incriminating evidence, and without having to provide any reason to anyone, prosecutors have the authority to charge or not with a crime and to prosecute or not prosecute the case (Bohm and Haley 2005, 278).

Like all attorneys, prosecutors are officers of the court. In addition, although police typically recommend that a suspect be charged with a crime, the final decision rests with the prosecution. To charge or not to charge and what to charge are all decisions within prosecutorial discretion, which is what gives prosecutors their formidable power. The only check on the power of the prosecutor's arsenal of legal weapons are the "rules of discovery" mandating that a prosecutor provide defense counsel with any exculpatory (favorable) evidence on behalf of his or her client.

Once the decision to prosecute has been made, prosecutors are then involved in virtually all stages of criminal adjudication, including whether or not to plea bargain a case (and the negotiated punishment to be doled out) or to take it to trial, the trial itself, and the sentencing phase as well. Other duties, depending on jurisdiction, that add to the power of prosecutors are recommending the amount and/or whether a person should receive bail; acting as legal advisers to other local governmental agencies; and managing a legal and political bureaucracy.

With few exceptions, partisan politics play a controlling role in the recruitment of prosecutors, both country and federal. For attorneys with any political aspirations or ambitions, choosing to work as a district attorney is a wise decision. As a political office engaged in the "war on crime" and as a political springboard to higher governmental posts, appointed or elected, the only office to rank higher is the mayor's. In short, it's not the money but the power, status, and political potential that attracts persons to prosecutors' offices, often cementing their allegiances to the political status quo and state-legal apparatuses in the process (Jacob 1980 [1973]).

Breakdowns of prosecuting attorneys by gender and/or race/ethnicity were not available; however, the number of chief and assistant prosecutors in 2005 belonging to the National Black Prosecutors Association was 800. Historically, women, blacks, Hispanics, and other minorities have been highly underrepresented. Although there are certainly more women prosecutors today compared to three decades ago (when there were virtually none), the presence of persons of color is still statistically marginal. In other words, the cultural gap between the majority of white, middle-class prosecutors and the overwhelmingly indigent majority of defendants, nonwhite or white, remains wide. Also, those who become assistant and chief prosecutors are not traditionally of the same class backgrounds as those members of the bar who take cases against big business and corporate America. As Herbert Jacob, the political legal scholar, pointed out (1980 [1973]) in one of his classic works:

There are substantial indications that in many cities, most of the assistant prosecutors come from local law schools. In Chicago, for instance, more assistants come from DePaul and Chicago Kent than from the University of Chicago or Northwestern University law schools. They are likely to come from more modest backgrounds than students in elite law schools; they are often graduates of local high schools and colleges and come from families that have lived a long time in the city. The backgrounds of prosecutors suggests that they are particularly sensitive to political implications of their work; they are usually part of the political clique that dominates their locale and, therefore, may be more protective of their fellow officeholders than others would be.

Little has changed about these fundamental political, social, and economic realities of prosecuting criminal defendants in contemporary America.

Defense Attorneys

Backgrounds of defense attorneys are similar to those of prosecutors, working class and middle class. Both groups of attorneys are usually homegrown and typically attended nonelite law schools within their native states. Unlike prosecutors, however, defense attorneys are generally not connected to the local political scene. It is also safe to assume that if prosecutors closed 2.4 million felony cases in 2005, then defense attorneys of some kind were present in each of these cases, although some of the 7 million misdemeanors might have been closed without the benefit of a defense counsel.

Criminal defense work is done by privately retained lawyers, court-appointed lawyers, public defenders, and contract lawyers. Regardless of the type of lawyer that one has, the Sixth Amendment to the U.S. Constitution as well as several twentieth-century Supreme Court decisions guarantee the right to "effective assistance" of counsel to people charged with a crime (Barak 1980; Loftus and Ketcham 1991). Besides the right to representation at trial, the right extends to several other critical stages in the criminal justice process where the "substantial rights of the accused" or convicted may be affected. These stages may include: police lineups, custodial interrogations, preliminary hearings, plea-bargaining sessions, first appeal of a negotiated or postconviction sentence, and probation and parole revocation hearings. The Supreme Court has also extended the right to counsel to minors in juvenile court proceedings.

Defense attorneys often receive a "bad rap" from the public for defending obviously guilty clients or for getting them off through legal loopholes or technicalities. However, the defense attorney is playing a part as an officer of the court by making sure the prosecutor can prove guilt beyond a reasonable doubt while playing by the accepted rules of procedure. The constitutional right to effective assistance of counsel and the adversarial nature of the adjudicative process would become meaningless if lawyers refused to defend their clients on the grounds that they knew (or believed, or the community generally believed) that a defendant was guilty. Hence, their jobs are to provide the best possible legal counsel and advocacy within the ethical standards of the profession and the limits of the law in order to compel the state to legally prove its case beyond a reasonable doubt.

On the whole, defense attorneys differ markedly from both prosecutors and judges. First, defense attorneys come on the stage after prosecutorial discretion has engaged in its gatekeeping functions, deciding which cases to drop, to negotiate, or to take to trial. In effect, prosecutors initiate cases and defenders respond. Similarly, though defenders may influence the decisions to plea or to try a case, they exert no systematic impact over the courtroom flow of criminal cases unless they are members of a large public defenders' office (Barak 1980). Moreover, unlike prosecutors and judges, criminal defenders are not elected public officials. They are all private citizens whether they are self-employed or salaried employees of local government.

Second, as a group, criminal defense attorneys are alienated and isolated from local politics; their chief alliances are with the vagaries of the legal marketplace and/or the civil service system to which they belong. In other words, not only are defense attorneys not part of a political patronage system, they are also generally not centrally located in one downtown office building, as prosecutors and judges are. Nor do they wield comparative influence with that of prosecutors with either bar associations or legislators.

Third, unlike prosecutors, not all lawyers who represent criminal defendants are adequately trained or prepared to specialize in the practice of criminal law. Most lawyers while in law school have typically taken one or two courses in criminal law and criminal procedure. Like most of the other law courses and like most practicing attorneys, the areas of law they specialize in relate to such lucrative fields as corporate, tax, or tort law or to the less remunerative, yet still financially secure, areas of the law such as probate, divorce, custody, or real estate. Comparatively speaking, the practice of criminal law provides its practitioners, with some notable exceptions such as Alan Dershowitz, Gerry Spence, or the late Johnnie Cochran Jr., less income, prestige, and status in the community.

This discussion provides some of the reasons why both academics and the U.S. Department of Justice estimate that about 34,250 persons are wrongfully convicted each year in American courts (Bohm and Haley 2005, 286). The wrongful convictions generally involve defendants who had public defenders or assigned counsel, and not the few who can afford nationally prominent, highly paid lawyers. Such high-end attorneys, however, are generally retained for one or more of three reasons: (1) the crime is sensational or highly publicized, (2) there are large legal fees involved, or

(3) the chance to make new law, usually in the area of criminal procedure, is a distinct possibility.

If defendants are upper-middle class, they may still have access to privately retained competent counsel. In most large cities, there is another small group of criminal lawyers who make very comfortable livings by defending professional criminals, such as gamblers, pornographers, drug dealers, and members of organized crime. Other defendants of the middle classes or working classes, who may or may not be able to afford private counsel, have access to the vast majority of criminal lawyers who practice predominantly in the large cities across this country. By and large, these solo criminal practitioners or small partnerships of two or three attorneys struggle to earn a decent living, often practicing other kinds of law to make ends meets.

The majority of criminal defendants who are too poor to afford to retain their own counsel must rely on one of three types of criminal attorneys: a court-appointed lawyer, a public defender, or a contract lawyer. Nearly 70 percent of state prison inmates had attorneys appointed by the courts; blacks (77 percent) and Hispanics (73 percent) had slightly higher rates (Bohm and Haley 2005, 287–88).

In sum, most practitioners of criminal defense work can be described as either "those who have failed to establish a successful practice and therefore accept criminal cases as a way of enlarging a legal practice, or those who relish the excitement in criminal work and feel that their practice secures some justice for the accused" (Quinney 1975, 213). However, in terms of the relatively few who fall into the latter category, most practice for many years as career civil servants in the public defenders' offices, justifying their roles "as mediators between the poor and the courts, resigned to seeking occasional loopholes in the system, softening its more explicitly repressive features, and attempting to rescue the victims of blatant injustices" (Platt and Pollock 1974, 27). As for most young defense attorneys who are busy learning and developing their litigation skills, they sooner or later become bored, cynical, and burnt out fighting for "justice for all," whereupon, if they have become competent in their trade, they leave the field of criminal law altogether for middle-class clients and the greener pastures of civil law.

Judges

The vast majority of judges at the state level oversee trial courts of general jurisdiction, with substantially fewer sitting on intermediate appellate courts or courts of last resort (state supreme courts). Judges who oversee most felony cases sit on the benches of what are variously called "district," "superior," or "circuit" courts (depending on jurisdiction). These trial courts, of which there are more than 3,000 across the nation, have the authority to try both civil and criminal matters and to hear appeals from the "lower courts" or trial courts of limited jurisdiction (i.e., city courts, municipal courts, county courts, justice-of-the peace courts, magistrate courts) that primarily handle misdemeanors, traffic violations, and ordinance offenses.

In several states, judges of the lower courts are not required to be lawyers or have any formal legal training. In other jurisdictions, before being elected or appointed to office, the judges will have been practicing lawyers, but many of them will have no background in criminal law before joining the judiciary. In jurisdictions where judges are elected to office, these may be partisan or nonpartisan elections. Where judges are appointed by city councils, mayors, legislatures, or governors, they are subject to the politics of local and state bar associations. Like prosecutors, then, whether elected or appointed, judges are also sensitive to the political process that generally serves the status quo rather than social change.

Like prosecutors and criminal defenders, most judges in the United States are overwhelmingly white and male. Judges tend to come from upper-middle-class families, average more than fifty years of age, attend college and law school in their home states, and are typically born in the communities in which they preside (Satter 1990). Better educated than the average citizen, a majority of these judges were previously in private legal practice, making more money than they usually do as judges. (In 2004, the average lawyer made $110,590 annually, while the average judge made $92,100 [Bureau of Labor Statistics 2004b].)

Compared to prosecutors and defenders, trial judges command more respect, status, and deference from citizens at large. According to imagery, judges are presumed to have enormous power over the adjudication or criminalization processes. Actually, though, judicial discretion is far more circumscribed than prosecutorial discretion because judges are subject to appeal and legal review by higher courts. Sentencing guidelines are established by legislators, and even when they are technically "advisory" they exert a great deal of control over the outcome. In effect, while trial judges do in fact possess a great deal of power, discretionary and otherwise, they are still less powerful in the administration of criminal justice than prosecutors are.

Since more than 90 percent of criminal cases are resolved by plea bargains, a judge's principal role becomes that of a "bureaucratic stamp" for negotiated deals worked out between prosecutors and defenders rather than one of an interpreter of complex legal matters. What Jacob (1980 [1973], 67) wrote about judges and criminal adjudication more than thirty years ago is just as accurate today as then:

> The massive flow of cases through their courts precludes anything but a cursory examination of the issues brought to their attention. Judges, like many factory

workers, sit on an assembly line. They repeatedly perform routine tasks, with each task consuming only a fraction more than a minute. For such judges, the role is exactly the opposite of the intellectual challenge a judgeship is presumed to pose; it is a mind demeaning, stupefying post.

Corrections Workers

When it comes to prisons and imprisonment, correctional officers represent the vast majority of workers. They are generally responsible for the security of the institution and have the most frequent and closest contact with inmates. As Hawkins and Alpert (1989) have observed, correctional officers experience a number of conflicts in their work, often become bored (tower workers) or overstimulated (cell block workers) depending on the nature of their jobs, and are subject to role ambiguity or role strain resulting primarily from the contradictions between custody and treatment objectives. Overall, these "officers generally have considerable discretion in discharging their duties within the constraints of rules, regulations, and policies. Yet, because they lack clear and specific guidelines on how to exercise their discretion, they feel vulnerable to second-guessing by their superiors and the courts" (Bohm and Haley 2005, 405).

Gresham Sykes's classic study, *The Society of Captives* (1958), pointed to some ambiguities in correctional officers' power and discretion because they are outnumbered by prisoners and depend on their compliance to keep the daily routine of prison, a situation he referred to as one of the "defects of total power." Hawkins and Alpert (1989) have identified three responses of officers to their working conditions. First, officers may become alienated and cynical and withdraw into some relatively safe niche within the prison. Second, some officers in their efforts to control inmates become overly authoritarian, confrontational, or intimidating. Finally, there are those officers who adopt a human-services orientation, seeking to make prisons a constructive place for themselves and for inmates. This latter orientation is not about waiting on the inmates and "serving" them in that sense, but a community policing type of orientation within the cell block rather than out on the streets (Johnson 2002).

While correctional officers are most directly engaged with inmates, there is a larger prison bureaucracy that accounts for many jobs. In 2001 adult correctional agencies employed about 440,000 people, about 220,000 were correctional officers (Bohm and Haley 2005, 404). By 2006, correctional agencies employed about 500,000 people. About three of every five jobs were in state correctional facilities, about 18,000 in federal institutions, and about 16,000 in privately owned and managed prisons. Median earnings in 2006 for correctional officers and jailers was $35,760, with the federal government paying more, local government paying less, and private prisons paying much less ($25,050) (Bureau of Labor Statistics 2008–2009). Salaries at both levels of government were subject to increases after completion of preservice training and/or a probationary period (Camp and Camp 2002, 168–69).

Although corrections workers for the federal bureau of prisons are required to have a bachelor's degree and some related work experience, paid or volunteer, applicants for state correctional systems only have to be eighteen or twenty-one years of age and possess a high school diploma or the GED. Slightly more than one-third (35 percent) had at least some college and about 10 percent of all correctional workers have a bachelor's degree or higher (Sumter 2008). At the same time, there are efforts to upgrade prison work from that of a mere job into that of a professional career. However, low pay, the nature of the work, the lack of prestige associated with it, and the remote or rural location of many prisons makes recruitment of better-educated officers difficult if the economy presents other opportunities. Conover (2000) sums up the situation from a discussion he had with a fellow guard:

> "officer after officer will tell you: there's no way in hell you'd want your kid to be a [correctional officer]." He said that probably ninety percent of the officers he knew would tell a stranger they met on vacation that they worked at something else—carpentry, he liked to say for himself—because the job carried such a stigma. Sure it had its advantages, like the salary, the benefits, the job security, and with seniority, the schedule: starting work at dawn, he had afternoons free to work on his land . . . but mainly, he said, prison work was about waiting. The inmates waited for their sentences to run out and the officers waited for retirement. It was "a life sentence in eight-hour shifts."

Some have argued that other obstacles to professionalizing corrections work have allegedly come from the backlash to affirmative action, tensions between the genders and races, and unionization of correctional workers (Owen 1985; American Correctional Association 2003).

In terms of gender and race, "77 percent of uniformed staff, including correctional officers, were male (though 35.5 percent of correctional officers hired in 2000 were female), and about 66 percent were white" (Bohm and Haley 2005, 404). When looking more broadly at all employees in state and federal prisons, about 33 percent are female (*Sourcebook* 2003, table 1.104, 96). And, while it is commonplace for women correctional officers to work in federal and state high-security institutions today, the first woman to do so was in 1978. Interestingly, women make up a greater percentage of employees in state facilities than they do in federal facilities, and there are a higher percentage of female employees in the South than in other regions.

The greater diversity in the workplace has also lead to greater tensions at times. As noted in chapters 5 and 9 especially, all groups can hold prejudices about others, but the dominant group has greater power to discriminate and harass. Women in a majority-male environment—especially one imbued with masculine values because of the quasi-military hierarchical organization—can be subject to both nonsexual putdowns as women and to offensive sexual comments or behaviors. Such comments or behaviors come from male inmates as well as a woman's fellow officers. As Conover (2000) has noted, "inmates sometimes tried to ejaculate on female officers," a common inmate rule violation and masturbatory fantasy portrayed on the popular MSNBC series *Lockup* during the 2009 season. All people of color, regardless of gender, can be subject to racial and ethnic slurs and stereotypes, similar to the dynamics discussed in the law enforcement section above. Women of color can be subject to all these forms of discrimination simultaneously. In addition, minority sexual orientations can also result in harassment of gays and lesbians, regardless of gender or race/ethnicity (Belknap 1995).

Finally, this discussion of corrections workers has focused its attention mainly on workers in prison. However, there are also probation and parole officers working in the field of "community corrections." Indeed, as inmate populations have soared over the past several decades, so have the number of persons on probation and parole. For example, between 1980 and January 2007, the increases for the number of offenders subject to probation have risen from 1.1 million to 4.2 million and parole has increased from 250,000 to almost 800,000 (Bohm and Haley 2005; BJS 2008b, tables 2 and 3). Statistics on employment, including race and gender breakdowns, are not available.

THE CHANGING NATURE OF THE CRIMINAL JUSTICE ENTERPRISE

Both the nature and context of criminal justice work continues to change because of changes in the nature of crime, perceived risk, and social trends like technological evolution and the changing worldwide political economy. This chapter closes with a brief review of four major developments that will continue to drive changes in the criminal justice enterprise: globalization, privatization, militarization, and homeland security. These developments are related to class, race, and gender not only because they are related to themes like diversity, otherness, inequality, and masculinity, but also because they represent the development of an emerging "security-industrial complex" (Klein 2007).

Globalization

Globalization refers to the growing interdependency among events, people, and governments around the world that are increasingly connected through trade, expanding communications, transportation, and computer networks. With a globalizing political economy, goods, labor, and money move more freely around the world, a situation that leads to some benefits but also intensified inequality of wealth and income. The chief economist of Wall Street investment bank Morgan Stanley noted: "Billed as the great equalizer between the rich and the poor, globalization has been anything but." Indeed, "only the elite at the upper end of the occupational hierarchy have been spared the pressures of an increasingly brutal wage compression. The rich are, indeed, getting richer but the rest of the workforce is not" (Roach 2006). Today, globalization emphasizes "free trade" and deregulation as corporations look for locations with the cheapest labor and fewest labor and environmental restrictions. Even after the 2009 economic crisis and pressure at the Global Economic Summit from the European Union, China, and India to establish international regulatory agencies, President Obama and the Wall Street and banking institutions he represented rejected the idea.

Globalization policies lead not just to inequality between countries but can lead to inequality within a country because of job losses, stagnating wages, and/or greater benefits to those at the top (through greater profits because of low wages and fewer restrictions) (Faux 2006; Klein 2007; Perkins 2007). In some countries, globalization has lead to an expansion in pain and social injustice as measured by higher rates of disease, poverty, and hunger. Studies carried out by the United Nations reveal that the top 20 percent of those living in high-income countries account for 86 percent of all the world's private consumer spending. At the same time, tens of millions of people succumb annually to famine and preventable diseases. For hundreds of millions of others, life has become a daily preoccupation with obtaining safe water, rudimentary health care, basic education, and sufficient nutrition (Barak 2007). Nations around the world are shrinking their welfare states while governments have been busy deregulating, downsizing, privatizing, contracting out, reducing taxes, and cutting social spending.

Ultimately, globalization and inequality create expanding opportunities for "legitimate" capitalists as well as criminals because the need for both licit and illicit goods or services grows in tandem. "Free trade" does not explicitly include the sexual trafficking of women and children, but encouragement of the "free flow" of goods also makes it easier to traffic persons, drugs, intellectual property, and weapons. It also encourages

> the fraudulent and unfair trade practices in commerce, the laundering of unauthorized drug and arms trade profits, the smuggling of illegal immigrants into

and out of nations, the dumping of toxic waste and other forms of ecological destruction, the acts of terrorism committed by and against various states, and the behavior of multinationals to move capital and technology to exploit cheap labor (Barak 2001, 66).

Meanwhile, the developing contours of some criminality are currently undergoing fundamental change as these become part of the growing transnational character of organized, financial, sex-related, immigration, and computer crime (Travis 1999; Edwards and Gill 2003; Sheptycki and Wardak 2005). As crime becomes transnational, crime control must do the same, requiring workers who are fluent in different languages and have an understanding of other regions of the world where the United States must collaborate with the crime control agencies in other nations.

An important aspect of globalization is immigration, which is also considered a security issue. A *New York Times* editorial noted that the Bush administration conducted "mass raids to net immigrant workers while leaving their bosses alone," using heavy weapons, dogs, and helicopters "to spread the illusion that something was getting fixed" (2009b, wk. 9). In eight years these policies netted 6,000 undocumented immigrants out of about 12 million and 135 employers out of who knows how many. In the process, they managed to destroy families, tearing parents and grandparents from children, many of whom are citizens of the United States. Raids, no matter how sensible or tactfully designed, will not fix the problems of immigration in a global economy. On the contrary, such policies have proven themselves to be counterproductive as the "fear they caused went viral in immigrant communities, driving workers further into the arms of abusive employers" (*New York Times* 2009b).

During the spring of 2009 the Obama administration issued new guidelines for Immigration and Customs Enforcement that emphasized prosecuting employers who knowingly hire illegal immigrants. Homeland Security secretary Janet Napolitano asserted during a CNN appearance that illegal immigration or "crossing the border is not a crime per se." She argued accordingly, "What we have to do is target the real evil-doers in this business, the employers who consistently hire illegal labor" as well as "the human traffickers who are exploiting human misery" (Quoted in Meyers 2009). However, the proposed shift on immigration policy is unlikely to have much of an impact on altering the lives of illegal immigrants or the working conditions of U.S. citizens. What these policies do not fix are the long backlogs in legal immigration.

The extended delays in processing paperwork and cases often extend years or decades, "forcing people who want to follow the rules to make an agonizing choice between intolerable separation from their families or lawbreaking" (*New York Times* 2009b). Nor do these policies protect illegal immigrants who are captured from the arbitrary cruelties of the detention and deportation system, in which due process is limited at best and unacceptable risks of sickness, injury, and death at worst prevail as a condition of confined imprisonment. As the editorial of the *New York Times* (2009b) succinctly articulated the situation:

> the new enforcement regime, like the old might lead employers to purge their payrolls of people they merely suspect are here illegally, to avoid the hassle and expense of a raid. . . . Without a path to earned legalization, undocumented workers who lose their jobs will have nowhere to go—except to endure ever-lower wages and worse abuse from bottom-feeding employers.
>
> While modifying raiding policies seem sensibly motivated and slightly more humane, the new guidelines as a whole are a smarter version of a bad idea that does not address the underlying problems of immigration. Far better, critics argue, would be for government to redouble its efforts to enforce the minimum wage, the right to organize, and health and safety protections. Such polices would have the effect of reducing the incentive to hire the undocumented while raising conditions for all workers.

Militarization

Although law enforcement has always been a quasi-military organization, the civil unrest of the 1960s led to the modern escalation in the militarization of the American police (Strauss 2007). Militarism is "a set of beliefs, values, and assumptions that stress the use of force and threat of violence as the most appropriate means to solve problems. It glorifies the use of military power, hardware, operations, and technology as its primary problem-solving tools" (Kraska 2007, 164–65). Accordingly, the militarization of law enforcement includes the processes of arming, organizing, planning, training for, and sometimes pursuing violent conflict.

Kraska argues that assessing the degree to which crime control in general and police behavior in particular have become militarized hinges on the clarity of its concepts. He has also argued that the "similarities between a police paramilitary drug raid [at home in the U.S.] and the latest Iraq war" represents "the cultural, organizational, operational, and material blurring of the line between war and law enforcement, on the one hand, and between U.S. military and civilian criminal justice, on the other hand" (Kraska 2007, 166). Certainly police departments across the United States have experienced dramatic growth and use of specialized units like Special Weapons and Tactics (SWAT) and Special Response Teams (SRT) that are based on similar units within the military. By 1995 more than 77 percent of police departments had specialized units, an increase of almost 48 percent from 1985 (Kraska 1999). Between 1980 and 2004, these units, mostly in the war on drugs, increased from 2,884 deployments to 45,000 per year (Kraska 1999, 2007).

Further, these units were once thought of primarily as *reactive* units for handling hostage standoffs and other unique situations, but in an "age" of zero tolerance policing these units have become *proactive* forces. In fact, by 2004, 85 percent were no-knock and quick-knock contraband raids inside private residences. Twenty-five years ago, these police paramilitary raids and "forced investigatory searches using the military special operations model, employed during hostage rescues, was almost unheard of and would have been considered an extreme and unacceptable police tactic. Today, it defines the bulk of activity most police paramilitary teams are engaged in, and this is true of both very small and large police departments" (Kraska 2007, 163).

Military personnel train and assist these specialized units, and they also arm local police with the latest in military technology, surveillance equipment, body armor, less-than-lethal use of force devices, "various gases, and explosives to breach doors" (Strauss 2007, 456). Most visible are the adoption of military weapons and devices including the 9mm Heckler, Koch MP5 submachine gun, and the M4 Carbine. The M4 Carbine is a smaller, modified version of the U.S. military's M16 assault rifle. "Other devices that are currently used by both the military and the police include thermal imaging technology, night vision goggles, body armor technology, and various modes of transportation including boats, armored personnel carriers, and helicopters" (Strauss 2007, 456).

The militarization of policing has been accompanied by an escalation in violence, lethal and otherwise. No-knock or quick-knock paramilitary raids—used to collect evidence, such as drugs, guns, or money—naturally surprise citizens and put both citizens and police in potentially volatile situations. Dealing with these potentially dangerous situations justifies further extraordinary measures:

> These include conducting searches during the predawn hours, usually in black military battle-dress uniforms, full body armor, ninja-style hoods, and an array of enhanced listening and seeing devices—sort of a twenty-first century cyborg style. It also includes a rapid entry into the residence using specialized battering rams or sometimes entry explosives, the use of flash-band grenades designed to temporarily disorient the occupants, a frantic room-by-room search of the entire residence where all occupants are expected to immediately comply with officers' screamed demands to get into the prone position. If a citizen does not comply immediately because he or she is confused, dazed, obstinate, or doesn't know that the people raiding the house are police, more extreme measures are taken. Finally, the police ransack the entire residence for contraband (Kraska 2007, 167).

The adverse affects from these raids includes situations like deaths of Branch Davidians in Waco, Texas, in 1993; the killing of children; unintentional (but still lethal) gun discharges; raids on the wrong house; and college students shot because of quick entry for violations of marijuana laws. The commonality of these types of tragedies is not known because data on SWAT teams gone wrong are not officially recorded. Kraska (2007), however, collected more than 300 cases between 1999 and 2004 of the same type of paramilitary deployment that resulted in similar tragedies, albeit on a smaller scale. The National Center for Women in Policing also notes that "many women are discouraged from applying to law enforcement agencies because of policing's aggressive and authoritarian image, an image based on the outdated paramilitary model of law enforcement" (2002, 3). This, in turn is detrimental to public safety because "women police officers utilize a style of policing that relies less on physical force and more on communications skills." Thus, when it comes to policing in general, "women are substantially less likely to be named in a citizen complaint, sustained allegation, or civil lawsuit" that results in a payout (2002, 3).

Privatization

Privatization refers to the process of government outsourcing certain tasks to for-profit businesses. While prisons have frequently contracted out food service and health care, privatization escalated in the 1980s with the creation of businesses that built, owned, and managed prisons. A number of private prison companies later had initial public offerings in which they raised money by selling shares to the public and became traded on the stock exchange (Selman and Leighton 2010). Indeed, in the opening of his book *The Perpetual Prisoner Machine*, Joel Dyer comments on the sign hanging outside the Northeast Ohio Correctional Center that reads, "Yesterday's closing stock price." The stock price is for the prison's owner, the Corrections Corporation of America (CCA), the leader in the private prison business. To Dyer, what the sign means "is that anyone—anyone with money, that is—can now profit from crime" (2000, 10). Dyer's concern with "turning the administration of justice into a free-market experiment" (2000, 12) is that "by placing a call to a broker, any American with a few bucks can begin to build wealth so long as the prison population continues to grow" (2000, 10).

The movement to private prisons started as a way to offset the high costs of correctional expenses, due to the incarceration binge in the United States. With the expansion of prison, jail, parole, and probation, Dyer's concerns are increasingly relevant because the number of companies involved in delivering services has expanded and they have diversified into providing more services (see chapter 10). For example, the privatization of punishment is not just the construction and management of prisons but also: housing illegal immigrants (including families), juvenile offenders, and the mentally ill; contracting to provide health care and food services for incarcerated persons; contracting to provide community-based forms of surveillance, including electronic monitoring; and, most recently, contracting for reentry services for the formerly incarcerated (Selman and Leighton 2010). Indeed, some local governments are considering using taxpayer money for private police as well—a notable departure from the historical situation where the clients of private security companies were private businesses.

The reality of contemporary corrections is that it includes several multinational prison businesses with billions of dollars worth of stock and billions more in debt to Wall Street banks. The money from investors and banks allowed private businesses to build many facilities and thus continue the unprecedented expansion of the prison population—an example of understanding the political economy of punishment, or how politics and economics exert influences on punishment more significant than arguments about retribution, deterrence, and sentencing guidelines (Rusche and Kirchheimer 1968 [1939]). Killingbeck (2005, 169) summarizes how at each stage of history, the reliance on imprisonment in its different forms was tied up in a political economy of punishment:

> When society was manual-labor based and dependent on the production of goods and cheap labor, imprisonment included prison labor. It was not until the use of prison labor was no longer economically viable and politically advantageous that reforms were instituted . . . With the advent of new technologies that reduced the demand for manual labor, imprisonment served to warehouse the surplus labor supply. As capitalism became more service oriented, imprisonment became a *service* to be provided. As capitalism becomes a combination of technology, service and information, so too does punishment, in the forms of electronic monitoring and GPS tracking (emphasis in the original).

With outsourcing and globalization, wages of most workers go down while those at the top do much better, leading to an overall situation of greater inequality. With private prisons, guards tend to be paid less and have fewer benefits than government workers, and the antiunion stance of private prisons makes it difficult for workers to substantially improve work conditions. As noted above, median earnings in 2006 for all correctional officers and jailers was $35,760, but private prisons paid $25,050 (Bureau of Labor Statistics 2008–2009). Meanwhile, the Chief Executive Officer (CEO) of private prison companies make more than the average head of a Department of Corrections who manages substantially more inmates. For example, the CEO of CCA had total compensation of almost $3.1 million for 2008 (CCA 2009), and the CEO of GEO made $3.8 million that year (GEO 2009; Selman and Leighton 2010).

The free-market ideology suggests that business will be more efficient and cheaper than government. But the research does not support the contention of cost savings. The argument about efficiency sounds plausible based on beliefs about government inefficiency, but private prison companies have substantial overhead because of executive pay, payment for the compensation committee to set executive pay, and executive compensation consultants; they also pay money to Wall Street banks and corporate attorneys for activities such as Securities and Exchange Commission filings, mergers, acquisitions, shareholder lawsuits, advertising, lobbying, campaign donations, and so on. In order to be competitive and turn a profit given all their overhead costs, they use cheaper, nonunion labor. The end result is staff turnover, apathy, and poor judgment—which combined in one case to precipitate a riot (Carceral 2005; Greene 2002; Selman and Leighton 2010). The other result is increasing inequality as states pay private prison companies, which pay their top leadership way more than the head of a department of correction would make and pay their employees in the prison less than what a state would pay.

In a larger sense, the issue is not just privatization but a prison- and criminal-justice–industrial complex. These terms were taken from the idea of a military-industrial complex that President Eisenhower warned of in his Farewell Address. He was concerned that the businesses with which the military contracted, increasingly outside of public scrutiny and accountability, were driving defense policy. He warned that "we must not fail to comprehend its grave implications. Our toil, resources, and livelihood are all involved. So is the very structure of our society" (Eisenhower 1961). Eisenhower saw the military-industrial complex as a new phenomenon because of WWII defense spending, and he warned that allowing it to acquire too much influence could "endanger our liberties or democratic processes." Similarly, while prisons and the criminal justice system have had contracts with businesses for supplies and consultants for much of their history, the nature of these relationships and the amount of money involved have reached a critical mass because of the war on crime that started in the 1970s. Table 2.2 notes that the United States spends upwards of $68 billion on corrections and $214 billion on criminal justice each year, which has created Las Vegas–style conventions for businesses selling goods and services. The increases in spending from the wars on crime and drugs have created a new type of permanent crime control industry with "grave implications" for criminal justice policy (Selman and Leighton 2010).

As more companies generate revenue from corrections, there is more potential for misplaced power in the multibillion-dollar prison-industrial complex to distort sentencing and criminal justice (and mental health and immigration) policy: the interests of corporate shareholders become increasingly important, causing increasing corporate lobbying and campaign donations, while public safety and public accountability become less relevant. Basic free-market principles dictate that companies with shares traded on a stock exchange have the duty to make money for shareholders. Thus, businesses involved in incarceration have no duty to balance their desire for ever-increasing profits with the larger public good that would come from, say, crime-prevention funding or money for schools. Indeed, sentencing reform and declining crime rates are "risk factors." Eric Schlosser summarizes the issues:

> Three decades after the war on crime began, the United States has developed a prison-industrial complex—a set of bureaucratic, political, and economic interests that encourage increased spending on imprisonment, regardless of the actual need. The prison-industrial complex is not a conspiracy, guiding the nation's criminal-justice policy behind closed doors. It is a confluence of special interests that has given prison construction in the United States a seemingly unstoppable momentum. It is composed of politicians, both liberal and conservative, who have used the fear of crime to gain votes; impoverished rural areas where prisons have become a cornerstone of economic development; private companies that regard the roughly $35 billion spent each year on corrections not as a burden on American taxpayers but as a lucrative market; and government officials whose fiefdoms have expanded along with the inmate population (1998).

The open question at the moment is whether the financial crisis will accelerate privatization—and thus lower-wage jobs—or whether it will cause a reduction in criminal justice spending and the size of the criminal justice–industrial complex. The complex will certainly not disappear, and Eisenhower stated that "We should take nothing for granted. Only an alert and knowledgeable citizenry can compel the proper meshing of the huge industrial and military machinery of defense with our peaceful methods and goals, so that security and liberty may prosper together" (1961).

Homeland Security

Immediately after the terrorist attacks of 9/11, a common expression was that "everything is different now." In many ways, everything is different now for criminal justice, even though the FBI did not include the victims of 9/11 in its usual tabulations of homicide in the Uniform Crime Reports (UCR) (Leighton 2002). Local law enforcement is now engaged in fighting terrorism and the FBI—originally devoted to domestic law enforcement—now has field offices in places like Afghanistan, Indonesia, and Uzbekistan.

Indeed, large portions of criminal justice, the military, intelligence, and security institutions have been reorganized to fight a war on terror that has no clear time frame or goals.

While terrorism is not new, international terrorism and the potential for cyberterrorism have emerged as serious new risks with the growth in globalization. The primary domestic response to these threats came after the terrorist attacks of 9/11, with the passage of the Homeland Security Act of 2002, which established the Department of Homeland Security (DHS). The creation of the DHS "represents the most dramatic transformation of the U.S. government since 1947, when President Harry S. Truman combined the various branches of the U.S. military into the Department of Defense. On an even grander scale, President Bush has combined 22 previously separate domestic agencies into the new department to protect the country from future threats" (Bohm and Haley 2005, 174).

The new department, whose development is ongoing, has five major "directorates" or divisions, including: Border and Transportation Security; Emergency Preparedness and Response; Science and Technology; Information Analysis and Infrastructure Protection; and Management (for budget and personnel matters). In addition to the directorates, several agencies have been reassigned to or especially created for the DHS, including the U.S. Coast Guard, the U.S. Secret Service, the Bureau of Citizenship and Immigration Services, the Office of State and Local Government Coordination, and the Office of the Private Sector Liaison.

Because DHS is a "work in progress," it is too soon to make pronouncements about all the effects of these changes that include jurisdictional modifications, conflicts, and integration of the separate, yet overlapping, responsibilities of those charged with law enforcement and homeland security. It is important to note, however, that the Homeland Security Act stipulates that "primary responsibility for investigating and prosecuting acts of terrorism shall be vested not in the Department, but rather in Federal, State, and local law enforcement agencies with jurisdiction over the acts in question" (DHS website). Even though law enforcement retains primary responsibility, the legislation has changed the nature of law enforcement in America.

Before the creation of the DHS, the FBI was primarily a federal police agency whose responsibilities for terrorism were limited to locating terrorist groups and preventing terrorist acts within the United States. Now, they have multiple international field offices, and with the establishment of the Directorate of Information Analysis and Infrastructure Protection—charged with analyzing the intelligence and information from other agencies—the FBI reorganized itself from a law enforcement agency whose top priority was policing crime to one whose top priority was intelligence gathering and counterterrorism. As part of this transformation, local field offices of the FBI are no longer allowed to establish their own distinct crime-control agendas. Other related changes at the FBI include:

- Restructuring the management hierarchy in Washington, D.C., to support counterterrorism efforts;
- Reassigning about one-fourth of the Bureau's 11,000 agents to work on counterterrorism;
- Establishing a National Joint Terrorism Task Force to include staffers from federal, state, and local agencies;
- Addressing directly the global terrorist threats by the opening of FBI offices in such places as Kabul, Afghanistan; Sarajevo, Bosnia and Herzegovina; Jakarta, Indonesia; Uzbekistan; London; Moscow; Seoul, South Korea; Ottawa, Canada; etc.

The consequences of these developments and changes in priorities has already had a detrimental effect on efforts of the FBI to combat white-collar and corporate crime at home, which ironically contributed to the current economic crisis, even though one main responsibility of DHS is to "ensure the overall economic security of the United States" (see box 2.3).

With the change from the Bush to Obama administration, the role of the bureau is changing because of the emerging "global justice" initiative of President Obama, which reverses some of the Bush administration's use of covert CIA actions and reinforces the expanded role of the FBI in the fight against terrorism (Meyer 2009). The new "approach effectively reverses a mainstay of the Bush administration's war on terrorism, in which global counterterrorism was treated primarily as an intelligence and military problem, not a law enforcement one. That policy led to the establishment of the prison at Guantanamo Bay, Cuba; harsh interrogations; and detentions without trials" (Meyer 2009). By contrast, the "global justice" approach begins with the premise that virtually all suspects should end up in either a U.S. or foreign court of law (and not be subject to military tribunals). Under the new guidelines, FBI agents will "expand their questioning of suspects and evidence-gathering to try to ensure that criminal prosecutions are an option" (Meyer 2009). Thus, on one hand, the shift in U.S. policy replaces the CIA-dominated system of clandestine detention and interrogation with one built around transparent investigations and prosecutions carried out by law enforcement agencies. On the other hand, under the new policy, the FBI and Justice Department will continue their already expanded role in global counterterrorism operations, leaving less resources and fewer agents to fight domestic crime.

In addition, President Obama brought some of the functions and responsibilities for the nation's digital security to the White House when he announced in late May of 2009 that he would appoint the "the nation's first

Box 2.3. Economic Crisis and the War on State-Corporate Crime?

Immediately after the terrorist attacks of 9/11 a common expression was that "everything is different now." In fundamental ways, many things are different in relation to counterterrorism strategies and the enforcement and administration of criminal justice both at home and abroad. More importantly, what has fallen below the radar are the connections between these changing legal–crime fighting operations and their effects on the missing war on white-collar and state-corporate crime. It is these omissions in controlling many financial practices from Wall Street to Main Street that may be linked to this country's current economic crisis. In the midst of an imminent worldwide recession, or even worse, a global depression occurring, this economic crisis of tsunami proportions will presumably last three to five years. Many people are calling for a new world economic order or global restructuring.

Whether such a fundamental change in international economic relations happens now or in the future, the primary response to 9/11 and to the larger war on terrorism by the United States had been the passage of the Homeland Security Act of 2002, which created the Department of Homeland Security (DHS). According to the legislation, the DHS was created for seven purposes, and the one that is most often ignored by public and private conversations alike is the legal charge that the DHS will "ensure that the overall economic security of the United States is not diminished by efforts, activities, and programs aimed at securing the homeland."

Although the DHS in its short history has certainly had its share of failures (the recovery in New Orleans in the wake of Hurricane Katrina), Homeland Security's most serious failure to date has been to bulk up its war on terror and remain heavily invested in a war on drugs while failing to replace those agents engaged in the fight against white-collar crime. The issue is not a choice between fighting terrorism or white-collar crime but placing a higher priority on a questionable drug war while white-collar and corporate crime control became "nonpriorities."

For example, following the September 11 attacks, the FBI shifted more than 1,800 agents, or nearly one-third of all agents, from law enforcement to terrorism and intelligence duties. So depleted were the ranks of the investigators in the areas of white-collar and corporate crimes that many executives in the private sector were complaining that they had been having difficulty attracting the bureau's intervention into even those cases that potentially involved frauds in the hundreds of millions of dollars. Moreover, since late 2003 and early 2004, the FBI had been requesting additional resources to the tune of $1 billion dollars as well as 800 more agents so that they could go after the perpetrators of mortgage fraud and other economic crimes that they viewed at the time as posing a looming threat to the financial markets.

While the agency did receive 50 million, or 5 percent, of their request for the "war on white-collar crime," the current number of investigators for these crimes is down 625 agents, or 36 percent from 2001. Finally, after trying to acquire the necessary resources and person power for more than four years, the FBI has recently launched more than 1,500 criminal investigations into this nation's mortgage-related business practices, including those financial and institutional transactions of such corporate giants as Fannie Mae, Freddie Mac, the American International Group, and Lehman Brothers.

Before there is another economic crisis of global proportions, perhaps the United States will learn, once and for all, the powerful lessons of the adverse effects of antiregulation policies and nonenforcement of upper-world white-collar and corporate crime on the wider society and world as a whole. Historically, that was not the case with either the savings and loans' scandals of the late 1980s or the corporate frauds perpetrated early in the twenty-first century by those CEOs in charge of Enron, HealthSouth, Adelphia, WorldCom, GlobalCrossing, Xerox, and Waste Management, to name the most conspicuous offenders. And, when the U.S. Congress has acted to reform the situation by passing legislation such as Sarbanes-Oxley in an attempt to control and regulate "corporate fraud gone wild," it was only a matter of time before those legal efforts were stripped of their enforcement teeth by lobbyists working on behalf of powerful antiregulation forces.

Even Alan Greenspan has finally come to the realization that "free enterprise" without regulation is no way to run the economy. In fact, it is criminal to run an economy that way, for which it is now costing the American taxpayers almost a trillion dollars as part of a plan to rescue the nation's financial system from a Wall Street–orchestrated, federally enabled, multibillion-dollar pyramid scheme.

Source: Adapted from Barak (2008)

cyber security czar to help protect the nation's telecom infrastructure and information systems that have grown so crucial to industry, the military and individual citizens" (*Denver Business Journal* 2009). On the heels of President Obama's declaration of a new security czar, the Pentagon announced "the formation of a Cyber-Command to both defend against cyber attacks and wage cyber warfare against our enemies" (ChattahBox.com 2009).

While many criminology students will find employment in the increased opportunities in security and related fields, the discipline of criminology—those who research and study crime—has done little to build on its understanding of violent crime and hate crimes to develop a better understanding of the mass murders of terrorists. Before 9/11, criminology as a field of study had a "grudging acceptance of terrorism" (Rosenfeld 2002, 1), and criminologists have written few books on terrorism. Among students, serial killers are popular, with much interest in psychological profiling and "mind hunting," so getting inside the head of Bundy, Gacy, or Dahmer is still more popular than understanding Osama bin Laden (who has killed far more people than those serial killers put together) (Leighton 2005, 2004). The issues go well beyond the simplistic slogan about how terrorists are crazy or hate us because we're free, which does a profound disservice to the cause of understanding the political worldview of terrorists (see Barak 2004a; Leighton 2005). Indeed, Benjamin and Simon—both former directors of the National Security Council—write in *The Age of Sacred Terror* about the "root causes" of terrorism:

> The United States is resented for its cultural hegemony, global political influence, and overwhelming conventional military power. Its cultural reach threatens traditional values, including the organization of societies that privilege males and religious authority. It offers temptation, blurs social, ethical, and behavioral boundaries, and presages moral disorder. America's political weight is seen as the hidden key to the durability of repressive regimes that fail to deliver prosperity while crushing dissent. Its support is cited to explain the power of Israel to oppress Muslims and degrade Islam. American military prowess is used to kill Muslims, as in Iraq, or is withheld to facilitate their extermination, as in Bosnia. The American cultural challenge to Islamic societies stands for a broader Western commitment to secularization, the relegation of religion to the private sphere, and a focus on the here and now instead of on either a hereafter for individuals, or a messianic era in which the righteous as a collective will partake (2002, 407–8).

For some Muslims, the Crusades were not just a historic event but a term that captures the ongoing battles between Islam and Christianity—a battle that has many more fronts because of globalization. While a small minority participates in actual violence, bin Laden is a "terrorist hero" similar to the Western outlaws and urban gangsters that Kooistra writes about in *Criminals as Heroes* (1989). Reeve, for example, notes that "scores of Pakistanis have named their newborn sons Osama," highlighting that the terrorists may be on the fringe "but those who applaud are the disenfranchised Muslims everywhere" (Reeve 1999, 203).

Kooistra suggests that hero status occurs when people find "some symbolic meaning in [an outlaw's] criminality" (1989, 152)—or his political violence, in the case of bin Laden. With criminals, support for the symbolic meaning happens when substantial segments of the public feel "'outside the law' because the law is no longer seen as an instrument of justice but as a tool of oppression wielded by favored interests" (1989, 11). In terms of terrorism, the message sent by the political violence finds support when large segments of the population are not just in poverty but feel disenfranchised within the social, political, and economic order in the global village (see also Armstrong 2005).

IMPLICATIONS

This chapter has provided a brief overview of some of the main categories of workers within the criminal justice system and highlighted some factors likely to change the criminal justice enterprise in the future. In examining workers, the overall conclusion is that while criminal justice work is becoming more diverse, it is still a white man's world. But proportional representation of women and people of color working in the administration of justice seems important for at least two reasons. The first issue is of fairness and confidence in the system: the more closely the criminal justice labor force represents the distribution of diverse groups in society, the more the system appears to represent "we the people." The second issue is of incorporating substantively different group backgrounds into the criminal justice process: women and people of color are more likely to bring experiences and insight into the field that a group of white males may not (Williams 1991 [1982]).

For example, the National Center for Women in Policing (2002) suggests that women have a positive impact on policing by helping to reduce police brutality, increasing the efficacy in police response to domestic violence, and more generally by promoting an emphasis on the use of conflict resolution over the use of force. Similar arguments are made about women correctional officers, emphasizing interpersonal communication and reducing the conflict and violence behind bars. The presence of women prosecutors and judges can challenge the patriarchal and paternalistic attitudes of the judiciary, and in the process, impact the treatment of women lawyers, victims, and defendants (Spohn 1990). Likewise, although the presence of women or people of color may result initially in "affirmative action" tensions and even backlash, over time the cognitive dissonance between the "in" and "out" groups dissipates and mutual identification sets in.

Nevertheless, scholars disagree on the extent to which a profession is changed by the increased presence of women or other minorities. Some hold that it is simply a white-male-dominated profession that forces women to adapt to a "man's world" or nonwhites to a "white world," not the other way around. Others maintain that it is simply the nature of the work people do and the working subculture that evolves from it that shapes the "working personality" or attitudes and values of workers. Certainly, when women and minority are token hires or represent a small portion of the workforce, they are less likely to be agents of change than when their numbers are greater. Thus, a third position argues that occupational roles and working subcultures are subject to modification, resistance, or negotiation by the substantial infusion of gender and racial/ethnic differences.

Even while the criminal justice system is slowly changing because of the infusion of more women and minorities, it is also being changed by forces of globalization, privatization, militarization, and homeland security. One aspect of globalization and privatization is outsourcing to the lowest bidder and moving where costs are cheapest. The result in both cases is the "increasingly brutal wage compression" as mentioned by Morgan Stanley's economist, Stephen Roach (2006). In other words, just as the United States is likely to continue to lose jobs because of globalization, it is also likely that more services of the criminal justice system will be privatized. The result will be more low-wage, contingent, nonbenefit employment for those at the bottom and greater wealth for those at the top. Additionally, the large increases in criminal justice expenditures have attracted the interest of many businesses, which want to find ways to tap into an expanding source of potential revenue brought about by the new securitization. As they do so, many of these penal-surveillance entrepreneurs also become advocates for "tough on crime" policies that lead to more expenditure—and potentially more business. Ironically, as more of criminal justice is directed by private-public enterprise for profits, concern for public safety and taxpayers becomes secondary.

Globalization creates issues related to immigration, terrorism, and cybersecurity (as anyone in the world with a computer can attack the United States). Robert Johnson offers a poignant reminder that "we forgot that our Global Village was a stepchild of technology, not the flowering of community" (2001). People around the world did not consciously decide they all wanted to be closer and set out to invent telecommunications technology and systems to easily move money around. Rather, "technology happened," and people are still catching up with its effects, good and bad. Likewise, the criminal justice system is playing catch up with homeland security and cybersecurity czars. Like with the military, it is not clear whether the criminal justice system is still fighting the last war or preparing for the future ones. But it is clear that the war on terror and emphasis on homeland security will lead to further militarization of the criminal justice system, even though the militarization accompanying the war on drugs has not lead to increased justice. Indeed, it may very well aggravate many existing concerns about racial profiling and other forms of discrimination such as disproportionate minority contact throughout the apparatus of criminal justice.

REVIEW AND DISCUSSION QUESTIONS

1. In the section on law enforcement, what do you think were the two most important points the authors made about the situation of women and minorities?
2. What are the similarities and differences between prosecutors, defenders, and judges?

3. In terms of adapting to the working conditions of prisons, what are the three common responses employed by correctional officers?

4. Define globalization, privatization, and militarization. What is one way that each is having an impact on the criminal justice system?

5. Since the Department of Homeland Security was created in 2002, how has the mandate and roles of the FBI changed?

Part II

3

Understanding Class and Economic Privilege

The novel Snow Crash *(Stephenson 1992) is set in an alternate United States at a time when the four things we do best are music, movies, software, and high-speed pizza delivery. Hiro lives in a 20' by 30' U-Store-It, formerly intended for people with too many material goods. The storage room has its own door and doesn't share walls with other units, so he tells himself there are worse places to live.*

Hiro is a freelance computer hacker; he also belongs to the elite order of Deliverators, those entrusted with the task of thirty-minute pizza delivery for the Mafia-owned businesses (specifically, CosaNostra Pizza franchise #3569). In contrast with his own residence, deliveries tend to be to burbclaves—a suburban enclave, gated community. All burbclaves have the same layout because the "Development Corporation will chop down any mountain ranges and divert the course of mighty rivers that threaten to interrupt this street plan," but not all of them are Apartheid Burbclaves like White Columns: "WHITE PEOPLE ONLY: NON-CAUCASIANS MUST BE PROCESSED." As he approaches the gate, a laser scans his bar codes and he rolls through the immigration gate and past "customs agents ready to frisk all comers—cavity search them if they are the wrong kind of people."

Hiro's partner, a skateboard courier named Y.T., gets arrested in the burbclave by MetaCops Unlimited ("DIAL 1-800-THE COPS All Major Credit Cards"), who also enforce traffic regulations for one of the major companies that operate private roads. But many of the FOQNEs—Franchise-Organized Quasi-National Entities—prefer to have their own security force rather than engage a general contractor. Security is a big deal because they're "so small, so insecure, that just about anything, like not mowing your lawn, or playing your stereo too loud, becomes a national security issue."

The burbclave doesn't have a jail because it would hurt property values and create potential liability, but "any half-decent franchise strip" has one, either the

69

cowboy themed Hoosegow or The Clink, Inc. The MetaCops quickly see the sign: "THE HOOSEGOW: Premium incarceration and restraint services. We welcome busloads!"

While Snow Crash is frequently considered science fiction, its author, Neal Stephenson, considers it an "alternative present." Indeed, the world he paints in the first pages of the novel satirize many features of the present day, including the shift from manufacturing to a service-based economy, rising income inequality, residential segregation, the popularity of gated communities, the privatization of justice functions, the predictable and franchise-based world George Ritzer describes in The McDonaldization of Society (2004), and the growth in corporate power to rival the resources of states and many nations in the global village.

While Americans like to think of themselves as a "classless" society, the United States has both a highly stratified workforce and an underprivileged category of people locked out of the economic expansion. Over time, this class-based society has also become spatially separated, divided into urban and suburban spaces, or what Sophie Body-Gendrot (2000) refers to as the new "geography of inequalities." Urban spaces elicit a recurrent fear of crime and lack of trust in the public institutions responsible for law and order. In contrast, the white flight from the "urban jungle" by the upper and middle classes have facilitated the development of "gated" and "walled" communities separated socially, mentally, and spatially from the poor.

In fact, by 1990, only 25 percent of whites lived in central cities, compared with 57 percent of blacks and 52 percent of Latinos (Body-Gendrot 2000, 30). In general, whites and minorities may be viewed as inhabiting worlds that rarely meet either socially or spatially, but there are also spillover communities of affluent whites and nonwhites and of impoverished whites and nonwhites. Nevertheless, for the most part:

> The residential environment of suburban whites is overwhelming white (82 percent), native born (92 percent) and non-poor (94 percent). In contrast, the living environment of most minorities is non-white, foreign, and disadvantaged. City-dwellers are twice as likely as suburbanites to live in female-headed families, 56 percent more likely to be unemployed, and their incomes are about 26 percent lower than those in the suburbs (Body-Gendrot 2000, 31).

These social realities of urban and suburban worlds of class difference also yield very different rates of arrest, for example. During the midnineties, when 30 to 40 percent of boys growing up in urban America were being arrested, only about 6 percent of suburban youth under the age of eighteen had never been arrested (Greenwood 1995, 92). These very real class differences in experiencing crime and the administration of juvenile/adult criminal justice have lasting consequences not only for these youths but also for the ways in which the larger society and its institutions come to view crime, criminals, and crime control.

As for life inside the overprotected, gated communities of suburbia, living has been redefined along with the meaning of community, engendering a sense of what used to be called the "me generation," along with twenty-first-century privatization and the notion that everyone must protect themselves and their families from the Other. This preference for living out in the suburbs and for the levy of separate taxes has caused drastic shortfalls in the fiscal budgets of urban America. In 2000, there were around 45 million residents, mostly white, living in such autonomous, unincorporated communities and about 9 million living in electronically or physically gated communities. By 2007, about one in ten U.S. households—more than 10 million households—resided in gated communities. That figure represented a tripling of such households since 1997 (Siegel 2009).

By the turn of the twenty-first century, Americans were spending about $65 billion for their private security, and the number of private police officers had exceeded the number of public. Much of the costs were not in the suburbs but in such inside cities as Los Angeles, New York, Chicago, and elsewhere because there is no access to the "defensible" spaces that are protected by new technologies of surveillance. Consequently, these urban areas claim to have private police on duty twenty-four hours a day because of the rising property values of such spaces and the needs of the affluent who live there. In this two-class divided society of rich and poor, "the privatization of safety . . . and the freedom to carry weapons in the public space (taken advantage of by one-third of U.S. citizens) distinguish the American landscape" at the turn of the twenty-first century (Body-Gendrot 2000, 32).

∽∾

The Constitution of the United States claims that everyone is entitled to equal protection under the law. The statues of Lady Justice that adorn many courts show her blindfolded so she can impartially weight the claims on the scales she carries. But most Americans know that being rich has its advantages, including in the areas of crime and law. Death row inmates joke that people who have capital do not get capital punishment, and the data support their observation. Being wealthy makes it more likely that someone can literally or figuratively get away with murder, while at the same time providing them greater access to politicians who can make the laws more favorable to the rich. Several observers see this pattern as so pervasive that they argue the criminal justice system is about controlling the poor and keeping them in their place (Chambliss and Seidman 1982; Quinney 1977; Shelden 2000). Further, "crime" refers to "crime in the streets" rather than "crime in the suites," or corporate crime, which is more prevalent and more costly to society. Inequality and roadblocks in achieving the American Dream are key concepts in strain theory and its offshoots. Thus, understanding class will be important for gaining insight into many facets of criminology and criminal justice.

Fundamentally, class revolves around questions of the distribution of income, wealth, and status. (At the same time, these questions are related to racial and gender identity, as many women and minority men tend to occupy the lower levels of the income distribution, as we will explore in subsequent chapters.) Despite its importance, class is currently less frequently discussed than race and gender. Today, especially in the context of the present economic collapse and recovery, many more people were briefly willing to speak about class and the transfer of wealth from all taxpayers to the very rich through bonus payments to companies bailed out by the government (Ritholtz 2009a). However, very few were willing to talk about "capitalism's dirty little secret: excessive lending was the only way to maintain the living standards of the vast bulk of the population at a time when wealth was being concentrated in the hands of an elite" (Funnell 2009). Outside of times when a financial crisis happens, conversation about class is more muted because getting vital information about class is still more difficult than with race or gender because basic sources, like the Census Department's *Statistical Abstract of the United States*, do not contain a table with basic information like how much wealth the top 10 percent of the country controls.

Consider that four members of the Walton family, whose wealth comes from Wal-Mart stores, are "wealthier than the bottom third of the U.S. population put together—about 100 [million] people" (Funnell 2009). The members of the Walton family appear on *Forbes* magazine's list of the 400 wealthiest Americans in ranks four through seven, with just more than $23 billion in wealth *each*. And, the level of inequality has generally become worse over time. But,

despite the extremely high and rising degree of wealth inequality in the U.S. and its adverse impacts on the economy and on civic and political institutions, the issue never was raised in the most recent Presidential election. The presidential debates contained no substantive discussions of wealth inequality or proposals to help achieve a more egalitarian distribution of wealth. The national media also failed miserably to bring this critical issue to the attention of the voters and to the candidates (Sum and Forsell 2009, 19).

Discussions of class are also problematic because information about the distribution of income and wealth can potentially disrupt deeply held beliefs about an America where everyone is middle class and anyone can get ahead—even become president like biracial Barack Hussein Obama—if they try hard enough. Indeed, since the mid-1970s, the distribution of wealth has become more unequal. Many people have experienced downward mobility and reduced expectations because of the decline in manufacturing jobs and the transfer of many service jobs to India. But saying that "the rich are getting richer and the rest of us are getting taken" is seen as inciting "class warfare" (Hightower 1998a, 105). The financial crisis and bailouts of "too big to fail" banks should have moved discussions of class, inequality, and privilege to the forefront of discussion, but popular outrage faded quickly.

This chapter starts an investigation into class to help illuminate aspects of criminology and criminal justice that were introduced in chapters 1 and 2. What follows is an overview of what class means, how income and wealth are distributed, and what studies say about the ease of mobility between classes. Although these issues often receive less attention than race and gender, a three-week series on class in the *New York Times* began by noting "class is still a powerful force in American life." It concluded that over the past thirty years or so, class "has come to play a greater, not lesser, role in important ways." Moreover,

> at a time when education matters more than ever, success in school remains linked tightly to class. At a time when the country is increasingly integrated racially, the rich are isolating themselves more and more. At a time of extraordinary advances in medicine, class differences in health and life span are wide and appear to be widening (Scott and Leonhardt 2005, A1).

SOCIAL CLASS AND STRATIFICATION IN SOCIETY

In a most generic sense, *class* may be defined as "any division of society according to status," or social ranking (*New Webster's Dictionary of the English Language* 1984, 186). For example, Horton and Hunt (1976, 234) defined social class as "stratum of people of similar position in the social status continuum." Consequently, the janitor and the college president are not of the same class and are not treated the same way by students. The *New York Times* series conceptualized class as a hand of cards, with the suits representing education, income, occupation, and wealth (Scott and Leonhardt 2005). Although class can cover many attributes that relate to social position, we use it here mostly to indicate income and wealth, which are strongly related to education and occupation. Elements of status—such as prestige, respectability, and celebrity—are also tied to income and wealth by way of occupation and education. But we believe primary attention should be placed on the stark inequality in the distribution of economic power and resources.

Further, income and wealth are more important than other aspects of class for understanding the nature of crime control and the functioning of the criminal justice system. Money is ultimately the primary factor involved in motivations and opportunities to commit crime, as well as in the responses of the criminal justice apparatus. For example, wealth means political influence to lobby for more favorable laws and less oversight; and, except for isolated cases related to widespread financial scandals, it is generally the case through history that poor defendants are the ones seen as "noncredible and/or disreputable persons regardless of their actual moral proclivities" (Emmelman 2004, 50, 63). Thus, the focus of our discussion of class is economic because it is convenient shorthand for understanding the larger issues, especially as these relate to crime, law, and justice.

Many social thinkers have tried to devise meaningful ways to divide up the spectrum of income and wealth. Karl Marx identified the capitalist class, or the *bourgeoisie*, who owned the means of production (factories, banks, and businesses); the *petty bourgeoisie*, who do not have ownership but occupy management or professional positions; and the *proletariat*, or workers, who need to sell their labor to make a wage. Marx also identified the surplus population or *lumpenproletariat*, which has no formal ties to the system of economic relations because they are unemployed or unemployable (see Lynch and Groves 1989). In developing his theory of class and class conflict, Marx also contributed a useful critique of capitalism, involving class struggle and his belief that history could be described in terms of an ongoing war of the rich against the poor for control of wealth. Although Marx himself did not write much about crime, his suggestion that law and criminal justice are tools used in this class warfare have been used by criminologists over time to provide important insights, as well as questions, that are explored throughout the text.

Many other attempts to describe the class system have been less useful because they are not tied to a theory of power relations or offer less useful insights for understanding law, crime, and justice. For example, eighteenth-century economist Adam Smith divided society into those who lived by wage labor, by renting out land, or by profiting from trade. Writing at the turn of the twentieth century, Thorstein Veblen (1969 [1919]) divided society into the leisure class and the working class: the former had become so wealthy that their main preoccupation was "conspicuous consumption," the latter so poor that they were forever struggling for their subsistence. Each of these descriptions of social class signifies that both the source of money and the amount of it separate people into different groupings.

Other attempts to describe the distribution of wealth tend to be variations on upper, middle, and lower classes, although there is some discomfort in describing others as "low class." To avoid possible value judgments, the lower segment of the income distribution has been described by such terms as *working class* and *working poor*, while *underclass* refers to the poorest of the poor who seem to lack class mobility and are locked into poverty. Comedian Jeff Foxworthy is something of an exception by becoming a multimillionaire with his "You know you're a redneck when . . . ," but part of its acceptance can be traced to the lack of jokes about race or racism. Also, a growing literature in the field of "white-trash studies" examines the poorest whites that have none of the power and prestige of most whites. These people tend to have resources equal to or even less than minorities but have white skin, so studying them can potentially shed theoretical light on issues of race and class (Wray and Newitz 1996).

One interesting attempt to describe the distribution is Paul Fussell's typology of nine classes: top out-of-sight (rich), upper, upper middle, middle, high proletarian, midproletarian, low proletarian, destitute, and bottom out-of-sight (1983). People in the first category included media mogul Ted Turner, who in the early 1990s gave $1 billion of his own money to the United Nations. One of Turner's seven properties is a New Mexico ranch that covers 578,000 acres, or enough room for 22 lakes, 30 miles of fishing streams, and more than 8,000 elk (Gilbert 1998, 90). The heirs of Sam Walton, founder of Wal-Mart, a more recent example of the out-of-sight, hold fortunes somewhat less than those of Microsoft founder Bill Gates, but who are largely unknown. People in the bottom category include homeless people, such as mentally ill people and veterans of recent wars who live in the subway tunnels of major cities (Barak 1991b; Toth 1995).

Many schemes for understanding class have difficulty placing women who work in the home and are not wage earners. Indeed, radical feminists often argue that women represent a social class. More generally, feminists argue that women's relationship to class structure is mediated by "the configuration of the family, dependence on men, and domestic labour" (in Gamble 1999, 206). Chapters 5 and 6 examine these issues in more detail, so for now the important point is that underlying all these ideas about how to create meaningful divisions are some basic concepts related to income, wealth, and financial assets. *Income* is the most straightforward indicator of class. It represents sources of individual revenue such as salary, interest, and other items reported on income tax forms. By contrast, *wealth* includes income plus possessions such as cars, savings accounts, houses, stocks, bonds, and mutual funds; it also subtracts out debts and loans. *Financial assets* is a measure of ownership of the economic system, so it excludes houses, cars, and items people could turn into cash at a garage sale. Instead, it focuses on stocks, bonds, and trusts—"the kind of ownership that gives a person distinct advantages in a capitalist society" (Brouwer 1998, 13).

The study of class is also part of a larger question about what sociologists call *stratification*, which is concerned with the distribution of social goods such as income, wealth, and prestige. Because most of these goods have an unequal distribution, part of stratification attempts to explain how small minorities maintain control over a disproportionate share of the social resources—an explanation that involves the role of the criminal justice system and the phenomenon of how *The Rich Get Richer and the Poor Get Prison* (Reiman and Leighton 2010a).

ECONOMIC DISTRIBUTIONS

Income, wealth, and financial assets are all distributed unequally in the United States. Americans have mixed reactions in their moral evaluation of this inequality. Some people believe it is unjust for some to starve and live in poverty while others have so much, a point highlighted during the 2001 corporate scandals when Tyco CEO Dennis Kozlowski was revealed to have paid $6,000 for a shower curtain for his multi-million-dollar mansion. Others see the inequality as a necessary part of the American Dream, where the possibility of nearly unlimited wealth motivates everyone to work harder to achieve the Good Life. In this section, we try just to describe the income and wealth distributions. Following these economic distributions, the rest of this section and the next one represent a discussion of social mobility and the American Dream in the context of economic influence, free markets, and power politics.

These concepts are important for furnishing a concrete picture of concepts like inequality and relative deprivation, which focuses on people's evaluations of their place relative to what others have and/or what they believe they are entitled to. As discussed further in chapter 8, Braithwaite argues "inequality worsens both crimes of poverty motivated by *need* for goods for *use* and crimes of wealth motivated by *greed* (1992, 81; emphasis in the original). Crime can be related to the powerlessness and exploitation of those at the bottom of the class system as well as by the unaccountability and manipulation by those at the top. Class mobility and crime are related to the notion of blocked opportunities and poverty in strain theory, yet it is seldom discussed in terms of class mobility, stratification, and greed.[1]

Income Distribution

To illustrate income distribution, Gilbert (1998) uses the example of a parade, where all the households in the United States pass by in one hour. The height of the marchers in the parade is used to represent their income, with the smallest being the poorest and the tallest being the richest. In updating Gilbert's idea with current data, the discussion of the parade is built around a 2006 median family income of $58,407 and a median height of approximately five feet seven inches.

First Twelve Minutes

Here are the lowest 20 percent of income earners who all together received 3.4 percent of all income.

Gilbert suggests that the parade opens on an odd note because "it seems that the first people are marching in a deep ditch" (1998, 86). These people have suffered income losses, such as self-employed people whose expenses are higher than their income. Many people in this opening part of the parade receive at least part of their income from public assistance, social security, or veteran's benefits. Women, minorities, and children are overrepresented in the first part of the parade, especially children in female-headed households. Over 12 million children live in poverty—including 33 percent of black and almost 27 percent of Hispanic children (*Stat-Abs* 2009, table 690).

The minimum wage in 2006 was $5.15 an hour, so someone who worked forty hours a week for fifty weeks out of the year would earn $10,300. They would appear in the parade as one foot tall. (As of July 2009, the minimum wage increased to $7.25 an hour, so those who work forty hours a week for fifty weeks out of the year earn $14,500.)

At the close of the first segment of the parade, marchers would be earning $20,035 and be just under two feet tall.

From Twelve to Twenty-four Minutes

Next come the 20 percent of income earners who collectively received 8.6 percent of all income.

In this category are families that have multiple-wage earners at marginal jobs and single-income families living off a wage from production or non-supervisory work (average salary was $16.06 before taxes in 2005). Wages for this group tend to appreciate at about the rate of inflation, so "the average worker's wages are stuck in neutral" (Porter 2005). That is an accurate assessment about the recent past, but a longer-term view shows slight erosion: in 1980, this group collectively received 11.6 percent of the income, about 3 percent more than they shared in 2006.

The poverty level for a family of four in 2006 was $20,614, and families earning this amount would be represented by a marcher two feet tall.

At the end of this part of the parade, with 40 percent of the families having passed by, those marchers would have been earning $37,774 and be just over three and a half feet tall.

From Twenty-four to Thirty-six Minutes

Now come the middle 20 percent of income earners who collectively received 14.5 percent of all income.

The median income of $58,407 crosses the line at thirty minutes into the parade. While there is a great deal of debate about who is included in the middle class, the median should be the midpoint of it. At the end of this part of the parade, more than halfway now, marchers earn $60,000 and would be about five feet nine inches tall.

From Thirty-six to Forty-eight Minutes

Now come the next 20 percent of income earners, who collectively received 22.9 percent of all income.

At the end of this segment, with the parade 80 percent over, the marchers would earn $97,032 and be nine feet four inches tall.

From Forty-eight to Sixty Minutes

These are the highest 20 percent of income earners who collectively received 50.5 percent of all income.

The last twelve minutes show a greater range—from just over nine feet to thousands of feet tall—illustrating the large income a relatively few households command. In the last three minutes, the top 5 percent of wage earners—who receive 22.3 percent of the income—would walk by, representing family salaries of at least $174,012 and a height of over sixteen feet. These marchers are likely to be professionals such as doctors and lawyers. Fifty-nine minutes into the parade, "we would be looking at 50-foot Goliaths, seconds after that, 200-foot King Kongs, and then the towering leviathans, thousands of feet tall" (Gilbert 1998, 89–90). Marchers from the last minute are likely to be corporate executives and a mix of celebrity entertainers and star athletes.

The average National Football Association coach makes $3 million, making them 287 feet tall. The average National Basketball Association coach did better: $4 million, making them 382 feet tall (Van Riper 2009). For CEOs, salary tends to be a small part of the overall pay or "compensation package," which includes stock options, spending allowances, and generous pensions that are frequently protected even during bankruptcy proceedings. Although the package helps CEOs build wealth, it can be compared with income because it is ultimately payment for the job they are doing. In 2008, *Forbes* magazine calculated that the average compensation for Fortune 500 CEOs was $11.4 million (DeCarlo 2009), meaning they would stand 1,090 feet tall in the parade (based on 2006 data). The highest paid CEO was Lawrence Ellison of Oracle, whose compensation (include certain stock gains) was $544 million, making him 53,288 feet tall.[2]

Historically this top group has managed impressive gains, which are described in the headline of one of the articles in the *New York Times* series on class: "Richest Are Leaving Even the Rich Far Behind" (Johnston 2005). A comparison with the average worker is even more striking: in 1980, CEOs of the largest companies were paid forty times as much as the hourly wage earners at their companies; by 1991, it was 140 times, and by 2003 the average CEO made about 500 times more than the rank-and-file worker (*Washington Post* 2002, E1; Revell 2003, 34). Put another way, *Fortune* magazine noted that if the minimum wage increased at the same rate as CEO pay since 1990, it would be $21.41 an hour instead of $5.15 in 2002 (Florian 2002, 30).

Increasing pay may make a certain amount of sense when tied to sustainable, long-term corporate growth. But, CEO pay and bonuses remained high even as the financial crisis hit and firms went bankrupt or received bailout money through TARP (Troubled Asset Relief Program). In a report, New York Attorney General Andrew Cuomo noted that "when the banks did well, their employees were paid well. When the banks did poorly, their employees were paid well. And when the banks did very poorly, they were bailed out by taxpayers and their employees were still paid well" (2009, 1). For example, his report notes that Citigroup and Merrill Lynch each together "lost $54 billion, paid out nearly $9 billion in bonuses and then received TARP bailouts totaling $55 billion" (2009). Other companies did not lose money but paid out more in bonuses than they made in income. Goldman Sachs, Morgan Stanley, and JP Morgan Chase together "earned $9.6 billion, paid bonuses of nearly $18 billion, and received TARP taxpayer funds worth $45 billion" (Cuomo 2009, 2).

In the end of the last minute are a number of celebrities—athletes and entertainers—who add some diversity to the largely white male CEOs. For example, in 2008, the top 100 best-paid celebrities according to *Forbes* (2009) included Oprah Winfrey, who was at the top of the list with $275 million (making her 26,288 feet tall), golfer Tiger Woods ($110 million), musician Madonna ($110 million), singer Beyonce Knowles ($87 million), basketball player Kobe Bryant ($45 million), basketball player Michael Jordan ($45 million), and comedian Chris Rock ($42 million).

Overall, income is unevenly distributed—a point especially notable when considering that median income at thirty minutes was the median height of five foot seven inches, but at fifty-seven minutes marchers are sixteen feet tall and several minutes later the last marcher is more than 53,000 feet tall. Further, income is becoming more unequally distributed over time. Since 1990, the top 5 percent has increased the proportion of income it receives, while the bottom 80 percent have seen their share shrink (*Stat-Abs* 2009, table 675). Finally, the market structure and venture capital system in the United States do provide degrees of openness and opportunity for changing income brackets, but an economist with the Federal Reserve Bank of Chicago notes that "income mobility has declined in the last 20 years" (Francis 2005). The article, "The American Dream Gains a Harder Edge," notes that most Americans do not believe mobility has declined, "but academic studies suggest that income mobility in the U.S. is no better that in France or Britain." Canada and the Scandinavian countries have more mobility than the United States (Francis 2005; Scott and Leonhardt 2005). The *New York Times* series on class noted the same phenomenon and aptly summarized the research as: "Mobility happens, just not as rapidly as was once thought" (Scott and Leonhardt 2005).

Wealth Distribution

Income is only one way of examining the finances of households, and in many ways measures of wealth are more important. Measures of income look at salary for a year, whereas wealth looks at the accumulated assets and debt over a lifetime. Wealth includes bank accounts, ownership of stocks and bonds, retirement accounts, houses, cars, and ownership of businesses; it also includes debts such as car loans, student loans, mortgages, and credit card balances. Of particular importance is the ownership of financial assets like businesses and stock—especially large blocks not held through a mutual fund or retirement account—that generate economic power.

To help see the difference between income and wealth, think of the difference between boxer Michael Tyson and businessman Michael Dell. During his boxing career, Tyson earned about $400 million in income but managed to spend it in ways that left him declaring bankruptcy after hitting $34 million in debt (Schlabach 2005, E1). In contrast, Dell makes a lower salary per year than Tyson received for many individual fights, but as founder of Dell computers he has substantial business and stock ownership. As with others, his wealth will rise and fall along with the value of his company's stock, but his ownership of the business will continue to provide economic and political power.

More generally, lists of people with high salaries tend to include minorities and women who are athletes and entertainers, but the lists of those with the largest wealth are much more likely to be white male businessmen. Whites have more than six times the wealth of African Americans, who collectively own 1 percent of all stock and 0.5 percent of business equity (Kennickell 2003, 35, 45). Indeed, out of the list of the 100 highest paid celebrities, only 3 are also in the *Forbes* 400 list of the wealthiest Americans: George Lucas is #91 on the wealth list ($4 billion); filmmaker Steven Spielberg is #131 on the wealth list ($3.1 billion); and Oprah Winfrey is #155 on the wealth list ($2.7 billion) (*Forbes* 2008).

To convey a sense of the wealth distribution, the income parade can be turned into a wealth parade, with the median height of five foot seven inches corresponding to median family wealth of $92,900 in 2004.[3] Data indicated the "typical" family:

has about $3,800 in the bank. No one has a retirement account, and the neighbors who do only have about $35,000 in theirs. Mutual funds? Stocks? Bonds? Nope. The house is worth $160,000, but the family owes $95,000 on it to the bank. The breadwinners make more than $43,000 a year but can't manage to pay off a $2,200 credit card balance (Irwin 2006, F01).

The "typical" family described above seems to be in slightly worse shape than the median family in the wealth parade, but they are quite close. Indeed, an increasing number of families in the lead up to the financial crisis took on increasing debt, meaning any loss of income or change in health insurance could have a drastic impact on their ability to pay on credit cards, mortgage, and cars. In such circumstances, families dip into any savings, then sell stocks, bonds, and retirement account holdings.

The basis of information for the parade is the Survey of Consumer Finances, which is done every three years. The survey deliberately excludes people in the *Forbes* 400, who are the 400 richest people in the United States. Because of the large amount of wealth held by those at the top, their exclusion means the survey results understate inequality. For example, the survey indicates that in 2004, the top 1 percent of wealth holders have 33.4 percent of the wealth, but this figure excludes about $1 trillion in wealth held by the *Forbes* 400. This amounts to 2 percent (Kennickell 2006, 7), so the top 1 percent in the United States own about 35.4 percent of all wealth.

While the discussion of the parade provides further breakdowns and additional information about wealth distribution, table 3.1 provides

Table 3.1. Shares of Net Worth and Distribution of Components, 2004

	Wealth Percentile Group				
	0–50	*50–90*	*90–95*	*95–99*	*99–100*
People are in this group if their net worth is above		$92,900	$827,600	$1,393,000	$6,006,000
Percent of All Net Worth Owned	2.5%	27.9%	12.0%	24.1%	33.4%
Percent of All Stocks Owned	0.6%	10.3%	10.1%	28.2%	50.9%
Percent of All Business Owned	0.3%	9.2%	5.7%	22.4%	62.3%
Percent of All Credit Card Debt	45.7%	46.9%	3.6%	3.1%	0.7%

Note: The *Forbes* 400, the 400 wealthiest families in the United States, were not included in the Survey of Consumer Finances used to produce table 3.1. In 2004, the *Forbes* 400 collectively had total wealth of over $1 trillion dollars; the minimum wealth to make the list was $750 million and the wealthiest family had $51 billion in wealth.
Source: Arthur Kennickell. "Currents and Undercurrents: Changes in the Distribution of Wealth, 1989–2004." Federal Reserve Board, 2006. http://www.federalreserve.gov/pubs/oss/oss2/scfindex.html.

Table 3.2   Wealth Held by Poorest 50 Percent of Families versus 400 Richest Families

Amount of wealth held by poorest 50 percent of population	$1.28 trillion
Amount of wealth held by Forbes 400 (the 400 richest families = 0.0004 percent of population)	$1.0 trillion

a summary of wealth and the distribution of certain assets. As noted above, direct ownership of stock and business are important measures of ownership of the economy that translates into economic and political power. Even the more general measures of net wealth indicate that the combined worth of the poorest 50 percent of the population (about 150,000 people) is only slightly higher than that held by the richest 400 families, which is represented in table 3.2 (Kennickell 2006; see also Sum and Forsell 2009):

First Thirty Minutes

While this is a large segment of the parade to discuss at once, this 50 percent of families in the United States collectively owned only 2.5 percent of all wealth in 2004. Seven percent of all families have negative net worth, meaning more debt than assets, so for almost five minutes the parade would be people who looked like they were marching in a ditch. Those at the tenth percentile, appearing at six minutes into the parade, have $200 net worth and would be less than a quarter inch tall. Those at the twentieth percentile, appearing at twelve minutes into the parade, have a net worth of $6,450 and would be almost five inches tall.

For these families, credit card debt tends to be high, along with auto loans that exceed the value of the car. Student loans contribute to the negative segment of the parade, but the education provides an increase in human capital, which relates over time to better income and jobs. Thus, while young people appear early in the parade, many of the students will start to accumulate some wealth over their lifetimes, while many of the women and minorities—who are also overrepresented here—will remain. The median wealth of African Americans was $20,006, representing a marcher just over one foot tall; the median wealth of Hispanics was $18,600 (Kennickell 2006, 34).

During the first half hour, assets tend to be in the form of checking and saving accounts plus vehicles. A majority of those marching after fifteen minutes own a home, although large mortgage balances mean the house does not contribute greatly to wealth. For example, putting 0 percent down as part of a subprime mortgage and financing 100 percent of a house means assets and debt balance out, so there is no net contribution to wealth. If housing prices increase, an owner will build wealth because of the difference between what they owe and what they can sell the house for. (In the quote above, the house was worth $160,000 and the family owed $95,000, meaning they had $65,000 in wealth from the house.) Homeowners who refinance during times of increasing prices and take cash out transform potential wealth into consumption—or money to cover other debts. When housing prices decrease, wealth decreases for many (and the ability to refinance decreases, leaving people without access to cash they had previously used to cover debts).

In the first thirty minutes, ownership of business is negligible: the bottom 50 percent owned 0.4 percent of equity in businesses, reflecting both low levels of ownership and relatively small businesses. On the other hand, this 50 percent of the population has almost 50 percent of all the credit card debt. At the end of this segment of the 2004 parade, marchers would have the median wealth of $92,900 and be the median height of five foot seven inches.

Thirty to Fifty-four Minutes

This segment, representing the fiftieth to ninetieth percentile, owned 27.9 percent of the wealth in 2004. In addition to larger checking and savings accounts, families are more likely to own stocks, bonds, and mutual funds; they are more likely to have retirement accounts that are better funded. They have larger houses, with less debt, and more likely to own rental property or second homes. This group still only owned 8.9 percent of all business equity. At the end of this segment, 90 percent of families would have marched by, representing 30.4 percent of all wealth. The net worth of the last people in this group was $827,600, which makes them about fifty feet tall.

Fifty-four to Fifty-seven Minutes

This part of the parade in 2004 represents the ninetieth to ninety-fifth percentile, which owned 12 percent of the net worth. Families at fifty-seven minutes had a net worth of $1,393,000, making them nearly eighty-four feet tall.

Fifty-seven Minutes to Fifty-nine Minutes and Twenty-four Seconds

This brief part of the parade covers the ninety-fifth to ninety-ninth percentiles, which owned 24.1 percent of all wealth in 2004. This 4 percent of the population owns 27 percent of the money in checking, savings, and money market accounts; 28.2 percent of stocks; 32.7 percent of mutual funds (other than money market); 25.2 percent of retirement account value; 24.9 percent of the cash value of all life insurance; and 22.4 percent of the value of businesses. The last marcher in this segment had a net worth of $6,006,000, making them 361 feet tall.

Fifty-nine Minutes and Twenty-four Seconds to Sixty Minutes

During this final thirty-six seconds, the top 1 percent parades by and in 2004 owned 33.4 percent of all wealth—3 percent more than were owned by the lowest 90 percent of families.

The last seconds of the parade would consist of the *Forbes* 400. For 2004, the lowest ranked person had wealth of $750 million (Kennickell 2006, 6)— about 45,075 feet tall (8.5 miles). There were 312 *billionaires* (Armstrong and Newcomb 2004). Being in the top hundred in 2004 meant wealth of $2.2 billion (Kennickell 2006, 6), making them 132,221 feet tall (over twenty-five miles tall)! Breaking the top ten requires wealth of at least $22.7 billion or 258 miles in height. The top person on the list, and the last marcher in the parade, was Microsoft's Bill Gates, whose worth was estimated at $51 billion (Kennickell 2006, 6). He would have a height of 580 miles.

By 2008 everyone on the *Forbes* list was a billionaire (*Forbes* 2008), with $1.3 billion necessary to make the list. The total wealth of the 400 on the list was just over $1.5 trillion. Given the general lack of gains by those on the bottom, these figures suggest a continuation of the trend

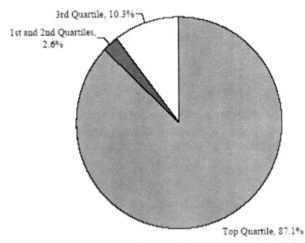

Figure 3.1. Percentage Shares of Net Worth Obtained by U.S. Households in Each Quartile of the Wealth Distribution, 2004
Source: Sum and Forsell (2009, 10)

from 1992 to 2004, when the distribution of wealth became more highly concentrated on a fairly steady basis. Rising inequality in the wealth distribution appears to have been ongoing although not continuously since at least the early 1980s. While figure 3.1 does not capture the change in inequality, it attempts to capture the picture in 2004. Certainly the financial crisis holds out the possibility that those at the top will have less wealth in absolute dollar amounts, and some measures will show less inequality because the rich had more to lose. But the real question will be if their share of the wealth—especially direct ownership of stock and business—is reduced and their economic and political power along with it.

POLITICAL SPHERE

For at least some purposes, American law treats corporations as "persons." The legal fiction of corporate "persons" means their size should also be considered to have a full understanding of how income and wealth affect the treatment of persons under the law. The intense concentration of wealth in corporations generates considerable political power, makes accountability increasingly difficult, and increases inequality in a way that is invisible to criminological theory.

Corporations now grow to unlimited size so that their money power now dwarfs that of (most) individuals. For example, Wal-Mart is the largest of the Fortune 500 companies with 2004 revenues of $288 billion (*Fortune* 2005), which would represent a height in the income parade of more than 31 million feet—well over 5,000 miles tall, compared to the average height of five foot seven inches! Such an income makes it gargantuan not only in relation to individuals but also cities, states, and even the federal government. Indeed, corporations make up more than half of the largest economies in the world. Because of mergers, they frequently grow faster than nations (such as with the merger of the oil companies Exxon and Mobil). Problems of jurisdiction compound problems of resources as we approach a time, in the words of Korton, "When Corporations Rule the World" (1995).

Moreover, the large concentrations of wealth by these megacorporations translate into political power that is also exercised through corporate lobbyists and Political Action Committees (PACs). PACs that donate thousands—or even millions—of dollars can achieve considerable clout at a time when during the late 1990s only 0.06 percent of the U.S. population contributed more than $1,000 to political parties or candidates (Hightower 1998b, 6). Many corporate interests donate heavily to both political parties to ensure access to legislators and favorable action on their legislation, regardless of which party wins the election. Further influence and consideration comes from the corporate use of "the slush fund, the kickback, the stock award, the high-paying job offer from industry, the lavish parties and prostitutes, the meals, transportation, housing, and vacation accommodations, and the many other hustling enticements of money" (Simon 1999, 24).

The result of this influence can be tax breaks, less regulation, or limits on the extent of punishment, such as the size of damages juries are allowed to award against businesses in product liability cases. An excellent example is the process to establish sentencing guidelines for corporate misconduct. In 1984, Congress established the U.S. Sentencing Commission to help create guidelines that would make federal sentencing more certain and uniform in criminal cases. The guidelines are a grid that judges use to plot both the severity of the offense and an individual's record to find an appropriate range for the sentence. The first set of guidelines in 1987 did not address corporate crime, although the 1990 ones did.

> Instead of $5,000 or less—the amount levied in four-fifths of all corporate convictions from 1975 to 1976—fines were set as high as $364 million. In addition, the commission had devised innovative new punishments—including probation and community service for convicted organizations (Etzioni 1990, C3).

After a "steamroller of business lobbyists" took notice, the Commission released a revised set of guidelines in which the potential fines were "slashed." Mitigating factors were given more weight, and aggravating factors (such as a prior record) were removed from consideration (Etzioni 1990, 3). Under the original plan, a level 10 carried a penalty of $64,000, while the postlobbying guidelines suggested $17,500; level 25 was revised down from $136 million to $580,000; and the maximum fine went from $364 million to $12.6 million. Later, then Attorney General Thornburgh, who had called fighting crime in the suites one of his top priorities, "withdrew the Justice Department's long-standing support for tough mandatory sentences for corporate criminals following an intense lobbying campaign by defense contractors, oil companies and other Fortune 500 firms" (Isikoff 1990, A1).

After the half *trillion* dollar savings and loan scandals of the late 1980s, Congress did increase penalties for some financial crimes and added some financial regulations. But, according to the authors of *Big Money Crime*, soon after the S&L crisis Congress went on a wave of "cavalier" financial deregulation, spurred on by lobbying and political donations, creating the "paradox of increasing financial deregulation coming on the heels of the most catastrophic experiment with deregulation in history" (Calavita, Pontell, and Tillman 1997). In turn, this deregulation created the conditions for the string of corporate corruption in 2001–2002 that included Enron, WorldCom, Tyco, Arthur Andersen, and many others (Leighton and Reiman 2002). Congress passed Sarbanes-Oxley to correct some of the systemic causes of widespread fraud. But with the passage of time, businesses felt increasingly comfortable lobbying against it and trying to undo many of the safeguards put in place to protect shareholders and retirement funds (Leighton and Reiman 2004).

Further, the financial services industry lobbied to be able to take on more risk, which resulted in the financial crisis of 2008–2009, and now they seem to be lobbying quietly behind the scenes to block much-needed reform after a $700 million bailout (Ritholtz 2009a). Indeed, Barry Ritholtz—the CEO of an investment research firm, blogger, and author of *Bailout Nation* (2009a)—argues that the financial crisis has been "wasted": there was "smoldering resentment" among people because of the "massive taxpayer wealth transfer to inept, corrupt, incompetent bankers." This provided the "best chance to clean up Wall Street in five generations," but "what we got instead, was the usual lobbying efforts by the finance industry. They own Congress, lock stock and barrel, and they throttled Financial Reform. It did not help that the Obama economic team is filled with defenders of the *Status Quo* . . . that fiddled while the economy burned" (2009b).

Although real people convicted of felonies lose their voting rights, corporations convicted of multiple felonies lose none of their political rights—and in some cases try to lobby Congress to weaken the law under which they were convicted. Further, corporate charters themselves act as a shield from the public and give the corporation permission to act in the best interests of shareholders rather than the larger public good. Thus,

> the corporation is now a superhuman creature of the law, superior to you and me, since it has civil rights but no civil responsibilities; it is legally obligated to be selfish; it cannot be thrown in jail; it can deduct from its tax bill any fines it gets for wrongdoings; and it can live forever (Hightower 1998a, 34).

While many of the individual men and women who work in the corporation make good neighbors, the corporation itself can be a problem because "the corporation's legally defined mandate is to pursue, relentlessly and without exception, its own self-interest, regardless of the often harmful consequences it might cause to others" (Bakan 2004, 2).

Indeed, Bakan asked Robert Hare, the noted expert on psychopathologies, to apply his diagnostic checklist to corporations and found a close match: they are irresponsible by putting others at risk; manipulative of everything, including public opinion; lack empathy for others and are unable to feel remorse; refuse to accept responsibility; and relate to others superficially (2004, 56–57). Just as psychopaths are known for their superficial charm, corporations may "act in ways to promote the public good when it is to their advantage to do so, but they will just as quickly sacrifice it—it is their legal obligation to do so—when necessary to serve their own ends" (118).

Thus, protecting people—citizens, workers, consumers, communities, and the environment—from the excesses of corporate behavior is an important function of law. But this social control is brought into question by donations and strategic lobbying on the part of corporations. When the size of corporate actors is combined with their institutional personality, the dark side of big business can be seen. Obviously not all businesses are bad all the time, and the point is that there is a problematic antisocial tendency that must be kept in check, but the control mechanisms to regulate and hold corporations accountable have become less powerful relative to the corporations.

IMPLICATIONS

This chapter began by noting the reluctance in our society to discuss issues of economic class. In spite of real differences in class, in popular media "people dwell in a classless homogenized American Never-Never Land" where "the pecking order of sex and looks has replaced the old hierarchy of jobs and money" (McGrath 2005). Class thus becomes less visible and less subject to honest conversation. But in some less guarded moments, even leaders of white supremacy hate groups admit that class is more of a problem than race. Many of their followers are poor whites who feel that no one represents them. One leader said that their literature was derogatory to blacks, but "we just use it as a vehicle to attract possible decent people" (in Ezekiel 1995, 112). Apparently, decent people feel that class is a taboo topic and will respond more favorably to an incorrect analysis that fosters hate by blaming blacks or a widespread Jewish conspiracy (the Zionist Occupied Government, or ZOG) for social problems (see Ezekiel 1995; Ridgeway 1995).

While criminal justice agencies do not share most of the beliefs of white supremacy groups, they too seem to feel that class is not a respectable topic and are reluctant to collect data about it. This observation did not hold for the 1960s and the first President's Commission on Crime in a Free Society, but it has become the current social reality. The problem of inequality and the growing gap between the rich and the poor are less frequently part of the "official knowledge" about crime and crime control, but they are important nevertheless. Indeed, a twenty-five-year retrospective on the President's Commission stated: "While evidence shows that criminal justice procedures are more evenhanded than in the past, it is also painfully obvious that the growing gap between rich and poor, and white and black, continues to make criminal justice a social battleground rather than a mechanism to increase social peace" (Conley 1994, 66).

Because of the long history of racism, blacks, Hispanics, and Native Americans are disproportionately poor, so issues of class and race are tied together in ways that will be explored in other chapters. The current and evolving problem is that criminal justice is contributing to the differences between rich and poor and the separation of whites from minorities. Current domestic policies of crime control operate as if "Americans have concluded that the problems of the urban poor are intractable and therefore they [apparently agreed to have their money] spent on a vast network of prisons, rather than on solutions" (in Welch 1996a, 101). Many taxpayers are willing to fund the construction of prisons to house the poor but are opposed to basic social and educational services for the poor. Some of these programs are cheaper than prisons and have the potential to reduce crime by preventing child abuse, enhancing the intellectual and social development of children, providing support and mentoring to vulnerable adolescents, and doing intensive work with juvenile offenders (Currie 1998, 81).

John Irwin and James Austin captured the essence of this problem almost a decade and a half ago, and the "enormous policy dilemma" they articulated ultimately as a problem of inequality and economic class has only intensified since then:

> On the one hand, we are expending a greater portion of our public dollars on incarcerating, punishing, treating and controlling persons who are primarily from the lower economic classes in an effort to reduce crime. On the other hand, we have set in motion economic policies that serve to widen the gap between the rich and poor, producing yet another generation of impoverished youths who will probably end up under control of the correctional system. By escalating the size of the correctional system, we are also increasing the tax burden and diverting billions of dollars from those very public services (education, health, transportation, and economic development) that would reduce poverty, unemployment, crime, drug abuse and mental illness (1997, 10–11).

While the levels of inequality, and the stability of it over time, have important implications for the American Dream and criminological theories like strain or conflict theory, criminology does not pursue these ideas in a way that would increase consciousness of class, inequality, and stratification. Sadly, the criminal justice system reflects the class biases in society—and helps to reinforce them. The United States continues to enlarge its apparatuses of criminal justice and crime control against the poorest members in society while the rich, especially corporations, continue to gather more wealth and feel unaccountable for the adverse consequences of their privileged behavior on the "teeming masses."

REVIEW AND DISCUSSION QUESTIONS

1. Why are many Americans disturbed by discussions of social classes, inequality, and the lack of class mobility in America?
2. Discuss the differences and overlaps between income, wealth, and financial assets. Why is it that female and minority celebrities have income but not the kind of wealth that would place them in the *Forbes* 400?
3. What are some of the current discussions or issues that involve explicit consideration of class?
4. What are some of the problems caused by inequality and the growth of corporations?
5. In what ways can you think of that class will be important for understanding criminology and criminal justice?
6. From reading sources outside this chapter, find out what the current arguments are for and against raising the minimum wage. How is a "living wage" different from a minimum wage, and what are the arguments on both sides of the debate about requiring a living wage?

4

Understanding Race and White Privilege

In Plessy v. Ferguson (163 U.S. 537 [1896]), the Supreme Court set the precedent of "separate but equal": separate facilities for blacks did not offend constitutional provisions about equal protection so long as they were equal to those provided whites. Louisiana law required separate railway cars for the races or partitions to separate the races if there was just one car. Plessy sat in a car designated for whites only, and the conductor told him to leave. As the Court described it, upon his "refusal to comply with such order, he was, with the aid of a police officer, forcibly ejected from said coach, and hurried off to, and imprisoned in, the parish jail" in New Orleans.

The Court found that the requirement of separate accommodations was a reasonable regulation, made "with reference to the established usages, customs, and traditions of the people, and with a view to the promotion of their comfort, and the preservation of the public peace and good order." Social prejudices, said the Court, cannot be overcome by legislation, and if the races "are to meet upon terms of social equality, it must be the result of natural affinities, a mutual appreciation of each other's merits, and a voluntary consent of individuals." Although Plessy argued that enforced separation "stamps the colored race with a badge of inferiority," the majority held that it is "not by reason of anything found in the act, but solely because the colored race chooses to put that construction upon it."

What is less known about the case is that Plessy "was seven-eighths Caucasian and one-eighth African blood; that the mixture of colored blood was not discernible in him," so the suit involved a claim "that he was entitled to every right, privilege, and immunity secured to citizens of the United States of the white race." Plessy argued "in a mixed community, the reputation of belonging to the dominant race, in this instance the white race, is 'property,' in the same sense that a right of action or of inheritance is property." The Court conceded it to be so, for the purposes of the case, but argued the statute did not take his property: either he was a white man who was entitled or a black man who was not. But who decides, and how? The train conductor seemed to have power to make racial classifications, which would result in arbitrary decisions, but the Court did not see that issue as properly before it. The state legislatures could guide decisions on racial classifications, but some said "any visible admixture of black blood stamps the person as belonging to the colored race; others, that it depends upon the preponderance of blood; and still others, that the predominance of white blood must only be in the proportion of three-fourths."

Justice Harlan was the sole dissenter, claiming that the decision would prove to be as "pernicious" as the Dred Scott case, which declared that escaped slaves who traveled North to freedom were still property and should be returned to their southern masters. For him, the statute seemed inconsistent, for example, in allowing black nurses to attend white children but not an adult in bad health. Harlan also pointed to another group that "is a race so different from our own that we do not permit those belonging to it to become citizens of the United States" and are "with few exceptions, absolutely excluded from our country." But under the law "a Chinaman can ride in the same passenger coach with white citizens" yet blacks "many of whom, perhaps, risked their lives for the preservation of the Union, who are entitled, by law, to participate in the political control of the state and nation, who are not excluded, by law or by reason of their race, from public stations of any kind, and who have all the legal rights that belong to white citizens, are yet declared to be criminals, liable to imprisonment, if they ride in a public coach occupied by citizens of the white race."

Harlan wondered if the Court's ruling about the reasonableness of separation would allow a town to assign the races to different sides of the street, a courtroom, or jury box. Unlike the majority, Harlan argued the purpose of the law was to compel blacks to "keep to themselves" while traveling rather than keep whites out of black areas, and "no one would be so wanting in candor as to assert the contrary." He acknowledged that whites were the dominant race and said that while "every true man has pride of race" that can be shown in appropriate situations, the Thirteenth Amendment abolished slavery and "prevents the imposition of any burdens or disabilities that constitute badges of slavery or servitude." Even though whites were the dominant race and "will continue to be so for all time," he was clear that:

> in the view of the constitution, in the eye of the law, there is in this country no superior, dominant, ruling class of citizens. There is no caste here. Our constitution is color-blind, and neither knows nor tolerates classes among citizens. In respect of civil rights, all citizens are equal before the law. The humblest is the peer of the most powerful. The law regards man as man, and takes no account of his surroundings or of his color when his civil rights as guaranteed by the supreme law of the land is involved.

～♦～

The previous chapter reviewed inequalities in income and wealth to establish the foundations for subsequent discussion of how economic bias undermines the ideal of equality before the law, so that the poorest is not the peer of the most powerful. This chapter provides an overview of race to set the stage for subsequent discussion of the extent to which racial and ethnic minorities are treated as equals under a criminal justice system that should be color-blind. While the election of a biracial man as president signals progress in overcoming discrimination, claims that the United States is now in a "postracial" era are wildly exaggerated. President Obama (2009) noted that,

> there's probably never been less discrimination in America than there is today. But make no mistake: the pain of discrimination is still felt in America. By African-American women paid less for doing the same work as colleagues of a different color and gender. By Latinos made to feel unwelcome in their own country. By Muslim Americans viewed with suspicion for simply kneeling down to pray. By our gay brothers and sisters, still taunted, still attacked, still denied their rights.

Despite the uneven progress that has occurred in the treatment of races and ethnicities, racial discrimination still persists in the administration of justice as exemplified by racial profiling and magnified through each step of the criminal process to result in serious minority overrepresentation of blacks and Latinos in prison.

While this chapter makes generalizations about the experiences common to all minority groups within a system in which the whites are the dominant group, it also recognizes the importance of diversity and that each minority group has its own unique experiences. In other words, just "as it is presumptuous to consider a Bostonian Irishman, an Anglo-California yuppie, a Jewish Greenwich Village artist, a Texas rodeo star, and a New Age Santa Fe vegetarian as all the same because they are coincidentally 'white,' it is just as unwise to render all 'Latinos' (or Asians or African Americans) as inherently alike" (Burnley, Edmunds, Gaboury, and Seymour 1998, 23). For instance, persons of about two dozen nationalities and cultures are all included in the "Asian and Pacific Islander" category. Among many differences, this masks how the median personal income for people from India (whose native language is English) and Japan is higher than that of whites, while the Cambodian, Laotian, and Hmong groups have a median personal income similar to African Americans (Le 2005). Also, among Hispanics, wide variations exist, with those of Cuban background generally being better situated in terms of income, employment, health, and education than Puerto Ricans or Mexicans and Mexican Americans. Further, women frequently have a different experience than men of a minority group because of *gendered racism*, a term used to reflect the overlapping systems of gender and racial discrimination (Essed 1991).

At the same time, members of diverse minority groups are all victims of ideological racism, in which dominant group traits are overvalued while those of other groups are devalued. Though we do not agree that race is merely a function of socioeconomic class, part of the common experiences of most minorities is their overall lower economic status, which makes them vulnerable to exploitation and control by the criminal justice system. Thus, understanding the political economy of an era, such as the need for cheap labor or a surplus of workers, is a key factor in understanding the relationship between minority groups and the administration of criminal justice. Historically, for example,

> The African slave trade began in earnest only after large-scale Native American slavery proved impractical in North America. The abolition of slavery led to the importation of low-wage labor from Asia. Legislation banning immigration from Asia set the stage for the recruitment of low-wage labor from Mexico. The new racial categories that emerged in each of these eras all revolved around applying racial labels to "nonwhite" groups in order to exploit them while at the same time preserving the value of whiteness (Lipsitz 2005, 68).

After the Civil War, the criminal justice system swept the newly freed slaves off the streets and leased them back to plantation owners for a profit (Oshinsky 1996). At other times, such as after the completion of the transcontinental railroad and the economic recession in the 1870s, the criminal justice system responded to surplus labor and white fears by passing the Chinese Exclusion Act of 1892, outlawing opium use among Chinese but not whites (Lusane 1991, 31). The desire for land and natural resources led to the forced relocation of Native Americans and the wholesale violation of all treaties signed by the U.S. government and sovereign tribes (Lazarus 1991). In each case, minority group entanglement with law and criminal justice related to changes in the political economy and was justified by an ideology of white supremacy that devalued minority groups. In each case, too, criminal justice served to maintain white privilege by regulating cheap labor, economic competition, and perceived social threats.

The racism that criminal justice both reflects and re-creates is thus part of the "sociology of waste" that squanders the talent and potential of minority groups (Feagin and Vera 1995). People of color pay the heaviest and most direct price because of white supremacy, but "few whites realize the huge amount of energy and talent that whites themselves have dissipated in their construction of antiblack attitudes and ideologies and in their participation in social discrimination" (Feagin and Vera 1995, 2). Racism diverts the attention of whites and causes them to scapegoat minority groups rather than "seeing clearly their own class exploitation and . . . organizing effectively with black and other minority workers" (Feagin and Vera 1995, 15).

The rest of this chapter is divided into three discussions. First, we discuss how race and ethnicity are not just about biology but are also socially constructed statuses and identities. We then define key terms such as racism, stereotypes, discrimination, and prejudice. Of particular importance is the idea of privilege and understanding that whites also have race. Finally, we examine the status of minorities in economic, political, and social terms.

One final note on the terminology of this chapter is necessary because so many terms are used to refer to racial groups. Of necessity, we must use the language of resources we consulted for this book. For example, governmental data and authors who follow the government classification system use "black" and "American Indian." We are aware that many minorities prefer "African American" and "Native American," and we use these terms as well, both when our sources do and as interchangeable with "official" terms. The designation "native American" means people of all races who were born in the United States, and contrasts with immigrants; "Native American" refers to American Indians, and the capitalization designates their status as aborigines or First Peoples on the land before it became the United States. Asian Indians are from India. At times, to capture the history of discrimination or someone's prejudice, we include quotations that are intended by the original speaker to be derogatory. We do not endorse these attitudes or the use of racial epithets but believe it is important to accurately portray the attitudes that have been held.

THE SOCIAL CONSTRUCTION OF ETHNICITY AND RACE

Race is socially defined by a constellation of traits that include physical characteristics, national origin, language, culture, and religion. *Ethnicity* has a great deal of overlap with race, which produces confusion and theoretical debate about their difference. As practiced as recently as 2000, the Department of Census had five categories of race (American Indian or Alaska Native; Asian; Black or African American; Native Hawaiian or Other Pacific Islander; and White) and one of ethnicity (Hispanic). For the Census, Hispanic ethnicity and race are two separate concepts, so that Hispanics can be White, Black, Hawaiian/Pacific Islander, Asian, or American Indian.

Explaining why we count this way is a political history that highlights the importance of how race is socially constructed. Back in the 1930s, in response to congressional debate about immigration restrictions, the Census created a category of Mexican to collect data. It created Mexican as an additional racial category, thus officially declaring Mexicans to be nonwhite, even though Mexicans had been slipped in with whites for purposes of school segregation and Jim Crow laws because their blood did not have "negro ancestry." After the Census, the Mexican government and Mexican Americans successfully lobbied to have the classification changed: "Although having their whiteness restored did not lessen discrimination, the Mexican government and Mexican Americans fully understood the implication of being officially recognized as a non-White group" (Foley 2005, 60). When Congress again called for the creation of statistics on people of Spanish culture, origin, and descent in the 1970s, political lobbying resulted in the current system so that Hispanics would not automatically be nonwhite.

The political lobbying should not be seen as defeating an "objective" system of classification because there are no genetic markers that allow for the identification of race, and geneticists are unable to determine race from a DNA sample (Marshall 1998).[1] Two randomly selected people from the world's population would have about 99.8 percent of their genetic material in common (Feagin and Feagin 1996). Scientists agree that modern humans originated from a small population that emerged out of Africa and migrated around the globe, so there is a continuum of genetic variation that makes the concept of race meaningless to geneticists (Marshall 1998). The various racial categories thus represent a social-political construct that reflects a negotiated definition of race recognized in the United States.

Indeed, the 2010 Census lists fifteen racial categories and provides space to write in specific "races" not listed on the form. As figure 4.1 reveals,

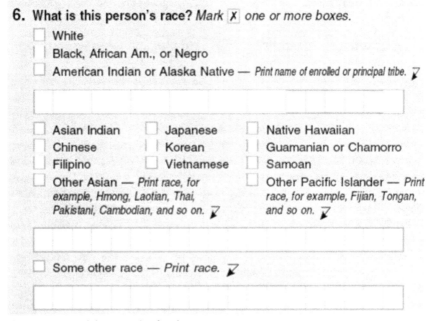

Figure 4.1.   Racial Categories for the 2010 Census
The Population Reference Bureau. Updated June 7 and retrieved June 9, 2009, from http://www.prb.org/Census2010/Questionnaire.aspx.

though, much of the new information about "race" is really capturing nationality—and the borders of many countries are arbitrary, constantly changing political compromises. For example, the form lists "Pakistani" under "other Asian," but Pakistan split in 1947 from what was then British India. The borders of British India were based on trade deals originally established by the British East India Company, which gradually came to colonize and rule India before turning it over to the British government. Pakistan's population was largely Muslim (and they are now an Islamic Republic) while India's population is mostly Hindu, so there are differences between the countries—just not racial or ethnic ones. Other nationalities listed on the form are similarly based on political, economic, and military history rather than reflecting "natural" home states for discrete "races."

Still, many people—not just white supremacists—believe race is an objective fact; they see race as part of their essence, inherent to them, even a property of the blood flowing through them (see box 4.1). Physical differences do exist among people and some of these traits are linked to biology and genetics, but the social construction approach recognizes that selecting the number of racial categories, deciding what characteristics determine the categories, and assigning people to the categories is ultimately a social and political act. For example, in *Plessy*, the Court ducked this very question of what makes a person black—a single drop of blood, half heritage, two-thirds, or any visible trace? All of these have been used by various state legislatures. Up to 1967, many states had antimiscegenation laws that prohibited whites from marrying members of a different race, which required specific definitions of race in order for state registrars to certify a person's racial composition. In Virginia, *white* meant "no trace whatever of any blood other than Caucasian; but persons who have one-sixteenth or less of the blood of the American Indian and have no other non-Caucasian blood shall be deemed to be white persons" (*Loving v. Virginia*, 388 U.S. 1). The fraction of Native American blood was based on the "desire of all to recognize as an integral and honored part of the white race the descendants of John Rolfe and Pocahontas."

The "mixed race" option introduced in the 2000 Census is another good example of the social construction of race. The Census had previously forced people of multiple races to specify only one, but they now have the option of reporting what they feel are the "important" racial identities in their background or just focusing on one. One of many who described himself as black has a white Jewish father and an African-Bermudan mother: "Checking more than one race," he contends, "would undermine the influence of blacks by reducing their number as a distinct group and so most likely diluting public policies addressing their concerns" (Quoted in Schemo 2000; see also Brune 1999). According to the Population Reference Bureau, the 2010 Census "continues the option first introduced in the 2000

Box 4.1.   Race and Blood

Hans Serelman was a doctor in Germany in 1935. His patient needed a blood transfusion, which at the time was done by finding a live donor ("donor-on-the-hoof") rather than using stored blood. Unable to find a suitable donor quickly enough, the doctor opened his own artery and donated his own blood. Instead of receiving praise, the Jewish doctor was sent to a concentration camp for defiling the blood of the German race.

In the succeeding years, Germany moved to eliminate the "Jewish influence" from medicine by limiting access to patients and medical school. To bolster claims of Aryan supremacy, the study of blood became a focus for distinguishing Aryans from Jews. The combined effects of these initiatives dealt a self-inflicted wound on the Nazi war effort. Hastily trained and inexperienced paramedics replaced the more than 8,000 Jewish doctors barred from practice. The infusion of mythology and misapplied anthropology set back serious scientific research on blood. The Nuremberg Blood Protection Laws severely limited the availability of blood for transfusions because of the possibility of being charged with "an attack on German blood" if the donor could not prove it was pure Aryan blood (Starr 1998, 26).

In the United States, the topic of "colored" versus "white" blood also stirred up controversy during World War II. The Red Cross knew that "blood was blood" and did not differ by race but followed the wishes of the military and refused to collect blood from African Americans. Following the attack on Pearl Harbor and the large demand for blood to treat many wounded soldiers, the Red Cross collected blood from blacks but labeled and processed it separately. As historian Douglas Starr notes, "The policy proved offensive to many Americans because the country was, after all, fighting a racist enemy" (1998, 108). A *New York Times* editorial commented, "the prejudice against Negro blood for transfusions is all the more difficult to understand because many a Southerner was nursed at the breast of a Negro nanny. Sometimes we wonder whether this is really an age of science" (in Starr 1998, 108).

In the late 1950s, Arkansas passed a law requiring the segregation of blood. Louisiana, home of the *Plessy v. Ferguson* case, "went so far as to make it a misdemeanor for physicians to give a white person black blood without asking permission" (Starr 1998, 170). The segregation of blood ended during the 1960s, more because of the civil rights movement than further advances in science.

Census for respondents to choose more than one race. Only about 2 percent of Americans identified with more than one race in the 2000 Census, but the percentage was much higher for children and young adults and will likely increase in 2010" (PRB 2009).

As these examples illustrate, people are not assigned to racial groups on the basis of genetics or "objective" factors. Thus, not only are the categories socially constructed but also placement of people in a category is itself based on numerous nonobjective social factors. People's willingness to claim a racial identity changes over time, further undermining any claim that race is an objective, fixed status. For example, Census figures indicate that between 1960 and 2000, the Native American population doubled, mostly because of increased self-identification. Stereotypes about the "drunken savage" remain, but the environmental movement and movies like *Dances with Wolves* have removed the perceived "taint" of being Native American and have replaced it with pride and a certain style or trendiness (Brune 1999; Hitt 2005). The increase in Native American population has continued with the popularity of genealogy, especially the increasing number of websites that serve to get people started, pushed by "ethnic shifting" or "ethnic shopping" (Hitt 2005). Research on Latino/as also finds that their "choice to identify as white or not does not reflect permanent markers such as skin color or hair texture but race is also related to characteristics that can change such as economic status and perceptions of civic enfranchisement" (Tafoya 2004, 2). Indeed, Hispanics "experience racial identity as a measure of belonging: Feeling white seems to be a reflection of success and a sense of inclusion" (Tafoya 2004, 3).

Further, no other country uses the same categories as the U.S. Census. This issue has important consequences for what criminal justice data is collected, how it is analyzed, and what "knowledge" is produced. For example, Canada only collects criminal justice data about "natives" and "non-natives." They are concerned that "'black' citizens have originated from many different countries over the last century, including the U.S., the West Indies, India, and Africa" (Lauritsen 2004, 70). Combining this diverse group into a single category makes analysis problematic, especially when there is no record of the country of origin or time of arrival in Canada. Criminologists then try to interpret white-black differences, even as "new 'white' immigrants continue to arrive from places as diverse as Russia or middle-eastern countries" (70). The broader question is how analysis using official data can provide "objective" knowledge about race if race itself cannot be objectively and consistently defined (Gabbidon and Greene 2005, 40).

Stating that race and ethnicity are socially constructed does not deny that some differences exist among people or that people experience very real oppression based on race and ethnicity. But far from reflecting inherent or essential racial identities, these racial categories reflect the social, economic, and political dynamics of the society that creates them, so there is a hierarchical ordering. Power and privilege are reflected in the schema of racial classification, which shapes people's lives and identities through stereotypes, prejudices, discrimination, and racism.

STEREOTYPES, POWER, AND PRIVILEGE

Stereotypes build on the dynamics of categorizing people, but they have the property of being fixed and are largely negative generalizations about a group of people. Many definitions stress the inadequate or problematic basis of stereotypes in personal experience—such as when people have stereotypes about groups they have never personally encountered but "know" about the group because of friends, the media, or social institutions that reflect prevailing beliefs. Stereotypes build on people's tendency to look for examples that confirm their beliefs and dismiss those contrary to how they see the world ("that's the exception that proves the rule").

Many Asians are stereotyped as the "model minority," and although this seems like a positive rather than negative evaluation, it has negative consequences for Asians since being "a paragon of hard work and docility carries a negative undercurrent" (Feagin and Feagin 1996, 404). Other evaluations about "exotic" women tend not to be truly positive but reinforce her status as a sex object and carry a history of racism and colonial conquest. The term *orientalism* is used to describe these attitudes toward the Middle East and Far East and reflects the values of the colonizing power. It also captures a tendency to focus on differences (from the Western "norm") and talk about the other in generalizations that suppress authentic human experience and complexity.

Prejudice refers to a negative or hostile attitude toward another social group. Psychologically, people project onto the minority group many of the negative attributes they wish to deny in themselves or the group with which they want to identify. Prejudice literally means prejudging someone, usually on the basis of a stereotype. While prejudice is a thought or attitude, *discrimination* occurs when people act on the basis of stereotypes and prejudice.

Because whites still have the vast majority of the power in society, they have the greatest ability to discriminate, so much of this chapter focuses on the problems associated with white prejudice and discrimination. In other words, people of all races can have prejudices or excessive pride of race, referred to as *individual* or *individualized racism*, and this describes individual people who consciously or unconsciously favor one race over another. Members of racial and ethnic minorities can certainly carry stereotypes and be prejudiced, but they generally do not have the power that can translate attitudes into substantial and recurring discrimination against whites in areas such as employment, business contracts, classrooms, department stores, and housing (Feagin and Feagin 1996). In this sense, the election of President Obama is a milestone of sorts in marking declining prejudice, but it does not radically change the overall power of minority groups and their ability to discriminate against the white majority.

Moreover, *racism* has conventionally been defined as a set of beliefs or attitudes—even a doctrine or dogma—in which "one ethnic group is condemned by nature to congenital inferiority and another group is destined to congenital superiority" (in Bonilla-Silva 1997, 20). From this perspective, racism is viewed as an irrational or flawed ideology because no such congenital relations exist. The term *institutional* or *institutionalized racism* acknowledges that racist behavioral patterns or consequences may have structural aspects to them that systemically stratify society, shape identity, and produce substantive differences. For example, Stokely Carmichael and Charles Hamilton observed:

> When white terrorists bomb a black church and kill five black children, that is an act of individual racism, widely deplored by most segments of society. But when in that same city—Birmingham, Alabama—five hundred black babies die each year because of lack of proper food, shelter and medical facilities, and thousands more are destroyed and maimed physically, emotionally, and intellectually because of conditions of poverty and discrimination, that is a function of institutional racism (1967, 65).

Bonilla-Silva expands on the notion of institutional racism by proposing the notion of *racialized social systems*, which refers "to societies in which economic, political, social, and ideological levels are partially structured by the placement of actors in racial categories" (1997, 132). This concept includes ideological beliefs as a component but also shows how the hierarchy of racial categories and the placement of people in them produce social relationships between the races.

A lack of understanding about race is perpetuated through the belief that race is about people of color and that whites do not have race. Being white or Caucasian involves having a race that affects identity and opportunity, even if whites have little race consciousness: "In the same way that both men's and women's lives are shaped by their gender, and that both heterosexual and lesbian women's experiences are shaped by their sexuality, white people *and* people of color live racially structured lives. In other words, any system of differentiation shapes those on whom it bestows privilege as well as those it oppresses" (Frankenberg 1993, 1).

Because whites are the dominant group, this social position and its privileges are naturalized through ideology so that being white seems neither privileged nor socially constructed. Ideology serves to naturalize the racial hierarchies, along with the prejudice and stereotypes that help re-create them. The ultimate point is not just that white traits come to be valued and minority traits devalued; but further, that *white privilege* is created when whiteness comes to be the norm, so that white people are not seen as speaking for whites but from and for a universal point of view. Richard Dyer explains:

> There is no more powerful position than that of being "just" human. The claim to power is the claim to speak for the commonality of humanity. Raced people can't do that—they can only speak for their race. But nonraced people can, for they do not represent the interests of a race (2005, 10).

Dyer believes whites have race, and he is speaking to the popular perception of whites having no race. The point of studying the race of whites is to make that point of view clearer:

> White people have power and believe that they think, feel and act like and for all people; white people, unable to see their particularity, cannot take account of other people's; white people create the dominant images of the world and don't quite see that they construct it in their own image; white people set standards of humanity by which they are bound to succeed and others bound to fail (12).

Because the majority group position is naturalized, members do not think of themselves as privileged and have few occasions to reflect on the "property interest" they have in being white. Box 4.2 contains a series of questions to provoke thoughts about naturalized or unrecognized privilege. Also, Frankenberg's work on white women explores the social construction of whiteness through interviews with women who have had to confront their whiteness though a variety of life experiences (including interracial relationships). Understanding whiteness involves asking many difficult questions, as indicated by a woman interviewed by Frankenberg: "I have an identity that doesn't have to do with my volition, but I've been profiting from it from birth. So what does that make me, and where does my responsibility lie? And where does my blame lie?" (1993, 175). Rather than confront some of these difficult issues, a small but increasing number of whites go ethnic shopping to see if there is an ethnic ancestor in their past they can use as a basis for a different identity—and Native American is one of the most popular. After all, "In a nation defined by ethnic anxiety, what greater salve is there than to become a member of the one people who have been here all along" (Hitt 2005)?

Andrew Hacker (1995) has created a classroom exercise to help students understand the value of being white. In "The Visit," an embarrassed official comes to a white person to say he (or she) was supposed to have been born to black parents. At midnight, he will become black and will have the features associated with African ancestry, so he will not be recognizable to current friends but inside he will be the same person he always has been. The white man is scheduled to live another fifty years as a black person, and the official's organization is willing to offer financial compensation, as the mistake is their fault.

Box 4.2.   You Know You're Privileged When . . . (Part 1)

In 1988, Peggy McIntosh's frustration with men who would not recognize their male privilege prompted her to examine her own life and identify ordinary ways in which she experienced white privilege. "I think whites are carefully taught not to recognize white privilege, as males are taught not to recognize male privilege" (1997 [1988], 292). Her list of forty-six forms of white privilege included the following:

- When I am told about our national heritage or about "civilization," I am shown that people of my color made it what it is.
- I can go into a music shop and count on finding the music of my race represented, into a supermarket and find staple foods which fit with my cultural traditions, into a hairdresser's shop and find someone who can cut my hair.
- Whether I use checks, credit cards, or cash, I can count on my skin color not to work against the appearance of financial reliability.
- I can talk with my mouth full and not have people put this down to my color.
- I can swear, or dress in secondhand clothes, or not answer letters, without having people attribute these choices to the bad morals, the poverty, or the illiteracy of my race.
- I can do well in a challenging situation without being called a credit to my race.
- I can be pretty sure that if I ask to talk to "the person in charge," I will be facing a person of my race.
- If I declare there is a racial issue at hand, or there isn't a racial issue at hand, my race will lend me more credibility for either position than a person of color will have.
- I can worry about racism without being seen as self-interested or self-seeking.
- I can take a job with an affirmative action employer without having my coworkers on the job suspect that I got it because of my race.

A few years later, Stephanie M. Wildman (1997 [1996], 325) suggested some additional conditions specific to dominant cultural white privilege, made with respect to her Latina/o friends, acquaintances, and colleagues. These included:

- People will not be surprised if I speak English well.
- People seeing me will assume I am a citizen of the United States. . . . People will never assume that my children or I are illegal immigrants.
- People will not comment about my sense of time if I am prompt or late, unless I am unusually late. Then people will assume that I have an individual, personal reason for being late. My lateness will not be dismissed as a joke about white time.
- People will pronounce my name correctly or politely ask about the correct pronunciation. They will not behave as if it is an enormous imposition to get the name right.

Hacker notes that white students do not feel it out of place asking for $50 million, or a million a year, which is a good indication of the value—the property interest mentioned in *Plessy v. Ferguson*—of being white. Students who say that because of affirmative action they would be better off as a black still come up with a figure to "buy protections from the discriminations and dangers white people know they would face once they were perceived to be black" (Hacker 1995, 31–32). In fact, other social indicators of well-being reveal none in which African Americans or Hispanics occupy a favored position. Indeed, Michael Tonry summarizes the situation as one in which "mountains of social welfare, health, employment, and education data make it clear that black Americans experience material conditions of life that, on average, are far worse than those faced by white Americans" (1995, 128; see also Johnson and Leighton 1999).

ECONOMIC, POLITICAL, AND SOCIAL SPHERES

This section presents a summary of how the various racial and ethnic groups compare to each other. Given the brevity of this section, it is important to remember that diversity within groups is masked by the broader categories. For example, Native American includes 562 federally recognized tribes, although there are actually more because the federal government has stringent requirements for recognition, which is the basis for certain grants, entitlements, and casinos. States and localities recognize a larger number of tribes, and there are also tribes that have no interest in recognition from governments that have systematically treated Natives so badly (see opening of chapter 7). Likewise, averages for other groups can conceal internal diversity even as they help illuminate the larger picture.

Table 4.1 presents an overview of the U.S. population to highlight the relative size of ethnic and racial groups for 2007. Note that while the Census lists most Hispanics as being white, 42 percent of Hispanics actually used the option of "some other race" (Tafoya 2004, 4–5). The Census notes that most of the descriptions for some other race were entries like "Mexican" or "Puerto Rican," so the Census blanked "some other race" and imputed a response based on a donor.

Economic Sphere

Chapter 3 mentioned that minorities were disproportionately represented in the early part of the income and wealth parades. For example, back in 1975, black median income was 60 percent of white median income, while Hispanic median income was nearly 72 percent of white median income. Thirty years later, in 2005, not much had changed: black

Table 4.1.   Population by Race and Ethnicity, 2007

Categories	*Population*	
Not Hispanic		**256,117,000**
One race:	251,912,000	
White	199,092,000	
Black or African American	37,037,000	
American Indian and Alaska Native	2,287,000	
Asian	13,080,000	
Native Hawaiian and Other Pacific Islander	417,000	
Two or more races:	4,205,000	
Hispanic		**45,504,000**
One race:	44,853,000	
White	42,075,000	
Black or African American	1,719,000	
American Indian and Alaska Native	652,000	
Asian	287,000	
Native Hawaiian and Other Pacific Islander	120,000	
Two or more races:	651,000	
TOTAL		**301,621,000**

Source: U.S. Census Bureau. 2009. "Resident Population by Sex, Race, and Hispanic Origin Status: 2000 to 2007." http://www.census.gov/compendia/statab/cats/population.html.

median income was almost 64 percent of white median income; Hispanic median income was about 74 percent of white median income (Lynch, Patterson, and Childs 2008, 3–4). Table 4.2 illustrates the large gap in median income and the disproportionate number of blacks and Hispanics in poverty for 2006. This reflects, in part, the differences in educational attainment, unemployment rates, and wage rates. For example, the occupations with the largest number of Hispanics include building/grounds work, cleaning/maintenance, and food preparation/service; occupations with the fewest Hispanics included legal, computer, and health care/medical (Pew Hispanic Center 2005, 10).

Some of the dynamics captured in the table can be understood through the research of Pager and Western, who sent whites, blacks, and Latinos to apply for real entry-level jobs. Job applicants were matched so their resumes would show the same basic level of education and work experience, although some whites also presented evidence of a felony conviction. The proportion of positive responses—being offered a job or called back for an interview—"depends strongly on the race of the job applicant. This comparison demonstrates a [clear] racial hierarchy, with whites in the lead, followed by Latinos, with Blacks trailing far behind" (in Reiman and Leighton 2010b, 73). In the experimental variation, the "white applicant with a felony conviction appears to do . . . better than his black [and Latino] counterpart[s] with no criminal background. These results suggest

Table 4.2.   Median Family Income and Individual Poverty Rate by Race and Hispanic Origin, 2006

Categories	Household Income	Individual Poverty Rate
All	$58,407	12.3%
White alone (non-Hispanic)	$61,280	10.3%
Black alone	$38,269	24.3%
Asian alone	$74,612	10.3%
Hispanic (all race)	$40,000	20.6%

Source: 2009 *Statistical Abstract*. Tables 674 and 689.

that employers view minority job applicants as essentially equivalent to whites just out of prison" (in Reiman and Leighton 2010b, 75).[2]

Income and wealth are important indicators because they relate to political power and the ability to shield one from hardships. Echoing the discussion of wealth in the previous chapter, research by the Pew Hispanic Center notes that "individual wealth is also known to provide access to superior health, education, and other services, and as a community, relative wealth is also correlated with social and political influence" (Kochhar 2004, 3). Table 4.3 illustrates the relative level of wealth held by Hispanics is about 9 percent of what is held by non-Hispanic whites, and blacks hold about 7 percent of the wealth of non-Hispanic whites. The wealth of minorities is also disproportionately in houses, cars, and checking accounts, as opposed to financial assets like stocks and businesses (which chapter 3 noted generates the most economic and political power).

Beyond the low level of minority wealth compared to whites, a striking finding is higher levels of wealth among Hispanics than blacks. Because 40 percent of Hispanics are immigrants, language, culture, and citizenship issues can serve as a barrier to jobs, which would contribute to low levels of wealth. Also, Hispanics (at least before the most recent financial crisis) remit more than $30 billion back to relatives in other countries—about

Table 4.3.   Net Worth/Wealth by Race and Ethnicity, 2002

	Median Net Worth of Household	Percent of Households with Negative or Zero Net Worth
Hispanic	$7,932	26%
Black non-Hispanic	$5,988	32.3%
White non-Hispanic	$88,651	13.1%
All Households	$59,706	Not reported

Source: Kochhar (2004, 5, 7). This survey uses slightly different data from the Federal Reserve study reported in chapter 3, so estimates may be slightly different. In particular, this survey oversamples low-income households, so median wealth estimates tend to be on the low side.

$2,500 per year per household (Kochhar 2004, 36). In spite of this large exporting of money, Hispanics still have greater wealth than blacks.

As a final note about the diversity within these categories, the distribution of wealth within the Hispanic community is more unequal than the distribution of wealth among whites. The richest Hispanics have less absolute wealth than whites, meaning they have less in terms of dollar amounts. But the wealthiest 5 percent of Hispanics control 49.8 percent of all Hispanic wealth; the top 25 percent accounts for 92.7 percent of the total Hispanic wealth (Kochhar 2004, 9–10). The richest blacks also have far less than the richest whites, but the concentration and inequality tend to be more similar between the groups (Kennickell 2003, 34).

Appreciating this diversity within racial and ethnic categories will be crucial to understanding the intersections of class, race, and gender in chapter 6. While the aggregate net worth of the poorest 50 percent of blacks is negative (Kochhar 2004, 9)—the debt of the lowest 33 percent cancels out the small net worth of the other 17 percent—2.4 percent of blacks had net worth above $500,000 (Kennickell 2003, 34) and included three black CEOs of Fortune 500 companies. There is also a sizable black middle class, evidenced by the 16 percent of blacks with net worth between $50,000 and $100,000 (34). Thus, blacks cannot be expected to have a single or unitary point of view. Indeed, in his analysis of comedian Bill Cosby's critique of the manners, morals, and habits of blacks, Dyson (2005) argues that this is a case of class warfare, with the black elite (what he calls the Afristocracy) criticizing the ghetto blacks.

Political Sphere

Racial and ethnic minorities continue to be underrepresented in politics, although the situation has improved. In the United States, voter registration and participation is especially low among minorities, adding to other difficulties electing minority officials. Table 4.4 highlights voter participation and minority representation at the national level. Compared with blacks and whites, Asians and Hispanics have larger numbers of noncitizens, rendering them ineligible to register and vote. The percent that voted for all groups is based on self reports, which tend to inflate the number of people who actually participated. Still, overall participation is low, which fuels registration and get-out-the-vote campaigns for both parties.

Not surprisingly the campaign and election of the first African American president in 2008 made a significant difference in voter participation by minorities. For example, black women had the highest voter turnout in history and overall the electorate was also the most racially and ethnically diverse, with nearly one-in-four votes cast by nonwhites according to a Pew Research Center analysis (Lopez and Taylor 2009). While the nation's three

Table 4.4.   Voting Participation and Members of Congress by Race and Ethnicity, 2008

	Percent of Population 18 or Older Eligible to Register	Percent of Total Population Who Registered	Percent of Total Population Who Voted	Number in U.S. Senate (Out of 100)	Number in House of Representatives (Out of 441)
White non-Hispanic	98	72	65	96	365
Black alone	94	66	61	1	41
Asian alone	68	37	32	2	6
Hispanic (any race)	63	38	32	1	24

Source: Census Bureau, Voting and Registration in the Election of November 2008. Available, http://www.census.gov/population/www/socdemo/voting/cps2008.html. Registration and voting percentage based on total population. Members of Congress from Congress.org, accessed October 16, 2009. The "Caucasian" category was the closest match to "White non-Hispanic" but may not be exact. The House of Representatives has 435 voting and 6 nonvoting members.

largest minority groups—blacks, Hispanics, and Asians—each accounted for unprecedented shares of the presidential vote, overall, "Whites made up 76.3% of the record 131 million people who voted in November's presidential election, while blacks made up 12.1%, Hispanics 7.4% and Asians 2.5%. The white share is the lowest ever, yet is still higher than the 65.8% white share of the U.S. population" (Lopez and Taylor 2009).

Representation for minorities is higher at the local level, but still low. In state government, 86 percent of legislators are white (and 90 percent of the legislative staff) (Kurtz and Weberg 2009). Because the Hispanic population is relatively young in the United States, they have great potential for gains in the future, especially if they can increase their voter participation rate. As a result, both parties are actively courting the Hispanic vote, with Republicans in particular hoping to improve minority participation in the party since only 8 percent of eligible blacks register Republican. Indeed, President Obama's nomination of Sonia Sotomayor created difficulties for Republicans who did not want her on the Supreme Court but who did not want to publicly oppose the first Hispanic to the Court.

Social Sphere

Educational attainment influences economic status and health. Since 1980, all racial and ethnic groups have experienced increases in their level of educational attainment; increases for blacks have been the most marked, while increases for Hispanics have been relatively small. Non-Hispanic whites and Asians are more likely than blacks, Hispanics, and American Indians to have completed education beyond high school.

Black Americans are more likely than whites or any other minority group to live in toxic physical environments. "In 1987 the Commission for Racial Justice of the United Church of Christ reported that three of every five black and Hispanic Americans live in a community with uncontrolled toxic-waste sites" (Austin and Schill 1991, 69; Lee 1992). Although poverty is an important factor, "the racial composition of a community was found to be the single variable best able to explain the existence or nonexistence of commercial hazardous waste facilities in a given community area" (Bullard 1990; Lee 1992, 14). Another survey indicated that, although attention has been focused on the problem of environmental racism, the concentration of toxic waste in low-income communities was *growing*, especially for low-income black Americans. Hazardous wastes were examined because nationally comprehensive data were easily available: "many other problems in minority communities, such as air pollution, workplace exposure, pesticides, lead poisoning, asbestos, municipal waste and others, are equally or more serious" but not subject to ready assessment (Lee 1992, 16; see also Bullard 1994; Kozol 1991; Lynch and Stretesky 1998).

IMPLICATIONS

The United States continues to be marked by a profound and persistent racial divide. This divide exists on numerous dimensions: "as a perception of others or in the form of stereotypes; in vastly different access to health care and education; and in the unequal distribution of economic goods and access to employment. And, despite society's best interests and intentions, there appear to be unconscious processes that continue to facilitate racial bias in criminal justice processes" (Lynch et al. 2008, 13). The ideology of racism can make it difficult for whites to understand the vulnerability minorities feel, which seems exaggerated to whites who have had few occasions to think about the privileges conferred on them. Even whites who would demand a large sum for a visitor telling them they had to live as a black are aware that being white does give them some protections, but it is a large step to internalizing the sense of social marginality that comes from living every day as a minority in a white country, even a highly multiracial one like the United States.

Unfortunately, even in the face of history and a mountain of social indicators that all illustrate minority disadvantage, many whites are still unable to see their racial privilege. In spite of a wide variety of data on the growing inequality in society and in the administration of criminal justice, politicians and media pundits support the same old practices for the most part that are responsible for these problems. Indeed, there were even calls to bring back the "chain gang" in spite of its long and obvious symbol as a tool of racial oppression (Gorman 1997). Meanwhile, communities are being destroyed, and the experience of incarceration makes it harder for inmates to be productive community members upon release. Even though released inmates have "done their time," the government has been developing increasingly sophisticated computerized records that help ensure that criminal record data is easily and widely available. Thus, "it is not fanciful to worry about the emergence of a sophisticated computer quarantine that had profound implications for social structure" because it isolates and separates and further marginalizes the poor, especially the black and Latino poor (Gordon 1990, 89; Gandy 1993; Lopez 2008).

This chapter should help clarify why many minorities picture themselves as profoundly marginal and expendable, leaving them with a sense of alienation perhaps best captured in Derrick Bell's "Chronicle of the Space Traders" (1990). In this story, blacks as a group are sacrificed to aliens for gold to retire the national debt, a chemical to clean up pollution, and a limitless source of clean energy. Following a national referendum and a Supreme Court decision, blacks are lined up and turned over to the aliens—in chains, just as they entered the country hundreds of years ago.

The moral of this story for Bell is that we have made no racial progress; whites would sacrifice blacks for their own gain today just as they did 400 years ago with the institution of slavery. Among blacks, the chronicle "captures an uneasy intuition" that black Americans "live at the sufferance of whites—that as soon as our [black] welfare conflicts with something they [whites] consider essential, all our gains, all our progress, will turn out to be illusory" (Delgado and Stefancic 1991, 321). Not too many whites share such a "pessimistic" view of the progress made (or not made) regarding racial relations in America, especially with the recent election of an African American president, but this is still likely tied to the inability to appreciate white privilege and the overall experience of minorities.

REVIEW AND DISCUSSION QUESTIONS

1. What is meant by the social construction of race? What are some of the examples the authors have given to support this point?
2. Highlight the distinctions between the following related terms: stereotypes, prejudice, discrimination, and racism. How are institutional and individual racism different?
3. What is meant by the term *white privilege*? What are the key points made in the quotes by Dyer?
4. Review the box on privilege. What do you think are the strongest examples? Are there any you think should be added?
5. What are some ways that all minority groups share similar experiences in the United States? Drawing on the chapter and your own knowledge, what are some of the differences between different groups?
6. What is meant by diversity within a minority group? What are some examples of this diversity, and when it might be important to advancing our social and criminological knowledge?

5

Understanding Gender and Male Privilege

The 1990s will be remembered for its attention to a relatively new kind of violence: "rampage school shootings." During this period, there was a "wave" of shootings by white males in middle and high schools across rural and suburban (but not urban) America. Between 1994 and 1998, there were approximately 200 violent deaths: 83 percent homicides; 13 percent suicides; and 4 percent combinations of the two (Hammond 1999). In peak years like 1998, forty-two school-related homicides happened. Among the homicides, there were no particular groups targeted by the all-male, adolescent and preadolescent perpetrators of these killings (Newman et al. 2004). (The 2006 shooting at an Amish school in Lancaster, Pennsylvania, did involve five female victims, but it was done by a man in his thirties and not a student peer.)

While media attention to school violence has declined, preliminary data for 2006–2007 showed that among youth ages five to eighteen, there were thirty-five school-associated violent deaths (twenty-seven homicides and eight suicides) or about one homicide or suicide of a school-age youth at school per 1.6 million students. Youth homicides at secondary schools remained less than 2 percent of the total number of youth homicides (Dinkes, Kemp, and Baum 2009). This is consistent with other years surveyed as well. There have also been fewer than a handful of acts of homicide and suicide on college campuses during the first decade of this century, the most infamous at Virginia Tech.

Those analysts who pay close attention to the wider organizational and societal features of community relations tend to distinguish between the more familiar revenge killings and the rampage shootings. The latter assaults involve a special kind of attack on multiple parties, selected almost at random. "The shooters may have a specific target to begin with, but they let loose with a fusillade that hits others,

113

and it is not unusual for the perpetrator to be unaware of who has been shot until long after the fact" (Newman et al. 2004, 15).

These explosions are not attacks aimed at the popular kids, bullies, athletes, and/ or harassers per se as many commentators and pundits have suggested. Instead, they are attacks on whole institutions—schools, teenage pecking orders, community social structures—and they represent "backlash" or "blowback" effects from male adolescents who are unable to successfully navigate the treacherous waters of doing teenage masculinity. Schools are the selected sites for these culturally played-out scripts of "becoming a man" and performing violence because "they are the heart and soul of public life in small towns" where there are "high levels of background violence, dysfunctional families, chaotic schools, [and] distracted adults too busy with town lives to pay attention to the local teens" (Newman et al. 2004, 15). These rampage school shootings thus contradict our most firmly held beliefs about childhood, home, and community: "They expose the vulnerable underbelly of ordinary life and tell us that malevolence can be brewing in places where we least expect it, that our fail-safe methods (parental involvement in children's lives, close-knit neighborhoods) do not identify nascent pathologies" that may be part and parcel of patriarchy, gender, and coming-of-age for socially and marginally adolescent males living in nonmetropolitan America (Newman et al. 2004, 15).

Many popular explanations for these rural and suburban shootings include mental illness, family problems, bullying, peer support, culture of violence, violent media, availability of guns, and the copycat effect. But most of these explanations on their own do not hold up, while some of these explanations in combination with others and with qualification—such as peer support and culture of violence—are more helpful. But what is missing from these types of analyses is the importance of young adolescent males as the perpetrators. Misfit girls have their problems, too, but they do not resort to rampage or any other kinds of mass shootings. Since all the perpetrators are male, masculinity should be a central part of the investigation—and certainly if all the perpetrators had been girls, the question would be "What's going on with girls?" (or "girls gone wild!") rather than "school violence" and "what's wrong with kids?" (Katz 1999).

Of course, both boys and girls seek status, perform for peers, find identities, and cope with their parents and other adults. The point is that the process of finding a workable niche in society is distinctive along gender lines. The all-male club of rampage shooters share at least in their own eyes and perceptions (if not in the eyes and perceptions of others, too) a dual failure—failing at adolescence and failing at manhood. For adolescent males, demonstrating masculinity is central to what makes a popular boy high on the social pecking order. As the authors of Rampage: The Social Roots of School Shootings *have stated:*

> *To be a man is to be physically dominant, competitive, and powerful in the eyes of others. Real men exert control and never admit weakness. They act more and talk*

less. If this sounds like Marlboro Man, it is because adolescent ideals of manliness are unoriginal. They derive from cultural projections found in film, video, magazines, and the back of comic books. In-your-face basketball players, ruthless Wall Street robber barons, and presidents who revel in being "doers" and not "talkers" all partake of and then reinforce this stereotype (Newman et al. 2004, 144).

The most powerful source of stigma for an adolescent boy coming of age in the United States today is being labeled "gay." The assumption is that being a man means being heterosexual, and even the specter of homosexuality compromises a boy's status and place on the social ladder because "gay" constitutes a failure at achieving masculine gender. "Gay" does not merely refer to a sexual orientation, preference, or reference, but also to a broader connotation now used as a slang term for any form of social or athletic incompetence to an array of other mistakes and failures. One fifteen-year-old girl explained: "Boys have a fascination with not being gay. They want to be manly, and put each other down by saying 'that's gay'" (in Newman et al. 2004, 146). Thus for boys, "the struggle for status is in large part competition for the rank of alpha male, and any kind of failure by another boy can be an opportunity to insult the other's masculinity and enhance one's own. It's a winner-take-all society, and any loss one boy can inflict on another opens up a new rung on the ladder that he might move into" (146).

As for those socially marginal and psychologically distressed youth who end up at the bottom of the social pecking orders as a result of their real or imagined failure to do masculinity, a few of them ultimately find themselves trapped in a limited repertoire of cultural scripts or strategies of action that resolve their feelings of shame, humiliation, and inadequacy. Various rampage school shooters all felt at the moment of crisis that they had no other options but to come forth and fire their weapons. They had all considered suicide, but that wasn't the manly thing to do. Going out in a blaze, perhaps shooting it out with the police, would certainly allow them to go down in school infamy as full of machismo. In carrying out these scenarios of killing, these adolescent males are not simply reacting to glorified violence, but rather they are immersing themselves in violent roles that they believed were powerful and would thus enhance their status as men.

In short, having violence, aggression, and domination as cultural norms for masculinity provides a framework for their behavior. These gendered rampage shootings provide these young males with a way to demonstrate their "anger with an entire social system that had rejected them. . . . For this purpose, any target [will] do just as well as any other, so long as the shootings [occur] on a public stage for all to see" (Newman et al. 2004, 152). In the process, these truly rare rampage killers, characterizing the extreme end of trying to do masculine gender, are able in a "twisted" way to claim the power and status their peers had denied them.

As with class and race, discussions of gender raise controversy. There's the F word—feminism—that many men and women resist even as they endorse basic tenets of treating women with dignity, respect, and equality. Discussing sex and gender means exploring what we mean by equality when men and women are different biologically in ways that go far beyond racial differences like skin color or hair texture. This problem is most evident in issues around human reproduction and biology, but it is also present in debates about whether men and women are "similarly situated" and thus deserve equal treatment as a matter of law. Women are 51 percent of the population but are considered a minority and part of the affirmative action plans. Should equality be based on what men were getting? Are both sexes to be treated equally based on what women are getting, or is there another alternative?

One flashpoint in these ongoing debates was the comments of Harvard's former president and current economic advisor to President Obama, Lawrence Summers, about diversifying personnel in science and engineering. The reasons he suggested for the small number of women in these fields was, in order of importance: (1) Women do not put in the long workweeks over the long run because they want to have children and value family; (2) innate differences between men and women lead men to outperform women; (3) discrimination and socialization (Summers 2005a). The comments created a great deal of dissent and discussion, much of it focused on the issue of innate differences—and much of it noting that since Summers became president at Harvard in 2001, the percentage of women getting a permanent tenured position at Harvard had declined by half to 12 percent.

Critics pointed out that the number of women in science and engineering had climbed from 3 percent to about 20 percent in thirty years, and the female genome and DNA had not changed that much in a few decades, so innate difference could not be a major factor. The chair of the sociology department asked, "Has anyone asked if he thinks this about African-Americans, because they are underrepresented at this university?" (Bombardieri 2005). Deborah Blum, a Pulitzer Prize–winning science writer, felt a sense of déjà vu: "Spend any time at all studying the biology of behavior and you will find it riddled with similar, nature-based defenses of the often less-than-perfect status quo. In the days before women were admitted to college, male scientists insisted that girls were born too fragile and emotional to even handle higher education" (2005). Critics also reported many studies showing the impact of socialization—women being steered away from a field, told they would not be good or interested, and finding no role models—and wished someone as educated as Summers and speaking from a place of such prominence had not reinforced the idea that "women were, well, dumb" when it came to math and science (2005).

In spite of supporters claiming he was the victim of political correctness, Summers (2005a) wrote a series of apologies in which he said he never meant to suggest "that girls are intellectually less able than boys, or that women lack the ability to succeed at the highest levels of science." He was just trying to be provocative, he claimed, and certainly did not wish to discourage talented girls and women, especially after all he learned about "the very real barriers faced by women in pursuing scientific and other academic careers" (2005a). Lost in the discussion was Summers's comment about women's willingness to put in the hours and sacrifice that it takes to get to the top, not just in engineering but corporate America as well. At least in this respect, his comments were similar to the analysis in a cover story of *Fortune* magazine, which noted some reluctance of women to make sacrifices for power and who instead looked for jobs that were satisfying or personally meaningful. But, "men, too, are growing dissatisfied with the price they pay to rise in corporate America and are looking for the same flexibility and balance that women want" (Sellers 2003, 100).

While this discussion has been about women in science and corporations, much of the same themes and lessons apply to criminology and criminal justice as well. One letter, signed by over a hundred scientists in response to Summers's comments, noted: "If society, institutions, teachers, and leaders like President Summers, expect (overtly or subconsciously) that girls and women will not perform as well as boys and men, there is a good chance many will not perform as well" (Borg 2005). Criminology recognizes the same phenomenon in labeling theory, and more generally the chapters in the third section of this book will review how stereotypes and expectations affect the treatment of men and women as both victims and offenders. Beliefs about women being too emotional and not able to handle the rigors of logic kept women out of law school and the practice of law for many years. Concerns about women's weakness continue to exert influence on women in policing and positions as correctional officers. Gender discrimination shapes opportunities in legitimate criminal justice work and also shapes the opportunities in crime, where women tend to be at the lower end of criminal organizations and participate in pettier criminality.

In taking up the task of analyzing gender, we recognize that, within the criminal justice system, men are the majority of offenders and victims. However, theoretical understandings of crime and violence up until recently did not consider why men have such high rates of offending relative to women, nor were theorists giving much attention to the roles of gender, socialization, and doing masculinity. Women are certainly still a small minority of the criminal justice caseloads, but they are the fastest growing proportion. As a consequence, until recently not much attention was paid to the differential treatment of male and female offenders, including the different needs of female inmates.

Because people's treatment within the administration of justice is shaped by what takes place outside the criminal justice system, this chapter, like the previous two chapters, locates its discussion—this time on gender—in terms of the larger economic, political, and social spheres of interaction. Before turning to a comparative discussion of the relative positions of men and women, we first address the relevant gender terminology. The point from the previous chapter about racial privilege is revisited in terms of male privilege—and in terms of how racial privilege impacts feminism. Finally, the implications of these relations for equal justice and the study of crime and social control are underscored.

GENDER AND SEX IN SOCIETY

Sex generally refers to nature and the biological components that characterize male and female. While sex tends to be thought of as limited to male and female, *gender* typically refers to nurture and the "dominant ideas about feminine and masculine traits and behaviors prevalent in any society at one time" (Hatty 2000, 111). Gender thus refers to the social expectations for males and females to be masculine and feminine, which involves the *social* processes through which people learn and are socialized into acting according to the notions of what is an appropriate role and behavior for men and women in our society. Understanding these social processes is crucial because it is both easy and convenient to attribute differences to biology ("innate") when the focus should be on socialization, role expectation, and factors that relate to how someone "becomes" a man/woman in our society. For example, people customarily identify women as being more in touch with feelings and nurturing than men. One explanation would be a biological one attributing those qualities to the women's reproductive functions in having a child. An alternate explanation would highlight the importance for women of understanding the feelings of others when society is male dominated, because women are frequently dependent on men economically and they are often subject to a great deal of male violence against women. In such a context, being attuned to the feelings of those in a dominant position and having the ability to comfort them would arise out of necessity and become part of the gender role expectation.

Essentialism is the belief in inherent qualities, an unchanging and indispensable quality. With gender, the debate is over *biological* essentialism, which refers to some innate and distinguishing qualities or personality traits that would exist in each sex that goes beyond cultural conditioning. The issue here is not to point to biological differences in, say, reproductive function, but to find out whether men or women have inherent traits that exist across cultures and throughout time. Feminists are generally skeptical about claims of essentialism because they tend to be used to justify inequality and male privilege. Just as Lawrence Summers (above) tried to point to innate differences when it comes to the hard sciences, Blum pointed to earlier justifications that women were innately unable to deal with college education. Similar thoughts have been behind denying women the right to vote and the ability to get a number of professional licenses (including law and medicine) because women were too emotional and/or seen as unable to handle the rigor of the field. Further, essentialism (be it based on sex, race, or class, or anything else), like Orientalism (see previous chapter), homogenizes a group of people; that is, it denies differences and diversity within a group of people (e.g., woman, blacks, the poor). Just as with racial stereotyping, this process is dehumanizing and normalizes the power relations so that inequality is not questioned because it appears to be the result of natural differences.

Gender is thus a social construction, a process though which gender is "done" (or "performed") through routine interactions with other people. By being aggressive and not displaying feelings, men can assert clams to masculinity; attacking gays reinforces the heterosexual aspect of masculinity, as does sexual aggression and domination of women. By making themselves up to look attractive, being sensitive to others, quiet and nonassertive, women accomplish femininity. In both cases, men and women "do gender" by handling situations in such a way that the outcome is considered gender appropriate and therefore heterosexual. Masculinity and femininity are never accomplished and secure in a final way; they are something that must be continually "done" and (re-)accomplished. (Such notions of femininity and masculinity also have a dire implication for female victimization and male perpetration in domestic violence.)

Gender roles are the socially scripted or appropriate behaviors for males and females, and they have traditionally reflected patriarchal values that have reserved for men public power and control of women (see box 5.1). Gender roles for women, for example, until recently have included those values and attitudes that often placed "women on a pedestal" representing "the idea that women need male protection and that they should be more virtuous than men, for example by not telling dirty jokes, getting drunk, or paying their share of the cost of a date" (Scully 1990, 79). The traditional corollary was that women who fell off the pedestal were seen as "legitimate

Box 5.1. You Know You're Privileged When . . . (Part 2)

a poem for men who don't understand what we mean when we say they
    have it
privilege is simple:
going for a pleasant stroll after dark,
not checking the back of your car as you get in, sleeping soundly,
speaking without interruption, and not remembering
dreams of rape, that follow you all day, that woke you crying, and
privilege is not seeing your stripped, humiliated body
plastered in celebration across every magazine rack, privilege
is going to the movies and not seeing yourself
terrorized, defamed, battered, butchered
seeing something else
privilege is
riding your bicycle across town without being screamed at or
run off the road, not needing an abortion, taking off your shirt
on a hot day, in a crowd, not wishing you could type better
just in case, not shaving your legs, having a decent job and
expecting to keep it, not feeling the boss's hand up your crotch,
dozing off on late-night buses, privilege
is being the hero on the TV show not the dumb broad,
living where your genitals are totemized not denied,
knowing your doctor won't rape you
privilege is being smiled at all day by nice helpful women, it is
the way you pass judgment on their appearance with magisterial authority,
the way you face a judge of your own sex in court and
are overrepresented in Congress and are not strip-searched for a traffic
    ticket
or used as a dart board by your friendly mechanic,
privilege is seeing your bearded face reflected through the history texts
not only of your high school days but all your life, not being relegated to a
    paragraph
every other chapter, the way you occupy
entire volumes of poetry and more of your share of the couch unchallenged,
it is your mouthing smug, atrocious insults as women
who blink and change the subject politely—
privilege is how seldom the rapist's name appears in the papers
and the way you smirk over your PLAYBOY
it's simple really,
privilege means someone else's pain, your wealth
is my terror, your uniform
is a woman raped to death here or in Cambodia or
wherever your obscene privilege
writes your name in my blood, it's that simple,

you've always had it, that's why it doesn't
seem to make you sick at stomach,
you have it, we pay for it, now
do you understand

Source: D. A. Clarke. 1981. *Banshee*. Peregrine Press.

victims" who deserved hostility and contempt—even vigilante punishment—whether in the form of harassment, domestic violence, or sexual assault.

Patriarchy refers to those societies organized around male privilege or hierarchy. Patriarchal societies vary in form and expression depending on whether they are agricultural, industrial, or service societies. The totality of their oppressive and exploitative uses of male authority and female subordination will also vary. *Sexism*, which can be present both at the individual and institutional level, describes the beliefs and social relations holding that men are superior to women. Sexism includes *paternalism*, the view that women need protection and are not fully responsible for their actions, and *chivalry*, the reluctance to inflict harm on a woman accompanied by unwillingness to believe that a woman could possess criminal intent (Moulds 1980). Adrienne Rich has defined *misogyny* "as organized, institutionalized, normalized hostility and violence toward women" (in Humm 1990, 139). Interestingly, the word for hatred of men, *misandry*, rarely appears in print or public discourse. *Phallocentrism* refers to social constructs that make men the focus of law and meaning (Gamble 1999). Taken together, these values, norms, and beliefs of patriarchy devalue women in society, setting them up for all kinds of unequal treatment.

One area in which patriarchy impinges on women through social, economic, and political forces is reproductive rights, as women's bodies have historically been subjected to control through control of their reproductive processes. According to World Health Organization, *reproductive rights*

rest on the recognition of the basic right of all couples and individuals to decide freely and responsibly the number, spacing and timing of their children and to have the information and means to do so, and the right to attain the highest standard of sexual and reproductive health. They also include the right of all to make decisions concerning reproduction free of discrimination, coercion and violence (2005).

While reproductive rights in the United States are often associated with the right to abortion, they encompass a much wider arena of woman's (and man's) reproductive processes and her right to choose or refuse treatments: abortion, sterilization, contraception, family planning, infertility treatment. Reproductive rights also include the right to be free from illnesses or other conditions that might interfere with sexual and reproductive functions. They encompass the right to provide for healthy children by meeting not only their physical needs but also their educational, emotional, and social needs (Flavin 2009).

Reproductive rights are "fundamental rights" that should receive the highest level of protection because they are related to "the right to bodily integrity, the right to privacy (including the right to an abortion), and the right to procreate" (Flavin 2009, 39). The right to privacy is frequently explained as "the right to be let alone" or "have government off our back" and establishes a personal sphere free from government intrusion. The right to bodily integrity is strong enough that organs cannot be taken from the dead without their prior permission. Indeed, "if a person cannot be forced to have criminal evidence removed from his body, or a father cannot be compelled to donate an organ to [save] his child['s life], then it follows that forcing a woman to be sterilized or take contraceptives similarly violates her right to bodily integrity" and privacy (Flavin 2009, 40).

Further, while it is important to think about individual rights, central concerns also include how the social, economic, and political conditions affect a woman's autonomy over her own body and her reproductive health. Thus, any analysis of these relations should not only look at a woman's (or man's) decision but also the role of poverty, racial discrimination, gender violence, abuse of technology, pharmaceutical and/or medical coercion, and family planning programs. For example, the United States has a history of coerced sterilization particularly of women of color, and several states in the early 1990s considered mandating the use of Norplant or Depo Provera (a type of long-acting contraceptive implant) to control younger, inner-city women on welfare and poorer women of color. "The consequences of this extends beyond the biological question of 'Who procreates?' It speaks to the question of 'Who matters?'" (Flavin 2009).

In the years leading up to the *Roe v. Wade* Supreme Court decision legalizing abortion, most white, middle-class feminists advocated for abortion and birth control. The radical feminists focused on the pursuit of sexual pleasure without fear of being forced into a marriage or getting pregnant; they fought for sexual liberation and voluntary motherhood. But then, as now, voluntary fertility control was never the driving force behind African American and Puerto Rican women's quest for reproductive rights. While they shared white women's desire to limit their own fertility on their own terms, their experiences and political agenda were quite different because they already suffered under persistent stereotypes that they were not just sexually liberated, but oversexed. Also, because of the legacy of widespread sterilization abuse, many minority women associated abortion rights with population control, racial genocide, and state coercion. Black and Puerto Rican women activists supported safe and legal abortion, but they, more than white women activists of the time, recognized the reproductive rights issues inherent in the need for state-supported child care services, decent wages and benefits, safe and affordable housing, and good medical care that would permit them to raise healthy children (Flavin 2009).

Sexuality may be thought of as combining elements of sex and gender as well as a person's subjective sense of himself or herself, or what is usually referred to as gender identification. Sexuality is an important site for patriarchal control as it has often been tied to men's control over female reproduction and reproductive rights, standards of beauty and body objectification, and attempts to ensure sexual access or availability. Part of the gender role for both men and women assumes heterosexuality, with modest allowances for female same-sex activity when done for the enjoyment of men. *Homosexuality*, male or female, refers to the sexuality of people who are characterized by a sexual interest in persons of the same sex. Gays and lesbians are frequently seen as "unnatural" because their sexual desire and gender orientation call into question aspects of masculinity, femininity, and gender roles that people would like to see as innate ("natural") but that are really socially constructed. Lesbians are frequently depicted in mass media as killers because the "unnaturalness" of their sexuality is seen as explaining the "unnaturalness" of the weaker and gentler sex committing violent crime. (In reality, most women who kill direct their violence against a chronic male abuser.)

In patriarchal societies, homosexuals are often represented or viewed as a threat to heterosexuals, especially by those who are "homophobic." The general prejudice against being gay is so strong that it affects many social interactions among men. Guys who have a deep friendship and intimate connection run the risk of being seen as gay, creating a problem for male bonding and *homosociality* (friendship with the same sex). Members of fraternities, sports teams, and sometimes those in the military have significant bonds with other men and thus pursue excessive heterosexual conquests to disavow the label of gay. A focus on scoring, using women, and being a player keeps the masculine heterosexual identity intact while allowing for close male friendships. Gang rapes can be a more extreme version of this phenomenon, where groups of men bond by using a woman (or series of women) and still maintain the masculine heterosexual identity (Miller 2008).

Feminism comprises both a basic doctrine of equal rights for women and an ideology for women's liberation from patriarchy. Feminism's basic task is consciousness raising about oppression and encouraging actions that undo the exclusions of women's opinions, experiences, and accomplishments. As discussed and elaborated upon in chapter 1, a wide diversity of perspectives are contained under this umbrella term, indicating that *feminisms* is more appropriate by not suggesting a singular woman's point of view. For example, women of color do not always have the same concerns and perspectives as white feminists, while "women of color" is a very diverse category itself because it includes women from different races (see the previous chapter on race). In addition, liberal feminism tends to seek equality for women within much of the existing political and economic system. In contrast, socialist and more radical feminisms tend to seek equality for men and women but under a different system, usually one that is less hierarchical and stratified than currently exists. (Third World feminism adds another layer of diverse women's viewpoints from developing countries, although that goes beyond the scope of this book.)

Chapter 4's discussion of race noted that people of all races could be prejudiced and have stereotypes, but discrimination implied a position of power to act on those prejudices, so the chapter emphasized discrimination against minorities by the white majority. Similarly, while men and women can both buy into stereotypes and harmful gender role expectations, men will be the primary initiators of sex discrimination because they tend to have the positions of power and decision-making ability. Further, while both men and women can engage in sexual harassment, male perpetrators are more of a problem because of the greater economic power of men combined with the prevalence of violence against women.

MALE PRIVILEGE

The chapter on race quoted Dyer about how whites had power because they could claim to speak for all people while people of color were normally considered to speak for their race. The same concept applies to gender, with men being seen as having no gender—and thus speaking for all ("mankind")—while women are seen as only speaking for women, a "special interest group." To further illustrate this point, substitute "men" for "whites" in Dyer's quote: "men have power and believe that they think, feel and act like and for all people; men, unable to see their particularity, cannot take account of other people's; men create the dominant images of the world and don't quite see that they construct it in their own image; men set standards of humanity by which they are bound to succeed and others bound to fail" (based on Dyer 2005, 12).

Men do not usually see this privilege (see box 5.1) because it is the purpose of gender roles and stereotypes to rationalize the inequality so that the status quo appears natural, inevitable, and just. But

> men's physiology defines most sports, their needs define auto and health insurance coverage, their socially designated biographies define workplace

expectations and successful career patterns, their perspectives and concerns define quality in scholarship, their experiences and obsessions define merit, their objectification of life defines art, their military service defines citizenship, their presence defines family, their inability to get along with each other—their wars and rulerships—defines history, their image defines god, and their genitals define sex (MacKinnon in Forell and Matthews 2000, 5).

And, law tends to see women as men see them because most laws are written, enforced, and judged by men.

Critiques of the "reasonable man" stand in law are a good illustration of male privilege. The standard arose initially because women were not allowed to sue in court or sign contracts, so questions about negligence or duties of care were based on a "reasonable man." But the standard remained even after women achieved more civil rights and were better integrated into the workforce, where the development of sexual harassment law exposed the problem of applying the reactions of a "reasonable man" to behavior that victimizes a woman. For example, one of the early cases involving a hostile work environment involved a female manager in an office with widespread pornographic pictures and a coworker the court majority described as "extremely vulgar and crude" who "customarily made obscene comments about women" (Forell and Matthews 2000, 37).

The majority, applying a "reasonable person" standard, found the environment to be "annoying" but not hostile in a way that raised sex discrimination issues. In the court's view, the pornographic posters had minimal effect "when considered in the context of a society that condones and publicly features and commercially exploits open displays of written and pictorial erotica at the newsstands, on prime-time television, at the cinema, and in other public places" (Forell and Matthews 2000, 37). For the majority, that such environments existed was a given, and the woman had "voluntarily entered" it; by showing intolerance of such conditions, the court implied that the woman was being hostile—not the environment. Besides, the law was "not meant to—or can—change" such workplaces, nor did the majority think it was "designed to bring about the magical transformation in the social mores of American workers" (37). Critics of the decision point out that the neutral-sounding "American worker" is "men who hold values allowing them to talk crudely about women and look at degrading pornography whenever they want to, including at work" (38).

The dissenting judge was one of the first to recognize that the appropriate standard was the reaction of a "reasonable woman." In addition to widespread pornographic posters, he noted that women in this office were "routinely" called "whores" and "cunts" (Forell and Matthews 2000, 40). The issue was not the personality of the woman bringing the suit, but the behavior of men in the office: "No woman should be subjected to an environment where her sexual dignity and reasonable sensibilities are visually, verbally or physically assaulted as a matter of prevailing male prerogative" (42). For this judge, the male perspective was disguised as "reasonable person." He suggested that "unless the outlook of the reasonable woman is adopted, the defendants as well as the courts are permitted to sustain ingrained notions of reasonable behavior fashioned by the offenders" (42).

One commentary on this case noted that the dissenting judge is an African American, "and his experiences as a black man may have made it easier for him to recognize discrimination—and that in certain situations the law needs to empathize with those who are viewed as the outsiders" (Forell and Matthews 2000, 42). While this example does help illustrate how men can be feminists and develop feminist sensibilities, it is also unfortunately the case that many men with the same experience as the judge focus on race and marginalize concerns about gender (sometimes arguing that they detract from the importance of race). Further, Dyer's quote about white privilege applies to feminism in that white women experience white privilege, even as they are discriminated against as women. Thus, there has been a tendency to write about white women's experience as "women's experience," while women of color speak for their race. Nonwhite feminists critiqued the feminist movement, especially its earlier phases, as being about the issues of middle-class white women. White feminists need to struggle with how they create white images and standards of humanity, even as they urge men to examine male privilege.

ECONOMIC SPHERE

Women make up slightly more than half of the total U.S. resident population and are thus a numeric majority in this country. However, because of their unequal position in the economic, political, and social spheres of American life, women are still considered a "minority group" on par with minority racial and ethnic groups. Women who worked full-time, all year in 2007, earned seventy-seven cents for every dollar that men earned for their full-time, year-round work (Census Bureau 2009, 5). The median earnings of full-time, year-round men were $46,367, compared to $35,745 for women (Census Bureau 2009). In explaining this discrepancy, the authors of the thoroughly researched book, *The Cost of Being Female*, noted that women

> are excluded from many good jobs. We are discriminated against in pay. More and more of us are supporting ourselves and our children with or without a husband's help. If we try to climb the corporate ladder, we bump our heads on a "glass ceiling," beyond which we cannot climb (Headlee and Elfin 1996, xiv).

Because of discrimination, child care and deadbeat dads, many women are unable to work full-time and year-round, so other economic comparisons show women to be more economically disadvantaged than the comparisons above. For example, in 2008, the median earnings of a female householder with no husband present were $33,073, compared to a male householder with no wife present whose income was $49,186 (Census Bureau 2009, table 1). Such disparities in wages mean that women are disproportionately in poverty: 13.8 percent of household with a male head and no wife present are in poverty, but 28.7 percent of female-headed households with no male were in poverty (table 4). The economic situation of single, female-headed families with children under age eighteen is particularly grim. Overall, nearly half of all such households live below the poverty line, compared to less than one-quarter of single male-headed households. One in three single, female-headed families owns a home, compared to more than half of single, male-headed families. These findings hold for white, black, or Hispanic families, although white families generally are better situated than black or Hispanic families. For example, around 39.7 percent of all black, single, female-headed households live in poverty and 39.6 percent of all Hispanic single, female-headed households, compared to 26.5 percent of comparable white families (Census Bureau 2008, table B-1). The situation of older, retired women tends to be worse than their male counterparts because lower earnings over a woman's lifetime means less money for retirement, along with fewer assets.

In addition to glass ceilings that prevent the advancement of women, a large amount of occupational segregation with "sticky floors" keeps women in low-paying occupations like secretaries and typists—jobs that are seen as "women's work" and devalued accordingly. Even women in higher-level jobs and professions earn less than their male counterparts. A common explanation for this discrepancy is that women have less education and work experience than men. However, women "in their thirties actually have more education than men in that age group, and are still paid less" (Headlee and Elfin 1996, 7). Other studies show that additional years of experience do not have the same rate of salary return for women as they do for men.

Although women have certainly made gains over the past forty years or so, they remain severely overrepresented in clerical and service occupations, making up over 90 percent of those employed as registered nurses and licensed practical nurses, secretaries and receptionists, kindergarten teachers, and childcare workers. Meanwhile, men are disproportionately employed in craft and laborer jobs; around 90 percent of all mechanics, construction workers, metal workers, truck drivers, and other motor vehicle workers are men, as are 90 percent of all architects and engineers, clergy, airplane pilots, police officers, and firefighters. Women make up less than 8 percent of the highest-ranking corporate executives of Fortune 500 companies and hold only 13.6 percent of the board positions (Catalyst 2004). In 2005, there were seven women CEOs at Fortune 500 companies, but none of those companies were among the 100 largest.

Chapter 3 noted that determining social class for women can be difficult, especially where they are dependent on men for income while they disproportionately perform unpaid domestic labor such as raising children. The especially difficult aspect of figuring class is determining the separate wealth and assets of men and women, but estimates exist for households headed by women and men. Not surprisingly, the sex differences for accumulated wealth are larger than differences in income. In 2002, non-Hispanic men had mean wealth of $86,370 while women had $51,405—about 60 percent of men's wealth; for Hispanic men, wealth was $13,154 and about three times more than women's median wealth of $4,489 (Kochhar 2004, 26–27). These differences are important in terms of women's security and power. (Note that the category non-Hispanic includes both blacks and whites.)

POLITICAL SPHERE

Final ratification of the Nineteenth Amendment occurred in 1920 and finally gave women the right to vote, fifty years after the Fifteenth Amendment granted former (male) slaves the right to vote. African Americans used their political voice to pursue a federal antilynching law, while white women pursued issues related to child labor and laws about women's working conditions. Women were united in the goal of getting the right to vote, but once they had it, "the lines that divided women—class, race, age, ideology—became more significant" (DuBois and Dumenil 2005, 483). The National Women's Party introduced an Equal Rights Amendment in 1923, which immediately exposed different views of equality. At a time before minimum wage law and a mass of New Deal legislation that many now take for granted, women had worked to pass laws that protected them from exploitation that existed in the workplace before unions, collective bargaining, and occupational health and safety laws. They feared equality would mean that hard-won protections would be repealed, while others "countered that such legislation treated women as invalids and could limit their economic opportunity" (483).

In 1986 the historical pattern of higher voter turnout rates for men than for women was reversed. Ever since then, the proportion of eligible female adults who voted has exceeded the proportion of eligible male adults who voted. But increased participation in voting has not lead to proportionate representation, especially at the national level. When the 111th Congress convened in January 2009, women held 17 of 100 Senate seats and 74

of 435 seats in the House of Representatives (plus three nonvoting positions representing Washington, D.C., Guam, and the Virgin Islands). On
the state level in 2005, women accounted for eight governors and fifteen
lieutenant governors; 23 percent of state legislators were women (Center
for the American Woman and Politics 2005). While women do not all see
issues the same way, the shortage of women's voices in national politics
hinders attempts to alter the status quo and effect lasting changes in social
and criminal justice legislation and policy.

SOCIAL SPHERE

Women have a life expectancy of seven to nine years longer than men, and
the gap is greater for blacks than for whites. Part of this difference can be explained by gender roles, which encourage men to be aggressive and to take
risks. Also, findings that men are more likely than women to die of stress-
related conditions such as heart attack and stroke suggest that the male role
model of being silent and not talking about feelings or seeking help may
mean men cope less well with stress than women do. Although women
have longer life expectancies, a study by the Society for the Advancement of
Women's Health Research showed that women fare worse than men when
it comes to several leading ailments. For example, three out of four victims
of autoimmune diseases (e.g., multiple sclerosis, rheumatoid arthritis, dia-
betes, and lupus) are women. Women are twice as likely as men to contract
a sexually transmitted disease and are ten times as likely to become infected
with HIV during unprotected sex with an infected partner. Women smokers
are at a greater risk of developing lung cancer than men smokers. Cardiovas-
cular disease actually kills 43,000 more women than men each year, yet virtually all randomized controlled trials on risk and treatment have focused
on men. Heart disease in women often goes undetected and untreated until
the disease has become severe. Consequently, 44 percent of women who
have heart attacks die within one year, compared to 27 percent of men. In
sum, gaps in our understanding of women's health exist and may impede
efforts to identify effective preventive methods, treatments, and cures.

Two major reasons for this gap in our understanding of women's health
are male privilege in the construction of medical knowledge and biological essentialism. Historically in the United States, "outside the specialized
realm of [women's] reproduction, all other health research concerned
men's bodies and men's diseases. Reproduction was so central to women's
biological existence that women's nonreproductive health was rendered
virtually invisible" (Kreiger and Fee 1994, 16). Some argue that "the lack of
[medical] research on white women and on men and women in nonwhite
racial/ethnic groups resulted from a perception of white men as the norm"

(16), while others argue that "for the most part, the health of women and men of color and the nonreproductive health of white women were simply ignored" (16).

In challenging this bias, whether it is based on false universalism or male-centered practice of medical science, the women's health movement since the 1960s has demanded that the medical community pay more attention to biology and illnesses specific to women and to conduct more research using women as subjects. It has also promoted women's empowerment through self-education and has lobbied for governmental changes on the local and national levels (e.g., establishment of governmental women's health organizations such as Office on Women's Health under the U.S. Department of Health and Human Services). While these efforts have led to some social change, the gap in the knowledge about women's health remains.

While the female gender role is increasingly accepting of female athletics, the cultural notion of ideal feminine beauty still emphasizes being thin, young, quiet, and pleasing—an image from mainstream mass media that causes a much higher rate of eating disorders linked to poor body image and low self-esteem among women than men. Indeed, Jean Kilbourne (known for her videos like *Still Killing Us Softly*) notes that women's magazines are "an invitation to pathology":

> A typical woman's magazine has a photo of some rich food on the front cover, a cheesecake covered with luscious cherries or a huge slice of apple pie with ice cream melting on top. On the back cover, there is usually a cigarette ad, often one implying that smoking will keep women thin. Inside the magazine are recipes, more photos of fattening foods, articles about dieting—and lots of advertising featuring very thin models. There usually also is at least one article about an uncommon disease or trivial health hazard, which can seem very ironic in light of the truly dangerous product being glamorized on the back cover (2000).

The impact of these messages is different across race, and the culture of thinness falsely universalizes the eating disorder experience of women of color. For example, one recent study found that "no Black women were found to have had anorexia nervosa, and the odds of detecting bulimia nervosa in White women were six times that of Black women" (U.S. Department of Health and Human Services 2004).

Beyond eating disorders, the media messages and low esteem lead to very different rates of cosmetic surgery for men and women. Body image is a much more salient aspect of the female gender role than the male, so women are encouraged to take physical beauty and weight much more seriously. Thus, according to the American Society for Aesthetic Plastic Surgery (2004), 90 percent of the cosmetic procedures and surgery in 2004 were performed on women. The top surgical procedures were liposuction and breast enlargement. While cosmetic procedures are also increasing for men, the overall level is still quite low because the male gender role emphasizes achievement, especially in the areas of wealth and power.

IMPLICATIONS

Studying gender, or how men and women accomplish masculinity and femininity, entails a consideration of how social structures constrain and channel behavior, which, in turn, may influence a person's criminal or law-abiding behavior or his or her actions in the workplace (Martin and Jurik 1996; Messerschmidt 1997; West and Zimmerman 1987). While great strides have been made in the last forty years toward achieving gender equality and justice, there is much ground yet to be covered. After reviewing the economic, political, and social evidence, it is apparent that most power is concentrated in the hands of men; the United States is still a male-dominated society. Men (particularly white) control key institutions such as the "military, industry, technology, universities, science, political office, and finance—in short, every avenue of power within the society" (Millett 1970, 5).

Increasingly, scholars are challenging the treatment of gender in existing theory and research, moving away from treating women as anomalies toward locating women at the center of research. This research also increasingly wrestles with the exploration of how race/ethnicity, class, and other social characteristics such as age intersect with gender to shape one's experience, as will be explored in the next chapter. But, as long as victims from either gender are stigmatized, blamed, or ridiculed for their situations; as long as women and men are harmed by purportedly "gender neutral" policies; as long as workers are sexually harassed in the workplace; as long as women and minority men are treated as "problems" or "anomalies"; as long as the institutions governing the treatment of men and women in the legislature, law enforcement, adjudication, or incarceration continue to be dominated by one sex, the fields of crime and justice have their work cut out for them.

REVIEW AND DISCUSSION QUESTIONS

1. What helps to explain why male students have only committed the "rampage school shootings," and what helps to explain why these killings have only occurred at rural and suburban, not urban, high schools?

Chapter 5

2. Distinguish between the following terms: sex and gender.
3. What is essentialism? What are the other terms that you thought most important for understanding gender?
4. What is male privilege? What are some examples, from the chapter and your experiences? How does privilege relate to feminism?
5. In the context of economic, political, and social spheres, how are men still privileged in relation to women in American society?

6

Understanding Privilege and the Intersections of Class, Race, and Gender

Rosa Lopez is a Salvadoran woman with a fourth-grade education who came to the United States more than thirty years ago. She became involved with the O. J. Simpson murder trial while working as a housekeeper for one of Simpson's neighbors. Rosa Lopez's testimony (which provided an alibi for Simpson) was given with the aid of an interpreter, and the attorney's questions to her were translated from English to Spanish. In her essay, "Rosa Lopez, Christopher Darden, and Me: Issues of Gender, Ethnicity, and Class in Evaluating Witness Credibility," associate professor of Law, Maria L. Ontiveros (1997 [1995]), counters the prevalent view that Lopez was a liar. She suggests that when one considers issues of culture, class, and gender, alternative views are possible.

During direct examination, Rosa Lopez established that O. J. Simpson's Ford Bronco was parked in front of his house after the alleged time of the murder. She also testified that she planned to leave the United States and not return. Among the reasons she cited for leaving was her fear that she would be physically harmed if she stayed in the United States. On cross-examination, prosecutor Christopher Darden attacked her credibility on several fronts. For example, he showed how Lopez had provided conflicting names, birth dates, and addresses on official documents that had been completed under the penalty of perjury. He argued that Lopez either manufactured the Bronco sighting or changed the time of the sighting at the suggestion of the defense. He argued that she had no reasonable fear for her physical safety.

Her demeanor and her answers further undermined Rosa Lopez's credibility during cross-examination. On dozens of occasions she responded to questions by saying "no me recuerdo" ("I don't remember"). Other times, she responded to Darden's questions by answering "if you say so, sir." Ontiveros notes that at times Lopez "appeared to concede or change her answers. She appeared hesitant and unsure. Sometimes her answers were non-responsive or did not seem to make sense" (Ontiveros 1997 [1995], 270).

A linguist sent a letter to the court pointing out that Rosa Lopez's tendency to answer people in authority by saying "if you say so, sir," is not altogether surprising given her humble background and gender expectations. Moreover, she is from a Spanish-speaking culture that is more subtle, more indirect, and less confrontational than that found in the United States. For example, while interpreters and court watchers alike agree that "no me recuerdo" translates to "I don't remember," the message Lopez sought to convey is less clear. Upon redirect examination, she confirmed that "no me recuerdo" meant "No," not "Positive yes," and that her usage of the phrase was common in El Salvador.

Darden also implied that Lopez must not have seen anything, because if she had, surely she would have mentioned it to her employers, whom she saw everyday. But even Court TV commentators recognized that this reasoning ignores the class differences between Lopez and her employers, which discourage intimate or even collegial conversations. Darden cast doubt on whether Lopez feared for her personal safety if she stayed in the United States, pointing out that no one had threatened her with physical harm. But Ontiveros raises a number of realities that Darden ignored. First, thousands of people "disappeared" during the war in El Salvador, including Lopez's own fifteen-year-old daughter. Further, Rosa Lopez had heard of the arrest of another defense witness for forgery charges. The prosecution justified Lopez's fears of arrest when they considered prosecuting her for the discrepancies on official forms. Given that being "arrested" could be life threatening in El Salvador, Rosa Lopez's fears become more understandable, even believable.

Rosa Lopez's credibility also appeared damaged because she used several different addresses. Yet among low-income people without a permanent address, it is not uncommon to give one relative's address as residence for mail even while living with another relative. Prosecutor Darden suggested Lopez was dishonest because she had used several last names, including Lopez, Reyes, and Martinez. Darden was ignorant of Latino naming conventions whereby people use the last names of both their parents, with the father's name appearing first. Moreover, "Reyes" could easily be a religious name given because Rosa Lopez was born on the Feast of the Three Kings.

Ontiveros concludes that she did not find Rosa Lopez to be totally believable, but neither did she find her to be the clear-cut liar depicted by the prosecution. The ordeal of Rosa Lopez, serves, nonetheless, to underscore the importance of "viewing all witness credibility through the lens of culture, class, and gender" (269). The case of witness Lopez also underscores the overlapping or intersecting spheres of class, race/ethnicity, and gender.

Imagine standing in the middle of an intersection with a view down several streets that run in different directions. If a friend stands at the end of one of those streets, she can share some of the same view, but her perspective will also be different: the features that are closest will be different and she will have a view down different side streets. Now, think of those streets as being social dimensions such as class, race, ethnicity, gender, age, and sexual orientation. To add to the analogy, imagine class as being represented by the height of the buildings and the floor one is on (including, perhaps, being in a basement). The view of those streets represents a person's life experiences, worldview, and "social location." Describing a person's social location based solely on race, for example, would be incomplete and possibly confusing; it would be like saying "main street" or "third street" in a large, diverse city without specifying a cross (intersecting) street. An indication of whether the location was in a penthouse or lower floor would also have value in describing both the location and the view. Thus, an accurate description requires other markers, such as gender and class, to get a "fix" on the location.

This chapter is about recognizing that all people are at the center of multiple intersections of power, inequality, and privilege as shaped by their class, race/ethnicity, and gender. Nobody fits into any one category alone; instead, everyone exists at the intersection of many categories that shape not only their view of the world and the actions they take but also other people's view of them (Wildman (1997 [1996]). To many people, this statement seems rather obvious. Their experiences of the world and actions within it are not divided up into categories (or chapters) that represent class, race, or gender. Even for those others who may not have an intuitive sense about the correctness of understanding intersections and privilege, it is still an important way to get beyond the frustrating generalizations about how men are different from women or the sweeping statements about the differences between whites and minorities. Further, as box 6.1 demonstrates, many simple questions—both about society and criminology—require an understanding of how class, race, and gender fit interdependently together.

As straightforward as this perspective seems, scholars of crime and justice have been slow to embrace the idea of "intersectionalities" applying to all groups of people. Research tends to focus on one social dimension at a time, independent of others. Even the widely used phrase "women and minorities" does not take into account that approximately 15 percent of the population is *both* women *and* racial or ethnic minorities. Women of color cannot choose to be treated as a member of the oppressed sex one day and a member of the oppressed racial group the next. They are—and will always be—both, although race may be more important in some situations and gender in others. Being both, however, frequently leads to invisibility, which came up during the 2004 vice-presidential debates. Moderator Gwen Ifill asked both candidates about AIDS: "and not about AIDS in China or Africa. But AIDS right here in this country, where black women between the

Box 6. 1.   Ask a Simple Question . . .

Fact: Men are more likely than women to be murdered in their lifetime. Blacks are more likely than whites to be murdered in their lifetime.

Question: Who is more likely to be murdered, a white man or a black woman?

Fact: Blacks constitute about 12 percent of the U.S. population, and around half of those are incarcerated in state or federal prisons. Women make up over half of the U.S. population, and around 7 percent of those incarcerated are in state or federal prisons.

Question: Are black women overrepresented or underrepresented in correctional facilities?

Having trouble answering these questions?

Answers: To take the first example, logic probably made it relatively easy to figure out that black men face the highest likelihood of being murdered relative to black women and whites. The conclusion that white women face the lowest likelihood of being murdered relative to white men and blacks was probably also straightforward. But to answer the question posed with any degree of confidence requires more information on race and gender combined—e.g., for black women, white men, and so on. This information ultimately reveals that black women actually face a higher likelihood of being murdered than white men.

The second question is probably best answered "Both." Black women are both overrepresented (as blacks) and underrepresented (as women) in prisons. Of course, black women incarcerated in a state or federal prison have more at stake than simply a choice of words. While the disproportionate incarceration of blacks has received a great deal of attention, most of this attention has been focused on black men. Similarly, a typical discussion of "women's experiences" has all too often assumed that black women share the experiences and needs of white women. It was this situation that the editors of a classic text on black women were addressing when they named their book *All the Women Are White, All the Blacks Are Men, But Some of Us Are Brave* (Hull, Scott, and Smith 1982).

The issues raised by these two questions go beyond mere semantics and wordplay. This exercise speaks in a small way to the importance of considering characteristics such as race and gender not as separate constructs but as interlocking ones.

ages of 25 and 44 are 13 times more likely to die of the disease than their counterparts." Between Dick Cheney and John Edwards, the candidates talked about AIDS in Africa, health insurance and genocide in Sudan, but "nary a word about Ifill's original question. The ball dropped, and bounced, and rolled away as if it were invisible" (Talvi 2004).

Further, even when research does try to discuss more than one dimension, it still lacks an understanding of privilege. Many studies that look at race differences do not acknowledge white privilege and how that can shape patterns of behavior, research questions, methods, and conclusions. Likewise, many studies of gender differences do not acknowledge male privilege and how that can shape patterns of behavior, research questions, methods, and conclusions. Many criminologists, in other words, still assume that gender is relevant only when discussing women, race is relevant only when discussing blacks and other people of color, and class is relevant only when talking about the very rich or the very poor. Similarly, many people assume that sexual orientation is relevant only when applied to gays and lesbians. The point is, on the contrary, that everyone is a member of a social class, an ethnic/racial group, and everybody also brings their sexuality and gender construction to their presentation and reception of self in everyday reality.

The intersections of class, race, and gender describe a way of viewing social inequalities or privileges as interrelated and interacting. But understanding how this intersectionality manifests itself within the criminal justice system presents challenges, including basic problems that theorists are still only just starting to develop the vocabularies and conceptual frameworks for grasping the multiple meanings and implications of these crosscutting social relations (Daly 1995; Baca Zinn, Hondagneu-Sotelo, and Messner 2005). Given the complex nature of the field and the early stages of theorizing, this chapter in the third edition still does not present the crisp and definitive answers that many might desire. Instead, we again remind readers not to *essentialize* groups by assuming that all women or all blacks or all poor people are a certain way and that there is a great deal of diversity found within class, race, and gender groups. But in dealing with the complexity of differences, it is also a mistake to become so focused on differences that one misses the larger patterns of class, race, and gender privilege that are present in crime and social control.

Within feminism, for example, Donna Haraway wants to recognize diverse feminisms but not create a "self-induced multiple personality disorder" (1991, 3) that would undermine a basis for sustaining theoretical coherence and effective coalition building for feminist politics. While each person's experience is unique, there are still structured patterns even after taking into account the diversity within a category like women. Baca Zinn and her colleagues use the analogy of a prism to capture this idea: light is made up of many colors that appear to be the same, but it "is not an infinite, disorganized scatter of colors. Rather refracted light displays an order, a structure of relationships among the different colors—a rainbow" (2005, 1). As we discuss more below, currently there are quite a few studies of individual groups, and the next major task is to build better understandings of the larger structure of relationships so that the "patchwork" of studies can be transformed into something even more understandable.

Thus, this chapter explores some of the challenges to understanding intersectionality, an awkward academic word used to capture the many dynamics involved in studying how the pieces of class, race, and gender "abrade, inflame, amplify, twist, negate, dampen and complicate each other" (in Baca Zinn et al. 2005, 7). Toward this end, the rest of the chapter is divided into three sections followed by a section on the implications. The upcoming section examines the question of whether one factor is more important than others, which would simplify the conceptual challenge if class or race or gender were always the most significant influence. The next section examines privilege, which may blind people to parts of their location and thus the dynamics involved in other situations. Finally, there is a section on the available data and techniques for modeling social phenomenon that present another challenge to the development of knowledge about intersectionality.

NO "MASTER STATUS"

Attempting to examine the interacting effects of class *and* race *and* gender is difficult, so a logical step to getting a handle on it is to ask which is the most important. If, for example, gender consistently had the most significant impact then it could be described as the *master status*. Unfortunately, though, neither class nor race nor gender is always the most important consideration. In some situations, one may be more important than the others in shaping the social reality of a situation, but existing theory is not sufficiently developed to predict what factor will be most important under what conditions. While this knowledge gap is frustrating, the less-than-perfect knowledge about how class, race, and gender interact does not undermine the advantages of trying to examine all of them rather than settling for a simpler but incomplete analysis.

Theorists who focus primarily on class or race or gender can make a strong claim about the importance of the attribute they study. Marxists, for example, point to class and argue that history is defined by the struggle between the rich and poor, the haves and have-nots. Law is a tool used by the rich, who make the law in this class warfare. Some feminists see "the battles of the sexes" as more fundamental and point to the failure of much traditional class analysis to examine women's unpaid household work and reproductive labor (which makes it difficult to place them in the class structure, as noted in chapter 5). Law tends to have a patriarchal bias because men tend to make the law and are the majority of judges. Others would argue that race is fundamental because it has been the basis of genocide (see chapter 7), slavery, and the Nazi Holocaust; chapter 4 noted that American history has included a succession of exploited minorities—blacks, Asians, Native Americans, etc. Laws made by the white majority defined the slave owner's property rights, reaffirmed segregation, and established the basis for the criminal justice system to police minorities—especially to maintain social control over excess labor. All three positions make important and strong claims, which is why this book highlights class, race, and gender. Yet, when combined the arguments do not support a claim that one factor is *always* the most important, so the emphasis must be on understanding how they work together.

To take a concrete example, consider the case of a minority congressman, Representative Harold E. Ford from Tennessee. Under many circumstances, being a member of Congress is the most important aspect of his interactions, so class would be the primary status (remember that class includes status as well as actual salary). But when he was stopped by a police officer at the airport in Washington, D.C., race was the important factor as even the congressman was affected by a version of Driving While Black. Ford said the officer "demanded to see identification, and when I showed it to him, he couldn't believe it was my car and that I was a member of Congress. . . . Finally, he let me go. No apology or nothing. It really hurt me. If I'm treated like this, I can imagine how folks who don't have access to the things I do as a member of Congress are treated" (Samborn 1999). In this situation, race was the reason for the stop and was so significant that the officer did not feel an apology was necessary even after discovering he had stopped a member of Congress. To his credit, though, Ford is aware that intersections are important and that in other situations being a member of Congress provides a privilege and access to power that other minorities do not have.

PRIVILEGE

As pointed out in each of the chapters on class, race, and gender, privilege makes inequalities seem "natural" and blinds people to many social dynamics. The rich are less likely to appreciate structural barriers to class mobility; male privilege will affect how men view gender equality; and white privilege will affect how whites view and understand racial issues. (Other races can also have privilege because there is a hierarchy of racial groups—consider people from Japan or India compared to those from African or poorer South American countries.) As we noted in the previous chapter on gender, women can draw attention to male privilege, but white women need to be aware of white privilege. Thus, researchers argue that social relations are a complex matrix of domination and oppression with few "pure" victims and few "pure" oppressors as people may be more or less privileged in relation to their multiple identities (Hill Collins 1990, 2004).

Further, class, race, and gender are only the starting point for understanding privilege. For example, the Social Work Code of Ethics requires those engaged in the provision of services to understand their clients in ways that include but are not limited to "race, ethnicity, national origin, color, sex, sexual orientation, age, marital status, political belief, religion, and mental or physical disability" (in Leighton and Killingbeck 2001). This statement is part of a larger requirement to understand diversity and oppression, so the National Association of Social Workers recognizes that privilege can potentially exist in all those areas. Finally, even those who are oppressed in multiple ways in the United States can still be privileged by living in the First World as a member of a superpower that uses its economic and military strength to maintain its "top dog" status.

Box 6.2 elaborates on the notion of privilege by examining some of the overlapping class, race, and gender privileges for a middle-class white male. Readers who do not fall in this category can still identify aspects of privilege they may share. The focus of attention should be on the idea of *privilege* rather than classism, racism, and sexism (Krisberg 1975; McIntosh 1997 [1988]; Wildman and Davis 1997). These "isms" and other forms of systematic discrimination would not exist if some people in the social order and hierarchy did not benefit from them. Also, discussions of the "isms" are much more common than candid discussions of privilege, but they may contribute to the very problems they identify by individualizing what is a systemic problem of power and inequality. For example, calling someone a racist or a sexist lays the blame on the individual rather than the cultural, social, and legal mechanisms that support and reinforce these expressions of racism and sexism. As a consequence, instead of being concerned about institutionalized racism and sexism, whites and men tend to focus on how to avoid the respective labels of racist and sexist while simultaneously benefiting from their privileged position in relation to these "isms" the labels refer to.

To the extent the "isms" discourse remains necessary, people should realize that patterns of domination and subordination are not interchangeable. In other words, someone subordinated under one form of discrimination or oppression is not similarly situated to someone under another form. This would mean, for example, there is a difference between a black or brown male subject to racial prejudice and a white, a black, and a brown female subject to sexual stereotypes; white women who view themselves as oppressed under sexism are in a privileged position based on heterosexism and racism. Drawing attention to a matrix of privilege and oppression is more complex but also more potentially productive because it highlights

Box 6.2.   You Know You're Privileged When . . . (Part 3)

In keeping with this section's focus on intersectionality, we have expanded on the forms of white privilege discussed in chapter 2 and male privilege discussed in chapter 3. This list attempts to identify some of the specific characteristics of middle-class, white male privilege:

- People who meet me for the first time will assume that I have a regular job and no criminal record.
- I get praise from women friends and colleagues when I demonstrate that I can cook, clean, or care for small children.
- If someone needs help with a technical activity such as setting up a new computer with necessary hardware or software, they assume I have the expertise and can be trusted with the responsibility.
- When making a major purchase, such as a car or a home, it will be assumed that I not only have the means to make such a purchase but also that I understand the business aspects of it, such as mortgage point and amortization.
- When I wear expensive clothing or jewelry or drive an expensive car, I will be treated as though I obtained these goods through the fruits of my own legitimate labor rather than through illegal activity or my association with a sexual intimate.
- If I am a parent of small children who works long hours outside the home, people will perceive me as a good provider who only wants the best for my family, rather than as someone who puts career above family or is otherwise a faulty, absentee parent.
- In the event I am assaulted while walking home at two in the morning, no one will assume I was involved in an illicit business transaction that went bad or blame me for being out late at night.
- If I am an attorney scheduled to appear in court, I can be reasonably confident as I enter the courthouse that I will not be mistaken for a secretary, court reporter, or defendant.
- At work, no one will imply that I got my job based on my race or sex.

the benefits of the current system for different groups as well as the ideological blinders that may prevent individuals from seeing those benefits.

As one of many examples, while there is still some public debate on "affirmative action" and admission to colleges and universities, there is relatively no mention of "legacy admissions." A study of all law school admissions found that twice the number of whites as blacks got into law schools on the basis of alumni preference, an elegant essay, or recommendations from powerful people (Wightman 1997). These students—largely white and of higher class—would not have been admitted on grades and test scores alone. These legacy admissions favor children of influential alumni or donors over other applicants—sometimes twice as many students were admitted through legacy admissions than through affirmative action (Padilla 1997, 2). Significantly, legacy students are perceived as deserving rather than unfairly privileged. However, many view students admitted under affirmative action as having received an undeserved advantage. In the case of legacies, nobody shouts "continued discrimination"; in the case of affirmative action, many shout "reverse discrimination."

Being aware of privilege is an important first step. Going further requires reading and seeking out knowledge "from the margins"; that is, created by the marginalized groups. This material relates experiences that more privileged groups do not have and may include theorizing about those experiences that are not recognized as valid "knowledge" or "truth." As Dorothy Smith discusses in her chapter "Women's Experience as a Radical Critique of Sociology" (1990), the insider's experience—"an experience distinctively of women, though by no means the experience of all women"—furnishes the basis for a critical standpoint. It can expose privilege in the existing bodies of knowledge, the creation of new languages, and in the methods, practices of knowing, and political strategies. Ideally, this knowledge should not be collected into a sociology of women but should "bring us to ask how a sociology might look if it began from a woman's standpoint and what might happen to a sociology that attempts to deal seriously with that standpoint" (1990, 12).

Reading and listening to voices "from the margins" does not require an uncritical acceptance as truth of whatever oppressed people write, but readers should approach marginalized knowledge with an awareness that privilege will color their willingness to see other truths—especially when it critiques their privilege, which people prefer to see as "natural" and just. The point of such discussions and writing should not be to make people feel guilt over privilege, because that is rarely the basis for a productive reaction and sustainable change. Rather, the point should be to raise awareness about privilege so that the person is in a better position to participate in the creation of a more equal and inclusive society through individual or collective actions.

DATA AND MODELING

A final challenge to studying intersections relates to the lack of complete data for systematic comparisons and the limitations of many models used to study social dynamics. It is simply not possible to discuss every permutation of class, race, and gender: simply examining "only" the upper, middle, and lower classes, two genders, and white and nonwhites would result in some thirty-six possible class, race, and gender offender-victim combinations (Lynch 1996). Describing these soon becomes too complex a process to be practical or meaningful, and many reports cannot include tables covering all these variations.

More fundamentally, though, important aspects of the data most needed to make many basic comparisons are lacking. Consider the table from chapter 4 on unemployment and race: unemployment data for Native Americans came from a separate source, and unemployment rates by race and gender were not reported. Further, common reference publications like the Census Bureau's annual *Statistical Abstract of the United States* contain no data on class. While such a publication cannot include all statistics about the United States, it does report that the per capita consumption of asparagus has risen from 0.3 pounds in 1980 to 1.1 pounds in 2006—but the percent of wealth owned by the top 1 percent of the country is not reported (2009, table 210). In studying crime, the FBI's *Uniform Crime Reports* contain no arrest or other information broken down by Hispanic ethnicity.

Even when race data are fully collected, some of the five categories are relatively small, so they get collapsed into "other" or omitted totally. Various chapters have already noted how internally heterogeneous racial categories can be, and adding together Native Americans, Pacific Islanders, and nonwhite Latinos creates a category so diverse it defies interpretation. Reports from governmental agencies typically use panethnic/racial categories such as black, Hispanic, and white (occasionally Asian and Native American) that mask great variations along generation, class, language, gender, and ethnicity lines within each of these groups. Also, government agencies tend to treat race and gender as separate variables rather than as overlapping social locations. Even reports published by the Bureau of the Census, the Department of Labor, and the Department of Justice seldom present breakdowns by race and gender simultaneously that would permit readers to compare, for instance, the offenses committed by white men to those committed by white women.

Another barrier to understanding intersections in relation to crime and justice is that most academic and government sources on criminal justice information reduce the social relations of class, race, and gender to static, categorical variables. With the widespread availability of computers and statistical software, researchers increasingly attempt to isolate specific effects of class, race, and gender on, say, a person's likelihood of being arrested or incarcerated. These mostly quantitative attempts to disaggregate effects come at the expense of understanding how these structuring factors interact with one another to yield, for example, *gendered racism* in a myriad of forms and shapes. That is to say, gendered racism is not the effect of simply adding gender to racism, nor is *racialized sexism* the product of simply adding race to sexism. Rather, each of these variables has a separate effect and is dependent on context, so their multiple combinations are likely to occur in complex ways not captured in a model based on 1 + 1 = 2.

Furthermore, the emphasis on quantitative methods and statistical analyses has resulted in a tendency among academics to conduct research from the assumption that we can "hold all else constant." For example, "What is the likelihood that a woman will be sent to prison, and how does that compare with the likelihood of a man being sent to prison if we hold constant prior record and offense seriousness?" But while holding all else constant and controlling for legal and extralegal characteristics make sense in a regression equation, it bears little semblance to the lives of the people who are represented by the variables. Moreover, when it comes to these interacting variables, Currie (1985, 149) has observed, "where both historical and current forces have kept some minorities disproportionately trapped in the lowest reaches of the economy, the distinction between economic and racial inequality itself is in danger of being uselessly abstract." But even though it is common knowledge that racial discrimination means blacks have lower income, researchers "control" for income to estimate the amount of racial discrimination, and the results of this sophisticated statistical control end up minimizing the amount of discrimination under the assumption that race and class are not related.

Using interactive terms, additional variables, and the incorporation of nonlinear or reciprocal dynamics has assisted quantitative analyses, but the fundamental problem is conceptual, not statistical. The lack of a consistent master status means the importance of class, race, and gender are quite fluid in ways that theory cannot yet capture. Much of the scholarship that best helps us understand how intersections play out in the social world tends to be qualitative, descriptive, and narrative, emphasizing the contextual aspects of people's day-to-day existence. Hence, we believe that qualitative studies, in combination with quantitative data, are best suited for demonstrating the nuanced meanings of class, race, gender, and their intersections. Here, the task is to go beyond what Baca Zinn and colleagues (2005) call the "patchwork quilt" phase of study, in which difference is acknowledged as important but done by "collecting together a study here on African American women, a study there on gay men, a study on working-class Chicanas, and so on."

IMPLICATIONS

A challenge remains to sort out the complex ways in which class, race, and gender simultaneously structure people's actions and others' reactions to them and to understand the complex ways in which these hierarchies are used to either sustain or resist the prevailing systems of inequality and privilege. Baca Zinn and colleagues (2005, 6) give an example of how women benefit from "their race and class position and from their location in the global economy, while they are simultaneously restricted by gender":

> Such women are subordinated by patriarchy, yet their relatively privileged positions within hierarchies of race, class and global political economy intersect to create for them an expanded range of opportunities, choices and ways of living. They may even use their race and class advantage to minimize some of the consequences of patriarchy and/or to oppose other women.

Nevertheless, the theoretical frameworks and orientations are still works in development that make sense of these situations in general and in criminology (see the introductory chapter section on studying criminal justice as a system and an apparatus). These attempts are further impeded by the shortage of official information that describes the distribution of social benefits and harms along class, race, and gender combined, not separately. Even with the limited information available, though, indicators of political, economic, and physical well-being indicate that social goods are not evenly distributed but rather are concentrated among the upper-class white men while poor racial and ethnic minority women incur the greatest social costs.

Nonetheless, the intersections of class, race, and gender in relation to inequality, privilege, and wealth/poverty may be further complicated by additional variables such as sexuality and marital status, or household living arrangements including cohabitation, once married, and serial marriages. For example, a nationally representative panel survey from 1979 to 2004 and a life-course of different group experiences revealed that whites generally had the most accumulated household wealth and that Hispanics also had more wealth than blacks (consistent with the tables from chapters 3 and 4 as well as the figures from chapter 5). This study revealed that whites' unadjusted average net worth was considerably more than blacks or Hispanics regardless of whether the cohabitation history was one of "directly married" ($160,000), "spousal cohabitation" ($160,000), "one-time cohabitation" ($162,000), or "serial cohabitation" ($158,500). But Hispanics' net worth was a bit more than blacks with respect to both spousal cohabitation ($60,000 to $58,000) and serial cohabitation ($61,000 to $57,000), and significantly more when directly married, $100,000 to $57,500. Yet conversely, the net worth of one-time cohabiting blacks was $60,500 compared to $57,500 for Hispanics (Painter and Vespa 2008, 10). The authors conclude "that race and ethnicity are associated with qualitatively different cohabitation experiences due to marriage markets, attitude, and non-marital childbearing" (Painter and Vespa 2008, 2).

While criminology has had a long-standing interest in class, only in the past thirty to forty years has this interest in social difference and privilege been extended to include race and gender; some argue that now the previous interests in class have almost been forgotten. In any event, the attention to the intersections of these social dimensions is an even more recent development. Since the late eighties, an increasing number of scholars have recognized the problems inherent in assuming that all women or all members of a particular race or sex, for example, stand on a similar footing.

Among the most promising of developments has been a focus on the ways in which class, race, and gender are not only social constructs but also are processes involving creative human actors. Structured action theory in particular highlights the ways in which our dominant cultural conceptions of doing masculinity and femininity intersect with the physical body, racial category, and social class, and how these relations, in turn, shape crime and justice. Hence, whether addressing the needs of victims, offenders, or criminal justice workers, we must not assume that "same treatment" is "fair" treatment, because too often equal treatment is defined by a male norm or reflects white, middle-class biases and ignorance of the challenges faced by poor men and women of color.

In evaluating proposed policies and legislation, for example, we should take care to consider their impact on people occupying a range of social locations rather than, for instance, assuming all women face the same challenges in leaving an abusive partner. We should ask: What is this program, policy, or law supposed to accomplish? How will it actually be implemented? What are the ramifications for historically marginalized groups? Upon what assumptions is it based? Who is included, and who is left out? What can be done to improve on this effort (S. Miller 1998; Renzetti 1998)?

REVIEW AND DISCUSSION QUESTIONS

1. From reading the opening narrative, how did class, race, and gender play into her testimony and the "credibility" of her testimony?
2. Explain how the intersectionalities of class, race/ethnicity, and gender apply to everybody, including men and women, whites, people of color, straights, and gays.
3. What is meant by "master status"? Do you agree with the authors that there is no *consistent* master status? Why or why not?
4. How does privilege impact the study of intersections? Specifically, what privileges do you think are most important for you to understand in approaching the study of class, race, and gender? What other types of privilege discussed in the chapter may also be important? Why?
5. What concerns do the authors have about data to fully study intersections, and how do they critique quantitative models of intersections?

Part III

7

Victimology and Patterns of Victimization

Because the deprivations of some minorities have been so extensive, some argue that these conditions amount to genocide, a powerful word used to describe extreme cases of mass violence and victimization that blends the Greek genos *(race or tribe) with the Latin-derived -cide (kill). The underlying concept of genocide involves an attempt to exterminate a group that shares common characteristics. Hence, charging genocide is claiming great harm and victimization; it not only indicts the perpetrators but also bystanders for doing nothing in the face of mass violence and it confers a moral authority on the victims to be heard and to demand change.*

The study of genocide has been confounded by a long and pervasive history of denial (Chalk and Jonassohn 1990). For example, traditional criminology takes great interest in serial killers and mass murderers but typically ignores genocide and other violations of human rights; there's even little interest in understanding a political mass murderer like bin Laden. In the context of victimology and victimization, the denial is a good reason to review claims that the majority population of the United States has committed genocide involving both Native Americans and African Americans.

Many citizens of this nation consider charges of genocide by minority populations to be overstated at best. They tend to associate genocide with the Holocaust in Nazi Germany, which has created a distorted standard because it is an extreme case rather than a more typical one. The core concept, however, is "an attempt to exterminate a racial, ethnic, religious, cultural, or political group, either directly through murder or indirectly by creating conditions that lead to the group's destruction" (Staub 1989, 8). Such destruction encompasses "not only killing but creation of conditions that materially or psychologically destroy or diminish people's dignity, happiness, and capacity to fulfill basic material needs"(25).

Every year on Columbus Day signs protest "500 years of genocide." Like many claims of genocide, this one is met with much denial. Indeed, for the 500th anniversary of Columbus arriving in North America, the National Endowment for the Humanities refused to fund any film that proposed to use the word genocide. Rather than look at events from the Native's point of view, people refuse to discuss whether Columbus himself was an "agent of genocide" and whether the colonization he set in motion has resulted in genocidal processes. Whether genocide is a fair characterization of the next 500 years revolves around Staub's definition of genocide as involving indirect murder through the creation of conditions leading to a group's social destruction. Raphael Lemkin (1900–1959), the man who coined the term genocide, understood it to be the "destruction of the essential foundations of the life" of the group and undermining the integrity of the group's basic institutions, which produces the "destruction of the personal security, liberty, health, dignity, and even the lives of the individuals belonging to such groups" (in Kuper 1985, 9). Moreover, very few instances of mass murder that have been acknowledged to be genocide involve the actual elimination of a group. Thus, the state of Israel and the presence of Jews worldwide today do not undermine a claim that the Holocaust was genocide.

With Native Americans, the low point of the population was down 90 percent from the level before the time Columbus arrived. Some population fluctuation was inevitable, but the drastic decline here is related to a number of practices that involved direct murder as well as indirect attacks on the well-being and cultural integrity of Native Americans. Consider, for instance, the aggressive appropriation (theft) of land that included forced marches—such as the Trail of Tears—that had a high death toll because hunger, exhaustion, and exposure to inclement weather killed many women, children, and the elderly. The removal of Native Americans from land that was sacred and had cultural significance eroded their cultural integrity, and their placement on desolate land further undermined the essential foundations of life. This process of forced relocation recurred multiple times with increasing numbers of white settlers or the discovery of mineral wealth on what was thought to be wasteland given to Native Americans (Lazarus 1991; Weyler 1992). Today, many reservations are still located on inhospitable land, which can also be a site for toxic and radioactive materials (Eichstaedt 1994).

To control the Native American population in the 1800s, settlers intentionally gave them disease-infested blankets that would kill large numbers who did not have immunity to European diseases. In addition, children were taken—sometimes at gunpoint—and put into boarding and reform schools where they were deprived of access to their culture and native language. Indeed, children were punished for doing anything "Indian" and were taught to be ashamed of their heritage. Even today, many Native Americans in prison are denied access to culturally appropriate practices like the sweat lodge and are coerced into Christian-based programs such as Alcoholics Anonymous, which further erodes their cultural integrity (Little Rock 1989).

The U.S. government—the representative of the American people—has broken every treaty it has made with the Native Americans (Lazarus 1991). The government's refusal to honor treaties negotiated in good faith by the native peoples has denied them rights to land, resources, and sovereignty in many ways that have imposed, both historically and currently, hardship and have destroyed their personal security, liberty, health, and dignity. Although several cases involving broken treaties have resulted in symbolic reparations for Native Americans, the ongoing problems remain. Indeed, most tribes, even on reservations, have little in the way of sovereignty and are subject to state and federal control. The tribal decision-making bodies are not always the same as those tribal members officially recognized as the leaders by the federal government. In addition, the Bureau of Indian Affairs has come under scathing criticism for being corrupt and not having the best interest of Native Americans at heart in administering their affairs (Lazarus 1991; Weyler 1992). In the latter part of the twentieth century, activism on the part of Native Americans, such as the American Indian Movement (AIM), was met with illegal surveillance and at times violent repression by the FBI and other law enforcement agencies (Churchill and Vander Wall 1990a, 1990b).

Although most of the direct killing of Native Americans is part of the past, the place accorded them by the white majority is one that destroys the essential foundations of their life. While the ongoing effort to undermine the integrity of Native American's basic institutions has occasionally met with spirited and creative acts of resistance to domination and colonization, these demonstrations have failed because of the unaltered structural relations of inequality between the majority of whites and marginalized minorities. What the National Advisory Commission on Civil Disorder noted about inner-city ghettos applies equally well to reservations:

> What white Americans have never fully understood—but what the Negro can never forget—is that white society is deeply implicated in the ghetto. White institutions created it, white institutions maintain it, and white society condones it (quoted in Pinkney 1984, 78).

In each case, whatever the intentions or consciousness of white society, both the inner city and reservations are places of extreme social deprivation and violence. Indeed, as African American and Harvard sociologist Sidney Willhelm (1970, 334) noted, "the Black ghetto evolves into the equivalent of the Indian reservation." Obvious questions thus arise as to whether the history or current conditions of blacks can be described as genocide as well.

Charges related to genocide of blacks start with the institutions of slavery and the forced removal of Africans from Africa to work in involuntary servitude on southern plantations, a process that resulted in 50 to 100 million premature deaths (Anderson 1995; Gorman 1997; Oshinsky 1996; Tolnay and Beck 1995). In 1951, black scholar William Patterson wrote a 240-page indictment against the United States called "We Charge Genocide" that he deposited with the United

Nations (Patterson 1970, 1971). Interestingly, U.S. delegates argued that the treatment of blacks was an economic rather than a racial dynamic, and therefore, that the genocide convention did not apply. In other words, the delegates maintained that it was an issue of social class rather than race because what had been done to poor blacks happened because they were poor—which ignores the obvious fact that it did not happen to poor whites.

Although the class dynamic is in operation with blacks, it is also racism that keeps blacks disproportionately in poverty. Furthermore, class cannot explain the history of lynching or of segregation that consistently condemned blacks to inferior accommodations. Blacks have certainly made gains since the 1950s, in terms of civil rights, income, and political representation. Despite these gains, the "mountains" of data discussed in chapter 4 demonstrate pervasive social, economic, and political disadvantage. Blacks are still much more likely to live in poverty and in inner-city neighborhoods that are places of concentrated poverty (Mandle 1978, 1992; Massey and Denton 1993; Wilson 1987).

The concentrated poverty and social disorganization of inner-city black communities function to compromise many essential foundations of life and the integrity of local institutions. The consequences of this racial stratification can be seen in a study of life expectancy done by Johnson and Leighton (1999) that compares the observed number of deaths for a race with what would be expected if it had the death rate of the other race. If blacks had the same death rate as whites in 1991, the expected figure would be 78,951 fewer untimely deaths of blacks that year (45,693 men and 33,258 women). If whites had the death rate of blacks, the expected figure would be 647,575 more premature deaths each year (376,992 men and 270,583 women).

The relatively shortened black lives are not always the result of direct intervention by whites but also reflect black-on-black violence and self-destructive behavior. The debate about genocide does not deny the personal responsibility blacks have for their actions, although it does take note that such behavior reflects adaptations to a broader social context marked by a "socioeconomic predicament which is itself profoundly antisocial" (Rubenstein 1987, 206). This theme was first articulated in 1899 by W. E. B. Du Bois in his classic study, The Philadelphia Negro, where he argued that Negro crimes were adaptations to a "lack of harmony" with their surroundings. Almost a century later, Chancellor Williams linked Du Bois's lack of harmony (similar in kind with Durkheim's anomie) to both black-on-black crime and white genocide:

> They, the so-called criminals and their youthful followers, expect nothing beneficial from the white world, and they see no reason for hope in their own. Hence, like caged animals, they strike at what is nearest them—their own people. They are actually trying to kill a situation they hate, unaware that even in this, they are serving the white man well. For the whites need not go all out for "genocide" schemes, for which they are often charged, when blacks are killing themselves off daily on such a large scale (1987, 325, emphasis in the original).

In the case of both blacks and Native Americans, white society has created conditions that undermine the essential life foundations and integrity of the group. Genocide still entails a certain—and unspecified—level of destruction and white involvement in those destructive processes. These elements are very much a subject of contention and cannot be resolved in this chapter. The goal here has been to overview the claim of genocide and to indicate why it should not be dismissed as "mumbo jumbo" or paranoia of "wild-eyed conspiracy mongers" (Jack White 1990, 20). Beyond the specific debate about genocide, Hacker (1995, 54) raises questions and uses logic that deserves further consideration:

Can this nation have an unstated strategy for annihilation of [black] people? How else, you ask yourself, can one explain the incidence of death and debilitation from drugs and disease, the incarceration of a whole generation of [black] men, the consignment of millions of women and children to half lives of poverty and dependency? Each of these conditions has its causes. Yet the fact that they so centrally impinge on a single race makes one wonder why the larger society has allowed them to happen.

Finally, the issue of genocide should lead into asking about the future of marginal groups, especially as technological developments and global capitalization make them increasingly expendable and their labor of decreasing value (Aronowitz and DiFazio 1994; Rifkin 1995; Wilson, 1996). Sidney Willhelm first raised the question in his 1970 book, Who Needs the Negro?, *which argued that impersonal forces and processes such as automation make the unskilled, uneducated poor expendable. Thus, even those who do not believe genocide is currently happening might be able to see the vulnerability felt by blacks, especially when more young black males end up in prison than in college.*

⁌⁊

Victimology is the scientific study of victims and victimization. The field can be traced back to 1937 when Benjamin Mendolsohn began gathering information about victims for his law practice. He subsequently conducted research on victims, including a rape study in 1940. In addition to coining the term *victimology*, he also introduced other related concepts such as *victimity* to suggest the converse of criminality. Initially, Mendolsohn and others "formulated a broad-based victimology that considered not merely crime victims, but all victims, including those produced by politics, by technology, by accidents, as well as by crime" (Elias 1986, 18). In 1948, Hans von Hentig provided the first landmark victimological study, *The Criminal and His Victim*, followed in 1954 by Henri Ellenberger's "Psychological Relations between Criminals and Victims." The field, research, and applications of victimology have continued to develop, as evidenced by numerous victimization studies, typologies, many international conferences on victimology, the emergence of *Victimology: An International Journal* in 1976, the creation of the World Society of Victimology in 1979, and the establishment of victim compensation programs in the United States and most of the developed nations of the world. Still, the struggle to maintain the broader perspective (beyond formal crime victims) envisioned by Mendolsohn has been a difficult one. Indeed, victimology has tended to follow the leads of Hentig and Ellenberger, narrowly focusing on criminal victimization, victim-offender relationships, and victim precipitation (the contribution the victim makes to his/her victimization) without examining the larger social, cultural, political, and economic relations that establish power arrangements between "offenders" and "victims." Thus, much victimology is limited to victims based on existing criminal law and is focused on individual (micro)level analysis that excludes structural sources and context for better understanding victimization.

In his treatise, *The Politics of Victimization*, Robert Elias captures the dilemma in victimology caused by a limited reality of victimization:

> Americans are a frightened people. We anticipate victimization even more than we experience it, although much actual victimization does occur. We mostly fear being robbed, raped, or otherwise assaulted, or even killed. Yet, while these crimes have captured our imaginations, they comprise only part of the victimization we suffer. We face not only the danger of other crimes, but also countless other actions that we often have not defined or perceived as criminal, despite their undeniable harm. We may have a limited social reality of crime and victimization that excludes harms such as consumer fraud, pollution, unnecessary drugs and surgery, food additives, workplace hazards and diseases, police violence, censorship, discrimination, poverty, exploitation, and war. We suffer victimization not only by other individuals, but also by governments and other social institutions, not to mention the psychological victimization bred by our own insecurities (1986, 3–4).

He suggests that the pathway to a more comprehensive victimology lies in the wedding of victimology with human rights, which can

> dissolve the "mental prison" that often characterizes how we think about victimization, and substitute a . . . broader conception that considers not only common crime but also corporate and state crime, that examines not only individual criminals but also institutional wrong-doing, and that encompasses not merely traditional crime but all crimes against humanity (Elias 1986, 7).

As indicated by the opening narrative on genocide and by our discussion of sociological contributions to crime and victimization, this chapter and book adopt a broader conception of victimization. This conception is also consistent with our concerns about social justice rather than just the narrow traditional focus on legally defined equal protection and criminal justice. The connection between these disparate type of victimization—the personal and the structural—is captured by Barak (2003, 116) when he writes about a sense of the collective experience of victimization and the nature of violence in the structural orders of the ghetto, the slums, poverty, and other forms of oppression: "all of those persons who inhabit impoverished environments, even if they have never been mugged, raped, or robbed by others living in their victimized neighborhoods, have been structurally violated every day of their lives."

Nevertheless, this type of emotional or psychic victimization is rarely, if ever, given official recognition or taken into account by the administration of justice. Chapters 1 and 8 in particular underscore the inherent problems and biases associated with the criminal law's role in shaping the notions of crime. In a parallel fashion, the criminal law also limits the boundaries of victimization and the scope of those who are considered victims. In other words, the "criminal law may provide the first narrowing of our consciousness of both crime and victimization, a process that continues in enforcement and subsequent stages of the criminal process" (Elias 1986, 32). Elias (33) continues that the penal code may "create an 'official' or 'social' reality of victimization which, among those harms it defines as criminal, stresses acts mostly committed by less privileged people, de-emphasizes and softens the acts committed by more privileged people, and then excludes from its definition other, extensive, and (usually more) harmful acts altogether, such as corporate crimes, state crimes, and what human rights advocates would call 'crimes against humanity.'"

While the criminal law, for example, excludes Quinney's "crimes of domination" (discussed in chapter 1), other examples that need to be included in studying victimology are actions committed with the authority of the state involving torture and other crimes against humanity (see box 7.1), those state-corporate crimes committed at the intersection of business and government, and those acts of commission and omission by agents of the criminal justice system in violation of the rule of law. (State-corporate crime is a recently developed hybrid involving the interplay of harmful social actions by governments and corporations; it extends the study of criminology to include injuries that violate neither criminal nor regulatory laws at the state level and may also include forms of social organization such as globalization and empire that may be in violation of international law or of crimes against humanity.)

The police or correctional officers typically carry out the most common types of state victimization, not necessarily with the backing of the state but often with the implicit or explicit approval of the larger society (Nelson 2000). (If these police or correctional personnel are private rather than public employees, then the victimization may be thought of as state-corporate crime.) The data surrounding police and penal victimization are sparse, but enough evidence of the use of excessive force and institutionalized violence exist to conclude that such behaviors do systematically occur,

Box 7.1.   Torture and the Bush Administration's Abuse of Power

In 2009, five years after the photographs of detainees being abused at Abu Ghraib aired on *60 Minutes II*, *New York Times* columnist Frank Rich wrote that it is important that we as a society "acknowledge that our government methodically authorized torture and lied about it." He (2009a, wk. 14) continues that:

> we also must contemplate the possibility that it did not just out of a sincere, if criminally misguided, desire to "protect" us but also to promote an unnecessary and catastrophic war, instead of saving us from "another 9/11," torture was a tool in the campaign to falsify and exploit 9/11 so that fearful Americans would be bamboozled into a mission that had nothing to do with Al Qaeda. The lying about Iraq remains the original sin from which flows much of the Bush White House illegality.

Rich is referring to a combination of events post-9/11 that led up to the second Iraq War, including the torture of the Al Qaeda operative Ibn al-Shaykh al-Libi in 2002, whose testimony became the centerpiece of Secretary of State Colin Powell's speech before the UN Security Council in 2003 to justify the invasion of Iraq. Libi was left unnamed, but Powell devoted nine paragraphs to "a senior terrorist operative" that linked Al Qaeda terrorists with Saddam Hussein and his weapons of mass destruction. Subsequently, Libi disavowed his torture-induced testimony and the facts on the ground totally discredited the existence of any connections between Al Qaeda and Hussein or any weapons of mass destruction.

Four interrogation memos released by the Justice Department in the spring of 2009 revealed in dispassionate legal prose that the CIA, with authorization from the White House, engaged in brutal interrogation techniques—including waterboarding, an act for which the United States prosecuted the Japanese after WWII. An editorial in the *New York Times* about the released memos stated: "Their language is the precise bureaucratese favored by dungeon masters throughout history. They detail how to fashion a collar for slamming a prisoner against a wall, exactly how many days he can be kept without sleep (11), and what, specifically, he should be told before being locked in a box with an insect—all to stop just short of having a jury decide that these acts violate the laws against torture and abusive treatment of prisoners" (2009, wk. 9). Other passages described forced nudity and the dousing of detainees with water as cold as forty-one degrees (Mazzetti and Shane 2009).

What these memos do not disclose is the number of detainees that were killed by these and other tortuous measures. Proof, however, of at least eight detainee deaths was documented in the 2007 Academy Award–winning film, *Taxi to the Dark Side*. Regrettably, as Rich (2009a, wk. 14) states, most Americans would rather:

cling to myths that quarantine the evil. If our country committed torture, surely it did so to prevent Armageddon, in a patriotic ticking-time-bomb scenario out of "24." If anyone deserved blame, it was only those identified by President Bush as "a few American troops who dishonored our country and disregarded our values": promiscuous, sinister-looking lowlifes like Lynddie England, Charles Graner and the other grunts who were held accountable while the top command got a pass.

Those scapegoated "grunts" that the U.S. military tried, convicted, and punished were only carrying out orders for which their military and civilian superiors had previously praised them. After all, the White House, the Justice Department, and the Pentagon had each authorized all those practices of torture performed inside the Bagram Air Force Base in Afghanistan, Abu Ghraib, and Guantanamo Bay prisons.

It does not look as though there will be any criminal prosecutions, independent investigations, or truth commissions involving the architects of these crimes of torture. In fact, the architects and high-level perpetrators of these crimes will never have to publicly face up to their violations of domestic and international law. The insistence by the Obama administration that we concentrate on the future and not dwell on the past, as well as the complacency of the American people to confront the truth of these crimes, are consistent with a long tradition of the United States avoiding and denying its numerous crimes against humanity. The continuation of denial does not bode well for building either peace or justice in the future because the wounds from these assaults run much deeper than most people realize:

> Even as the torturer shatters the world of his victim, he assaults the foundation of his own world, although he does not know it. Indeed, his blindness is a consequence of the torture, even a condition for it. The torturer and his victim are close to each other. There is physical contact. Yet in every other respect they are as distant as it is possible for one person to be from another. In the moral and affective vacuum that has been generated, sympathy, empathy, pity, understanding—every form of fellow-feeling—have been reduced to absolute zero. That is why torture is always . . . an "undoing of civilization," and probably more reliably than anything, it foretells the descent of a civilization into barbarism (Schell 2009, 17).

although not uniformly across the United States. For example, in 1999, the U.S. Department of Justice held a national summit on police brutality as one of a number of planned initiatives designed to improve police-community relations and to increase police accountability. During the same year, Amnesty International (AI) held hearings on police brutality in Los Angeles, Chicago, and Pittsburgh. The organization documented patterns of ill treatment across the nation, including police beatings, unjustified shootings, and the use of dangerous restraint techniques to subdue suspects (Amnesty International 1999a). Moreover, although only a minority of the many thousands of law enforcement officers in the USA engage in deliberate and wanton brutality, [AI] found that too little was being done to monitor and check persistent abusers, or to ensure that police tactics in certain common situations minimized the risk of unnecessary force and injury. The report also noted that widespread, systemic abuses had been found in some jurisdictions or police precincts. It highlighted evidence that racial and ethnic minorities were disproportionately the victims of police misconduct, including false arrest and harassment as well as verbal and physical abuse (Amnesty International 1999a, 147).

Abuse of police authority and discretion ranges from verbal slurs and racial profiling to brutality and murder; reports are widely circulated about the misuse of pepper spray, tasers, and police dogs; deaths resulting from dangerous restraint holds; and police shootings in disputed circumstances. Rogue officers may commit these acts alone or in small teams, or they may be endemic to a police force. Some of this behavior is spontaneous and personal in response to a specific incident, like a high-speed chase. Some of it is more planned and organizational, such as the Rampart scandal, involving the Rampart Division of the Los Angeles Police Department (LAPD), where a federal judge ruled in 2000 that the government's antiracketeering statute—known as the RICO (Racketeer Influenced and Corrupt Organization) Law and created for the purpose of dealing with drug bosses and organized crime figures—could be applied to the LAPD (Cannon 2000).

Penal violence, associated with incarceration and punishment for criminal convictions, is probably a more significant and common experience than police violence. The range and variety of penal abuse is also much broader. Common concerns involve the physical and sexual abuse of inmates as well as the excessive use of batons and electroshock weapons. Each year, dozens of inmates kill other inmates, and thousands are injured seriously enough to require medical attention. Many of these acts, including some instances of prison rape, are indirectly state crimes because they are facilitated by and/or overlooked by the correctional workforce. Mentally ill inmates, who constitute 15 percent to 25 percent of the prison population, are not adequately treated for their conditions and are then punished when they act out. Increasingly, public and private prisons are relying on administrative lockdowns or on policies of segregation and isolation. Accordingly, prisoners deemed to be particularly disruptive and dangerous are secured in small, often windowless cells for twenty-three hours a day. At any given time in the contemporary United States there are tens of thousands of prisoners subjected to this modern solitary confinement, "a form of numbing mental torture that drives about one-third of them psychotic, induces irrational anger in 90 percent, and ups the likelihood they will commit violent crimes upon release" (Ross 2009, 1).

Whether the victimization is done by police force or penal violence, the victims of these acts are in the vast majority of persons with little power, status, or stake in American society. These same groups, unfortunately, tend to be disproportionately victims of street crime, especially violent victimization. In each of the four sections that follow, we try to report both what is known about victimization and some of the missing elements of this official picture of the "reality" of victimization. The data for the tables below comes mostly from the National Crime Victimization Survey, one of the largest victimization surveys and based on a nationally representative sample of 42,000 households comprising some 76,000 persons each year. Because the survey, done by the Bureau of Census, is nationally representative, researchers can draw some conclusions about the distribution of victimization across income, race, gender, and several aspects of intersections. The picture is still not complete—for example, there is no data on wealth (just annual income) and gender victimization is not broken down by income levels. The survey also uses the criminal law as its basis for asking about victimization, so it does not measure the incidence of corporate crime or workplace harms, let alone crimes by the criminal justice system, the state, or various types of environmental or structural violence. Thus, the amount of actual victimization recorded by the survey is small in relation to the harms suffered by people each year in the United States. We do try to comment on several notable exclusions and ask readers to become aware of the *analogous social harms* discussed in chapter 8.

VICTIMIZATION AND CLASS

Researchers have found that the overall level or amount of victimization in rates of urban criminal violence are due largely to the differences in racial inequality and socioeconomic conditions. For example, a classic study by Judith Blau and Peter Blau in the early 1980s found that increases in the rates of criminal violence were positively associated with the socioeconomic inequality between races as well as with economic inequality generally. In making a case for *relative* rather than absolute deprivation, Blau and Blau (1982, 114) concluded, "if there is a culture of violence, its roots are pronounced economic inequalities, especially if associated with ascribed position." A quarter of a century later in a replication of Blau and Blau's classic study, Stolzenberg, Eitle, and D'Alessio concluded that the overall data support the "relative deprivation thesis" which holds that increases in economic inequality, particularly race-based inequality, result in increases in violent criminality: "Cities with large income disparities between Whites and Blacks had higher rates of violent crime, controlling for other factors" (2006, 303). Thus, from a sociological perspective, making sense out of criminality or victimization involves more than understanding individual behavior. It is also, from an integrated or holistic perspective, about understanding the structural conditions, the institutional arrangements, and the social and cultural relations of a society—and how these impinge on individual and group adaptations.

Unfortunately, victimization data from the National Crime Victimization Survey, whose results are distributed by the Bureau of Justice Statistics, reveal nothing about the structural context of victimization. Widely used publications like the *Sourcebook of Criminal Justice Statistics* use the survey data, and because the *Sourcebook* is available on the Internet, users can search all tables and figures using keywords. A search for information relating to "income" turned up several tables related to victimization (see below), but "wealth" turned up a sentence about how "The Bureau of Justice Statistics' (BJS) Federal Justice Statistics Program provides a *wealth* of data on the U.S. District Courts"—but the wealth of data did not include anything on victimization (or any other aspect of criminal justice) related to economic wealth. Searching for "class" results in references to "classification" and classes as they relate to schools, but no matching information on social class.

The victimization data distributed by the Bureau of Justice Statistics for household income are presented in table 7.1. In general, rates of overall property crime were higher for lower-income households compared to higher-income households. More specifically, households earning less than $7,500 per year were victims of property crime at a rate that was about 1.5 times higher than households earning $75,000 per year or more. Households earning less than $15,000 per year had higher property crime rates than households in all other income categories. Patterns in the rates for household burglaries and property thefts were similar to that of overall property crime: with those households in the two lowest income categories—less than $7,500 per year and $7,500 to $14,999—victimized by "burglary and theft at higher or marginally higher rates than households in all other income categories" (Rand 2008, 5). Various thefts or personal larcenies that do not involve contact with the offender have less clear patterns by income. The distribution could well change if the table further broke down the upper income levels, because those with substantial income live in gated communities and purchase security services that could affect victimization levels at higher incomes.

The data released recently by BJS do not include a breakdown of violent victimizations by income. Such data have been presented in the past, and the last edition of this book contained more detailed victimization data by income from supplementary tables posted to the BJS website. Thus, table 7.2 reprints the more complete victimization data to add to the picture of victimization by income and as an illustration of the limits of current data

Table 7.1. Property Crime Rates, by Household Income, 2008

Type of Crime	Less than $7,500	$7,500–$14,999	$15,000–$24,999	$25,000–$34,999	$35,000–$49,999	$50,000–$74,999	$75,000 or More
Property crimes	204	175	162	151	143	126	133
Completed household burglary	57	53	32	33	27	21	16
Motor vehicle theft	9	8	6	6	8	8	6
Theft	138	115	123	112	109	97	111

Source: Bureau of Justice Statistics, 2009. *Criminal Victimization, 2008*. U.S. Department of Justice (September, NCJ 22777), table 5.

Table 7.2. Victimization Rates (Per 1,000 Age Twelve and Older) by Income, 2003

Type of Crime	Less than $7,500	$7,500–$14,999	$15,000–$24,999	$25,000–$34,999	$35,000–$49,999	$50,000–$74,999	$75,000 or More
All personal crimes	51.1	31.9	27.0	25.8	22.0	23.3	18.5
Crimes of violence	49.9	30.8	26.3	24.9	21.4	22.9	17.5
Completed violence	18.7	10.7	10.3	10.5	5.3	5.5	3.7
Rape/sexual assault	1.6*	1.8*	0.8*	0.9*	0.9*	0.5*	0.5*
Robbery	9.0	4.0	4.0	2.2	2.1	2.0	1.7
Assault	39.3	25.0	21.5	21.8	18.3	20.4	15.4
Aggravated	10.8	7.9	4.5	5.0	4.8	5.2	2.7
Simple	28.5	17.0	17.0	16.9	13.5	15.2	12.6
Property crimes	204.6	167.7	179.2	180.7	177.1	168.1	176.4
Completed household burglary	48.4	34.9	34.2	28.2	22.1	20.6	17.0
Motor vehicle theft	6.3	7.3	8.9	12.3	9.5	8.4	11.9
Theft	140.3	118.3	131.9	133.1	140.0	134.7	143.7
Completed	138.4	115.7	126.6	128.7	134.0	130.1	139.0
Less than $50	40.4	28.2	34.3	42.9	43.0	43.5	45.2
$250 or more	35.3	25.1	35.0	30.0	32.0	30.7	34.4

Note: Detail may not add to total shown because of rounding. Table excludes data on persons whose family income level was not ascertained. *Estimate is based on about ten or fewer sample cases.
Bureau of Justice Statistics. 2005. *Criminal Victimization in the United States, 2003*. Statistical Tables (July 2005, NCJ 207811), tables 14 and 20. Available, http://www.ojp.usdoj.gov/bjs/abstract/cvusst.htm.

about class. The data clearly show that people at the low end of the income distribution were more than twice as likely to be the victim of a violent crime as those at the upper range of this income distribution. This pattern is consistent for all types of violent crimes, including rape, robbery, and assault—and is even more pronounced in cases where the crime of violence was completed or involved an injury. The one unmistakable pattern in the table is that the crimes most Americans fear and regard as most serious happened disproportionately to lower-income households.

Tables 7.1 and 7.2 present incomplete pictures of victimization in several respects. For example, many harmful acts of business and government are not part of the criminal law, so many types of injury are excluded from official data. Reiman and Leighton recalculate figures from the FBI's *Uniform Crime Reports* on how Americans are murdered to include workplace hazards, occupational diseases, and preventable medical errors—"How Americans Are Really Murdered." While the FBI reports information on about 14,000 murders where the weapon is known, "How Americans Are Really Murdered" includes information on more than 170,000 (2010, 88). The category of "Occupational Hazard and Disease" contributes significantly to the revised estimate, and because the victims in this category work in blue-collar manufacturing and industrial jobs, these victimizations are disproportionately located in the lower-income groups. As noted in chapter 4, toxic waste facilities also tend to be in poor and especially minority areas, increasing the victimization for a range of diseases.

In a similar vein, businesses and other institutions are excluded from estimates of victimization. However, because of their concentrated wealth and social organization, businesses are able to publish supplementary statistics on the victimization they suffered from, say, employee theft or credit card fraud. Insurance companies may also produce additional information on fraud related to false claims by patients and doctors. But there is a profound lack of data in criminology and elsewhere, for example, about the pain and suffering experienced by some 45 million Americans who have no health insurance. Nor is there any accounting of victimization related to medical services that are denied and/or exceedingly difficult to obtain because of the health insurance industry's desire to secure greater profits. People who have no dental insurance and pull their own teeth out with pliers (Gladwell 2005) are not part of the discussion of victims.

Further, the victimization for any year would not pick up the mass financial victimization caused by corporate frauds at Enron, WorldCom, Tyco, and many others. Most of these losses would be to middle- and upper-income, largely white victims. The losses range up to millions of dollars but would not be captured by the "theft greater than $250" category or by questions about other personal larcenies. Neither would the further impacts on the victims of these losses, including people delaying retirement, rejoining the workforce, and scaling back on college education for their children (Leighton and Reiman 2002). Enron has been found guilty of illegal activities related to California's power crisis, and on audiotapes made by Enron employees, "traders joked about stealing money from California grandmothers and about the possibility of going to jail for their actions." But the grandmothers would have nothing to report to the victimization survey. Neither would all those persons who had their mortgages foreclosed and lost their homes in 2007–2009 as a result of fraudulent lending practices. The exclusion of these types of victimization from crime surveys and most discussion in criminology add to the sense that these harms do not amount to "real" crime. To help counter this absence of victimization or a false sense of a lack of victims, some insight into the harms done by corporate and white collar are reproduced in box 7.2.

Box 7.2.   Victim Impact Statements about Corporate and White-collar Fraud

The outbreak of financial fraud in 2001–2002 resulted in mass victimization. One of the clearest examples of the harm done by financial fraud is this victim impact statement that was prepared in August of 2005 for submission at the sentencing of Scott D. Sullivan, former chief financial officer of WorldCom. It has been edited for brevity.

My name is Henry J. Bruen Jr. I am a former shareholder, and former employee of WorldCom's NYC National Sales Group. I requested the opportunity to address this court out of a sense of duty, honor, and an obligation to give voice to individuals that have suffered as a result of the fraud perpetrated primarily by Scott Sullivan and Bernard J. Ebbers. I represent the working professional . . . and the average investor that has suffered indescribable trauma financially, personally and professionally as a result of the criminal activities of Scott Sullivan and his co-conspirators. I want to take this opportunity to be a witness to justice being done in this matter.

I have never met Scott Sullivan personally but the effect of his activity of being the principal architect of this scheme, and implementer of this heavy-handed fiscal fraud, [has] affected me deeply and personally. On June 28, 2002, articles began appearing in newspapers which depicted Sullivan's palatial hideaway in Boca Raton, Fla. There were descriptions of the then 40-year-old being the financial brain of a devastating profit-rigging scheme to cook up nearly $4 billion in cash flow that never existed.

The pictures alone of his "palatial villa" had at best a chilling effect on WorldCom business in Manhattan. I was forced to defend to my customers[,] both existing, and potential[,] how a 40-year-old executive was able to afford such a monstrosity of a home. The next comment from my customers was "obviously the rates that you are charging for your service are far too high. . . . I need to look at renegotiating my contract with your company." This turned out to be the tip of an ongoing escalating death spiral of revenues and new business opportunities. Not to mention the obliteration of any personal credibility, trust and goodwill that I may have built with a customer as a result of these new revelations. As the amount escalated by the billions so did the intensity of abuse and skepticism that I experienced on a daily basis. Not to mention the fact that my retirement funds and bonuses, were tied up in stock options which eventually became worthless.

I was a member of the National Accounts Group that was the most profitable sales channel of all six WorldCom sales channels dealing with global, multinational and national size enterprises. I had brought in major new business accounts resulting in over $5 million in new business. I had become a top 5 percent Presidents Club winner four consecutive times in a row and had been recognized in my branch over 15 times for outstanding sales performance with an average income of $180,000. After the fraud announcement on June 26, 2002, my commission income dwindled to next to nothing due to an inability to attain new business from customers that was previously committed and contracted with WorldCom.

Over the next six months after the fraud announcement, I was saddled with the stigma of being a legacy WorldCom employee in addition to being tasked with explaining the accounting fraud and subsequent scandals that unfolded in the media daily to customers and personal friends alike. Rounds of layoffs began immediately starting at the senior management levels and worked their way down. Finally I was laid off in the sixth company-wide layoff in early 2003. During my tenure at WorldCom I experienced the agony of watching over 30,000 co-workers get laid off [,] while each day wondering when my name would be on the list. The psychological effect of finding out what new disaster awaited you at work each day from the media coverage was both savage and demoralizing. The daily pounding and constant assault of improprieties in the newspaper was mind-numbing and debilitating. This experience embodied the definition of hell on earth if there ever was one.

Over the last two years I have suffered the loss of all my personal savings, medical benefits, retirement funds, stock market investments, and personal property assets as a result of my inability to replace my personal income due to no fault of my own. I was just one of thousands of hard-working professional employees that put their faith and belief in what was a great company, which was destroyed solely by the greed and avarice of Scott Sullivan and his co-conspirators. What happened to me as a result of Scott Sullivan is representative of tens of thousands of other employees and investors who had their careers, retirement and livelihoods literally destroyed by the layoffs and bankruptcy of WorldCom Inc.

My only hope and prayer is that this sentencing proceeding reflects to Scott Sullivan the severity of his crimes, which led to the disintegration of WorldCom, and demonstrates, that this type of activity will not be tolerated in corporate America[,] for he can never repay me or the tens of thousands of people like me[,] whose lives disintegrated before them in the blink of an eye. I hereby respectfully submit this statement to be entered into the record which reflects my personal feelings, and the sentiment of many people like me trying to piece back the broken pieces of our lives in the wake of this disaster.

The subprime mortgage fraud of 2007–2008 had a more devastating and widespread impact than the earlier fraud. But the deregulation causing the

(continued)

Box 7.2. (*continued*)

crisis meant that there were few laws to break, so there have been almost no criminal charges filed against those who caused a global economic meltdown. But this time period involved the discovery of another unrelated fraud: the Ponzi scheme of Bernard Madoff. Although it has been estimated that investors since 1995 had lost some $13.2 billion, the November 2008 account statements at the time of the collapse of Madoff's empire showed that losses could be as high as $65 billion.

Ponzi schemes essentially involve using the money from new investors to pay back earlier investors and to support the perpetrator's lifestyle. Paying back earlier investors and meeting requests from people who want to take some of their money out establishes legitimacy. Madoff seems to have started the scheme to cover losses that he thought would be fleeting: "When I began the Ponzi scheme, I believed it would end shortly and I would be able to extricate myself and my clients from the scheme." But "as the years went by I realized that my arrest and this day would inevitably come" (Frank and Efrati 2009a, B1).

Though Madoff did not look directly at any of the victims when they spoke of their pain and suffering in U.S. District Court during the sentencing phase, he did turn to them during his remarks before the sentence was announced and simply uttered: "I'm sorry. I know that doesn't help you." He added:

> I cannot offer you an excuse for my behavior. How do you excuse betraying thousands of investors who entrusted me with their life savings? How do you excuse deceiving 200 employees who spent most of their working life with me? How do you excuse lying to a brother and two sons who spent their entire lives helping to build a successful business? How do you excuse lying to a wife who stood by you for 50 years? . . . I will live with this pain, with this torment, for the rest of my life . . . I have left a legacy of shame . . . to my children and grandchildren . . . (Frank and Efrati 2009b, A1).

The thousands of victims who knowingly and unknowingly invested with Madoff came from all walks of life; they included the world's largest banks and wealthiest people as well as folks of modest means. However, just 113 of them filed letters with the federal court and only nine victim statements were recorded live the day of sentencing. The victims who spoke that day, with one exception, were not wealthy. They were ordinary people with median incomes, including a physical therapist, a retired correctional officer, and an accountant. Collectively, their stories of financial devastation where life savings were lost lasted about one hour.

Tom FitzMaurice, sixty-three, who was working three jobs to make ends meet, stated, "there will be no retirement, no trips to California to visit our 1-year-old grandson." He also read from a statement by his wife, Marcia, who stood by his side: "I cry every day when I see the pain in my husband's eyes." . . . "I cry for the life we had." In a letter shared by Judge Chin from one widow who had gone to see Madoff two weeks after the death of her husband to invest their life savings, he was quoted as saying, "Your money is safe with me," as he put his arm around her. Another victim, Miriam Siegman, born blocks away from the District Court in NYC and now living a new life of poverty in Stamford, Connecticut, stated, "I now live on food stamps. . . . I scavenge in dumpsters at the end of the month." On the other hand, Burt Ross, a former mayor of Fort Lee, New Jersey, having lost $5 million in retirement funds and trusts for his children, stated that he was not in bad shape personally but was speaking on behalf of other victims. He noted that renowned Holocaust survivor and author Elie Wiesel had invested millions of dollars on behalf of nonprofit charities. Ross commented, "As if Mr. Wiesel hasn't suffered enough in his lifetime" (Lattman and Lobb 2009, A12).

Recognizing that sentencing a seventy-one-year-old man to 150 years is largely symbolic, Judge Chin explained that "symbolism is important for victims" because a "substantial sentence may in some small measure help the victims in their healing process." Similarly, Jayne Barnard, a law professor who had written a 2001 law review article that was influential in the change in the law in 2004 and who has argued with others that fraud victims also suffer emotionally and socially, was in attendance at the sentencing and had this to say: "The proof of the value of the process is exactly what we saw in the courtroom today. The victims were eloquent, they were dignified, and they told very powerful stories" (Lattman and Lobb 2009, A12). They also referred to Madoff as a "monster" and a "low-life" (and who can argue?). The victims present at the sentencing also burst into applause and cheers when the tough sentence was given (Frank and Efrati 2009b).

VICTIMIZATION AND RACE

As the previous section indicated, crime victims are disproportionately from the lower economic classes. While whites make up the majority of the poor, minorities are disproportionately poor, so it follows that they are also disproportionately victims of crime. The figures that follow illustrate some of the racial differences, but official statistics, as noted earlier, do not capture the structural violence experienced by marginal folks, minorities in particular, day in and day out (Barak 2003; see also Robert McAfee Brown [1987]). Nor do they expose the impact racial inequality has on the level of patterns of victimization.

For example, William J. Wilson in *The Truly Disadvantaged* (1987) wrote about the "cycles of disadvantages" and how the deindustrialization of the United States and the associated economic and social changes eliminated hundreds of thousands of manufacturing and other jobs from urban areas by the 1980s. This created a permanent underclass of residents, especially African Americans. Subsequently, other researchers also linked the costs of social inequality, urban poverty, and racial discrimination to social problems generally, including violence and other forms of victimization, particularly drug consumption and trafficking often found in marginal, distressed communities (Sampson and Wilson 1995; Hagan 1994). Similar lines of inquiry have also developed out from the sociological schools of social disorganization and social ecology as well as from neighborhood studies, all of which link crime and victimization to "kinds of places" rather than "kinds of people." For example, Rodney Stark's "theory of deviant places" explains why urban areas with more dense housing and poor neighborhoods are more likely to facilitate crime than suburban and rural areas where communities are more spread out (Stark 1987).

In one of the most comprehensive and imaginative analyses of the contradictions of capitalism in relation to marginally oppressed African Americans, victimization, and crime, Becky Tatum has provided a hybrid formulation that employs social psychology and Marxist notions of oppression in her "neocolonial model of adolescent crime and violence." In particular, "the theory examines the relationship between structural oppression, alienation, and three adaptive forms of behavior—assimilation, crime and deviance, and protest" (Tatum 1996, 34). Building on models of colonialism and internal colonialism, Tatum's model shifts the study of crime "from the victims of oppression to exploitative structural systems" (48). Tatum's model assesses behavioral adaptations to blocked structural opportunity from the perspective of race as the primary variable, followed by class. By specifically combining the perspective of racial conflict and anomie, she argues that African American and lower-class youth experience greater structural exclusion than white or middle-class youth. At the same time, the social psychology of a lack of bonding interacts with perceptions of oppression and feelings of alienation, so that crime and violence are also viewed as dependent on the local environment. Ultimately, Tatum suggests a dynamic reciprocal model where lower-class youths, especially African Americans, experiencing structural exclusion, perceived oppression, and fewer systems of community support result in higher levels of alienation and in higher inter- and intrapersonal levels of crime, violence, and victimization.

Probably the most provocative thesis that links social inequality, racism, and biology to socioeconomic and racial/ethnic group victimization is the "weathering framework" by Arline Geronimus, a professor of health behavior and a social epidemiologist at the University of Michigan. Her approach is based on studies of African Americans and whites living in Detroit and demonstrates "that blacks are, biologically speaking, older than whites of the same chronological age" (Blitstein 2009, 56). This victimization is due, Geronimus argues, to a combination of racism and stress that can weather the systems of the human body, fueling the progression of disease, aging, and death. As stressors ranging from environmental pollution to high crime to racism-induced anger accumulate and feed on each other, they alter the culture and behavior of a community, which can lead, for example, to higher rates of smoking, drinking, and drug use.

Geronimus and her colleagues have already shown that blacks having experienced repeated exposure and adaptation to the above types of stressors are also experiencing earlier health deterioration. These racial differences are not explained by poverty because "poor and nonpoor Black women had the highest and second highest probability of high [stress] scores, respectively, and the highest excess scores compared with their male or White counterparts" (Geronimus et al. 2006a, 826; see also 2006b). Other similarly focused research has "established that the health of Latino immigrants declines as they stay in America longer and improve their lots in life, and that South Asian Indian mothers, who have socioeconomic profiles comparable to whites, suffer from birth outcomes as poor as those of low-income blacks" (Blitstein 2009, 53).

Finally, as discussed earlier in the chapter, there is a relationship between health disparities and racial inequality. Consistent with the Geronimus thesis, there are some very revealing comparative data on the disparities between blacks and whites living in the United States. For example, the following figures illustrate the health differences between African Americans and whites:

- black residents of high-poverty areas are as likely to die by the age of forty-five as American whites are to die by sixty-five;
- the disability rates of black fifty-five-year-olds approach the rates of seventy-five-year-old whites;
- in impoverished urban areas like Harlem, one-third of black girls and two-thirds of boys who reach their fifteenth birthdays don't reach their sixty-fifth—a rate that is almost three times higher than among average Americans;
- in 2009, blacks were dying at rates comparable to that of whites from 1979; and
- in 2000, black cancer death rates were 30 percent higher than among whites; a half century earlier in 1950, black rates were slightly less than whites (Blitstein 2009, 49–51).

All of these health disparities in accelerated rates of mortality, including the findings by Geronimus and her colleagues regarding comparative rates for teen pregnancy, motherhood, and infant mortality strongly support the argument that this victimization is a byproduct of social disadvantages and racial inequality (Kaufman, Geronimus, and James 2007).

As with official data on class and victimization, BJS data do not mention or measure contributions from the larger social context. Table 7.3 presents victimization rates of violent crime by race. Blacks were somewhat more likely than whites to be victims of overall violence, except for those who identify as being two or more races. For that year, less than 1 percent of the population self-identified as being of more than one race (multiracial), so that category is small and heterogeneous (comprising people of all races in various mixtures), which makes meaningful analysis difficult. (However, the violent victimization rates are twice as high as those for blacks, so something dramatic is happening with the statistics or in the lives of mixed-race people that deserves further investigation.) Hispanics had a lower overall rate of violence compared with non-Hispanics, a pattern that plays out to a slight degree in all categories but is mostly driven by the substantially higher rate of simple assaults reported by non-Hispanics.

The previous section noted that BJS currently just reports property crime by income, which we supplemented with earlier data on violent victimizations. With race, BJS currently only reports violent victimization, so table 7.4 presents the more complete data that was available for the earlier edition of this book. Overall, the data show that minorities, whether black or Hispanic, have higher levels of victimization than whites. This pattern holds for both violent and property crimes, with the minor exception of small completed thefts. Unfortunately, a limitation of the survey is that the relatively small number of people of other races makes it difficult for the sample to generate reliable estimates of the victimization rates of

Table 7.3. Victimization Rates (Per 1,000 Age Twelve and Older) of Violent Crime by Race/Ethnicity, 2008

Type of Crime	White Only Rate	Black Only Rate	Hispanic Rate	Other Race Rate	Two or More Races Rate	Non-Hispanic Rate
All	18	26	16	15	52	20
Rape/Sexual Assault	0.6	1.9**	0.6**	0.9**	1.9**	0.8
Robbery	2	6	3	3**	7	2
Assault	16	19	12	11	43	17
Aggravated	3	5	4	3	7	3
Simple	13	13	9	9	36	14

Bureau of Justice Statistics. 2009. *Criminal Victimization, 2008* (December, NCJ 22777), table 4. *Other race includes American Indians, Alaska Natives, Asians, Native Hawaiians, and other Pacific Islanders. **Based upon ten or fewer cases.

American Indians/Alaska Natives, Asians, and Native Hawaiian or Other Pacific Islander. By pooling data from 1992 to 2001, the Bureau of Justice Statistics came up with data for Native Americans and found they had exceptionally high rates of violent victimization—101 per 1,000 persons age twelve and older, compared with fifty for blacks, forty-one for whites, and twenty-two for Asians (BJS 2004c, 4). BJS did a similar analysis for Asian, Native Hawaiian, and Pacific Islanders using data from 2002 to 2006. They found that Asians had a lower rate of violent victimization—10.6 per 1,000, compared with 24.1 for non-Asians; property crime was also lower, though not as dramatically, with a rate of 115.3 for Asians and 162.3 for non-Asians (2009b, 1).

Most victimization involves offenders and victims of the same race and are thus *intraracial* crimes, although American Indians are the most likely

Table 7.4.   Victimization Rates (Per 1,000 Age Twelve and Older) by Race, 2003

Type of Crime	White Only Rate	Black Only Rate	Hispanic Rate	Non-Hispanic Rate
All personal crimes	22.1	30.7	25.3	23.0
Crimes of violence	21.5	29.1	24.2	22.3
Completed violence	6.1	11.3	7.8	6.8
Rape/sexual assault	0.8	0.8*	0.4*	0.9
Robbery	1.9	5.9	3.1	2.4
Assault	18.8	22.3	20.8	19.0
Aggravated	4.2	6.0	4.6	4.6
Simple	14.7	16.3	16.1	14.4
Property crimes	159.1	190.2	207.8	158.2
Completed household burglary	23.7	30.6	26.5	24.3
Motor vehicle theft	7.8	15.3	14.0	8.4
Completed theft	118.6	132.5	152.6	16.8
Less than $50	37.1	36.5	31.5	37.5
$250 or more	29.7	29.5	43.7	28.1

Bureau of Justice Statistics. 2003. *Criminal Victimization in the United States, 2003.* Statistical Tables (July 2005, NCJ 207811), tables 5, 7, 16, and 17. Available, http://www.ojp.usdoj.gov/bjs/abstract/cvusst.htm.
* Estimate is based on about ten or fewer sample cases.

of any racial group to experience a violent victimization by someone of a different race (BJS 2004c, 14). For 2008, out of the homicides for which the FBI had data on the race of victims and offenders, 3,036 homicides were white-on-white and 2,722 were black-on-black (UCR 2008, table 6). The absolute number of black-on-black homicides is lower than that for whites, but blacks make up 12 percent of the population, so the rate is very high and the problem is compounded because the homicides are concentrated among black men. The pattern of intraracial offending for whites and blacks is consistent with strong patterns of racial segregation (Massey and Denton 1993; Krivo and Peterson 2009).

One subset of crimes involving different races or *interracial* crimes is "hate crimes," or bias-motivated offenses. The FBI defines hate crimes or "bias crimes" as involving crimes against persons or property motivated at least in part by the perpetrator's bias against a "race, religion, sexual orientation, ethnicity/national origin or disability" (UCR 2008). This definition excludes gender and thus does not conceptualize any violence against women, including rape, as a hate crime, although ongoing efforts to revise the definition and other background are discussed in box 7.3. Terrorist acts are not included in hate crime statistics, although some (like the bombing of the federal building in Oklahoma City), appear in the homicide section of the Uniform Crime Reports. The 3,000 deaths from 9/11 were excluded from the New York homicide figures of the Uniform Crime Reports for 2001 (Leighton 2002) and were also not recorded as hate crimes, which was consistent with the Bush administration's efforts to define terrorism as a war rather than a crime.

In 2008, race and ethnicity combined accounted for almost 65 percent of bias crime incidents, with religion comprising about 20 percent and sexual orientation comprising 15 percent (UCR 2008, table 1). Of the offenders for whom race was known, 73 percent were white and 21 percent black, with the other racial groups comprising the rest (UCR 2008, table 3). The FBI does not report offenders by ethnicity, just race. Even though race is frequently dichotomized into "white" and "minority" (or just "black"), not all crimes by minorities involve antiwhite bias, because members of some minorities have prejudice and antipathy toward other minorities. For 2008, the largest category of hate crimes was antiblack (3,413 incidents), followed by anti-Jewish (1,055), antimale homosexual (948), and antiwhite (812) (UCR 2008, table 5).

Hate-crime statistics should be interpreted with caution. First, the number does not reflect all hate crimes but simply those hate crimes that were recorded as such by the police. For 2008, the state of Alabama officially recorded eleven hate crime incidents and Mississippi recorded four (UCR 2008, table 12). Any biases present in the police force will affect the likelihood of officers being willing to record the offense as bias motivated and

Box 7.3. The Controversy over Hate-crime Legislation

Hate speech typically involves actual speech or writing that expresses hostility to a group, and it may also include symbolic speech like burning a cross. In *R.A.V. v. St. Paul* (507 U.S. 377 [1992]), the Supreme Court decided to invalidate a law making it a crime to display objects such as a burning cross that "arouses anger, alarm or resentment in others on the basis of race, color, creed, religion or gender." In addition to other problems with the ordinance, the majority of the court found it was an impermissible regulation on the content of free speech guaranteed by the First Amendment. On the other hand, in a subsequent case, *Virginia v. Black* (538 U.S. 343 [2003]), the Court modified its position somewhat by upholding a Virginia law prohibiting the burning of crosses where it was done with an attempt to intimidate.

Sentencing enhancement laws for bias-motivated crimes, by contrast, go much further than merely prohibiting hate speech or symbolism, by adding additional penalties to personal or property crimes because of the bias/hate shown in victim selection. For example, for bias-motivated assaults, the Supreme Court unanimously upheld sentencing enhancement for bias-motivated assaults in *Wisconsin v. Mitchell* (508 U.S. 476 [1993]). In that case, Mitchell, a black teenager, had been watching the civil rights film *Mississippi Burning* with friends. When they were outside later, the group saw a young white boy and Mitchell asked the group if they felt "hyped up to move on some white people." He added: "You all want to fuck somebody up? There goes a white boy; go get him" (quoted in *State v. Mitchell* [485 NW2d 807, 809, 1992]). The Court held that the Wisconsin statute was not aimed at punishing protected speech or expression and that motive could be a consideration of the sentencing judge. Likewise, previous speech and utterances by defendants are frequently admitted into evidence in court to establish motive.

Interestingly, those who oppose sentencing enhancement penalties for hate crime do so, among other reasons, because "crimes against some type of victims will incur greater penalties, with this injustice spurring resentment" (Cockburn 2009b, 9). The point being that such laws—based on a victim's actual or perceived race, color, religion, and national origin—value some victims over other victims, creating disparate or unequal treatment of victims. But much current law punishes bias against the majority as well as the minority (antiwhite and antiblack, anti-Christian as well as anti-Islam). Valuing other victims thus could mean expanding the types of bias that result in punishment. Indeed, the 2009 Matthew Shepard Act, which was signed into law by President Obama, was controversial because it added federal penalties for bias-motivated crimes based on the victim's actual or perceived sexual orientation, gender, gender identity, or disability. (Although the FBI collects data on some of the categories based on state law offenses, federal law had no provisions to enhance penalties for these types of bias-motivated crimes before the 2009 act.)

(continued)

Box 7.3.   (*continued*)

Opponents also argue that these types of laws create thought crimes. The difference between a regular assault and a bias-motivated one is the perpetrator's thoughts about some characteristic of the victim. Instead of creating new categories of crime, opponents maintain that "federal and state hate crime laws are unnecessary and dangerous" because the object of criminal adjudication should be "to apply existing laws in a manner that constitutes justice, no matter who the victim may be" (Cockburn 2009b, 9). In contrast, the Supreme Court in *Mitchell* found that the state provided an adequate basis for singling out bias crimes for enhanced penalties because they are "more likely to provoke retaliatory crimes, inflict distinct emotional harms on their victims, and incite community unrest" (508 U.S. 476 [1993]).

The debate over hate-crimes legislation also has to do with whether activist groups favor or oppose the sentence-toughening business. The Obama administration and the gay lobby generally back the Matthew Shepard Act and others at the state level. It is also favored, for example, by all those groups affiliated with the Leadership Conference on Civil Rights except for the American Friends Service Committee. Like the AFSC, the gay National Coalition of Antiviolence Programs opposes enhanced sentencing penalties for those convicted of hate crimes.

fill out the additional paperwork. For example, white privilege may make some white officers more sensitive to aspects of bias in crimes involving white victims and minority offenders; at the same time they may be less likely to see bias in crime involving minority victims and white offenders. Also, future increases in the number of reported hate crimes might be viewed cautiously as they could be due to more complete reporting practices as well as greater sensitivity on the part of police. Increases in *reported* hate crime may or may not reflect trends in the actual occurrence of hate crimes.

VICTIMIZATION AND GENDER

The previous sections on class and race argued that inequality lead to greater levels of victimization. The argument, summarized by Braithwaite (1992), is that inequality increases crimes of "need"—people motivated to commit property crimes to satisfy basic needs as well as culturally constructed material "needs." The poor and minorities also find the inequality structurally humiliating, which can lead to property or violent crime. He writes that "the propensity to feel powerless and exploited among the poor and the propensity of the rich to see exploiting as legitimate both . . . enable crime" (1992, 94). Similar dynamics apply to race, but gender inequality plays out in a different way. The key variable of humiliation, which turns to violence and victimization through rage, is less likely in women because of gender socialization: "women, instead of feeling humiliation and rage, feel guilt and shame" (1992, 95). This can lead to self-destructive behaviors as well as victimization by the privileged. Gender inequality and degradation of women "enables rape and violence against women on a massive scale in patriarchal societies, not to mention commercial exploitation of the bodies of women by actors who might ambiguously be labeled white-collar criminals" (1992).

Braithwaite's analysis indicates that some victimization caused by gender inequality will not be seen as crime and thus excluded from official statistics. And, making sense of official statistics requires going beyond his analysis to draw in the critique of masculinity and the problematic values—violence, domination, etc.—that comprise it (chapter 5). With this background, it makes sense that men make up the majority of victims of officially defined crime, and the vast majority of the perpetrators are other men. Women suffer smaller numbers of victimizations, but these are largely also perpetrated by men—and men frequently known to the woman rather than strangers. Certainly violent women do exist and some women batter some men, although these examples are exceptions to main trends despite their cultural prevalence in movies and other media perpetuating an antifeminist edge. (Indeed, the authors' informal survey of websites about battered men revealed that the concern about victimized men was limited to ones victimized by women; rarely was there an acknowledgement about the high level of victimization by other men, and no discussion of rape in men's prisons.)

Table 7.5 provides the most recent available data for rates of violent victimization by gender. For all categories except rape/sexual assault, men experienced higher levels of victimization. Overall, males were victims

Table 7.5. Victimization Rates of Violent Crime by Gender, 2008

Type of Crime	Male	Female
All personal crimes	21	17
Rape/sexual assault	0.3*	1.3
Robbery	3	2
Assault	18	14
Aggravated	4	3
Simple	15	12

Bureau of Justice Statistics. 2009. *Criminal Victimization, 2008* (December, NCJ 22777), table 4. *Based upon ten or fewer sample cases.

of violent crime, robbery, and aggravated assaults at rates higher than females. Males also had higher but not significantly higher rates of violence for simple assault. The exception to higher victimization rates for the male gender is rape/sexual assault where women/girls were eighteen times more likely to be victims than men/boys. As with class and race, the most recent victimization data leaves out significant information, so we are again reprinting the more detailed table from the previous edition of this book. The additional information in table 7.6 indicates that men and women have roughly similar rates of completed violence, and the category of attempted or threatened violence elevates the overall rate of violent victimization for men.

Going beyond the tables, the FBI reports that for 2008, 4,351 murders involved a male offender and male victim, whereas only 455 involved a female offender and male victim (and this category includes an unknown number of battered women who kill their abusers) (UCR 2008, table 6). Male offenders also killed 1,710 females, with only 200 homicides involving female-on-female dynamics. This general pattern holds for other types of violent crime. According to the Bureau of Justice Statistics (2005b, 14): "Between 1998 and 2002, nearly 4 out of 5 violent offenders were male. Males accounted for 75.6 percent of family violence offenders and 80.4 percent of nonfamily violence offenders. Among violent crimes against a spouse, 86.1 percent of the offenders were male; against a boyfriend or girlfriend, 82.4 percent; and against a stranger, 86 percent of the offenders were male."

Besides men's greater risk of most types of victimization, the most striking differences between men and women's victimization patterns emerge when we consider the victim-offender relationship. Men are more likely to

Table 7.6.   Victimization Rates (Per 1,000 Age Twelve and Older) by Gender, 2003

Type of Crime	Male	Female
All personal crimes	26.7	20.2
Crimes of violence	26.3	19.0
Completed violence	7.3	6.5
Attempted or threatened violence	19.0	12.5
Rape/sexual assault	0.2*	1.5
Robbery	3.2	1.9
Assault	23.0	15.7
Aggravated	5.9	3.3
Simple	17.1	12.4

Note: *Estimate is based on about ten or fewer sample cases.
Bureau of Justice Statistics 2005. *Criminal Victimization, 2003.* Statistical Tables (July, NCJ 207811). Table 2. Available, http://www.ojp.usdoj.gov/bjs/abstract/cvusst.htm.

be victimized by another male who is a stranger, while women are more likely to be victimized by a male known to them. According to findings from the National Crime Victimization Survey, 32 percent of women's violent victimization occurred at the hands of strangers, including 30 percent of rapes recorded by the survey. In contrast, 54 percent of men's violent victimization involved a stranger, including 58 percent of aggravated assaults (BJS 2004a, 9). A separate survey of college women revealed that about 90 percent knew their attacker: "For both completed and attempted rapes, about 9 in 10 offenders were known to the victim. Most often, a boyfriend, ex-boyfriend, classmate, friend, acquaintance, or coworker sexually victimized the women" (BJS 2000, 17).

Historically, the law has been reluctant to define women as victims who have crimes committed against them in their homes or as part of a relationship. For centuries, men benefited from not being held accountable for their crimes against women. The failure to recognize domestic violence as criminal behavior reinforced the patriarchal idea that "a man's home is his castle." Since the 1970s, however, society has begun to consider violence against women in the home a crime. Likewise, over the next twenty years, "private matters" such as acquaintance rape, marital rape, and stalking also became treated as criminal offenses. Nevertheless, while women are gaining the right to be treated like any other assault victim and to have their battering husband, for example, arrested and punished, the reality is that many women face social, economic, and cultural barriers that may prevent them from taking full advantage of their legal rights.

The question of why women stay in an abusive relationship is in part a reflection of male privilege in criminology if it is not also accompanied by a searching examination of why men batter. Chapter 5 on gender noted the sexual harassment case in which the male judges decided that sexist environments were a given and decided that women had "voluntarily" entered into it. With battering, the violent behavior of man is taken for granted, so the question has been focused on the woman's behavior. The assumption seems to be that she "voluntarily" stays, with the mistaken idea that she enjoys it more implicit than in the past but still present. Box 7.4 further discusses this issue to clarify that a variety of social and other factors are important in understanding the dynamics of women staying in abusive relationships.

One of the other crimes with a distinct gendered pattern is stalking, which is "a course of conduct directed at a specific person that would cause a reasonable person to feel fear" (BJS 2009c, 1). Legal definitions vary widely from state to state in the activities they consider harassing, in threat and fear requirements, and in how many acts must occur before the conduct can be considered stalking. Both men and women can be victims and offenders of stalking, but data from a 2006 BJS survey indicated women are almost three times more likely to be stalking victims (20 per 1,000 females

Box 7.4. Why Some Battered Women Sometimes Stay

Asking "Why does she stay?" rather than "Why does he batter—and why doesn't he leave?" ultimately privileges men and oppresses women. The question about women's behavior invites scrutiny and finding fault while treating the man's behavior as unremarkable. This is similar to sexual assault, where drinking privileges men and oppresses women: "he was drunk" tends to excuse sexual violence and "she was drunk" invites blame. So, the questions people should be asking are "Why is he violent? Why does the community let battering happen? And, how can we all better support abused women?"

Still, the question about barriers to women leaving abusive relationships is important and helps expose dynamics of domestic violence. So, the first point is that most battered women do leave several times and work to minimize the violence that they—and their children and pets—face. Second, leaving is the most dangerous time period. Batterers do not need anger management; they want control of their partners and leaving the relationship threatens that control, so it is met with increased violence. In an article entitled "Why Battered Women Stay," Susan McGee (1995 [2004]) further discusses the barriers abused women face, and some of the more significant ones are summarized below.

McGee (1995 [2004]) notes that "battered women sometimes stay for their children." They do not want the abuser to get custody and "reason that they will sacrifice themselves so their children can have a father, good schools, a safe neighborhood, or financial security." They may not have the money for divorce and a custody battle. Battered women are typically in a catch-22 situation: they get blamed for breaking up the family if they leave and blamed for endangering the children if they stay. Further, "some battered women stay because there is no place for them to go" (McGee 1995 [2004]). Shelters do not exist in all parts of town, and some areas, especially rural, may not have a shelter. Funding for shelters and domestic violence services is precarious. Abusers frequently try to isolate a woman from her friends and family—and difficult economic times mean people are working harder to survive and have less capacity to help. After staying at a shelter, a woman must get an apartment, which requires money and a credit rating (both of which an abuser may prevent her from having). Also, "women face discrimination in the rental market, and landlords are often reluctant to rent to formerly battered women, believing that their assailant will show up and cause property damage or physical harm."

Some battered women also stay "because they are not given accurate information about battering. They are told that they are codependent or enablers of his behavior—if they would change, their assailant would" (McGee 1995 [2004]). Women keep trying to change their behavior and themselves, only to be blamed for not trying harder. They may believe that therapy will stop the violence because they want to believe in him and hope "the violence will end and their relationship can resume. All women want the violence to end; many do not want the relationship to end." Indeed, sometimes battered women stay because "they believe in love and they still love their partners." McGee (1995 [2004]) writes that this is difficult to understand but emphasizes that "women may love their partners and at the same time hate their violent and abusive actions." She notes that "many people have been in difficult relationships (or jobs) that they should leave but couldn't, or needed time to be able to depart." Finally, "love is glorified in our culture. Popular songs and movies reinforce the idea that love is the most important thing in life and that people (especially women) should do anything for it."

In addition, some battered women stay "because they believe what most people in our society think about battered women: that they imagine or exaggerate the violence" and "that they provoke or are to blame for the violence" (McGee 1995 [2004]). They may believe that abuse does not happen to women like her (Weitzman 2000), in families like hers, and/or in communities like hers. Friends, family, clergy, and professionals may also believe myths about domestic violence and/or make excuses for the abuser ("he's under a lot of stress"). The result is that she will feel blamed, "hysterical," or selfish for wishing to escape abuse, and she is offered ideas that will not help her situation and may actually make it more difficult to escape.

Some battered women also stay "because their assailants deliberately and systematically isolate them from support" (McGee 1995 [2004]). Abusers desire control, so they try to isolate a woman from friends and family—as well as try to get them to become his ally. Abusers "accuse the partner of infidelity every time she speaks to someone" and pick fights when she contacts people, so she gradually gives up communicating with them. Abusers take car keys and phones, even nail "the windows shut and put a lock on the outside of the door." They may also threaten her ("if I can't have you, no one will"), her family, friends, and pets if she escapes; they may threaten suicide and/or exaggerate the devastating effects of prison. Some assailants may even "play on homophobia and tell their partners that shelters are lesbian recruiting stations, are staffed by lesbians, or are places where she will be attacked by lesbians or become one." An abuser may also harass her at work, make her late or engage in other activities so that she loses her job—and the ability to support herself. Economic resources are an important predictor of not just leaving but permanent separation, so inequality in income (see chapter 5) and the disproportionate number of minority women in poverty (see chapter 6) are real barriers to escaping abusive relationships.

Finally, "some battered women stay because they are addicted and their addiction prevents them from taking action." Women may drink or take drugs to deal with the physical and emotional pain caused by the relationship. An abuser may encourage the consumption or even coerce her into doing it, then sabotage efforts at recovery. "Doctors may prescribe tranquilizers for a battered woman's 'nerves.'" Drinking and drug use, even short of addiction, "make the women less able to act on her own behalf and give the assailant a handy tool for discrediting and blaming her."

(continued)

Box 7.4. (*continued*)

Just because there are real and substantial barriers to leaving does not mean that a battered woman should stay in a relationship. As McGee (1995 [2004]) notes:

> Although leaving may pose additional hazards, at least in the short run, the research data and the experience of advocates for battered women demonstrate that ultimately a battered woman can best achieve permanent safety and freedom apart from the batterer. In sum, leaving requires strategic planning and legal intervention to avert separation violence and to safeguard survivors and their children.

For McGee's article and additional information, including safety plans to help a battered woman escape, explore the domestic violence resources at http://www.stopviolence.com.

age 10 and over) than men (7.4 per 1,000 males age 18 and over) (BJS 2009c, table 3). In general, no difference was found in stalking prevalence between white women and minority women, but some evidence suggests that American Indian/Alaska Native women report proportionately more stalking victimization than women of other racial and ethnic backgrounds (BJS 2009c, table 3; BJS 1998d). People who identified as being more than one race had noticeably higher rates of victimization (BJS 2009c), indicating (again) that something dramatic is happening with the statistics or in the lives of mixed-race people that deserves further investigation.

An earlier study found that nearly 95 percent of female victims and 60 percent of male victims identified their stalker as male (BJS 1998d), while the more recent one found that "female victims of stalking were significantly more likely to be stalked by a male (67%) rather than a female (24%) offender" (BJS 2009c, 4). The earlier survey found that some type of intimate partner stalks most women, while men tend to be stalked by strangers and acquaintances (BJS 1998d). The more recent one did not break down victim/offender relationship by gender, but noted that "about a tenth of all victims were stalked by a stranger, and nearly 3 in 4 of all victims knew their offender in some capacity" (2009c, 4). Also, a strong link exists between stalking and other forms of violence in intimate relationships. Four out of five women who were stalked by a current or former husband or cohabitating partner were also physically assaulted by that partner, and nearly one-third were also sexually assaulted by that partner.

VICTIMIZATION AND INTERSECTIONALITY

In chapter 6 on privilege and intersections, box 6.1 asked about the relative rates of victimization for white men and black women. Men have higher victimization rates than women, but the rates for blacks are higher than for whites, so the question reinforced the importance of understanding intersections. Indeed, while the data in the previous sections are accurate, examining intersections reveals some exceptions and important variations that are not clearly visible with more limited comparisons. For example, official statistics support the contention that men are more likely to be victimized than women, but this will vary by racial/ethnic and class backgrounds. In particular, young black men—especially those who are poor—are at a greater risk for homicide victimization. Their risk of being murdered is four to five times greater than that of young black women, five to eight times higher than that of young white men, and sixteen to twenty-two times higher than that of young white women. Furthermore, a breakdown of official victimization rates by both race and sex revealed that some groups of men are less likely to be victimized than some groups of women.

The most current victimization report from the Bureau of Justice Statistics has only one table breaking down sex and race (in terms of reporting crimes to the police). Thus, table 7.7 displays earlier victimization rates broken down by race, ethnicity, and gender. The men in each category have higher victimization rates than women in the same racial or ethnic category. But black women and white men have similar rates of victimization, including the same rate of aggravated assault and a substantially higher rate for black women of overall victimization from completed violence. Indeed, the category of completed violence (as opposed to the "threatened and attempted violence") shows black men having the highest victimization rate, followed by black women and Hispanic women.

Given the strong pattern of people with low income experiencing greater victimization, part of this dynamic may be class based because minority women have the least income. Unfortunately, the data are not published in a form that breaks down gender by income. However, table 7.8 presents victimization rates by race and income and shows that for most crimes, blacks have a higher victimization rate than whites of the same income. While the victimization rates of blacks sometimes lack a clear pattern across increasing income, the higher rates of black victimization can be clearly seen by focusing on the lowest and highest levels of income, especially for summary categories like all crimes of violence and completed violence.

Table 7.7. Victimization Rates (Per 1,000 Age Twelve and Older) by Race, Ethnicity, and Gender, 2003

Types of Crime	Male White Only Rate	Male Black Only Rate	Male Hispanic Rate	Female White Only Rate	Female Black Only Rate	Female Hispanic Rate
All personal crimes	25.1	39.2	n/a	19.4	23.8	n/a
Crime of violence	24.7	38.4	29.0	18.5	21.4	19.3
Completed violence	6.1	13.7	7.4	6.1	9.4	8.2
Rape/sexual assault (a)	0.2*	0.2*	0.0*	1.4	1.4*	0.8*
Robbery	2.3	8.7	3.5	1.5	3.6	2.7
Assault	22.3	29.5	25.6	15.5	16.4	15.9
Aggravated	5.6	6.6	6.6	2.8	5.5	2.7
Simple	16.6	22.8	19.0	12.7	10.9	13.2

Note: Excludes data on persons of "Other" races and persons indicating two or more races.
*Estimate is based on about ten or fewer sample cases.
(a) Includes verbal threats of rape and threats of sexual assault.
Source: Bureau of Justice Statistics. 2005. *Criminal Victimization in the United States, 2003* (July 2005, NCJ 207811), tables 6 and 8. Available, http://www.ojp.usdoj.gov
/bjs/abstract/cvusst.htm.

Table 7.8. Victimization Rates (Per 1,000 Age Twelve and Older) by Race and Income, 2003

Types of Crime Whites Only	Whites Only Less Than $7,500	White Only $7,500–$14,999	White Only $15,000–$24,999	White Only $25,000–$34,999	White Only $35,000–$49,999	White Only $50,000–$74,999	White Only $75,000 or More
Crime of violence	47.8	30.7	21.3	23.5	22.7	22.4	17.4
Completed violence	16.4	8.3	8.1	9.6	5.6	4.8	3.6
Rape/sexual assault (a)	1.5*	1.6*	0.8*	1.1*	1.0*	0.4*	0.5*
Robbery	7.1	2.9	2.5	1.3*	2.1	1.5	1.7
Assault	39.2	26.2	18.1	21.1	19.6	20.5	15.1
Aggravated	10.5	7.1	3.6	3.8	5.1	5.0	2.4
Simple	28.7	19.1	14.6	17.3	14.5	15.6	12.7
All household burglaries	52.5	40.9	35.1	35.6	27.7	24.5	19.8
Theft	138.7	115.1	127.4	129.8	139.5	133.9	140.0
Completed theft	36.9	29.9	33.3	43.1	42.1	44.9	45.0
Less than $50							
$250 or more	38.5	26.3	34.9	29.6	31.8	29.2	33.9

(continued)

Table 7.8. (*continued*)

Types of Crime Blacks Only	Black Only Less Than $7,500	Black Only $7,500–$14,999	Black Only $15,000–$24,999	Black Only $25,000–$34,999	Black Only $35,000–$49,999	Black Only $50,000–$74,999	Black Only $75,000 or More
Crime of violence	58.6	24.9	42.6	34.8	15.9	31.3	26.9
Completed violence	19.7	14.7	16.9	15.4	3.5*	15.0	6.4
Rape/sexual assault (a)	1.1*	2.2*	1.3*	0.0*	0.7*	1.6*	0.0*
Robbery	12.4*	5.7*	9.7	7.8*	2.0*	9.6*	2.4*
Assault	45.0	17.0	31.5	27.0	13.2	20.1	24.5
Aggravated	13.2*	8.2*	3.1*	11.0	3.9*	5.5*	5.7*
Simple	31.8	8.8*	28.5	16.0	9.2	14.6	18.8
All household burglaries	55.8	45.8	55.7	31.5	31.7	29.7	34.6
Theft	141.5	120.8	153.1	151.9	165.3	129.9	244.8
Completed theft	50.2	24.7	37.2	41.6	56.2	28.8*	65.1
Less than $50							
$250 or more	26.6	15.0*	36.0	34.2	34.8	42.7	54.9

Note: Detail may not add to total shown because of rounding. Excludes data on persons whose family income level was not ascertained and data on persons of "Other" races and persons indicating two or more races.

*Estimate is based on about ten or fewer sample cases.

(a) Includes verbal threats of rape and threats of sexual assault.

Source: Bureau of Justice Statistics. 2005. *Criminal Victimization in the United States, 2003. Statistical Tables* (July 2005, NCJ 207811), tables 15, 21, and 22. Available, http://www.ojp.usdoj.gov/bjs/abstract/cvusst.htm.

The victimization rates for whites generally tend to decline with higher income, though theft tends to be more consistent across income categories. For blacks, however, rates of victimization for income categories has less or no discernable pattern, even if one discounts figures marked by an asterisk that are potentially problematic estimates based on very few cases. With crimes like assault, victimization rates increase toward the upper levels of income, and the pattern is even more pronounced with theft. In such cases, having data beyond income may be helpful. For example, credit rating can impact what apartments and rental opportunities are available, thus presenting different neighborhoods to people who have the same income; for those who are buying, accumulated savings and wealth could influence opportunities in different regions of cities and suburbs.

While the National Crime Victimization Survey data provide a snapshot of the amount of victimization, the data does not capture the cumulative lifetime chances of being a victim. Being at higher risk of victimization is rarely a one-year event, but it means that one's overall chances of being a victim of a certain crime is greater, as well as the chances of being a victim of multiple crimes. Indeed, the lifetime chances of criminal victimization need to be added to the probability of victimization from other acts not formally labeled as crimes as well; to the likelihood of criminal assault should be added, for example, the chances of increased exposure to toxic waste, unsafe work places, and brutality at the hands of the criminal justice system (to name just a few). For women, the victimization rate for, say, acquaintance rape needs to be added to the likelihood of a relationship involving domestic violence, sexual harassment at work, catcalls on the street, and unwanted exposure to pornography in a variety of settings. Women of color will have additional factors related to racial discrimination to also factor in.

Further, perceptions of the victim and his or her "worthiness" will shape the reaction to these individual and lifetime profiles of victimization in ways that vary by class, race, gender, and their combinations. For example, when a black man is assaulted, many people may be more inclined to assume he was doing something that precipitated the violence, perhaps by being involved in the drug trade or some other illicit business. A white, middle-class woman may be seen as the ultimate "victim," deserving of the most sympathy, especially when her behavior was consistent with the "pedestal values" described in the beginning of chapter 5 on gender.

A final limitation of the survey data is that it does not reveal the experience of victimization, the barriers to getting help, or many aspects of life related to the victimization. For example, while the physical experience of being battered is the same for all women, a victim's ability to obtain help in escaping the abuse is strongly related to class, race, and ethnicity. Box 7.4 noted this dynamic general, and Rivera's work (1997 [1994]) on the experiences of battered Latinas offers some more specific insights, some of which hold true for other racial and ethnic minorities. She observed that a shortage of bilingual and bicultural criminal justice workers creates a system ill prepared to address many battered Latinas' claims—a problem that exists for many immigrant women. Racial and ethnic minority women must decide whether to seek assistance from an outsider who "may not look like her, sound like her, speak her language, or share any of her cultural values" (261). Frequently stereotyped, minority women such as Latinas are often seen as docile and domestic, or sensual and sexually available. This kind of racial and ethnic stereotyping devalue some minority groups of women in particular and may place even more social distance between these women and those assigned to handle their complaints.

Similar problems exist within the Asian/Pacific Islander community. In addition, "the low status they hold in the traditional Asian/Pacific family hierarchy as children and as females, compounded with a culturally based emphasis on maintaining harmony even if it is at the cost of the individual's well being, continues to discourage these teenagers from asserting their rights and needs" (Yoshihama et al. in Levy 1998, 192). It can also be a barrier for adult women, and it combines with shame and guilt to further increase the barriers to reporting and to receiving help. Thus, when the Bureau of Justice Statistics (2009b, table 5) reports that Asian females are less likely than non-Asian females to be victimized by an intimate (and more likely to be victimized by a stranger), caution is warranted in interpreting the results. It is not clear how much of this difference is based on the woman's place in the family hierarchy, maintaining harmony, etc., and how much reflects real differences in victimization.

The economically marginalized position of many women of color also means they have limited resources to fill the gaps in available support services to assist them (e.g., by securing an attorney, seeking counseling, hiring a translator, telephoning family and friends who reside outside the United States). An immigrant woman may face additional challenges to seeking help. If she doesn't speak English, police officers may rely on the batterer to provide the translation. Immigrant women's families may be far away, contributing to the experience of isolation. Or, as Tina Shum, a family counselor at a social service agency, observed, many battered Asian immigrant women share a house with extended family members where there is no privacy on the telephone and no opportunity to leave the house. Some immigrant women are basically held hostage by their boyfriends or husbands, who threaten the women with deportation if they report their abuse. Even if such threats are unfounded, they may still intimidate women with no independent access to information. Many women do not realize that even if they are not U.S. citizens, they are still entitled to police protection from abuse.

Some minority women are reluctant to seek help from the police. They may fear the police will do too little and not take their victimization seriously. Or they may fear the police will do too much and deal with the abuser too harshly, thus compounding the problem of minority overrepresentation in prison (see chapter 10). Many women of color have had experiences with police—either in the United States or in their country of origin—that led them to distrust or place little confidence in the police. Interviews with operators of domestic violence shelters in Harlem, for example, revealed that police brutality was the dominant issue in minority communities, while violence against women was not even a close second. "Women of color fear that the protections they seek could result in their men being beaten or even killed by cops. And if the batterer, often the sole source of support for the victim and her children, is charged with a felony, he could spend his life behind bars under the 'three-strikes-and-you're-out' mandate" (Swift 1997, B7).

Responses to battered women need to acknowledge not only that women of color experience sexual and patriarchal oppression at the hands of their male partners but also that they "at the same time struggle alongside them against racial oppression" (Rice 1990, 63). For black women in particular, the emphasis on racial solidarity and not "airing dirty laundry" has often meant placing the needs of collectivity (family, church, neighborhood, or race) over their own individual needs. This emphasis on in-group survival often "promotes a paradigm of individual sacrifice that can border on exploitation" and that may have dire consequences in terms of their need for help escaping abuse (Collins 1998, 29).

IMPLICATIONS

The U.S. government has been well aware of racial disparities in crime, violence, victimization, criminal justice, and health care for decades. As far back as 1984, the Department of Health and Human Services established a Task Force on Black and Minority Health. In 2000, Congress elevated the National Institutes of Health Office and Minority Health, turning it into the higher-profile National Center on Minority Health and Health Disparities. Nevertheless, no major legislation on the problem was ever submitted by Congress to G. W. Bush for his signing even though most health disparity measures are either stagnant or getting worse. Unfortunately, Obama's health care and civil rights agendas describe only vague plans to address these disparities, and the types of traditional interventions that focus on individuals (e.g., increased heart disease screening for black males) have all failed miserably to make a dent in what are systemic problems. On the other hand, a "weathering"-inspired public policy would aim to reduce the social and racial disparities and to lower the environmental or structural stressors that "weather" some bodies more quickly than others. Geronimus's plan, for example, is not about managing stress on the individual level:

Sending armies of yogis and therapists to Americas' ghettos wouldn't address the larger crisis. Simplistic paeans to racial harmony won't work either. The issues are too systemic (Blitstein 2009, 57).

Structural victimization is difficult to separate from institutional and individual forms of victimization as each of these three spheres of intersection become consumed with emotional issues of self-esteem and social respect. At the same time, the issues of shame, humiliation, and anger associated with institutionalized abuse are less about individual-behavioral characteristics and more about group-cultural characteristics associated with variables of class, race, gender, and age. These variables and other social indicators of value or status serve to differentiate the forms of abuse and nonabuse that are socially constructed as appropriate for men, women, boys, girls, heterosexuals, homosexuals, whites, African Americans, Asians, Hispanics, the rich, the poor, the homeless, immigrants, the mentally ill, and so forth.

Furthermore, what differentiates institutionalized expressions of victimization from interpersonal and structural expressions of victimization is that the former are often interwoven with the normative practices of socialization found in the home, at school, in the street, at the workplace, and in the criminal justice system. In the case of crime control, the institutional forms of victimization carried out by the administration of justice are part and parcel of the cultural attitudes, social identities, and relations of power and conflict that parents and children, teachers and students, adolescents and adults, and agents and enemies of the established order occupy. At the same time, victimization by agents/agencies of the criminal justice apparatus are supported by ideologies that rationalize, justify, or excuse such behavior by helping to blur the distinctions between abuse and discipline, harassment and teasing, assault and defense, and punishment and reform.

Finally, acts of victimization—interpersonal, institutional, and structural—do not survive because the majority formally or overtly endorses these kinds of behavior. On the contrary, most of these acts are denied, ignored, or dismissed as exceptional events rather than general patterns of structural and cultural interaction. Accordingly, most attempts at criminal justice reform are "reformist" rather than "structural" in nature. They do not upset or challenge existing power relations, nor do they address the larger social and cultural roots of these patterns of victimization. Instead, these efforts in criminal justice reform or victimization reduction are aimed almost exclusively at controlling and/or changing the individual perpetrators ("bad apples") of excessive abuse. Services for victims are still secondary concerns. What are called for, in contrast, are much wider strategies of recovery that include an array and diversity of services, programs, and resources that revolve around "restorative" and redemptive practices of justice. Such policies strive to reconcile the collective interests of perpetrators, victims, and bystanders alike in the processes of rehabilitating, reaffirming, and reconstructing the personal and social sense of well-being. These strategies of intervention are also aimed at strengthening community, and they are designed in the spirit of establishing community efficacy (Barak 2003).

REVIEW AND DISCUSSION QUESTIONS

1. What is meant by the term *genocide*, and how is it accomplished? Based on your answer, what are the important arguments for and against the position that "the majority population of the U.S. has committed genocide involving both Native Americans and African Americans"?
2. What is the difference between the "narrower" and "broader" approaches to victimology? Which approach does this book take, and why?
3. How is inequality linked to the overall level of victimization for class, race, and gender?
4. What are the other important conclusions you can draw about the patterns of victimization in relationship to class, race, and gender? Please answer in terms of official and unofficial data.
5. What are the barriers to women leaving an abusive situation? How many of these—and what other barriers can you think of—that apply to minority women, abused heterosexual men, and gays and lesbians abused by their partners?

8

Lawmaking and the Administration of Criminal Law

In 1964, a court sentenced William Rummel to three years in prison after being convicted of a felony for fraudulently using a credit card to obtain $80 worth of goods. Five years later, he passed a forged check in the amount of $28.36 and received four years. In 1973, Rummel was convicted of a third felony—obtaining $102.75 by false pretenses for accepting payment to fix an air conditioner that he never returned to repair. Rummel received a mandatory life sentence under Texas's recidivist statue. He challenged this sentence on the grounds that it violated the Eighth Amendment's prohibition of cruel and unusual punishment by being grossly disproportionate to the crime.

In Rummel v. Estelle *(1980) the Supreme Court affirmed Rummel's life sentence for the theft of less than $230 that never involved force or the threat of force. Justice Lewis Powell's dissent noted "it is difficult to imagine felonies that pose less danger to the peace and good order of a civilized society than the three crimes committed by the petitioner" (445 U.S. 263, 295). However, Justice William Rehnquist's majority opinion stated there was an "interest, expressed in all recidivist statues, in dealing in a harsher manner with those who by repeated criminal acts have shown that they are simply incapable of conforming to the norms of society as established by its criminal law" (445 U.S. 263). After "having twice imprisoned him for felonies, Texas was entitled to place upon Rummel the onus of one who is simply unable to bring his conduct within the norms prescribed by the criminal law" (445 U.S. 284).*

Now consider the case of General Electric, which is not considered a habitual criminal offender despite committing diverse crimes over many decades. In the 1950s, GE and several companies agreed in advance on the sealed bids they submitted for heavy electrical equipment. This price-fixing defeated the purpose of competitive bidding, costing taxpayers and consumers as much as a billion dollars.

GE was fined $437,000—a tax-deductible business expense—the equivalent of a person earning $175,000 a year getting a $3 ticket. Two executives spent only thirty days in jail, even though one defendant had commented that price-fixing "had become so common and gone for so many years that we lost sight of the fact that it was illegal" (in Hills 1987, 191).

In the 1970s, GE made illegal campaign contributions to Richard Nixon's presidential campaign. Widespread illegal discrimination against minorities and women at GE resulted in a $32 million settlement. Also during this time, three former GE nuclear engineers—including one who had worked for the company for twenty-three years and managed the nuclear complaint department—resigned to draw attention to serious design defects in the plans for the Mark III nuclear reactor because the standard practice was "sell first, test later" (Hills 1987, 170; Glazer and Glazer 1989).

In 1981, GE was convicted of paying a $1.25 million bribe to a Puerto Rican official to obtain a power plant contract. GE has pled guilty to felonies involving illegal procurement of highly classified defense documents, and in 1985, it pled guilty to 108 counts of felony fraud involving defense contracts related to the Minuteman missile. In spite of a new code of ethics, GE was convicted in three more criminal cases over the next few years, plus paying $3.5 million to settle cases involving retaliation against four whistle-blowers that helped reveal the defense fraud. (GE subsequently lobbied Congress to weaken the False Claims Act.) In 1988, the government returned another 317 indictments against GE for fraud in a $21 million computer contract.

In 1989, GE's stock brokerage firm paid a $275,000 civil fine for discriminating against low-income consumers, the largest fine ever under the Equal Credit Opportunity Act. A 1990 jury convicted GE of fraud for cheating on a $254 million contract for battlefield computers, and journalist William Greider reports that the $27.2 million fine included money to "settle government complaints that it had padded bids on two hundred other military and space contracts" (1996, 350; see also Clinard [1990]; Greider [1994]; Pasztor [1995]; Simon [1999]).

Because of tax changes that GE had lobbied for and the Reagan tax cuts generally, GE paid no taxes between 1981 and 1983 when net profits were $6.5 billion. In fact, in a classic example of corporate welfare, GE received a tax rebate of $283 million during a time of high national deficits even though the company eliminated 50,000 jobs in the United States by closing 73 plants and offices. Further, "Citizen GE," whose advertising slogan has been "brings good things to life," is one of the prime environmental polluters and is identified as responsible for contributing to the damage of fifty-two active Superfund sites in need of environmental cleanup in this country alone. In 1999, they agreed to a $250 million dollar settlement to clean up the Housatonic River in Massachusetts. GE is responsible "for one of America's largest Superfund sites, the Hudson River, where the company dumped more than a million pounds of toxic wastes including cancer-causing polychlorinated biphenyls over a period of decades, according to the EPA" (Center *for Public Integrity 2007). Instead of cleaning up their part of the 197-mile site, they mounted an eight-year challenge to the Superfund law that requires polluters to remedy toxic situations they created. (GE's corporate environmental counsel during part of this time, Ignacia Moreno, was appointed by President Obama to be Assistant Attorney General for the Environment and Natural Resources Division in the Department of Justice.)*

Even though felons usually lose political rights, GE donated almost $18 million to candidates in federal elections between 1989 and 2009 (Center for Responsive Politics 2009a), and they spent $191 million for lobbying between 1998 and 2009 (Center for Responsive Politics 2009b). In spite of having been convicted of defrauding every branch of the military multiple times, GE is frequently invited to testify before Congress. GE also has the ability to shape public opinion through its ownership of NBC Universal, which owns NBC television (and A&E, USA, and others), MSNBC, and the financial news outlet CNBC. Some call CNBC an "economic infomercial" because there's a rather obvious but little discussed conflict of interest between owning a financial news outlet, being one of the world's largest financial operations, and receiving government support during the economic crisis. GE created a number of finance arms to help people and companies buy its products, and those activities accounted for nearly half of their earnings in the last five years (Gerth and Dennis 2009). Most people know GE "for light bulbs and home appliances, but GE Capital is one of the world's largest and most diverse financial operations, lending money for commercial real estate, aircraft leasing, and credit cards for stores such as Wal-Mart. If GE Capital were classified as a banking company, it would be the nation's seventh largest" (Gerth and Dennis 2009). Although GE was not originally eligible for government support through programs enacted to help with the financial crisis, they engaged in lobbying and received $74 billion in loan guarantees that helped the company finance its operations at low cost (Gerth and Dennis 2009).

For 2008, GE was the sixth largest company on the Fortune 500 list. If the corporation's revenue were compared to the gross domestic product of countries, it would be in the fifty largest economies in the world. With this kind of political, economic, and social power, it is easy to understand why "three strikes and you're out" does not apply to the "big hitters" like GE.

The pattern outlined by these examples was reinforced in 2003, when the Supreme Court upheld a fifty-year sentence for two acts of shoplifting videos from K-Mart. Under California's "three strikes" law, Leandro Andrade's burglary convictions from the 1980s counted as the first two, and the prosecutor decided to charge the shoplifting incidents as strikes, which carry a mandatory twenty-five years each. The Supreme Court, citing Rummel v. Estelle, *held that the sentences were neither disproportionate nor unreasonable (Lockyer v. Andrade, 538 U.S. 63).*

At the same time, Enron's Chief Financial Officer Andrew Fastow negotiated a plea bargain for not more than ten years in prison and was subsequently sentenced to six years based on his cooperation with prosecutors. (He is eligible for "good time" reduction in sentencing and a year reduction for undergoing drug treatment for his dependence on antianxiety medicine, so Fastow could serve as little as four years.) Fastow had been instrumental in the fraud, which resulted in the largest bankruptcy in U.S. history at that time. He had worked the deals to launder loans through allegedly independent entities to make them appear as revenue for Enron, and he helped push the accountants to approve the deals and used the massive banking fees Enron paid to silence Wall Street analysts who asked questions about Enron's finances. Fastow was originally charged with about a hundred felony counts, including conspiracy, wire fraud, securities fraud, falsifying books, as well as obstruction of justice, money laundering, insider trading, and filing false income tax returns. And the sentence was negotiated in the environment where getting tough on corporate crime was seen as a high priority (Leighton and Reiman 2004).

❧

Contemporary legal scholar Donald Black states: "Law itself is social control, but many other kinds of social control also appear in social life, in families, friendships, neighborhoods, villages, tribes, occupations, organizations, and groups of all kinds" (1976, 6). However, law is a special form of social control because it represents "governmental social control" (Radcliffe-Brown 1965 [1933]) over the citizenry. The government has a monopoly on the "legitimate" use of coercion—detention, arrest, incarceration, and execution—and the law serves to identify the acts (crimes) and actors (criminals) that power is to be used against. Robin Miller and Sandra Lee Browning capture this sentiment in their introduction to *For the Common Good*:

> Law is a structural force that, at least theoretically, reaches everyone. It can be powerful in its scope, its frequency, and its intensity. . . . And a law that is not commonly accepted by the people still has the power to shape behavior through sheer force of the punishments handed down for violations of it (2004, 6).

The criminal law thus represents the first stage at sorting though annoying, troublesome, harmful, and deviant behavior to see what acts should be crimes and subjected to formal social control. The criminal law, by what it includes as well as the seriousness of the punishment, signals to the police how to prioritize their efforts. It does the same for prosecutors. Sentencing guidelines, while advisory, shape the behavior of judges by indicating which defendants should be sent to prison (and for how long) and which can be subject to execution.

The criminal law not only shapes the priorities of those in the criminal justice system but it also plays an important role in shaping people's attitudes about what is dangerous and harmful behavior. In this sense, the criminal law not only reflects consensus that rape, robbery, and street crime are serious harm but it also helps create consensus that these are the worst harms and many white-collar and corporate behaviors are not really crimes. This effect is magnified through the media, which uses the criminal law as the basis for reporting on crime, including story frames about the "crime problem" and "crime waves."

For example, Rummel was convicted of three property crimes and received a life sentence, while Andrade was convicted for four property crimes over the course of decades and received a mandatory fifty years. But the criminal law seemingly has no provisions to penalize those who cause a global financial crisis that wipes out trillions of dollars in wealth. The reporting of the crisis, even on those who profited handsomely from billions of dollars in bonuses paid for from a taxpayer funded bailout, was not from the framework of crime. In general, the corporate-owned media did little to expose massive problems before the economic collapse, and they have tended to expose a few "bad apples" rather than systemic problems that require a systemic overhaul to protect people from future property losses caused by behavior of the powerful.

This chapter examines the ways in which law, lawmaking, and the administration of justice in particular are subjected to and shaped by class, race, and gender. The foundation of this chapter is that criminal law is not a "natural" or "objective" reflection of harm, but it is the result of a political process where money and privilege matter. While some laws reflect widespread consensus of what conduct should be prohibited, other laws reflect the interests of powerful groups with special access to and influence over lawmakers. In pursuing this topic, the current chapter elaborates on many ideas introduced in chapter 1, such as the importance of examining the types of harms written into the criminal law.

The next section of this chapter provides many examples of how class—and thus wealth and ownership of the economic power—shape the law. At times, this influence means harms done by the rich and powerful are not part of the criminal law, or they receive sentences that are much less harsh than comparable street crimes. At other times, laws have been passed to help big business avoid paying taxes on their profits and to enable corporate fraud.

Comparatively, class presents striking examples of bias in the law because most of the obvious racial examples, like Jim Crow, have slowly been erased from the books and laws now look facially neutral (there are no acts on the books where the wording of the text indicates it only applies to blacks or minorities). So, the section on race in this chapter reviews some of the history of race-based law and then turns to an examination of race and differential treatment in the administration of justice. Although traffic laws are facially neutral, they are applied differentially and create the problems of Driving While Black (DWB) that we will discuss. This section on race also builds on the earlier discussion of classical criminology and provides a foundation that will be explored further in the chapters on law enforcement, criminal adjudication, punishment, sentencing, and imprisonment.

This chapter's section on gender examines the many ways of trying to make sense of equality, given that men and women have important differences (including, but not limited to, reproductive functions). Feminist analyses differ on where they locate the sources of inequality and what they see as the goal of change; they question whether women should direct themselves to equality with men based on a male standard within the current economic system. While feminism does make gender inequality a primary question, the diversity of analysis and goals suggest the discussion should be about *feminisms* rather than a singular feminism. Such an understanding is important for subsequent chapters that will be discussing gender inequality in relation to specific practices and policies of criminal justice administration.

CLASS, CRIME, AND THE LAW

The rich and powerful use their influence to keep acts from becoming crimes, even though these acts may be more socially injurious than those labeled criminal. The concept *analogous social injury* "includes harm caused by acts or conditions that are legal but produce consequences similar to those produced by illegal acts" (Lanier and Henry 2004, 19). Much of the harmful and illegitimate behavior of the elite members of society has not traditionally been defined as criminal, but nearly all the harmful and deviant behavior perpetrated by the poor and the powerless, the working and middle classes, is defined as violating the criminal law. Thus, basing crime control theory and practice on a neutral criminal law (as discussed in chapter 1) ignores the fact that the legal order and the administration of justice reflect a structural class bias that concentrates the coercive power of the state on the behaviors of the relatively poor and powerless members of society. These omitted relations of class justice reveal the importance of two systemic operations in the administration of criminal justice: "selective enforcement" and "differential application" of the law. Selective enforcement of harms by the law refers to the fact that most harms perpetrated by the affluent are "beyond incrimination" (Kennedy 1970) and not part of the criminal law. When harms committed by the politically and economically powerful are part of the criminal law, differential application means that the police, prosecutors, and other agents of the criminal justice system use their discretion to ignore or minimize the consequences.

Criminologist Stephen Box suggests that one of the most important advantages of "corporate criminals" lies "in their ability to prevent their actions from becoming subject to criminal sanctions in the first place" (in Braithwaite 1992, 89). Although certain behaviors may cause widespread harm, the criminal law does not forbid abuses of power in the realm of economic domination, governmental control, and denial of human rights (Simon 1999). As we saw in the opening narrative of this chapter, being a habitual offender is against the law in most areas, where "three strikes and you're out" applies to street criminals. But habitual offender laws do not apply to corporate persons (like GE) that can repeatedly commit serious crimes without being subjected to these statutes or to the legal possibility of a state revoking a corporation's charter to exist (Hartmann 2002).

In some cases, harmful actions will be civil offenses rather than criminal ones, but the difference is significant because civil actions are not punishable by prison and do not carry the same harsh stigma. A plea to civil or administrative charges does not amount to an admission of guilt and thus cannot be used against a business in other related litigation. Other destructive behavior may not be prohibited by civil law or regulations created by administrative agencies. In this respect, the tobacco industry produces a product that kills about 450,000 people a year, but its actions are not illegal and are not a substantial part of the media campaign of the Office for National Drug Control Policy or Partnership for a Drug Free America.

The Rich Get Richer and the Poor Get Prison suggests that the result of these relations is that law is like a carnival mirror. It distorts our understanding of the harms that may befall us by magnifying the threat from street crime because it criminalizes more of the conduct of poor people. At the same time, it distorts our perception about the danger from crime in the suites by downplaying and not protecting people from the harms perpetrated by those above them in the class system. As a consequence, both the criminal law and the administration of justice do "not simply *reflect* the reality of crime; [they have] a hand in *creating* the reality we see" (Reiman and Leighton 2010, 64, emphasis is original). Thus, to say that the criminal law appropriately focuses on the most dangerous acts is a problematic statement because the criminal law shapes our perceptions about what is a dangerous act.

Reiman and Leighton also argue that the processing of offenders serves to "weed out the wealthy." Selective enforcement means that many harmful acts will not come within the realm of criminal law, "or, if technically criminal, not prosecuted, or, if prosecuted, not punished, or if punished, only mildly" (2010a, 64). This observation is consistent with the analysis in Donald Black's highly acclaimed book, *The Behavior of Law* (1976). Black sought to discover a series of rules to describe the amount of law and its behavior in response to social variables such as stratification, impersonality, culture, social organization, and other forms of social control. When it comes to issues of class, the variables of stratification and social organization are the two most relevant. Black proposed that the law varies directly with hierarchy and privilege, so that the more inequality in a country, the more law. He also applied his proposition to disputes between two parties of unequal status and wealth. Based on a wide variety of cases, Black concluded there is likely to be "more law" in a downward direction, such as when a rich person is victimized by a poorer one. This means the use of criminal rather than civil law, for example, and a greater likelihood of a report, an investigation, arrest, prosecution, and prison sentence. In contrast, when the wealthier harms the poorer, Black predicted there would be less law—meaning civil law, monetary fines rather than jail, and therapeutic sanctions rather than punitive ones. Further, Black argued that there is likely to be "more law" in the downward direction when an individual victimizes a group high in social organization, such as a corporation or the state. Conversely, "less law" and a pattern of differential application are likely to be the result of a corporate body or the state victimizing individuals or groups of individuals that have lower levels of social organization, such as poor communities.

When corporations are charged, they can use their resources to evade responsibility. Criminologist James Coleman (1985) did an extensive study of the enforcement of the Sherman Antitrust Act in the petroleum industry and identified four major strategies that corporations employ to prevent full application of the law. First is endurance and delay, which includes using expensive legal resources to prolong the litigation and obstruct the discovery of information by raising as many motions and legal technicalities as possible. Second is the use of corporate wealth and political connections to undermine the will of legislators and regulators to enforce the law's provisions. Third is secrecy and deception about ownership and control to prevent detection of violations and make them more difficult to prove. Fourth are threats of economic consequences to communities and the economy if regulations are passed and/or fully enforced.

Corporations and those with economic power are also able to use mass-mediated communication to shape the public discourse and moral outrage about "crime" (Barak 1994). In short, the corporate elite's relative monopoly over the "free" airways allows them to act as "transmission belts" for creating consensus over what is and is not a crime. For example, Reiman and Leighton (2010a) note that multiple deaths that result from unsafe workplaces tend to get reported as "accidents" and "disasters," while "mass murder" is reserved exclusively for street crime. While there are differences between the two, it is not clear that one should be a regulatory violation and the other should be a crime—especially since the criminal law recognizes harms done knowingly, recklessly, and negligently.

In spite of the influence of the criminal law and media in shaping beliefs about harm, the American public occasionally regards white-collar crimes as at least as serious as street crime and that corporate criminals are treated too leniently for the harms they do to workers, consumers, and the environment (Grabosky, Braithwaite, and Wilson 1987; see also Lanier and Henry [2004]). For example, respondents in polls have supported stiffer sentences than had been handed down under the Food, Drug, and Cosmetic Act. People in other surveys favor incarceration for false advertising, unsafe workplace, antitrust offenses, and the failure by landlords to make repairs, resulting in the death of a tenant. The offense of "knowingly manufacturing and selling contaminated food that results in death" was ranked in seriousness behind assassination of a public official and killing a police officer during the terrorist hijacking of a plane; the selling of contaminated food was considered more serious than "killing someone during a serious argument" and the "forcible rape of a stranger in a park" (Grabosky et al. 1987, 34–35). Even though people do see some corporate crimes as being as serious as street crime and as deserving of punishment, these sentiments are not reflected in the mass media or criminal law because such rules would adversely affect the interests of the rich and powerful who have better access to lawmakers.

The remainder of this section discusses various harms committed by the poor and the powerful to illustrate the class bias in the criminal law and administration of justice. The starting point is injuries and violations of bodily integrity, some of which are analogous to violent street crime. Later in the section, we review fraud, the economic crisis, and acts analogous to theft because they involve an illegitimate appropriation of resources.

Not all injuries committed by corporations are analogous to violent crime, but consider that as far as the criminal justice system was concerned, there was no crime committed in the 2005 deaths of twelve miners in West Virginia, even though:

> Time and again over the past four years, federal mining inspectors documented the same litany of problems at central West Virginia's Sago Mine: mine roofs that tended to collapse without warning. Faulty or inadequate tunnel supports. A dangerous buildup of flammable coal dust (Warrick 2006, A04).

In the two years before this explosion, the mine was cited 273 times for safety violations, one-third of which were classified as "significant and substantial," and "16 violations logged in the past eight months were listed as 'unwarrantable failures,' a designation reserved for serious safety infractions for which the operator had either already been warned, or which showed 'indifference or extreme lack of care'" (Warrick 2006, A04). This state of affairs seems to fit within the criminal law categories of knowing, reckless, or negligent, but most matters like this stay within the realm of administrative sanctions and the civil law. Despite the obvious importance of human decisions, events like this tend to be reported as "disasters" or "accidents."

Outside of mining, the situation is the same. From 1982 to 2002, the Occupational Safety and Health Administration (OSHA), which has primary responsibility for the nation's workplace safety, identified 1,242 deaths it concluded were related to "willful" safety violations. But only 7 percent of cases were referred for prosecution, and "having avoided prosecution once, at least 70 employers willfully violated safety laws again, resulting in scores of additional deaths. Even these repeat violators were rarely prosecuted" (Barstow 2003). One of the many barriers is that causing the death of a worker by willfully violating safety laws is a misdemeanor, with a maximum sentence of six months in jail, so such cases are of little interest to prosecutors. This level of punishment was established by Congress back in 1970, which has repeatedly rejected attempts to make it tougher, so currently harassing a wild burro on federal lands carries twice the maximum sentence of causing a worker's death through willful safety violations (Barstow 2003). Compare the lack of change in the punishment for a worker's death with the escalating toughness for all types of street crime, where Congress continued to be "tough on crime" even during the height of the war on crime and enacted three-strike laws, expansion of the number of strikeable offenses, increased the number of criminal acts covered by a mandatory minimum sentence, increased the mandatory minimum sentences, and made more offenses eligible for the death penalty. During the same period and into the present, Congress has voted down all laws to increase penalties for workplace deaths that result from willful behavior, even modest proposals to increase the maximum penalty to ten years (Barstow 2003).

Also, on twelve occasions the Peanut Corporation of America knowingly shipped out peanut products contaminated with salmonella, which killed at least 8 people and sickened 500 more (Layton 2009). But a year later, no criminal charges have been filed either under criminal laws for adulterated foods or homicide laws. The news media and others did not report or treat this incident as "crime," let alone mass murder. Media did provide information about the thousands of recalled peanut products, but the amount and intensity of coverage was different than if, say, a street gang rather than a corporate gang had killed eight people and hurt hundreds of others. Few noted that the Food and Drug Administration has no power to require a recall of contaminated foods but must negotiate with the corporation for a voluntary recall of food that laboratory tests show to be infested with *E. coli* or salmonella. People would find it intolerable if police had documented evidence of drugs but could not seize them and had to negotiate with the drug manufacturers to destroy the drug, but efforts to give the FDA the power to order recalls of contaminated foods have repeatedly been defeated by corporate interests.

The analysis provided here also applies to financial crimes, including several episodes of massive and widespread fraud. For example, Representative Frank Annunzio, who was chairman of the House subcommittee on financial institutions that investigated the prosecution of criminals involved in the savings and loan (S&L) wrongdoings of the late 1980s, makes the same points in his opening remarks to one congressional hearing:

> Frankly, I don't think the administration has the interest in pursuing Gucci-clad white-collar criminals. These are hard and complicated cases, and the defendants often were rich, successful prominent members of their upper-class communities. It is far easier putting away a sneaker-clad high school dropout who tried to rob a bank of a thousand dollars with a stick-up note, than a smooth talking S & L executive who steals a million dollars with a fraudulent note (Hearings 1990, 1).

These comments highlight how hard it is to prosecute upper-class criminals, even though the harm done is much greater than street crime, and how reluctant the system is to prosecute them. Some S&L executives personally stole tens of millions of dollars, and others were responsible for the collapse of financial institutions that needed government bailouts to the tune of $1 billion (Binstein and Bowden 1993; Calavita, Pontell, and Tillman 1997; Pizzo, Fricker, and Muolo 1991). The total cost of the S&L bailout ultimately climbed to about $500 billion (Day 1993), yet few S&L crooks went to prison (Pizzo and Muolo 1993), and the ones who had received a prison sentence received an average of two years compared with an average of nine years for a bank robber (Hearings 1990).

After such expensive and widespread fraud, Congress briefly decided to "get tough," but soon removed all the regulations put in place to safeguard against similar fraud taking place. These actions set the stage for the 2002 financial scandals involving Enron, WorldCom, Global Crossing, Tyco, and others. The *New York Times* captured the subsequent situation with the headline: "Now Who, Exactly Got Us Into This? Enron? Arthur Andersen? Shocking Say Those Who Helped It Along" (Labaton 2002, C01; see also Leighton and Reiman [2004]). With respect to the economic meltdown and recession/depression of 2008–2010, the same types of questions are once again being raised and the same types of financial offenders appear to be avoiding responsibility, let alone criminal culpability. They also were able to keep their million-dollar corporate bonuses for helping to run the U.S. and global economies into the ground, necessitating trillion dollar bailouts that dwarf the bailouts associated with the earlier savings and loan scandals from twenty years ago. While some of the bailout money has been repaid, other loans and investments will result in losses, and the government has had to spend large sums for economic stimulus, meaning taxpayers have had to pay a substantial "Wall Street incompetence tax" (Ritholtz 2008a). Barry Ritholtz, CEO of a financial research firm and author of *Bailout Nation* (2009a), stated that a consistent element of the problem has been "an abdication of responsibility from the various entities assigned to supervise and regulate" our financial system (2008b). He suggests that we would not allow the Super Bowl to be played without referees because "we *know* that players would give in to their worst impulses" (2008c, emphasis original) and the financial system is the same. In an article explaining the crisis, Ritholtz (2008d, 100) writes in the form of a memo from Wall Street to the government, admitting that Wall Street has some responsibility for the massive losses of money and damage to the economy:

> We on Wall Street . . . used excessive leverage, failed to maintain adequate capital, engaged in reckless speculation, created new complex derivatives. We focused on short-term profits at the expense of sustainability. We not only undermined our own firms, we destabilized the financial sector and roiled the global economy, to boot. And we got huge bonuses.

But, he continues in "A Memo Found in the Street: Uncle Sam the Enabler": "D.C.: We could not have done it without you. We may be drunks, but you were our enablers: Your legislative, executive, and administrative decisions made possible all that we did. Our recklessness would not have reached its soaring heights but for your governmental incompetence."

At the root of the financial crisis are complex securities based on mortgages that may never be repaid because lax underwriting standards encouraged lenders to give mortgages to borrowers without resources to repay them (unless housing prices continued to increase indefinitely). The Federal Reserve had power to regulate mortgage underwriters but failed to do so. At any point in time, they could have imposed tighter lending standards or prohibited mortgages where borrowers did not have to verify income or assets (a "NINA" or "liar's loan"). Mortgages were in great demand by investment banks that made large profits pooling and reselling as mortgage-backed securities. Mortgage underwriters were paid if the borrower made the required payment for the first several months, so they invented numerous mortgages that had low interest rates and payments for the first year or so then reset to higher rates that the borrowers could not afford.

In spite of underwriters giving hundreds of thousands of dollars to people so poor "they did not have a pot to piss in" (*This American Life* 2008), credit ratings agencies like Standard & Poor's and Moody's gave them high credit ratings, which encouraged investors all over the world to buy them. The credit agencies have minimal oversight and regulation, and lawmakers were not concerned about the obvious conflict of interest inherent in the business model of being paid by the investment bank to rate their product. Ratings agencies that gave out anything less than the best credit ratings were not used by the investment bank for rating other mortgage-backed securities.

To make matters worse, the Securities and Exchange Commission (SEC) waived its leverage rules for five big Wall Street firms. "Leverage" is essentially how much a firm can borrow for the amount of assets it has. Before 2004, the permitted debt-to-capital ratio was 12 to 1, but after lobbying by investment banks, the SEC allowed these firms to use whatever leverage they wanted. Firms increased their leverage to 30 to 1 and even 40 to 1, essentially borrowing $30 and even $40 for each dollar of assets (Ritholtz 2008d, 101). Many invested this borrowed money into problematic mortgage-backed securities. Further, many companies were involved in buying or selling "credit default swaps," which can be thought of as insurance against a company's inability to pay its debt. But unlike insurance, no federal or state agencies regulate the trillions of dollars of swaps, and there is no centralized clearinghouse to keep track of what parties have sold, how much protection, and whether they would be able to pay if the situation required it. Thus, as Wall Street firms started to run into financial trouble, no one knew who might run into problems due to their exposure to credit default swaps. The lack of transparency caused a lack of trust that froze up the credit system because no one wanted to lend money in case the borrower turned out to be in deep financial trouble.

When the economic crisis hit, taxpayer bailouts became one of the main policy tools, "with approximately $12 trillion dollars to date deployed to support or rescue private companies in total" (Jordan 2009). But private investors in troubled companies received substantially better deals than the government did. Also, neither the government nor shareholders have pushed for organizational change in the companies receiving bailout money. Emma Jordan, a law professor who studies corporate governance, noted that the prospects for reform to create a "robust prudently guided financial sector have been substantially clouded by the fact that both the corporate governance structure and the executive leadership of the financial sector remain largely unchanged—92 percent of the management and directors of the top 17 recipients of TARP funds are still in office" (Jordon 2009). Worse still, the financial institutions that previously posed "systemic risk" because they were "too big to fail" are now even larger because of government policy to provide financial support for combining weaker institutions with stronger ones. Critics charge that financial reform legislation is riddled with loopholes and exceptions from lobbying efforts.

In summary, the massive systemic fraud with the S&Ls is followed by massive systemic fraud of Enron, WorldCom, etc., which is followed by massive systemic financial shenanigans that lead to a global economic crisis. Most of the people who caused this are not only still in place at their jobs but also received bonuses, and the companies that required bailing out because they were too big to fail are now even bigger. Serious financial reform is being undercut by the financial institutions receiving taxpayer bailouts. The stage is being set for bigger problems and a more expensive taxpayer bailout. To understand this frustrating situation, consider that banks and securities firms spent $193 million to fund political campaigns for the 2008 elections—and they raised additional money through trade groups (Ritholtz 2009c). The more general problem is with corporate power, discussed in chapter 3. Comparing the revenues of corporations with the Gross Domestic Product (the total value of all goods and services produced by a nation) reveals the relative size and power of corporations. As table 8.1 demonstrates, seven financial institutions involved in the financial crisis are among the top 100 largest economies in the world. Overall for 2008, thirty-seven of the top one hundred economies are corporations; the two biggest corporations—Wal-Mart and Exxon Mobil—are about the same size as Iran, the twenty-sixth largest country. As Braithwaite notes, "power corrupts and unaccountable power corrupts with impunity" (1992, 89).

Finally, because the government (the state) makes the laws, many of its own abuses of power are not considered to be crime. Government-

Table 8.1.   The Largest Economies in the World: Gross Domestic Product of Countries Versus Revenues of Corporations, 2008

Overall Rank	Company Rank	Company/Country
58	8	Citigroup
59		Hungary
60		Kazakhstan
61		New Zealand
62		Peru
63	9	Bank of America
66	12	JPMorgan Chase
67		Kuwait
68	13	AIG
76		Vietnam
77	19	Cardinal Health
78	20	Goldman Sachs Group
79	21	Morgan Stanley
80		Morocco
92	30	Merrill Lynch
98		Belarus
100	37	Lehman Brothers

Source: World Bank, Gross Domestic Product 2008, and *Fortune*, Fortune 500 for 2008, http://siteresources.worldbank.org/DATASTATISTICS/Resources/GDP.pdf,   http://money.cnn.com/magazines/fortune/fortune500/2008/full_list/.

sponsored genocide of Native Americans in order to secure their land and its mineral wealth violated basic human rights and treaties, but these acts were never subject to criminal law, nor were the victims ever counted in terms of the numbers of people murdered in this nation (Barak 1998). Following 9/11, Congress passed the PATRIOT Act as part of the effort to fight the "war on terrorism" and removed some of the legal rights that had protected U.S. citizens from invasion of privacy by government agents—some laws requiring search warrants, for example.

One of the classic statements on this topic, first referred to by President Dwight Eisenhower as the "military-industrial complex," is a book by C. Wright Mills called *The Power Elite* (1956). He contended that an elite composed of the largest corporations, the military, and the federal government dominates life in the United States. Mills argued that these three spheres of power are highly interrelated, with members of each group coming from similar upper-class social backgrounds, attending the same private and Ivy League universities, even belonging to the same social or political organizations. In addition to their mutual "ruling class interests," corporate elites also make large political donations to both the Republicans and Democrats to ensure their access to the law-making process.

RACE, CRIME, AND THE LAW

The classic analysis of "punishment and social structure" by Georg Rusche and Otto Kirchheimer (1968 [1939]) revealed the relationship between the type and form of punishment in society and the changes in the political economy. Important aspects of the analysis are the notion of surplus labor and the costs of production. While the idea of surplus labor can be used in a class-based analysis, frequently minorities are the labor pool that is regulated through punishment. One striking example is the rise of black imprisonment following the Civil War—and which some would argue apply to the rise of black imprisonment rates today through the developments in a changing industrial-service and global economy (see chapter 4).

The Civil War abolished involuntary servitude and freed the slaves, although "the transition from bondage to freedom was more theoretical than real" (Gorman 1997, 447). Millions of blacks were "suddenly transformed from personal property to potential competitors" (Tolnay and Beck 1995, 57). Southern whites in particular had to compete with blacks for jobs, and plantation owners would now have to compete with one another for good help with higher wages. In addition, many whites feared "domination" by the newly freed blacks that outnumbered the whites, and they feared black men in regard to white women, especially since many young white men were killed or wounded in the war. Some whites, on the other hand, "believed that blacks would perish in freedom, like fish on the land. The Negro's 'incompetence,' after all, has been essential to the understanding—and defense—of slavery itself" (Oshinsky 1996, 19). One southerner summed up the situation:

> I think God intended the niggers to be slaves. Now since man has deranged God's plan, I think the best we can do is keep 'em as near to a state of bondage as possible. My theory is, feed 'em well, clothe 'em well, and then, if they don't work whip 'em well (in Oshinsky 1996, 11).

In the latter part of the nineteenth century, actual imprisonment was not much of an option as there were few prisons, and the Civil War had destroyed many buildings in the South. The solution lay in leasing inmates out to the plantations from which they had just been freed. After all, the economic base of the South was the same, involving labor-intensive crops like tobacco and cotton. Leasing the former slaves out to plantation owners meant the owners had cheap labor, the blacks were back under control, and—as a bonus—agents of the criminal justice system took a share of money involved in the leases. Blacks were the ultimate losers of the new system of criminal laws and the administration of justice, and many were returned to the plantation so quickly they hardly noticed emancipation. The threat of plantation prisons kept many other blacks in servitude under labor contracts that re-created the conditions of slavery: "The horror of the ball and chain is ever before [blacks], and their future is bright with no hope" (in Gorman 1997, 71).

Worse still, under the lease system, owners no longer had the same economic interest in blacks as property, which removed some restraints against brutality. If a slave died, the owner had to buy another, but leased blacks that died were easily and cheaply replaced. One employer of leased convicts noted in 1883 that with "these convicts we don't own 'em. One dies, get another" (in Robert Johnson 2002, 43). The situation is summarized by the title of Oshinsky's book, *Worse Than Slavery*, and he notes that in Mississippi in the 1880s not one leased convict lived long enough to serve a sentence of ten years or more (1996, 46). However, because of the social control, cheap labor, and fees generated by the leases, the system expanded. Blacks were put to work not just on plantations but in a variety of grueling and dangerous jobs that included mining, building roads, clearing swamps, and making turpentine.

The nominal basis for arrests was laws based on slave codes: "The slave codes of the antebellum period were the basis of the black codes of 1865–1866 and later were resurrected as the segregation statutes of the period after 1877" (in Gorman 1997, 447). When able-bodied black men had not actually done anything wrong, the police would falsely charge them with crimes. When the men could not pay off the court fees, they were forced to go to work to "pay back their debts." These bogus arrests were sometimes orchestrated by "employers working hand-in-glove with local officials to keep their [work] camps well stocked with able-bodied blacks" (Oshinsky 1996, 71).

The picture that emerges is of black convicts as slaves and the state functioning as slave master (Gorman 1997). Understanding black "criminality" at this juncture involves the perspective Darnell Hawkins (1995, 34) described in which arrest is "less a product of their conduct than their social standing" (similar to the contemporary Driving While Black issues discussed in chapter 9). The folk song, "Standin' On De Corner" captures this dynamic:

> Standin' on the corner, weren't doin' no hahm,
> Up Come a 'liceman an' he gab me by d'ahm.
> Blow a little whistle an' ring a little bell;
> Heah come 'rol wagon a-runnin' like hell.
> Judge he call me up an' ast mah name
> Ah tol' him fo' sho' Ah weren't to blame.
> He wink at 'liceman, 'liceman wink too;
> Judge he say, "Nigger, you got some work to do."
> Workin' on ol' road bank, shackle boun'.
> Long, long time fo' six months roll aroun'.
> Miserin' fo my honey, she miserin' fo me,
> But, Lawd, white folks won't let go holdin me
> (in Franklin 1989, 104–5).

Variations on this pattern occur for other minorities at different points in history. For example, after the transcontinental railroad was completed, Asian (Chinese mostly) labor was no longer needed. To control this surplus population, the United States passed new criminal laws that selectively prohibited "Orientals" from possessing drugs (e.g., the Chinese Exclusionary Act of 1882 outlawed opium use among Chinese but not whites) or differentially applied existing drug laws against them. At the same time, both moral panics and the criminalization of minorities could occur for reasons other than political economy; bigotry and racism on their own were enough.

For example, the use of racism and drug laws to further the social control of minorities is revealed in a 1910 report that detailed "the supposed superhuman strength and extreme madness experienced by Blacks on cocaine, and explained that cocaine drove Black men to rape" (Lusane 1991, 33). Rumors circulated that cocaine made blacks bulletproof. In fact, an article in the *New York Times* ("Negro Cocaine 'Fiends' Are a New Southern Menace") reported that southern police were switching to larger caliber weapons to protect themselves from drug-empowered blacks (Lusane 1991, 34). Just to be sure, Georgia kept its pre–Civil War statutes where black men faced capital punishment when convicted of the rape or attempted rape of a white woman (however, for white men convicted of raping black women, the penalty was a fine, prison, or both [Scully 1990]).

For much of the nation's history, laws like the one at issue in *Plessy v. Ferguson* explicitly required differential treatment for minorities in the form of "separate but equal." Of course separate facilities were never equal to what whites had, and the recognition of this inequality lead the Supreme Court to strike down segregated systems. For example, separate law and medical schools for blacks were never equal to white institutions, so the Court struck down these arrangements and forced integration in a series of cases that would culminate in the famous *Brown v. Board of Education* case. In *Brown*, the Court finally recognized not just that separate was unequal, but contrary to the majority holding in *Plessy* (see opening of chapter 4), separation stamps a badge of inferiority on those segregated.

After *Brown* and the 1960s civil rights legislation, these laws had made racial classifications largely disappear. However, "facially neutral" statutes can still have a disproportionate impact on minorities, and that is the current problem. Such laws may or may not be racist in their intent, but they are in their effects and impact. Traffic laws are racially neutral, but one important controversy is about DWB and the large number of black men who are pulled over. The other significant example is the federal sentencing guidelines that have penalized the possession of crack cocaine more heavily than powdered cocaine in a 100 to 1 ratio. Originally, federal law required a mandatory five-year sentence for possession of 500 grams (about a pound) of powder cocaine or five grams (about one-sixth of an ounce) of crack cocaine. The sentence for first-time crack offenders (without possession of a weapon or other aggravating factors) is longer than the sentence for kidnapping, and only slightly shorter than the sentence for attempted murder. About 85 percent of those sent to prison under the crack provisions of the original and amended laws have been black (Bureau of Justice Statistics 2001, 11), so this sentencing pattern contributes directly to problems of disproportionate minority confinement.

Whatever the intent of lawmakers, if arrests had been proportionate to use, then the ratio of black to white arrest and incarceration rates would have been very different, suggesting that there is an additional differential application of this allegedly neutral law. Indeed, as the former drug czar William Bennett acknowledged during his reign, the typical crack smoker is a white suburbanite despite the urban stereotypes of crack houses filled with blacks (Lusane 1991). As the U.S. Department on Health and Human Services reported, 4.5 percent of whites, but only 0.6 percent of blacks, aged eighteen to twenty-five had done crack cocaine during their lifetime; 1.1

percent of whites and 0.3 percent of blacks had done it in the previous year according to the 2004 survey (SAMHSA 2004, table 1.45B).

In many ways, establishing actual racial intent is beside the point and should not be necessary for remedial action. In the areas of employment and housing discrimination, for example, evidence of patterns of discrimination or disparate impact is sufficient. Further, Congress knew the impact of this law from protests, reports, and recommendations from the U.S. Sentencing Guidelines Commission itself to end the disparate penalties. In 1995, 1997, and 2002, the U.S. Sentencing Commission recommended ending the 100 to 1 disparity between powder and crack penalties, and, in an unusual display of bipartisanship, Congress rejected their recommendation and kept the 100 to 1 disparities (Smothers 1995; Hinojosa 2008). In 2007, the Chair of the Sentencing Commission stated: "The Commission believes that there is no justification for the current statutory penalty scheme for powder and crack cocaine offenses," and it "remains committed" to its 2002 recommendation that any ratio "be no more than 20 to 1." Congress has not acted to remedy the situation and racial disparities, but the Sentencing Commission used the authority it had to revise the drug sentencing guidelines, which were higher than the mandatory minimums set by Congress (Hinojosa 2008). So, the guidelines are closer to the (still problematic) mandatory minimum sentences, but there is still disparity between coke and crack, which will continue to fuel the problem of disproportionate minority confinement because of differential application of the law. As a candidate, Barack Obama (2007) said "let's not make the punishment for crack cocaine that much more severe than the punishment for powder cocaine when the real difference between the two is the skin color of the people using them."

There was an obvious degree of complacency on the part of legislators with disproportionate minority imprisonment that fuels a debate over whether legislators are racist. Rather than trying to debate their character, we believe it is important to understand the moral status of such complacency by applying the distinction between direct and oblique intention that moral philosopher R. M. Hare (1990, 186) has articulated:

> To intend some consequence directly one has to desire it. To intend it obliquely one has only to foresee it. . . . We have the duty to avoid bringing about consequences that we ought not bring about, even if we do not desire those consequences in themselves, provided only that we know they will be consequences. I am to blame if I knowingly bring about someone's death in the course of some plan of mine, even if I do not desire his death in itself— that is, even if I intend the death only obliquely and indirectly . . . this is very relevant to the decisions of legislators (many of whose intentions are oblique), in that they have a duty to consider consequences of their legislation that they can foresee, and not merely those that they desire.

While Hare highlights the moral responsibilities of legislators for the foreseeable results of laws, the larger point for purposes of this book is that disparities can arise from facially neutral legislation because of the administration of justice. This includes the police, courts, and especially sentencing. Laws are written in categorical language that call for arrest and processing of persons engaged in legally prohibited acts, but police officers and other agents of crime control do not apply these laws uniformly. Rather, when deciding whether or not to give a traffic violator, for instance, a warning, a ticket, or an intensive search, law enforcement will exercise a certain amount of discretion. The question becomes to what extent is discretion exercised as a reflection of institutionalized (rather than individualized) racial bias against nonwhites, over and above any bias created by enforcing laws that have a disproportionate impact on minorities.

After reviewing an extensive number of studies some two decades ago, the *Harvard Law Review* (1988, 1496) stated: "The argument that police behavior is undistorted by racial discrimination flatly contradicts most studies, which reveal what many police officers freely admit: that police use race as an independently significant, if not determinative, factor in deciding whom to follow, detain, search, or arrest." Because most people then and now violate the law at some points during their lives, this heightened scrutiny continues to result in higher levels of arrests, and creates a picture of the "typical criminal" as being young, black, and inner-city (Reiman and Leighton 2010a). The racially based profile of the typical criminal is then used to justify the belief that "race itself provides a legitimate basis on which to base a categorically higher level of suspicion" (*Harvard Law Review* 1988, 1496). In turn, the cycle becomes a self-fulfilling prophecy as the criminal justice system often operates on stereotypes and profiles that define some groups "as having a propensity to be morally depraved, thus endorsing a view of those who share in that culture as unworthy of equal respect" (*Harvard Law Review* 1988, 1514).

The excessive identification of minorities with crime is not only a problem of local law enforcement agencies or of state legislatures; it also extends to the elite federal agencies as well. For example, the National Narcotics Intelligence Consumers Commission (NNICC) has consisted of representatives of the Central Intelligence Agency, the U.S. Coast Guard, U.S. Customs Service, Department of Defense, Drug Enforcement Administration, Federal Bureau of Investigation, Immigration and Naturalization Service, Internal Revenue Service, National Institute on Drug Abuse, Department of State, and Department of Treasury. Their report on the supply of illicit drugs to the United States mentions Colombian drug mafias, Mexicans, African American street gangs, Dominicans, Cubans, Haitians, Jamaicans, and Puerto Rican criminal groups, Chinese, Nigerian, and West African groups, Middle Eastern traffickers, Lebanese, Israelis, Pakistanis,

Turks, Afghans, Burmese, Thai, Laotian, Cambodian, Russian, Filipino, Taiwanese, and Korean.

There are also a few references to domestic production, but only one specific reference to whites, the market for LSD being white college students. Although whites own airplanes and boats, they seem to be one of the few groups in the world not involved in drug smuggling according to the NNICC. Given low levels of minority wealth and ownership of the economy, one would expect that whites might make an appearance as money launderers, but the report mentions only casinos and notes that Native Americans operate them in almost every state. Money laundering also involves Pakistanis and Southwest Asia's underground banking system as well as Russians in the United States, according to the report. Technology generally, but apparently not whites specifically, also appear to facilitate the laundering of drug money. From reading the report, it appears that laundering does not occur in white-controlled banking and financial institutions, like those in the Caymans and other tax-haven locales.

GENDER, CRIME, AND THE LAW

One of the main themes of this text is examining inequality, which is easiest to do along the lines of class and race. With gender, analysis requires attention to the ways that men and women are different—which goes beyond the physical differences that are included in constructions of race and ethnicity and beyond the material differences that are included in the constructions of class. Remedying gender inequality also requires addressing the question of whether equality in the current system, which is based on male norms, is the appropriate measure. What does equality look like when women (but not men) can get pregnant and society treats all women of childbearing age as if they were "pre-pregnant" (Flavin 2009)? Feminists have contributed different perspectives on these questions, making it more correct to discuss *feminisms* rather than a monolithic feminism. At times, "feminism" tends to refer to a privileged white, middle-class liberal feminism, but just as we have encouraged readers to be aware of the diversity within gender, we now consider the diversity of feminism—itself reflective not only by women's different economic class and ethnic locations in society but also by their sexual orientations or lifestyle practices.

What feminisms have in common is a concern with women's oppression and marginalization; all feminism makes women's experiences central to the social, political, and economic analysis. But feminisms differ in where they locate the source of oppression, what they consider to be the most salient issues, and thus what the central policy implications are. Thus, there's not a single analysis of gender discrimination or of how to reconcile sexual differences with equal protection and gender equality. So, this section reviews the main strands of feminist legal thinking and politics of change that are helpful in understanding gender issues related to law and the administration of justice. While it attempts to identify and articulate core beliefs of different feminisms, they have overlap. Also, individuals may think in terms of liberal feminism on one issue but be more radical or socialist on another.

Liberal feminism has focused on discrimination and considers legal and customary restraints to be the main barriers to women getting their fair share of the pie. Thus, the goal is to ensure that women and men have equal civil rights and a level playing field when it comes to economic opportunities. Liberal feminists concentrate on discrimination against female offenders, prisoners, and workers as well as the criminalization of deviance among women for behaviors such as prostitution. Their project for change revolves around achieving sexual and gender equality vis-à-vis equal opportunity programs such as affirmative action and antidiscrimination policy.

Critical feminists of whatever strain—Marxist, socialist, radical, and postmodern—object to liberal approaches not only for failing to question the existing legal and economic system but also for wanting equality in it. As Colette Price framed the issue more than thirty years ago: "Do we really want equality with men in this nasty competitive capitalist system? Do we want to be equally exploited with men? Do we want a piece of the pie or a whole different pie?" (Redstockings 1978, 94). As a diversified group, critical feminists differ in the emphasis they place on economic, biological, racial, and sexual sources of oppression, privilege, and inequality.

Marxist feminism has been concerned with the way the criminal justice system under capitalism serves the interests of the ruling class at the expense of the lower classes. Marxist feminists view the oppression of women as an extension of the oppression of the working class. They argue that it is impossible for anyone to obtain genuine equal opportunity in a class society in which the wealth produced by the powerless mainly ends up in the hands of the powerful few. These relatively few powerful are disproportionately male, which makes it even harder for women, as the privileged have a vested interest in maintaining their higher status, especially as reflected in the laws and capitalist legal order. Moreover, Marxist feminists argue that women are at a disadvantage in general and in relation to the law specifically because they are less likely than men to be lawmakers, attorneys, judges, and other types of criminal justice workers. Hence, they maintain that if *all* women are to be liberated—not just the middle class and affluent—then the capitalist system and its "bourgeois laws" must be replaced by a system of "people's laws."

Socialist feminism argues that women are oppressed not only because of their subordinate economic position but also because of their "class" as women. Social feminists were among the first of the feminist theorists to recognize exploitation rooted in racism, ageism, and heterosexism. Like Marxist feminism, socialist feminism clarifies how economic conditions alter labor market demands for women. In addition, socialist feminism highlights how sexist ideology legitimates women's exclusion from higher-paying men's jobs and their dominance in the domestic sphere. Patriarchal ideologies and exclusionary practices produce pools of marginal women who resort to crimes of survival such as transporting drugs or exchanging sex for money or other goods and services. Hence, socialist feminists call for widespread economic and cultural changes to dismantle the twin evils of capitalism and patriarchy. They place special emphasis on the needs of the poor and working women—women who suffer the consequences of a system that not only exalts men over women but also those who have over those who do not. They advocate equal work opportunities for men and women as well as policies that would alleviate women's "second shift" by increasing childcare and family-leave programs while at the same time increasing men's involvement in domestic work.

Radical feminism tends to focus on female victims, particularly survivors of gendered violence like domestic violence and sexual assault. Radical feminists argue that the source of the problem is male-dominated society. They criticize liberal and Marxist feminists for not going far enough. It is not sufficient to overturn society's male-dominated legal and political structures; transformation must also happen to all the social and cultural institutions (such as the family, the church, and the educational system) that reinforce women's roles in devalued activities like child bearing and nurturing—as well as devaluing women's activities. (Teaching and nursing, for example, are important professions, but the vast majority of workers are women, so those professions are "feminized" and devalued.) Radical feminists focus attention on how men attempt to control females. They argue that one of the pathways to women's liberation involves self-determinism inside and outside their sexual and parental roles. That includes, for example, permitting each woman to choose for herself when to use or not use reproduction-controlling technology (i.e., contraception, sterilization, abortion) and reproduction-aiding technologies (i.e., artificial insemination, in vitro fertilization, surrogate/contract motherhood).

Postmodern feminism questions both the essentialism of other feminisms and the absolutism of truth. Postmodern feminists argue for multiple truths that take context into account, so they emphasize the importance of alternative accounts or narratives to show the privilege embedded in dominant social constructions. Postmodern feminists, for example, examine the effects of language and symbolic representation, especially how legal discourse constructs different "types of Woman" such as "prostitute," "bad mother," "worthy victim." Postmodern feminism may be divided into two camps: *skeptical* and *affirmative*. The skeptical postmodernists embrace a more extreme relativist perspective where there are no objective truths, and therefore they do not adopt policy stances and remain noninterventionist, relying on critique and deconstruction alone. By contrast, affirmative postmodernists address the possibilities of reconstruction, of rebuilding through policies based on contingent truths. They tend to emphasize the power of agency, self-determinism, and how humans actively build and rebuild their social worlds rather than being merely passive subjects or legal objects of external forces only (Henry and Milovanovic 1999). Postmodern feminist scholars tend to recognize a responsibility to build legal bridges across diverse groups in order to work collectively—not to arrive at a universal understanding of justice, but "to do our best to make judgments that make the world a good place to be" for everyone (Wonders 1999, 122).

The feminisms reviewed above adopt three approaches to gender inequality: the sameness perspective, the difference perspective, and the dominance perspective. Each of these perspectives has its strengths and weaknesses. Advocates of the *sameness perspective*, also referred to as the "gender neutral" or "equal treatment" perspective, support a single standard governing the treatment of women and men. Take, for instance, the lack of vocational and educational programs in women's prisons relative to what is found in men's prisons. One solution is to give women the same programs that men have. If men have programs designed to rehabilitate sex offenders, then these programs should be available to women prisoners as well. However, few women prisoners (less than 2 percent) are rape and sexual assault offenders (Greenfeld 1997). In other words, women prisoners on the whole do not have the same need for sex-offender programs as men prisoners do. In contrast, many women—but few men—were primary caretakers for children before incarceration, so setting policies and programs about children based on men's prisons is also problematic.

Our analysis and others' suggest caution in equating equality with justice. The sameness approach may actually harm women, as the approach is not neutral but tends to be based on the treatment of men. As the narrative at the beginning of chapter 10 illustrates, "equality with a vengeance" is a real concern if sentencing for women is based on the "get tough" standard that applies to men. Further, gender bias in sentencing cannot be eliminated simply by stipulating (as is done in the U.S. Federal Sentencing Guidelines) that gender is not to be considered. Gender neutrality, in other words, cannot be legislated because society is not gender neutral. In the area of purportedly gender-neutral training, for example, Britton (1997) observed that the rhetoric of correctional officer training in her study was explicitly gender neutral, yet closer examination revealed that the training model was based on the experiences of male officers, particularly those working in male-dominated institutions. Similarly among women and employment, the gender-neutral framework is most likely to benefit those women whose biographies and class backgrounds most resemble those of successful white males.

Advocates of the *difference perspective* call for differential treatment of women and men. After all, some very real differences exist in the situation of men and women, such as women's capacity to bear children. Some critics of this perspective, such as Catharine MacKinnon (1991 [1984]), view it as both patronizing and necessary. Others talk about how women might be seen as getting "special treatment" or receiving "special rights," while other critics raise concerns about reinforcing gender stereotypes. For example, a policy of permitting single parents to receive a "downward departure" from sentencing guidelines would primarily benefit women and would likely be seen as a special right for those playing a traditional gender role.

Both the sameness and the difference approaches to gender equality do not measure up for two reasons. First, they both assume a male norm. As MacKinnon has argued, "gender neutrality" is simply the male standard and the "special protection" rule is simply the female standard, "but do not be deceived: masculinity, or maleness, is the referent for both" (1991 [1984], 83). Second, both perspectives reflect a preoccupation with gender differences while ignoring the role of power and domination. An alternative to the sameness and difference perspectives is the dominance perspective that takes up the neglected aspect of the other two approaches, namely *power*.

The *dominance perspective* recognizes that men and women are different and that the sexes are not equally powerful. Most differences between men and women can be attributed to a society in which women are subordinate and men are dominant. Advocates of the dominance perspective maintain that the solution to gender inequality is not to create a single standard (sameness) or a double standard (difference) but to address the inequality in power relations between the sexes. For example, proponents of the dominance approach have exerted pressure on the U.S. legal system to abandon its "hands off" attitude toward domestic violence, to redefine wife battering and marital rapes as crimes on the same level as injuries caused by strangers, and to expand the meaning of and protection from sexual harassment.

The dominance approach is not without weaknesses, too. It has also been criticized for its overconfidence in legal recognition and its failure to acknowledge that "legal rights are sometimes overshadowed by social realities" (Chesney-Lind and Pollock 1995, 157). For instance, while women have the legal right to be treated like any other assault victim and to have their battering husband arrested and punished, the reality is that women also face social, economic, and cultural barriers that may impede or prevent them from taking full advantage of their legal rights. The dominance perspective, like the other feminist perspectives on gender equality, has each been critiqued for being "essentialist" and "reductionist" in its approaches. In short, each of these perspectives assumes one monolithic "women's experience" that can be described independent of other characteristics such as race, class, age, and sexual orientation.

Essentialism and reductionism occur when a "representation" or a "voice"—mostly white, straight, and socioeconomically privileged—claims to embody or speak for everyone (see chapter 5). In a one-dimensional or essentialist world, for example, "Black women's experience will always be forcibly fragmented before being subjected to analysis, as those who are 'only interested in race' and those who are 'only interested in gender' take their separate slice of our lives" (David Harris 1999, 255). However, critical race feminism attempts to simultaneously address the importance of an antiessentialist and intersectional approach to race, gender, crime, and the law.

INTERSECTIONALITY, CRIME, AND THE LAW

In understanding the larger processes of criminal justice, many aspects of the class analysis and race analysis overlap. The idea is that the criminal justice system does not criminalize crimes of the rich, described by Quinney as many of the crimes of domination (see chapter 1). In contrast, the crimes of the poor become the main focus of criminal law, and the processes of criminal justice become a tool in class warfare to control the poor, especially the unemployed surplus labor pool that contains a disproportionate number of minorities. The class analysis focuses on the poor, while the race analysis equates the controlled "dangerous classes" with racial minorities. Given that most minorities are disproportionately poor, the class and race analyses are similar, though the race analysis would consider minorities more vulnerable to entanglement in systems of control because of prejudice and stereotypes. Racism and racist assumptions are frequently involved in creating "moral panics" or other situations thought to justify increased social control (e.g., drug and immigration laws) of the *other*.

The current widespread perception that black men are engaged in criminal activity, for example, is facilitated by the inundation of images of black criminals that not only contributes to what Katheryn Russell (1998) refers to as the *criminal blackman* but also to an uncritical acceptance of different punishments for the same crimes. Russell (1998, 71) argues, "crime and young Black men have become synonymous in the American mind." She cites such evidence as the racial hoax cases in which someone fabricates a crime and blames it on another person because of his race and gender or in which an actual crime has been committed and the offender falsely blames someone because of his race and gender.

The impact of class and race can also be seen in Shine and Mauer's (1993) research on the discrepancies in punishment between drug users and drunk drivers. According to the Uniform Crime Reports, there were 8.5 million arrests for criminal offenses nationwide for the year they analyzed. Of those, drug abuse violations accounted for 1,101,302 arrests and driving under the influence (DUI) accounted for 971,795 arrests. Shine and Mauer report that drug use resulted in an estimated 21,000 deaths a year (through overdoses, diseases, and violence associated with the drug trade) at an estimated annual cost of $58 million. Alcohol was associated with 94,000 deaths annually, with estimated societal costs of $85 million.

Although the criminal uses of illicit drugs and alcohol both cause great harm to society, the responses to these crimes are strikingly different. In particular, the criminal justice system punishes the possession of illicit drugs much more severely than it punishes drunk driving. While persons convicted of drug possession are typically charged with felonies and are likely to be incarcerated, drunk drivers are typically treated as misdemeanants and receive nonincarceration sentences. In New York State, for example, persons convicted of drug possession are twenty-four times more likely to be sentenced to prison as those convicted of drunk driving.

Shine and Mauer suggest that this differential response to similarly harmful behavior may stem from the different profiles of the perceived "typical" drug offender and drunk driver. For both drug abuse and DUI offenses, the overwhelming majority of arrestees are male (over 80 percent). However, nearly 90 percent of all those arrested for drunk driving are white, compared to less than two-thirds of those arrested for drug abuse violations. Blacks made up approximately one in ten of all those arrested for driving under the influence but over one in three of all persons arrested for drug abuse violations. Shine and Mauer note that DUI offenders are typically white, male, blue-collar workers, while persons convicted of drug possession are disproportionately low income or indigent African American and Hispanic males. The authors conclude: "Although substantial numbers of deaths are caused by drunk drivers, our national approach has emphasized prevention, education, and treatment. . . . For drug abuse, particularly among low-income people, treatment initiatives have lagged behind the move to 'get tough'" (Shine and Mauer 1993, 35). Even if states have made some progress in increasing penalties, there is still a large discrepancy in public opinion about the problems and flow of offenders through the system.

Similarly, Meda Chesney-Lind (2006, 10) argues in "Patriarchy, Crime, and Justice" that "to fully understand the interface between patriarchal control mechanisms and criminal justice practices in the United States, we must center our analysis on the race/gender/punishment nexus." She explains how media demonization, the masculinization of female offenders, and the criminalizing of women's victimization—all part of the feminist backlash starting in the 1980s—has resulted in greater increases in rates of arrests and incarceration for both women and girls compared to those of men and boys. And this increased incarceration rate has disproportionately and negatively affected girls and women of color. Between 1994 and 2003, the arrests of adult women increased by 30.8 percent whereas male arrests for the same offense fell by 5.8 percent; between 1989 and 1998, girl's detentions increased by 56 percent compared to a 20 percent increase for boy's detentions. Similarly, a joint study by the American Bar Association and the National Bar Association published in 2001 found that nearly one-half of the girls in detention were African American girls, and they constituted about 12 percent of the girl population, and conversely, white girls, who constituted 65 percent of the girl population, accounted for 35 percent of those in detention (Chesney-Lind 2006).

A final important example of intersections is fetal protection laws, through which the criminal law enhances punishment for harms to pregnant women. Although many states have chosen enhanced penalties for assaulting a pregnant woman, the federal Unborn Victims of Violence Act of 2004 "and most state fetal homicide laws treat the fetus as an independent second victim that has legal rights distinct from the pregnant woman harmed by the criminal act: that is, when a pregnant woman is murdered or injured, two victims are claimed—the woman and her fetus—not one" (Flavin 2009, 99). The concern about these laws is that they have been passed based on concern about domestic violence to pregnant women, but those who support the laws have little concern for the Violence Against Women Act or related initiatives. In addition, the laws are used as a back door to prosecute pregnant women for drug addiction, when drug counseling is not available to many poor pregnant women. Fetal protection laws have not been applied against men, even though studies find a correlation between men's exposure to certain chemicals (pesticides, solvents, etc.) and increased risk of miscarriage or fetal defects.

The recognition of fetal "rights" has important implication for women's bodily sovereignty by giving it a legal cause of action against the mother and turning her into a "baby carrier" or "bystanders to their own bodies" (Flavin 2009). The criminal law thus not only erodes women's rights but also the differential application of such laws target poor and minority women. Rather than more directly confronting domestic violence, universal health care, or a drug war that has not made treatment a priority, attention is focused on "bad" pregnant women.

IMPLICATIONS

Ideally, the study of lawmaking, criminal law, and the administration of justice should take the intersectionality of class, race, gender, sexuality, and age into consideration. This is difficult, on the one hand, because the law does not take into account or define crimes based on the class, race, and sex/gender of the offender. The criminal law is most obviously biased in a class-based way, while it is more race- and gender-neutral on its face. But what the law regards as a crime and whom society sees as the criminals are reflective of the statuses of class, race, and gender. Indeed, the problem is that facially neutral laws still result in disparate treatment because of the administration of criminal justice.

For example, while blacks are overrepresented in street crime and underrepresented in suite crime, Blumstein (1995) found that 20 to 25 percent of the black incarceration rate (representing about 10,000 blacks annually) is not explained by disproportionate offending. As the *Harvard Law Review* noted: "Substantial underenforcement of antidiscrimination norms" and "increasingly sophisticated empirical studies indicate disparities in the treatment of criminal suspects and defendants that are difficult to explain by reference to decisional factors other than racial discrimination" (1988, 1476). This finding applies to both men and women, with the absolute number of minority men involved in the criminal justice system at very high levels and the number of minority women at relatively lower levels, but increasing at the fastest rates.

This disparate treatment is corrosive of justice and generates the very different perceptions of the justice system held generally by whites and minorities. A biased law enforcement like pretextual stops (DWB), for example, can "undermine the legitimacy of the use of coercive power and can make the criminal justice system no better than the criminals it pursues. In the process, such stops based on racial bias erode trust in the system of justice, create public cynicism and hostility, and make police work more difficult and dangerous" (Cole 1999; see also David Harris [1999]). As the New York State Office of the Attorney General (1999) reported, civil rights do not exist unless the personal safety of all citizens is secured lawfully; policing without respect for the rule of law is not policing at all.

Legislators, policymakers, and criminal justice practitioners alike argue that they cannot foresee all the consequences of proposed and enacted laws. One way to assist them and to provide constant feedback on the fairness and justness of the administration of justice would be to implement class, race, and gender "impact statements" modeled after current environmental and financial impact statements. These types of analyses of the impact of new laws and the enforcement of old laws on class, race, and gender in relationship to the practices of crime control would specifically collect the relevant data necessary for evaluation.

Lawmakers could still pass laws that would make the situation worse for victims and/or offenders based on class, race, and/or gender, and criminal justice practitioners could continue to make exceptions to the "rule of law," but neither the makers nor the enforcers of law could maintain any longer that they did not know the consequences of their actions, especially if impact reports continued to be updated to reflect the actual changes related to the law taking effect. Moreover, public officials would have to dialogue with and answer to an empowered community armed with the knowledge of how class, race, and gender impact the differential administration of justice in America.

REVIEW AND DISCUSSION QUESTIONS

1. How do class, race, and gender affect lawmaking and affect the administration of criminal law and justice? What were the best examples from the text, and are there others you can think of?
2. What is meant by the concept of *analogous social injury*? What are some examples, and why are these acts when done by elites "beyond incrimination"?
3. How has the treatment of ethnic and racial minorities by the administration of justice both improved and not improved over the past century?
4. Discuss the differences between both the various types of feminism and the various feminist approaches to addressing law and gender inequality. Which of these models/approaches do you ascribe to, and why?
5. Using the examples of drunk driving and drug possession, discuss the relationship between the different profiles associated with each and the intersectionality of class, race, and gender.

9

Law Enforcement and Criminal Prosecution

The movie review headline in the entertainment section read in bold and large type: Racism, raw and modern. *The subtitle read: "Crash bravely admits that prejudice isn't a thing of the past." This critically acclaimed and controversial film takes place in cosmopolitan Los Angeles in 2005, not in the Deep South in 1955. In a documentarylike day-in-the-life montage of overlapping racist explosions, the audience watches as over the course of two days cars—and life—begin to collide. "There's a traffic stop. A fender-bender. A fiery car crash. A carjacking. And as the accidents mount, the accidental collisions of different people build, and the result is always some ugly, revelatory racism"(Whitty 2005, E2). All of the scenarios that unfold convey a sense of equal-opportunity racism: Black, brown, red, yellow, and white, male and female, rich and poor, powerful and powerless, nobody has yet escaped the prejudices, biases, and stereotypes of the other.*

While it is true that every group has prejudices, chapter 4 noted that an important difference was in the power whites generally had to act on their biases and create discrimination. There's the issue of white privilege, which makes conscious and unconscious racism "an amalgam of guilt, responsibility, and power—all of which are generally known but never acknowledged" (in Bell 1998, viii). The protection of white privilege in turn has important consequences for the treatment of minorities. In this vein, Laura Fishman (1998) writes about "the black bogeyman and white self-righteousness" by which she and other authors of color like Derrick Bell are commenting on how "whiteness" or white racism continues to serve as "a connector spanning the gargantuan gap between those whites at the top of the economic ladder and most of the rest scattered far below" and how "politicians and others can so easily deflect attention from what they are not doing for all of us to what whites fear" people of color might do to them (Bell 1998, viii).

Only the white racism analysis, and not the "equal opportunity racism" view presented in Crash, recognizes the differential treatment and consequences of racial power. The very concrete and tangible consequences for those who lack the necessary privilege include aspects of the administration of justice like racial profiling. While built on myths about the alleged propensity for blacks and browns to be involved with drugs and carry weapons, police scholars and the courts largely discredit such findings. For example, like other criminal justice research that has found burdens associated with being young, minority, and male (Miller 1996; Spohn and Holleran 2000), Engel and Calnon's (2004, 84) very thorough examination of racial profiling found that after relevant legal and extralegal factors were controlled, young minority males were "at the highest risk for citations, searches, arrests, and use of force during traffic stops." Yet those same black and brown drivers were no more likely to be carrying contraband than white drivers.

This chapter will present additional data later about Driving While Black (DWB), but consider for the moment a study done by New York's Attorney General based on 175,000 "UF-250" forms—paperwork that NYPD officers are required to complete after a wide variety of "stop" encounters (New York State Office of the Attorney General 1999). This data goes beyond driving to include a wider range of stop and frisk practices related to the Supreme Court's decision in Terry v. Ohio (392 U.S. 1, 1968) under which a police officer can detain a civilian if the officer can articulate a "reasonable suspicion" that criminal activity is "afoot." The report found that:

> Blacks comprise 25.6 percent of the city's population, yet 50.6 percent of all persons "stopped" during the period were black. Hispanics comprise 23.7 percent of city's population, yet 33.0 percent of all "stops" were of Hispanics. By contrast, whites are 43.4 percent of the city's population, but accounted for only 12.9 percent of all "stops" (NYSOAG 1999).

The Office of the Attorney General, with the aid of Columbia University's Center for Violence Research and Prevention, also performed a regression analysis to see if differing rates of street crime for minorities could explain the increased rate of stops of minorities. But even after accounting for the effect of differing crime rates, the analysis showed blacks were stopped 23 percent more often than whites and Hispanics were stopped 39 percent more often (NYSOAG 1999).

While disproportionate focus on minorities is a problem, national evidence also indicates that many traffic stops involved extensive searches. Police would start by looking under seats and in the trunk but continued by deflating tires, prying off door panels, and taking apart sunroofs. In at least one instance, officers handed the driver a screwdriver, saying, "You're going to need this" to put the car back together (Harris 1999). The belongings of blacks have been strewn on the highways, blown around by passing trucks, and urinated on by dogs sniffing for drugs. Other stops involved officers who were quick to unholster firearms. Some of these stops happened to rich or famous blacks, including politicians. As part of the settlement to lawsuits charging discrimination, several jurisdictions started requiring *data collection on police stops. Other studies were undertaken directly on behalf of minority groups and still others were done proactively by localities concerned about discrimination. The overall results confirm the experience of minorities that they are disproportionately targets of police power and "vulnerable to the whims of anyone holding a criminal justice commission" (Doyle 1992, 75.) The situation is better than, but still reminiscent of, the problem described by the song "Standin' on De Corner" in the previous chapter.*

These incidents amount to abuses of police discretion because of prejudice and stereotypes. The concern is not only with the individuals harmed by such incidents but also damage done to the rule of law, which helps protect individual liberties by demanding clearly articulated law and due process, applied equally to all. The notion of a rule of law is contrasted with a rule of men, which can be arbitrary and unclear; it is frequently used to benefit the ruler and differentially applied at the whim, caprice, or prejudice of those who hold power. Thus, violations of the rule of law can undermine respect for the law and institutions of criminal justice, which can come to be seen as exercising an arbitrary or discriminatory power—and are consequently seen as unjust.

More specifically, Harris (1999) addresses the question of why DWB matters and points out that it has substantial impact on the innocent: "the great majority of black people who are subjected to these humiliating and difficult experiences but who have done absolutely nothing to deserve this treatment—except to resemble, in a literally skin-deep way, a small group of criminals." Because the majority of those stopped are innocent, but the stops themselves are legal, blackness is, in effect, criminalized. Further, while most profiles are based on flawed data and assumptions, the profile focuses increased police attention on the group, which can uncover additional wrongdoing that becomes evidence in support of the profile. Discrimination is rationalized through a self-fulfilling prophecy that denies the presence of drugs in white suburbia, and without a profile does not deploy massive resources there to investigate.

In addition, Harris contends that DWB distorts the legal system by fostering deep cynicism of its fairness, both because of its impact on the innocent and because the increased scrutiny of blacks means disproportionate numbers of them end up in prison—so black communities "bear a far greater share of the burden of drug prohibition" (1999). DWB matters further, he says, by distorting the social world, by which he means that it imposes a "spatial restriction on African-Americans, circumscribing their movements" and basically ensuring that blacks stay out of areas where whites and the police feel they "do not belong" (see also Lee [2000]; Withrow 2006). Finally, DWB undermines community policing, which requires mutual trust of police and the citizens they patrol. In the end, Harris notes, "aside from the damage 'driving while black' stops inflict on African-Americans, there is another powerful reason to change this police behavior: it is in the interest of police departments themselves to correct it" (1999).

༄

Like other institutions of social control, a primary role of criminal justice administration—law enforcement, adjudication, and punishment—is to persuade people to abide by the dominant values of society. As noted in the previous chapter, the criminal justice system is different in being able to exercise coercive power. Police can stop, detain, arrest, and use deadly force; courts can imprison, order execution, or sentence people to intensive regimes of surveillance through probation or parole. While the politicians play an important role in defining crime, police are more visible because of their presence on the streets and the numerous TV shows devoted to their work.

In the United States "criminal justice" is administered by a loose confederation of more than 50,000 agencies of federal, state, and local governments, each carefully limited by law or subject to *jurisdiction*—"the right or authority of a justice agency to act in regard to a particular subject matter, territory, or person" (Bohm and Haley 2005, 147). Beyond the statutes that create and direct law enforcement and other criminal justice agencies, the procedural law (derived mainly from the U.S. Supreme Court decisions) also imposes limitations on the authority of those agencies, as do civilian review boards, ombudsman, departmental policies and procedures, and civil liability suits.

An individual enters the criminal justice system first as a suspect, next as a defendant, and finally as a convicted criminal. The criminal justice response to crime typically begins when a crime is reported to the police, or far less often, when the police themselves discover that a crime had been committed. Solving a crime is sometimes easy, for example, when a victim or witness knows who the perpetrator is or where to find him or her. In these situations, an arrest supported by either victim and/or witness statements and by crime scene evidence is sufficient to close the case. More often, however, the police must conduct an in-depth investigation or engage in a manhunt to find suspects. In either situation, if the investigation is successful, a suspect is arrested, then brought to the police station for booking.

The court subsystem consists of four basic stages: charging, pretrial, trial, and sentencing. Soon after the suspect is arrested and booked, a prosecutor reviews the facts of the case and the available evidence. The prosecutor decides whether to charge the suspect with a crime or crimes. If no charges are filed, the suspect must be released. When it comes to the less serious crimes such as misdemeanors or ordinance violations, the prosecutor prepares a *complaint* specifying that the named person has committed an offense. If the offense is a felony or a more serious crime for which a person may be confined in a prison for more than one year, then the prosecutor prepares either an information or the grand jury issues an *indictment*. Both the information and the indictment, each used in about 50 percent of the jurisdictions, consists of a formal charge or written accusation of the crime or crimes committed.

After the charge or charges have been filed, the pretrial stages begin when the suspect, who is now the defendant, is brought before a lower-court judge for an *initial appearance*. The defendant is presented with the formal charge (or charges) against him or her and advised of his or her constitutional rights. For a misdemeanor or an ordinance violation, a *summary trial* without a jury may be held. For a felony, a *probable cause hearing* is held to determine whether or not there is enough evidence to make a "reasonable person" believe that, more likely than not, the proposed action is justified, and to decide whether or not *bail* is appropriate. If there is not sufficient evidence, then the suspect is released. If there is sufficient evidence, the suspect is next subject to a *preliminary hearing* whose purpose is for the judge to determine whether or not there is probable cause that the defendant committed the crime or crimes. If the judge finds probable cause, then an indictment or information is filed with the court, and the defendant is scheduled for an *arraignment*. The primary purpose of the arraignment is to hear the formal information or indictment, ensure the defendant knows the charges, and allow the defendant to enter a plea. Upwards of 90 percent of criminal defendants plead guilty to some of the charges against them, based on a *plea bargain* arrangement between the prosecutor, the defense attorney, and the defendant. It typically occurs between the time of the preliminary hearing and the time of the arraignment, but it can occur up to and even after the trial has begun.

If the defendant pleads not guilty or not guilty by reason of insanity, a trial date is set. Of those cases, a mere 10 percent actually go to trial, with about half being a jury trial and about half consisting of a bench trial because the defendant has decided to waive his Sixth Amendment right to a jury trial. If the jury or the judge finds the defendant guilty as charged, the judge and/or the jury, depending on the jurisdiction, participate in the *sentencing process*. Of course, if acquitted (found not guilty), the person is set free; if the jury is "hung" and cannot reach a decision, then the defendant may be released but could be subject to retrial.

Those who are convicted of a crime will be sentenced, based on statutory law and philosophical as well as political considerations. After sentencing, the convicted person then becomes subject to the penal-correctional subsystem. Options here usually consist of *incarceration* in prison (for sentences greater than one year), jail (for sentences less than one year), or community *probation*. In some jurisdictions, incarcerated criminals may be eligible for *parole*, in which they finish their sentences outside of prison and are subject to special conditions of behavior, violations of which may result in reimprisonment. Once offenders have served out their whole sentence in one form or the other, they are formally released from criminal justice authority. However, "invisible punishments" may still affect them, including the exclusion from public housing, denial of student loans, and the right to vote (Mauer and Chesney-Lind, 2002).

This descriptive overview of the criminal justice system highlighted the formal workings of law enforcement, prosecution, adjudication, and punishment bureaucracies according to the formal rules of law. Embedded throughout this system, however, at literally every decision-making point, are numerous informal opportunities for discretion that create variations in police, prosecutorial, and judicial behavior that often result in unequal treatment for many. The exercise of "discretion" (Susan Miller 1999; Skolnick 1996 [1967]; James Wilson 1972) is explored in this and the next chapter as a means of trying to appreciate the relationship between the formal and informal practices of law enforcement and criminal adjudication. More specifically, in each of the next three sections we examine the identification of criminals and labeling of crime in the context of class, race, gender, and intersections.

CRIME, CRIMINAL IDENTIFICATION, AND CLASS CONTROL

On November 20, 1993, the front page of the *New York Times* carried two stories about crime. The first was about the U.S. Senate approving what would become the 1994 Omnibus Crime Bill. That legislation provided $8.9 billion for hiring 100,000 police officers, $6 billion for prisons and boot camps, and increased federal penalties for a variety of gang-related activities. The second story's headline read: "Anti-Drug Unit of CIA Sent Ton of Cocaine to U.S. in 1990." This pure cocaine was sold on the streets of the United States, where federal penalties at the time were a five-year mandatory minimum for possession of 500 grams of powder cocaine or just five grams of the cheaper crack cocaine. (There are 907,000 grams in a ton.)

The Omnibus Crime Bill and the unprosecuted crimes of the CIA do not only serve to selectively enforce and differentially apply laws against illegal drug distribution but together they also help to reproduce various stereotypes associated with drug-related behavior. For example, the new police officers paid for by the crime bill were among those out on the streets searching for gang members and busting numerous poor people with small amounts of cocaine, who ended up in the prisons built with an influx of federal dollars. Meanwhile, little comparable effort was invested in law enforcement going after the more affluent consumers of the powder cocaine, who rarely ended up in prison, and when busted, often found their way into detoxification or drug treatment facilities (Humphries 1999). At the same time, the CIA was not identified as a drug trafficker, nor were any officials arrested. One CIA officer resigned and a second was disciplined in what was called "a most regrettable incident" that involved "instances of poor judgment." And while a federal grand jury was supposed to investigate and Representative Maxine Waters of East Los Angeles, a member of the House Intelligence Committee, suggested closer scrutiny of the CIA antidrug activities, nothing ever came of this political scandal in the "drug war" waged against the gangs of East LA.

This episode in law enforcement reflects a larger pattern in which police focus their efforts on controlling the behavior of the poor, identifying criminals as predominantly members of the lower economic classes. Similarly, investigative tools such as the use of "profiles" are constructed around street criminals and gangs rather than on suite crime and corporate criminals, even though the recidivism rates of offenders like "citizen GE" are habitual in practice (refer back to the opening narrative in chapter 8). As Edwin Sutherland found in his classic study of corporate crime in America more than a half century ago:

> The records reveal that every one of the seventy corporations had violated one or more of the laws, with an average of about thirteen adverse decisions per corporation and a range of from one to fifty adverse decisions per corporation. . . . The "habitual criminal" laws of some states impose severe penalties on criminals convicted the third or fourth time. If this criterion were used here, about 90 percent of the large corporations studied would be considered habitual white-collar criminals (in Reiman and Leighton 2010a, 125).

More recent studies confirm the high prevalence of repeat criminality and habitual corporate crime, even after they successfully prevent many of their harmful actions from becoming categorized as crimes. For example, a Justice Department study examining the years 1975–1976 found that more than 60 percent of 600 corporations had at least 1 enforcement action initiated against them, and half of the companies were charged with a serious violation. A later study by *U.S. News & World Report* found that during the 1970s, 20 percent of the Fortune 500 had been convicted of at least one major crime or paid a civil penalty for serious illegal behavior. From 1975 to 1984, almost two-thirds of the Fortune 500 "were involved in one or more incidents of corrupt behavior such as price fixing, bribery, violation of environmental regulations and tax fraud" (Etzioni 1990, C3). As one observer of corporate crime noted, the "corporate structure itself—oriented as it is toward profit and away from liability—is a standing invitation to such conduct" (in Hills 1987; see also Bakan [2004]).

While it is often noted that in the area of elite deviance hardly anyone ever goes to prison, less attention is given to the law enforcement reality that the U.S. regulatory and judiciary systems "do little if anything to deter the most damaging Wall Street crimes" (Leaf 2005, 38). Such a situation exists for two reasons: (1) most state regulators and prosecutors do not make white-collar crime a priority; and (2) the FBI does not make white-collar and corporate crime a priority, leaving substantial aspects of the problem to agencies like the SEC that have also not made enforcement a priority—and that work in an environment encouraging deregulation and industry self-regulation.

First, state regulators and prosecutors, with a few notable exceptions like former New York attorney general Eliot Spitzer, shy away from complicated cases involving financially powerful entities. Resources and training are issues, so are politics. Corporations and wealthy individuals can be large campaign contributors and exercise substantial political influence. Regulators also know that if they cooperate with industry, they have a better chance of landing a lucrative job with the industry after they finish working for the government. After getting industry experience, they are valued as regulators, which then increases the chance they can land a better-paying job with the industry. This revolving door is described as *agency capture*, which refers to the process by which regulatory agencies come to be dominated (from the inside) by the industries they regulate through the revolving door of personnel. Prosecutors typically enter private practice or politics after government service and do not want to make enemies of the wealthy and powerful who could be a source of campaign donations or a job.

Second, white-collar task forces of the FBI are stretched too thin and tend to focus on such wide-ranging schemes like Internet, insurance, and Medicaid fraud, abandoning traditional securities and accounting offenses to regulatory and administrative agencies like the Securities and Exchange Commission. The FBI has been conspicuously absent from the recent financial crisis, even though FBI officials in 2004 said that mortgage-related problems had "the potential to be an epidemic" (Schmitt 2008). Many media reports note that the agents have been reassigned from white-collar crime to the war on terror. But, the percentage of inmates in federal prisons for drugs has continued to increase, indicating that the war on terror has been used to justify reducing the forces fighting white-collar crime, but not the drug war. Thus, the "limited resources for white collar crime" masks a decision to make fighting the drug war a higher priority than costly white-collar crime that has destabilized the economy and thus national security (see box 2.3: Economic Crisis and the War on State-Corporate Crime?).

The shift in priorities reflects a lack of will to combat white-collar crime even as the nation was experiencing the impact of Enron-related fraud. At the close of the Bush II presidency, the FBI was devoting so few resources to white-collar crime that companies had to turn to private investigators to prepare "courtroom-ready prosecutions" that they can take to the FBI because they are unable to get the agency's attention, even in cases of multimillion dollar cases of loss (Lichtblau, Johnston, and Nixon 2008). The former lead prosecutor of Enron's Ken Lay and Jeffrey Skilling commented that "most sitting U.S. Attorneys now staring at the subprime crisis find scant resources available to pursue sophisticated financial crimes" (Schmitt 2008). The FBI found a small number of additional agents and resources to look into mortgage fraud and investigate firms at the center of the financial crisis after the crisis happened, but then Attorney General Michael Mukasey repeatedly rejected calls for an equivalent of the Enron Task Force that was used to prosecute earlier widespread complex financial crime (Lichtblau et al. 2008).

The other source of referrals to prosecutors is federal regulators. In the area of securities, regulators, "while determined and well trained, are so understaffed that they often have to let good cases slip away." Even when referrals are made, discretion means cases are not always pursued: "Prosecutors leave scores of would-be criminal cases referred by the SEC in the dustbin, declining to prosecute more than half of what comes their way" (Leaf 2005, 38). Indeed, by 2008, federal officials brought fewer prosecutions of securities fraud than in 2000, the year before Enron.

Former SEC chair Christopher Cox said, "We've done everything we can during the last several years in the agency to make sure people understand there's a strong market cop on the beat," but he required staff to get approval for an increased number of actions from SEC commissioners. According to former SEC chair Arthur Levitt, this has effectively "handcuffed" the inspection and enforcement division (Paley and Hilzenrath 2008). An SEC press release claimed that under Chairman Cox, the percentage of staff working on enforcement has increased, but the actual number of enforcement staff declined from 2005 and the percentage increased only because other SEC divisions had bigger cuts. (*New York Times* columnist Floyd Norris asks, "Is there anyone at the commission with the nerve to tell Mr. Cox that the enforcer of disclosure laws ought to be particularly careful to avoid misleading hype?" [2008a]). Further, "the commission delayed settlements while commissioners negotiated to impose smaller penalties than the companies had agreed to pay" (Norris 2008b). (Imagine a chief prosecutor who delayed a plea bargain to try to impose a smaller penalty than requested by the lawyer for a burglar or drug dealer.)

Thus, despite the impressive record of habitual criminality on the part of corporate America and the occasional reference to upper-world crime, the Reagan, Bush I, Clinton, and Bush II administrations have all consistently worked to get government "off the backs" (e.g., deregulate) of corporations as they ratcheted up their war on the crimes of the poor. For example, while President Reagan's "tough on crime" legislation expanded the use of mandatory and minimum sentences along with federal use of the death penalty, his administration eliminated many federal regulators and inspectors who acted as police in the corporate neighborhood. Some have suggested that such strategies of crime control (actually policies of class control) are the equivalent of removing police from a high crime area because the free will of criminals is being interfered with. Rather than "get tough," deregulation of business affairs has produced an environment of expanding criminal activity as it has reduced enforcement and penalties.

Finally, the so-called self-regulatory organizations such as the National Association of Securities Dealers are relatively toothless, and other trade groups like the American Institute of Certified Public Accountants stubbornly protect their own. Self-regulation frequently involves a minimal effort to promote good behavior in order to prevent stricter outside regulation. News media conglomerates rarely give more than superficial coverage and analysis of the structural roots of these crimes, in addition to which they avoid coverage wherever possible of stories that involve the larger corporations who own them. Perhaps worst of all, "corporate chiefs often wink at (or nod off to) overly aggressive tactics that speed along the margins of the law" (Leaf 2005, 38).

Bernard Madoff, mastermind of a $64 billion financial swindle—one of the largest in history—highlights shortcomings of the regulatory system and of financial watchdogs, particularly the SEC, which failed to catch the crime despite repeated warnings over a ten-year period. And, although others are expected to be criminally charged by prosecutors as part of the financial fraud, at the time of Madoff's sentencing on June 29, 2009, only one other person, David Friehling, auditor of Bernard L. Madoff Investment Securities, was being prosecuted. As noted in figure 9.1, the SEC was suing a few others for civil fraud, New York attorney general Andrew Cuomo was suing one person, and several others were under prosecutorial scrutiny.

The "bottom line" for corporate illegality is that the powerful know that the odds favor their never getting caught and charged in the first place with a crime, let alone having to defend themselves of the same in a court of law. According to the *U.S. Attorney's Annual Statistical Report,* for the year 2008, there were 6,117 white-collar or business crimes filed against 8,684 defendants, with an impressive overall conviction rate for the year of 90 percent. Of those convicted, 63 percent were sentenced to prisons, and of those 29 percent were given sentences greater than three years. During the same year, there were only 149 individuals charged with corporate fraud, of which 120 were convicted, representing an 81 percent conviction rate; seventy-three of these convicted defendants were sentenced to prison. However, there were only forty-seven corporations charged with fraud cases against a mere seventy-four defendants in 2008 (U.S. Department of Justice 2009, 7 and 42). Eight years earlier in 2000, federal prosecutors had charged 8,766 defendants, slightly more than in 2008, with what the government terms

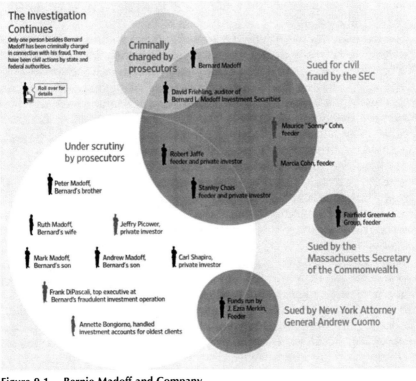

Figure 9.1. Bernie Madoff and Company
Source: *Wall Street Journal* (June 27–28, 2009).

white-collar crimes, convicting 6,786 or 78 percent of the cases brought. Of that number, about 4,000 were sentenced to prison; nearly all of them for a term of less than three years, averaging around sixteen months (Leaf 2005). But, like the conviction figures for 2008, the ones for 2000 were also highly misleading.

As Henry Pontell, coauthor of *Big-Money Crime: Fraud and Politics in the Savings and Loan Crisis*, has stated: "I've seen welfare frauds labeled as white-collar crimes" (in Leaf 2005, 38). Moreover, further investigation by Clifton Leaf of the Justice Department's 2000 statistics revealed that only 226 were cases involving securities or commodities fraud. Moreover, according to TRAC data (Syracuse University's web data clearinghouse, which has been tracking prosecutor referrals from virtually every federal agency for more than a decade) from 1992 to 2001, SEC enforcement attorneys referred 609 cases to the Justice Department for possible criminal charges. Of that number, U.S. attorneys decided what to do on about 525, declining to prosecute just over 64 percent, successfully convicting 76 percent of those, with only some 20 percent or eighty-seven of those criminals finding their way into prison (Leaf 2005, 39).

The situation has only changed a little after Enron and the Year of Corporate Financial Scandals. In the immediate aftermath of the scandals, President Bush created a new corporate fraud task force, although critics pointed out the official responsible for this "financial SWAT team" directed a credit card company that had paid more than $400 million to settle consumer and securities fraud suits. Businesses—lead by the U.S. Chamber of Commerce—mounted a heavy public relations and lobbying effort to carry the message about "overregulation" and regulatory "overreach" (*Business Week* 2005).

Similarly, the Sarbanes-Oxley Act of 2002 (SOX) was a reaction to a number of major corporate and accounting scandals, including those affecting Enron, Tyco International, Adelphia, Peregrine Systems, and WorldCom. These "criminal enterprises" shook the confidence of the nation's securities markets when the share prices of affected companies collapsed, costing investors billions of dollars. The SOX law was created for the purposes of getting tough on systemic fraud. The number of companies reporting fraud was high, and an examination of Enron reveals the nature of systemic fraud. Enron paid accountants Arthur Andersen large amounts of money for consulting on how to structure deals, then would pay another branch to audit the books. The large consulting fees create an obvious conflict of interest, because the Arthur Andersen auditors are not going to report problems with the work the Arthur Andersen consultants just received big money to do. Enron paid large sums to Wall Street firms to help with deals, then used those fees to persuade those firms to fire or remove analysts who had questions about Enron's stock. In the end, stock analysts privately ridiculed stocks and companies while publicly maintaining a "Buy" rating (Leighton and Reiman 2004). Further, many CEOs and a wide range of very well-paid executives claimed to have no knowledge of wrongdoing.

To remedy these issues, SOX required some separation between auditing and consulting firms, as well as a degree of independence on the part of stock analysts. It required CEOs to sign off on financial results and made companies assess the integrity of financial controls in auditing procedures designed to detect fraud. Other provisions attempt to make corporate boards more independent, so when potential problems arise the CEO is less likely to be able to tell his board member friends that everything is fine and move on (as happened at Enron and other firms). Additional reforms attempt to break the cycle whereby compensation committees vote higher pay for CEOs, who then approve higher pay for board members, and each party scratches the others' back even while the company is heading into fraud-induced bankruptcy. So far, SOX has not been weakened despite many complaints from businesses.

Still, as the previous chapter noted, financial regulations were weakened soon after they were put in place following the savings and loan scandals. While debate over the costs and benefits of SOX continues to this day, high-risk corporate misbehavior and financial fraud from Wall Street to Main Street eventually tanked the national and global economies, helping to bring about the worst financial crisis that the world has seen since the Great Depression of the 1930s. However, despite the widespread and systemic nature of the upper-world crimes, prosecutions seem to be rare, and when they occur, civil rather than criminal lawsuits are more likely to occur. For example, America's biggest subprime mortgage lender, Countrywide Financial, was slapped with a prosecution for unethical business practices in the summer of 2008, hours before its shareholders were due to vote the company out of existence. The attorney general of Illinois filed the civil action against Countrywide for deceitful conduct and lax standards in the way it provided subprime mortgages to customers. As "part of a single-minded quest" to dominate the U.S. home loans industry, the suit accused Countrywide of "using misleading marketing to sell mortgages packed with hidden fees and risky terms" that resulted in tens of thousands of foreclosures and losses to investors of nearly $2 billion for 2007 and the first half of 2008 (Guardian.co.uk 2008).

More importantly, it is an open question as to whether the Obama administration will achieve meaningful reform. No doubt some legislation will come out of the financial crisis, but the question is how extensive and deep they will be—whether they ask and answer the hard questions about what caused the breakdown and what needs to be done to avoid these or similar fiascos from happening in the future. While the financial crisis seemed to help his candidacy for president because there was more confidence in him to deal with the situation, his administration and most of Congress have tight relationships with Wall Street. A Public Citizen study of public finance records calculated that Wall Street had spent $5 billion in campaign contributions and lobbying between 1998 and 2008. Similarly, International Monetary Fund economists have shown that between 1998 and 2006 the average FIRE (finance, insurance, real estate) firm increased its lobbying costs by 25 percent compared to other industries that had only raised theirs by 10 percent (Hayes 2009).

In this sense, the regulatory system was not overwhelmed by modern financial practices; rather, it was systematically gutted and dismantled by the government at the behest of banking interests. Unfortunately, Obama's economic advisers—including Larry Summers and Tim Geithner—"participated directly in unwinding prudential rules and regulations. Cheers were led by the Federal Reserve, with heavy lifting by both political parties" (Greider 2009, 8). History also makes it clear that one of the reasons that old regulations failed is because "modern" banking and finance shifted credit functions outside regulated banks and into a variety of unregulated money pots—the so-called shadow banking system of hedge funds and private-equity firms. These interact intimately with traditional banks and give them profitable ways to evade rules or conceal the condition of balance sheets from regulators and investors. These interactions are dazzlingly complex, but this was not an accident. It was the goal of financial deregulation enacted by Bill Clinton, arm and arm with the GOP Congress (Greider 2009, 8).

Because of the powerful interests at work lobbying for their own interests over the public interest (see chapters 1 and 8), campaign finance may be necessary before meaningful financial regulation can happen. Until then, the individuals who either created the mess in the first place and/or did not see the trouble coming in the second place have captured the agencies needed to protect the public interest.

Outside of financial reporting, though, enforcement tools against big business are not in good shape either. Antitrust provisions designed to keep firms from becoming too big, too powerful, and unaccountable are rarely invoked (for example by allowing Exxon and Mobil to merge into ExxonMobil by just divesting a few gas stations in California). As of 2005, the Occupational Safety and Health Administration (OSHA) and its state partners had had 2,400 inspectors to cover the nation's 7.2 million work sites (Department of Labor 2006, 4–5). The advisory system for notifying consumers about dangerous or defective products is weak, and an editorial in the *Journal of the American Medical Association* harshly critiqued the system of checking on the safety of drugs once they were on the market. In an article called "Postmarketing Surveillance—Lack of Vigilance, Lack of Trust," the authors conclude that without a "long overdue major restructuring" the United States will be "far short of having an effective, vigilant, and trustworthy system of postmarketing surveillance to protect the public" from problematic prescription drugs or contaminated food products (Fontanarosa, Rennie, and DeAngelis 2004, 2650). In these and other areas of public concern, such as those involving health care and climate change, which also call for stricter enforcement and prosecution of violators, there are at least well-organized consumer lobbies and a permanent infrastructure pushing lawmakers in a progressive direction and doing battle against the interests of the insurance or oil industries.

In sum, when it comes to crime, criminals, and class control the old legal axiom still stands: while rich people don't hold up Dairy Queens, and poor people don't price-fix or swindle the consumer, police and prosecutors seem to pursue only those who do, in fact, hold up DQ's—namely, the poor and marginal. Indeed, writing for the 6–3 majority that declared unconstitutional Michigan's 1999 law denying legal representation to poor people in criminal appeals, Supreme Court justice Ruth Ginsburg noted: "Seven out of ten inmates fall into the lowest two out of five levels of literacy" and without counsel are incapable of "navigating the appellate process" (in American Civil Liberties Union of Michigan 2005, 1).

As for the rich, like in the "game of Monopoly®," they seem to have no need for the "get out of jail free" cards, since very few resources in law enforcement are earmarked for the task of reducing white-collar and corporate crime. But even when they are arrested, they can hire attorneys to help escape or minimize the charges. In contrast, findings of public hearings in 2003, conducted by the American Bar Association's Standing Committee on Legal Aid and Indigent Defendants, indicate:

- Absence of sufficient training, qualification standards, and performance evaluations for indigent defense counsel;
- Inordinately high caseloads of indigent defense counsel;
- Lack of indigent defense system standards, accountability, and statewide oversight;
- Inadequate compensation for individual defense counsel and funding for indigent defense services, including lack of resources for investigative, expert, and other support services;
- Disparity in funding and resources for indigent defense versus prosecution (American Civil Liberties Union of Michigan 2005, 1).

For example, in 2004, Johnny Lee Bell was convicted of second-degree murder and received an automatic mandatory sentence of life in prison, despite his public defender's admission that she had spent only eleven minutes preparing for his trial. The National Association of Criminal Defense Attorneys (2004) notes that the "case is egregious, but not unsymptomatic given the trend of substandard legal representation that has become common in many states."

CRIME, CRIMINAL IDENTIFICATION, AND RACE CONTROL

The single biggest issue involving minorities and law enforcement has been DWB, a topic introduced in the opening of this chapter. A number of lawsuits have been filed against the police for a variety of abusive and discriminatory behaviors. In 1999, for example, the U.S. Justice Department filed a federal lawsuit against the New Jersey State Police for an alleged pattern and practice of discrimination or "racial profiling" involving traffic stops. Various state and local police departments also faced similar lawsuits filed by civil rights groups. Beyond the lawsuits, this topic generates heated debate and helps account for some of the different attitudes whites and minorities have toward police and the criminal justice system, so it will be the focus of this section.

Table 9.1.   Attitudes toward Prevalence of Racial Profiling

Percent of Each Race Agreeing That Profiling Is Widespread			
	White	*Black*	*Hispanic*
When motorists are stopped	50%	67%	63%
When passengers are stopped in airports	40%	48%	54%
When shoppers are questioned in malls or stores	45%	65%	56%

Source: *Sourcebook of Criminal Justice Statistics*, 2003, table 2.26.

Many of the early complaints about this practice were ignored or discounted by many whites (see the discussion of privilege in chapter 4), and table 9.1 indicates ongoing racial differences regarding the perceived prevalence of racial profiling. Some settlements for lawsuits alleging discrimination and civil rights violations during the 1990s included requirements to collect more extensive data, which became a practice in numerous jurisdictions with racial tensions. Other researchers also undertook to find ways to see if minority overrepresentation in traffic stops was related to race or simply worse driving. The first data were anecdotal but indicated that police targeted black, brown, and other nonwhites frequently for minor violations—no seat belt, titled license plates, or illegible (dirty) plates. For example, one of the earliest studies to demonstrate racial profiling was a 1988 study of vehicles on the New Jersey Turnpike, which showed that African American motorists with out-of-state plates accounted for fewer than 5 percent of the vehicles but 80 percent of the stops. A decade later, in Illinois Hispanics made up less than 8 percent of the population and took fewer than 3 percent of the personal vehicle trips, but they made up approximately 30 percent of the motorists stopped for discretionary offenses, such as the failure to signal a lane change or driving one to four miles over the speed limit (David Harris 1999).

Two studies conducted at the end of the 1990s, one on "driving interventions" and the other on "stop and frisk" practices, both revealed significant adverse consequences for minorities. In the state of Maryland, observers who watched an interstate near Baltimore and recorded information on 5,741 cars over 42 hours reported that 93.3 percent were violating traffic laws and thus were eligible to be stopped by the state police. Of the violators seen by the study's observers, 17.5 percent were black and 74.7 percent were white. However, the Maryland State Police reported that 72.9 percent of the vehicles they stopped had black drivers (Harris 1999). (The New York stop and frisk study was discussed in the opening narrative of this chapter.)

More recent research from Engel and Calnon (2004, 69–72) concluded that:

- men, younger drivers, blacks, Hispanics, drivers of other races . . . were significantly more likely to receive citations than were women, older drivers, and whites;
- the odds that black drivers would receive a citation were 47 percent greater compared to the odds for white drivers, and the odds for Hispanic drivers were 82 percent higher;
- the percentage of minority drivers who reported having their person or vehicle searched was double that of white drivers—5.4 percent of white drivers were searched, compared to 10.9 percent of blacks, 11.2 percent of Hispanics, and 6.5 percent for other;
- only 2.6 percent of white drivers reported being arrested, compared to 5.2 percent of black drivers, 4.2 percent of Hispanic drivers, and 2.1 percent of drivers of other races and ethnicities; and
- 2.7 percent of whites reported having force used against them, compared to 6.7 percent of blacks, 5.4 percent of Hispanics, and 1.7 percent of drivers of other races and ethnicities.

While a study for the Bush administration found no evidence of blacks being disproportionately pulled over, the report, "Contacts between the Police and Public," supports the general findings above about the *consequences* of the stop. The Bureau of Justice Statistics reviewed evidence from across the nation and found "evidence of black drivers having worse experiences—more likely to be arrested, more likely to be searched, more likely to have force used against them—during traffic stops than white drivers" (BJS 2005a, 9). While the final report still contains the information quoted in the previous sentence, the *New York Times* reported that "political supervisors within the Office of Justice Programs ordered Mr. Greenfeld [head of the Bureau of Justice Statistics] to delete certain references to the disparities from a news release that was drafted to announce the findings, according to more than a half-dozen Justice Department officials with knowledge of the situation." Greenfeld refused and "was initially threatened with dismissal and the possible loss of some pension benefits," an event that the *Times* notes "caps more than three years of simmering tensions over charges of political interference at the agency." He ultimately moved to a lesser position, and the report was posted to the BJS website without a news release or congressional briefing, leading to charges that the results were being buried (Lichtblau 2005).

Many traffic stops, especially for concerns like dirty license plates and minor violations like failing to signal a lane change, are really a pretext for searching for drugs or weapons. But the Supreme Court upheld their validity in *Whren v. U.S.* (1996), saying that as long as the police saw a violation for which they could stop a car, it did not matter that the stop was a pretext (Blast 1997). But *Whren* did not decide any racial discrimination issues raised under an equal protection challenge based on other precedents, such as *Yick Wo v. Hopkins*, in which the Court held that even if "the law itself be fair on its face and impartial in appearance, yet if it is applied and administered by public authority with an evil eye and an unequal hand the denial of equal justice is still within the prohibition of the Constitution" (118 U.S. 356 [1886]).

Pretextual stops based on racial bias erode trust in the system of justice and create the cynicism and hostility that was discussed in the opening narrative of this chapter. Harris, for example, contends that "pretext stops capture some who are guilty but at an unacceptably high societal cost" because they "undermine public confidence in law enforcement, erode the legitimacy of the criminal justice system, and make police work that much more difficult and dangerous" (1999). In addition, "pretextual traffic stops fuel the belief that the police are not only unfair and biased, but untruthful as well" because if the stop was about enforcement of the traffic code, there would be no need for a drug search:

> Stopping a driver for a traffic offense when the officer's real purpose is drug interdiction is a lie—a legally sanctioned one, to be sure, but a lie nonetheless. It should surprise no one that those who are the victims of police discrimination regard the testimony and statements of police with suspicion. If jurors don't believe truthful police testimony, crimes are left unpunished, law enforcement becomes much less effective, and the very people who need the police most are left less protected (Harris 1999).

These observations tend to be supported by polling data reported in the *Sourcebook of Criminal Justice Statistics* for 2004 and 2008 (see table 9.3 on reported confidence in the criminal justice system and police by race just before the implications section below).

On the other hand, the opposite of pretextual stops and aggressive policing may be referred to as underenforcement. As Donald Black (1983) articulated in his theory, "Crime as Social Control," among the socially disadvantaged, "crime is commonly moralistic and can be characterized as self-help in the pursuit of justice when legal protection fails" (Wilkinson et al. 2009, 25). In fact, studies of New York City, Philadelphia, and elsewhere, discussed in chapter four, revealed the need for marginalized urban males—absent the access to legal security—to rely on self- and group/gang protection from violence and as a means of indigenous social control.

While police are frequently considered the gatekeepers of the criminal justice system, prosecutors also make important decisions about who is released from the system and who gets processed further into it—and for what crimes. Prosecutors have wide discretion about which cases to pursue, the charges to make, and what bargains to offer in exchange for guilty pleas. These decisions become all the more important in relationship to the federal and state sentencing guidelines, which have removed a great deal of discretion from sentencing judges and made prosecutorial decisions more important. (The Supreme Court did strike down the guidelines in 2005 and made them advisory, but data from the Sentencing Guidelines Commission indicates that judges still tend to follow them, and sentencing practices in the year before and after the Supreme Court decision are quite similar.)

However, there is virtually no independent review of prosecutorial decisions as there are with judicial decisions or rulings, so bias at this stage of the criminal justice system is the least likely to be scrutinized. Often overlooked in the evaluation of "equal justice" and due process is the fact that when it comes to black defendants, "statistical studies indicate that prosecutors are more likely to pursue full prosecution, file more severe charges and seek more stringent penalties than in cases involving nonminority defendants" (*Harvard Law Review* 1988, 1520). At the same time, in those jurisdictions where the percentage of black prosecutors is more representative of the black population at large, the odds of receiving incarceration as opposed to probation are more racially equitable (Farrell, Ward, and Rousseau 2009).

Decisions about the severity of a crime can easily reflect conscious or unconscious stereotypes and racism that relate to dangerousness, moral depravity, and so on to nonwhite defendants. For example, Native Americans receive harsher treatment related to notions of "drunken Indians" or "wild savages." They may be seen as "outsiders" to the larger community, and court decisions may reflect paternalistic attitudes that "locking up the drunken Indians was the best thing they could do for them" (in Lynch and Patterson 1991, 108). Also with Native Americans, cultural factors can hinder communication about Anglo legal concepts or procedures as well as other important contextual aspects of the case (Welch 1996a, 284).

Moreover, as the *Harvard Law Review* (1988) article, "Developments in the Law: Race and the Criminal Process," concluded, a variety of studies indicate that black-on-white crime is most likely to be seen and treated as more serious in contrast to white-on-black or black-on-black crime. Similarly, both empirical data and mock trial experiments indicated that minority defendants face a greater risk of receiving unjust verdicts when their jury does not adequately represent minorities. That is, when the defendant was a minority, "white jurors [were] less likely to show compassion, and are less likely to be influenced by group discussion," so the defendant is more likely to be "found guilty and to be punished severely" (*Harvard Law Review* 1988, 1560). The same review also found that nonminority defendants who have had minority attorneys to represent them have not fared as well as those who have nonminority attorneys.

In fact, some argue that the race of the defendant and the victim matter more than any other personal characteristics. A survey of experimental research led the author of "'The Impact of Racial Demography on Jury Verdicts in Routine Adjudication" to conclude that "there is a tendency among white jurors to convict black defendants in situations where whites would be acquitted" (Levine 1997, 528–29). Further, as Harris noted with respect to pretextual stops, minorities' experience with racism and a greater distrust of the police, based partly on a history of excessive use of force and partly on a history of racial profiling, make minorities more suspicious of the prosecution's case, especially when based substantially on police testimony.

In contrast, whites' more favorable or benign interactions with police lead to less skepticism about the latter's testimony, and hence is given greater weight. And, while it is empirically demonstrable that juries with more black and Hispanic representation tend to acquit more than all-white juries do, this pattern may or may not be based on a form of jury nullification (or the acquittal of an obviously guilty person as a protest or expression of solidarity with the defendant by the jury). As Levine (1997, 537) noted, "Even when cases entail heart-wrenching mitigating circumstances or absurd laws, jurors are reluctant to acquit those whose guilt is indisputable."

CRIME, CRIMINAL IDENTIFICATION, AND GENDER CONTROL

Chapter 7 noted that most offenders and victims are male, so much of the law enforcement and adjudication involves largely male criminal justice employees processing mostly male perpetrators for crimes against other men. According to the FBI's Uniform Crime reports, for 2008, 76 percent of all arrests were men, including 82 percent of arrests for violent crime. Women, although a majority of the U.S. population, were a majority of those arrested only for the crimes of embezzlement (52 percent), prostitution and commercial vice (69 percent), and runaways (56 percent) (table 42). While the exact numbers and percentages change over time, the basic proportions have held constant for many years.

In some ways, UCR arrest data understates gender differences because the offense categories are broad and derived from a wide variety of criminal acts. For example, as Steffensmeier (1995) points out, "fraud" includes shoplifting a $10 item, stealing a radio from a parked car, stealing merchandise from one's workplace, and cargo theft worth thousands of dollars. Even though larceny-theft is considered a "serious crime" according to UCR definitions, most of the crimes women commit tend to fall at the lower range of offense seriousness. Most arrests of women are for shoplifting, passing bad checks, credit card fraud, and welfare fraud—not serious corporate frauds, let alone physically injurious acts like product defects, industrial pollution, or unsafe workplaces. Crimes women commit have tended to be extensions of women's domestic and consumer role activities (i.e., paying family bills and obtaining family necessities) rather than evidence of women becoming more like men in committing violent crimes.

In the 1970s, explanations of women's lower level of criminal involvement were often based on an assumption that women have benefited from police officers' and judges' paternalistic and/or chivalrous attitudes. As a result, the argument went, women were less likely to be arrested, convicted, or incarcerated. Over the past quarter century or more, assumptions of paternalism have been criticized on a number of grounds. First, most studies asserting paternalism have not empirically evaluated whether it is in fact responsible for the differences (Daly 1994). Second, there is ample reason to question whether all women have benefited equally from judicial paternalism—and, indeed, whether black women have *ever* benefited from it (see Raeder 1993; Young 1986). Klein (1995 [1973]) notes that chivalry is "a racist and classist concept . . . reserved for the women who are least likely ever to come in contact with the criminal justice system: the ladies, or white middle-class women" (10, 13).

Historical evidence of the lack of chivalry toward black women includes the fact that they were placed in chain gangs with men while white women offenders were placed in reformatories (Rafter 1990). Similarly, white women's rebellion against gender roles may lead to psychiatric treatment, while black women are more likely to wind up in prison (Hurtado 1989). Moreover, black women have been characterized by larger society and popular culture as "welfare queens," "Mammys," and "Jezebels," tough, masculine, "black Amazons," and castrating, dangerous "sinister Sapphires"—not the sorts of women upon which chivalry is generally bestowed (Mullings 1994; Young 1986). In contrast to the widely held but false belief in chivalry is the longstanding denial of police services to female victims of male domestic violence by the mostly male police force. Indeed, as chapter 7 noted the historical reluctance to define women as victims who have crimes committed against them in their homes or as part of a relationship, and the police have had a key role in using their discretion to not hold men accountable for their crimes against women. For example, Carol Jordan notes, "historically, studies have shown low rates of arrest of domestic violence offenders, ranging from 5% to 18% of cases" and "low arrest rates are documented even when victims have received physical injury from the abuse" (2004, 1416).

In response to widespread concerns and lawsuits claiming that policies denied women equal protection, jurisdictions passed mandatory arrest policies or preferred-arrest policies. Such policies reinforce the message that battering is a serious crime and aim to encourage police action, sometimes by creating conditions where the police should arrest even if the victim does not want to press charges. Although such actions taken against a woman's wishes may further disempower her and cause economic problems if the family is dependent on the batterer's income, the strategies were in response to police claims that they did not arrest because the battered women would not follow through and the case would be dropped anyway. Many jurisdictions also added prosecution "no drop" policies to make sure that police arrests would be matched by activity in the prosecutor's office.

The unfortunate result of these policies has been greater arrest rates of battered women because the police go into a situation and simply arrest both parties if there is evidence each side has hit the other. In this sense, "it is ironic to note, but holding the state accountable for women's safety through changes in law enforcement practices, many victims of ongoing battering have ended up with less protection and fewer services and have been labeled as a defendant. The consequences of mandatory arrest policies may be exacerbated for women of color, in part, because they are more likely to fight back" (Miller and Meloy 2006, 92). The perceived gender neutrality of the policy hurts domestic victims who need to contend not just with the abuse, but also an arrest and subsequent problems that may include denial of access to shelters because of an assault conviction, child custody issues, victim assistance, difficulties with employment or housing, and being mandated to attend a batterer intervention program (Miller and Meloy 2006).

Miller and Meloy note the problem is also partly caused by a criminal justice system based on incidents and not understanding the long-standing patterns of systemic—physical, sexual, and verbal—abuse that are frequently the context for the woman's actions. They further note that women are disadvantaged in the system because "women are not socialized to use violence, so they remember every incident" and thus "more readily admit their violence than do men" (2006, 92). Women also are "less savvy" about the criminal justice system, and all "these tendencies backfire for women but may fuel the perspective that women are mutually combative and violent in relationships" (2006, 92). (Remember the findings from the Bureau of Justice Statistics, reported in chapter 7, that "among violent crimes against a spouse, 86.1% of the offenders were male; against a boyfriend or girlfriend, 82.4%" [2005b, 14]).

One recent trend has involved trying to train police to identify a primary aggressor as a way to cut down on the number of victims who get arrested. However, advocates for battered women who do trainings with police report frustration in dealing with "the prevalence of sexism in the larger culture and the persistence of hegemonic masculinity in police departments in which women are denigrated and excluded" (Huisman, Martinez, and Wilson 2005, 795). Women represent a little more than 10 percent of all sworn officers and even fewer are in upper-level management, so there are few counters to male privilege. Trainers who pointed out the basic fact that most batterers are men were "accused of being sexist or man-hating" and questioned "sometimes belligerently" about resources for battered men

(Huisman et al. 2005). Female trainers seemed to be judged by their appearance and received feedback about being "man-hating lesbians with an agenda" (Huisman et al. 2005).

Some scholars have suggested that prosecutorial discretion has made it likely that women (particularly white, middle-class women) will be pursued less than men because women's crimes are typically less serious than men's and women do not present as great a threat to society as men do. In some cases, however, the reverse is true, and women may actually be subjected to more vigorous prosecution than men, such as with the criminal prosecution of pregnant, drug-using women. For example, beginning in the late 1980s and continuing throughout most of the 1990s, despite the harms associated with legal drugs, efforts to criminalize pregnant women's drug use had singled out cocaine users—particularly crack or rock cocaine users—for prosecution (Flavin 2009). "Drug-addicted pregnant women" tend to conjure up an image—not of a suburban white, middle-class woman who smokes, drinks, and takes prescription medications but rather of a poor, urban-dwelling, crack-addicted black woman trading sex for drugs. Few images generate less compassion than the latter, even though an article in the *Journal of the American Medical Association* reviewed seventy-four studies of prenatal cocaine exposure and found that while maternal cocaine use does increase risk, concerns have been exaggerated (Flavin 2009, 107). Moreover, the response has been an increased willingness to criminalize the woman's behavior rather than expand the availability of drug treatment and prenatal care, particularly for women who have small children or are infected with HIV. As a result, most of the women prosecuted have been low-income women of color.

Furthermore, criminalizing maternal conduct may discourage women from seeking prenatal care and drug treatment out of fear that they will be subjected to prosecution. One woman reports:

> I know a lot of mothers say that they don't get prenatal care 'cause they feel like as soon as they walk through the door, they will be judged, "Oh, you're a crack-head. Why the ____ did you get pregnant anyway?" So they don't get prenatal care . . . they have those commercials about addicts that don't get prenatal care because they just don't give a ____. They do give a ____, but they are thinking about how they gonna be looked at when they walk in the hospital door, like they not good enough to be pregnant (quoted in Rosenbaum and Irwin 1998, 315–16).

More generally, the criminalization of maternal drug use—especially when combined with fetal protection laws like the Unborn Victims of Violence Act discussed in chapter 8—presents a slippery slope; the precedent it sets could potentially justify prosecuting pregnant women for driving recklessly, getting in cars with reckless drivers, ignoring a doctor's advice to stay in bed, drinking alcohol or smoking tobacco, being homeless, or being involved with a violent partner.

In sum, in subtle and not so subtle ways, gender helps to shape the type of crime a person commits and the forms it takes as well as the responses of the criminal justice system, such as those involving domestic violence assaults, police behavior, and nonenforceable restraining orders for abusers to stay away. Further, prosecutorial decisions are helping shape areas of law like fetal rights and regulating women's reproductive behavior. By issuing no-procreation orders and prosecuting pregnant women for their actions, the law and the criminal justice system are deployed to establish what a "good woman" looks like and how conception, pregnancy, birth, care, and socialization should take place.

INTERSECTIONALITY AND THE IDENTIFICATION OF CRIMINALS

As previously discussed, men disproportionately commit crime, with black men overrepresented in many offense categories and women overrepresented in a few. And even though a variety of studies have indicated that black-on-white crime and white-on-white crime are most likely to be seen as serious in contrast to white-on-black and black-on-black crime, Radelet (1989), for example, has shown that the key dynamic involved was class, not race. Radelet reviewed the records of almost 16,000 executions that had occurred in the United States between 1608 and 1989 to look for cases in which whites had been executed for killing blacks. He was able to find only thirty cases—less than two-tenths of 1 percent. Some of these cases occurred during slavery, indicating that class was of more importance than race. In the remaining cases, Radelet (1989, 534–35) found examples where defendants had killed whites but could not be prosecuted because of lack of evidence, when defendants had long records or previous sentences to life imprisonment, and where the occupational status of blacks "clearly surpassed that of the white assailant," including cases "in which the defendants were marginal members of the community, perhaps being labeled as 'white trash.'"

Discussions of crime and offender characteristics have focused to such an extent on black men that, as noted earlier, "criminal" has almost become a synonym for black men. While official statistics that fail to combine race and gender make the task of criminal identification awkward, certain crimes seem to qualify as "white men's crimes" on the basis of their overrepresentation compared to women in general and minority males in particular. For arson, tax, gambling/lottery, pornography/prostitution, civil rights, environmental/wildlife, antitrust, and food and drug offenses, 70 percent or more of the offenders are white and 70 percent of the offenders are male (U.S. Sentencing Commission 1999). Of course, the serious underrepresentation of women and minority men as CEOs and in other executive positions of large corporations effectively blocks them from the access necessary to engage in large-scale white-collar crimes. Hence, it is not surprising, for example, that all forty-six of the individuals convicted in Operation Ill Wind, a large-scale defense procurement fraud investigation, were white males (Pasztor 1995), and the vast majority of those convicted in the Enron-style corporate frauds also have been white men.

A fundamental point of this and other chapters is that the intersections of class, race, and gender shape not only perceptions of crime but also the nature of criminal behavior itself and the responses of the criminal justice system. In short, opportunities to engage in legal and illegal behavior and to be pursued for the latter are shaped or framed by relations of class, race, and gender. Drawing on interviews from women cocaine users, Murphy and Rosenbaum (1997) identified ways in which race and class interact to profoundly influence the type of cocaine (powder versus crack/rock), patterns of use, and the consequences of drug use for different categories of women. Murphy and Rosenbaum consider two young women "who used cocaine too much": Monique, a poor underclass black woman living in an impoverished inner-city neighborhood, and Becky, a white, middle-class woman. Although there were similarities between the two women's experiences (e.g., both first snorted cocaine in a mixed-gender group with friends, both continued to use cocaine not because of the high but to be part of a social scene), several factors differentiated Monique and Becky's experiences with cocaine.

Monique, growing up in housing projects, was exposed to powder cocaine in early 1985 and was shown how to smoke crack within a year. The availability of crack in the neighborhood (with less risky drugs being harder to find) and the prevalence of crack use or dealing among her friends contributed to the escalation of Monique's crack use. By contrast, Becky lived in a white, middle-class neighborhood. Her first cocaine source was someone at an upscale rock and roll club. During the first two years, Becky's cocaine use was limited to the one night a week she worked at the club, though her cocaine snorting increased once she began to work more steadily at the club and as more of her friends used powder cocaine. Becky, with her own private room at work and at home, was able to conceal her drug use, whereas Monique's crack use kept her outside her house and on the streets. While Becky's avoidance of detection helped her to avoid the criminal justice system and the label of "deviant" despite her rising drug use, Monique was arrested, was stigmatized both formally and by her family, and she suffered many losses.

As the example of Becky and Monique illustrates, being black and poor places a person in closer geographical proximity to opportunities to buy and/or smoke cocaine and to become a criminal subject of the administration of justice. By contrast, class and race help to structurally protect someone who is a white, middle-class person with a stake in conformity from serious consequences of drug use. Such privileges as those shared by Becky and other white, middle-class drug users can make a "period of heavy [drug] use a mere detour on the road to a solid future" (Murphy and Rosenbaum 1997, 109). This type of complex and institutionalized selective enforcement and differential application of the law is, once again, reflective of the dynamic interactions of class, race, and gender.

Understanding the working of class, race, and gender requires an appreciation of structural inequalities embedded in society, which runs counter to the focus on individual acts, individual deviants, and individual pathologies. This is the focus that characterizes many media depictions as well what the police do in evaluating potential violation of the law. Further, "without an understanding of institutional aspects [of inequality], students decontextualize social interactions; they equate prejudice with oppression and argue that members of privileged groups are also oppressed" (in Huisman et al. 2005, 802). The decontextualized understanding sees society in terms of the "equal opportunity racism" described in the opening narrative of this chapter. The contextualized understanding sees the inequalities of class, race, and gender—dynamics that shape the attitudes and choices of the perpetrators, the treatment of victims, and the power that the criminal justice system can both reflect and re-create.

Finally, the combined differential application and selective enforcement of law by class income and racial composition is reflected in the reported confidence that these groups have for the criminal justice system and the police. Not surprisingly, data about public trust in the criminal justice system and police tends to reflect different sentiments by income as reported in table 9.2. As income increased in 2004, people had more confidence in the criminal justice system overall and the police specifically. While the category of a "great deal/quite a lot" of confidence showed increasing numbers as income goes up, the category of "very little" confidence showed very strong movement through the income distribution. For example, only 5 percent of those in the top income category had very little confidence in police; four times that number—more than 20 percent—of those in the lowest income category expressed very little confidence. Likewise the number expressing very little confidence in the criminal justice system doubled from the upper- to lower-income categories.

Four years later, the reported confidence in the criminal justice system had changed significantly. Across all five income brackets, confidence

Table 9.2. Reported Confidence in Criminal Justice and Police by Income, 2008

Income Level	Reported Confidence in the Criminal Justice System		Reported Confidence in Police	
	Great Deal/ Quite a Lot	*Very Little*	*Great Deal/ Quite a Lot*	*Very Little*
More than	35% (2004)	17%—23%	69%—66%	5%—6%
$75,000	22% (2008)		(2004) (2008)	
$50,000–$74,999	39%—23%	14%—27%	70%—65%	9%—7%
$30,000–$49,999	32%—20%	24%—34%	60%—59%	9%—9%
$20,000–$29,999	31%—12%	33%—9%	57%—42%	12%—14%
Under $20,000	31%—27%	31%—42%	60%—47%	21%—16%

Source: *Sourcebook of Criminal Justice Statistics*, 2005 and 2009, tables 2.11 and 2.12, respectively.

or favorables that ranged from 31 percent to 39 percent in 2004 had declined in 2008 by almost one-third. Most notably, it was the two higher income brackets whose confidence dropped the most. Police confidence in 2004 ranged from 57 percent to 70 percent, averaging almost twice as much confidence as in the criminal justice system. Four years later, police confidence had declined by about 10 percent. Noticeably, it is the two lower income brackets whose confidence had declined the most. While one could offer interpretations or speculations about these contradictory trends and findings between 2004 and 2008, we prefer not to because we think that for this data to be more meaningful, the income distribution or spread needs to be expanded above the $75,000 level to include at least $75,000–$100,000; $100,000–$150,000; and $200,000 and above.

There are some parallels between income and race in terms of the relative confidence in the criminal justice system and in the police as demonstrated in table 9.3. Regardless of income bracket and race—black or white only— the ratio of confidence in the police to the criminal justice is about 2:1. The confidence rates by income and race declined for both the criminal justice system and the police from 2004 to 2008. Comparatively, income appears

Table 9.3. Reported Confidence in Criminal Justice and Police by Race, 2008

Income Level	Reported Confidence in the Criminal Justice System		Reported Confidence in Police	
	Great Deal/ Quite a Lot	*Very Little*	*Great Deal/ Quite a Lot*	*Very Little*
White	36%—21%	21%—31%	70%—62%	8%—8%
Black	25%—17%	32%—31%	41%—36%	13%—21%

Source: *Sourcebook of Criminal Justice Statistics*, 2005 and 2009, tables 2.11 and 2.12, respectively.

to be far less important than race. While black and white confidence in the criminal justice system and the police had both declined, they also moved closer together, as the confidence of whites and higher-income persons declined at steeper rates than that of blacks and was irregular with respect to income. The income group that lost the most confidence in both the criminal justice system and the police was $20,000 to $29,000. The most significant difference between black and white confidence had to do with the police, with about 1.67 more whites than blacks expressing high levels of confidence in the police and about 2.15 as many blacks expressing very little confidence compared to whites for 2004 and 2008 combined.

IMPLICATIONS

A history of pseudoregulation of illegitimate white-collar and corporate behavior over the past three decades is the major reason for the current economic recession that came to a head in the United States at the end of 2007 and quickly spread around the world as the first serious global downturn in the new age of globalization. To put it simply, when America's financial markets fail to do what they are supposed to do, namely manage risk and allocate capital effectively, the results are nothing short of a global economic meltdown. Whether we are talking about the U.S. economy, the economies of the G-20's, or the global economy as a whole, unless all of these develop regulatory systems with teeth and confront the key structural issues of protectionism and international cooperation according to Joseph E. Stiglitz, recipient of the Nobel Prize in Economics in 2001, we lose some of the important benefits of globalization. Stiglitz chairs the UN Commission of Experts, which was given the task by the General Assembly of preparing an interim report for the G-20's summit in June 2009. Stiglitz (2009, 13) and the Commission identified ten policies that needed to be implemented immediately and "ten deeper reforms to the global financial system on which work needs to begin."

The point is there are more than a few experts out there who understand how these economies work and what needs to be done to restructure the economies of developed, developing, and underdeveloped countries in the context of both globalization and the world economy itself. Unfortunately, neither the United States nor the other members of the G-20's are willing to make the required substantive changes because these essentially hurt the interests of the privileged few from these countries. Domestically, the only way that special interests will not continue to dominate the U.S. political and economic policies is for the transmission belts of power (e.g., the lobbies) to be neutralized, if not eliminated by law. Otherwise, it will be "business as usual," where the rich and the powerful financial corporations they run will remain beyond incrimination. Hence, these white-collar and corporate acts of questionable and fraudulent intent will continue unabated. We are not calling for stiffer penalties for the unlucky few who end up facing criminal prosecutions, but instead, we seek real regulation, control, and oversight of the various financial empires and of their accountants, feeders, and those private investors involved in securitization. We are also calling for the restructuring of an economic system that works to the advantages of the few at the expense of most everybody else.

Unlike the underpoliced, privileged world of white-collar and corporate crime that victimizes virtually all members of society, the overpoliced, disadvantaged world of marginalized offenders victimizes mostly other poor people, especially those of color. In these differential processes of enforcement and in the context of class and race control, violations are often commonplace. For example, the Detroit, Los Angeles, and New York police departments have been under recent federal investigation for systematic human rights abuses, especially related to members of minority groups and to cases involving mentally or emotionally disturbed individuals who were killed under questionable circumstances. Other reports document police ill treatment of demonstrators, both in the street and in custody in jail, who were in Seattle protesting during the World Trade Organization talks in December 1999 and in New York City protesting the policies of the Bush administration during the Republican Convention in the summer of 2004. During the Seattle protests, police behavior was found to include indiscriminate use of pepper spray and tear gas against nonviolent protesters, unresisting residents, bystanders, and the excessive use of force by police against people held in the King County jail after arrest. Similar complaints were lodged in response to the police handling of demonstrators at the 2001 Biotechnology Industry Organization trade show in San Diego. As one member of the BioJustice Legal Team stated, police worked "to squash public debate over genetic engineering by harassing, intimidating and otherwise criminalizing the public for our concern with these issues" (McDonald 2001, A1).

Some of the violence in police-citizen encounters and police shootings may be attributed to disturbed officers, alcohol abuse, the game of "cops and robbers," and especially to the role of fear. But the bulk of this behavior has more fundamentally to do with issues of respect. As Hans Toch (1990) notes, police violence is often in response to taunts, because

the officer's self-love is gauged by "respect" from others. "Respect" for law, when a man feels he embodies the law, inspires private wars under color of law. Few officers may be violent, but these are backed by others—by peers who see police bonds as links to survival . . . violent suspects often tend to be counterparts of violent officers. These suspects also prize respect, and view it as a measure of self-esteem. This suggests that much police violence comes about when either party to a confrontation engages the other in a test of respect. Violence becomes probable where issues of self-esteem are mobilized for both contenders (230).

Where police forces are obsessed with real and imagined dangers, and where various communities are in fear of the police, polarization and distance between the two are inevitable. Fear, on both sides, increases in-grouping and/or protective behavior among police and increased alienation and distrust among citizens, which leads to further isolation, cynicism, and police abuse/violence. Across the United States, for example, the evidence is quite consistent that African Americans represent a disproportionate share of police shooting victims and that "this disproportion is greatest where elective shootings of non-assaultive, unarmed people are concerned" (Fyfe 1990, 238).

There is also evidence that police behavior can change to reduce the discrimination experienced by minorities and other marginal members of society compared to whites and other middle-class people. In the area of racial profiling, for example, media and public scrutiny resulted in changed leadership and in stronger commitments to fairness, the first steps toward reducing biased behavior in policing. One study of racial profiling involving traffic stops and searches in Rhode Island, between 2001 and 2005, found that disparities between whites and blacks were "significantly reduced when news media coverage [put] more pronounced pressure on police organizations and police departments" (Warren and Farrell 2009, 52).

While nobody can expect the police to engage in full enforcement of the criminal law and few expect that every observed and reported infraction of the legislative statutes could be formally prosecuted and adjudicated, the selective enforcement and differential application of the rule of law should, nevertheless, be carefully examined and officially monitored at all times, because individual and organizational discretion by police, prosecutors, and judges has historically reproduced patterns of crime control that adversely affect the poor and marginal members of society while they positively benefit members of the middle and upper classes. These patterns of law enforcement and prosecutorial discretion reflect not only the relations of class, race, and gender but also other factors as well, including but not limited to: the nature of the crime, departmental policies, the relationship between the victim and the offender, the amount of evidence, the preference of the victim, the demeanor of suspects, the legitimacy of the victim, and local politics (Bohm and Haley 2005).

REVIEW AND DISCUSSION QUESTIONS

1. With respect to class control, street and suite crime, and the administration of criminal law, discuss the workings of selective enforcement and differential application. Provide examples.
2. What are some of the reasons for inadequate prosecution of corporate or executive crimes?
3. In terms of race control, how does the criminal justice system work to the disadvantage of minorities and to the advantage of nonminorities? Provide examples.
4. Regarding gender control, use examples to describe the different ways in which men and women offenders are responded to by the administration of criminal justice.
5. How has the identification of criminals been affected by the intersections of at least two of any combination of the three variables—class, race, and gender? Provide examples.

10

Punishment, Sentencing, and Imprisonment

In 1984, Federal Sentencing Guidelines were adopted to curb the power and discretion of judges in sentencing criminals. The primary goal of the guidelines was to provide more uniformity in sentencing nationwide and to create sentencing policies that would be entirely neutral with respect to the offender's race/ethnicity, sex/gender, national origin, creed, and class/socioeconomic status. But many judges complained that these rules for punishment placed rigid constraints on their ability to make refined decisions based on defendants' circumstances (e.g., child abuse, mental illness, family situation, etc.). U.S. District Court judge David O. Carter, for example, has been quoted as saying: "Uniformity under the sentencing guidelines [is] a shield for defendants who deserved harsher sentences and a sword that struck down rehabilitation for those who deserved leniency. . . . Experience shows that uniformity [is] a bad proxy for justice"(in Weinstein and Rosenzweig 2005, 12A).

In 2005, the U.S. Supreme Court ruled in U.S. v. Booker (125 S. Ct. 738) and U.S. v. Fanfan (125 S. Ct. 1) that the guidelines are no longer binding, but advisory only (rather than completely invalid). Calling the Court's new approach to sentencing "wonderfully ironic," Justice Antonin Scalia wrote in his dissent: "In order to rescue from nullification a statutory scheme designed to eliminate discretionary sentencing [by judges], it discards the provisions that eliminate discretionary sentencing" (in Weinstein and Rosenzweig 2005, 12A). While this decision has the potential to restore more of a balance between the extremes of "indeterminate" and "determinate" sentencing systems, monitoring by the Sentencing Commission indicates no noticeable changes in sentencing practices since the decision.

At the heart of the guidelines controversy is the issue of the extent to which judges should be able to take into account the individual offender as well as the individual offense in determining the proper sentence for a convicted person. For example, Bobbi Brandt pleaded guilty to a one-count indictment charging her with the distribution of a tiny amount (two grams) of cocaine. The guidelines stated an applicable range of ten to sixteen months of incarceration. The court imposed a sentence of five years' probation and a $5,000 fine, a downward departure (more lenient) from the guidelines that the state of West Virginia appealed.

The sentencing court took into account that she had two young children whom she would lose in a custody battle because she was separating from her husband. Their father, however, would not be the one raising these children. As the court noted, "Strangers will be taking care of [her] children" (United States v. Brandt 907 F2d 31 [1990]). The court further considered that Brandt had been a teen mother and had dropped out of high school but was trying to stay employed and be a good mother: "The carrying forward of the guideline range of imprisonment . . . would have a devastating impact upon the emotions, mind and the physical well-being, just every aspect, of the two innocent youngsters to be separated from" their mother.

The state of West Virginia appealed the downward departure because the Sentencing Guidelines Commission had included wording that "family ties and responsibilities and community ties are not ordinarily relevant in determining whether a sentence should be outside the guidelines" (Nagel and Johnson 1994, 201). The appeals court framed the question as to whether Brandt's family responsibilities were "extraordinary" as called for in the guidelines and concluded that "the district court's implicit finding that the situation was extraordinary was clearly erroneous. . . . Mrs. Brandt's situation, though unfortunate, is simply not out of the ordinary . . . a sole, custodial parent is not a rarity in today's society, and imprisoning such a parent will by definition separate the parent from the children."

Under the same reasoning, other appeals courts had also denied to other single parents downward departures for a lack of extraordinary circumstances. In one case, a father was denied a downward departure even though he had three children and his wife was totally disabled, thus requiring care and being unable to help raise the children. The majority likened the situation to a single-parent family. Judge Heaney's dissent included such words as "unbelievably to me, we have held [single-parent families] to be absolutely ordinary, apparently without exception," and went on to say that while "Congress did not intend to make calculating machines out of district judges, yet time and time again this court has seen fit to . . . transfer that discretion to prosecutors whose actions remain utterly unreviewable" (United States v. Goff 20F3d 918 [1994]).

Significantly in U.S. v. Brandt, the appeals court did comment that having Brandt's children placed with strangers "would have been perfectly relevant before the advent of the Sentencing Guidelines and, obviously, quite sufficient even if there had been sentence review." In other words, as part of the shift from the "rehabilitation" model ("let the treatment fit the criminal") to the "just deserts" model ("let the punishment fit the crime") and the determinate sentencing system *that began in the late 1970s, Congress directed the Sentencing Commission to downplay "individualizing" factors such as ties to family and community, occupation, and education (U.S. Sentencing Commission 1992).*

With the Supreme Court's 2005 ruling in the Booker *and* Fanfan *cases making the guidelines advisory, it is uncertain whether these and other extenuating factors will become more relevant. On the one hand, judges—including the late Supreme Court Chief Justice Rehnquist—dislike guidelines because they deny judges their traditional powers of discretion, independence, and ability to impose alternative sentences no matter what mitigating circumstances may have been involved. On the other hand, advisory guidelines may be better than any new system politicians may come up with to replace the old sentencing guidelines.*

Indeed, Attorney General Gonzales, noting that the sentencing guideline system "made Americans safer and our system of justice fairer," suggested replacing the guidelines with a system of minimum guidelines. In his vision, "the sentencing court would be bound by the guidelines minimum" and "the guidelines maximum, however, would remain advisory, and the court would be bound to consider it, but not bound to adhere to it" (Gonzales 2005, emphasis in original). So, in effect, the Attorney General's proposal would make mandatory minimums that would deny discretion that might result in leniency or alternative punishments, but the advisory maximum punishments would only allow judges great discretion to get as tough as they wanted to be.

⟡

Punishment is an important aspect of the administration of justice in the United States and the effort to prevent and control crime. Historically, there have been several rationales or justifications for punishment, based in very different or contradictory approaches, and reflected in this chapter's opening narrative. Today, there are basically five rationales used to explain or justify the various punishments imposed by the criminal courts: retribution, deterrence, rehabilitation, incapacitation, and restoration.

From biblical times through most of U.S. history, the dominant justification of punishment has been retribution, whose essential idea is that the punishment should fit the harm done by the crime. Retribution implies some kind of repayment for an offense committed, with variations in terms of the more emotional *revenge* and the more rational *just deserts*. The former refers to paying the offender back by making him or her suffer; the latter to the proportional punishment deserved for the harm inflicted. Unlike the other rationales for punishment, retribution is the only one that focuses exclusively on the past criminal offense without consideration given to future criminality.

The classical school of criminology (see chapter 1) introduced the rationale of deterrence in the late eighteenth century. Classical theorists such as Beccaria believed that retribution by itself was a waste of time and that the only legitimate purpose for punishment was the prevention (or deterrence) of crime. Other classical theorists like Bentham were informed by a utilitarian philosophy of "the greatest good for the greatest number," under which the pain of punishment was morally valid if it produced a larger good, like a reduction in criminal victimization through deterrence or rehabilitation. Sentencing actual offenders so the punished individual will not engage in future crime involves *specific* deterrence; *general* deterrence refers to preventing other potential offenders from engaging in crime by the example set by punishing specific offenders. With the deterrence rationale, no longer is punishment solely dependent on the nature of the offense. In addition, consideration is focused on offenders—actual and potential—and the deterrent effects to be derived from the severity of the punishment.

Rehabilitation involves the attempt to "correct" the personality and behavior of offenders through educational, vocational, and therapeutic intervention or treatment. The goal of rehabilitation is not based on the fear of punishment but modifying the character of the offender so that she/he finds crime to be morally unacceptable or giving the offender skills (education, job training, etc.) so they can secure legitimate employment. "Treatment" may be carried out while an offender is incarcerated or while she/he is living in the community at large. Early U.S. efforts were religious in nature, with the *penitentiary* built around the idea of penance, a process through which sins are forgiven after they are confessed with true sorrow and promise to follow through on the priest's requirements. Penitentiaries gave way to *reformatories*, which offered a wider range of educational and vocational programs, although current "correctional institutions" tend to emphasize warehousing rather than actual correction (Irwin 2006).

Incapacitation usually refers to the removal (or restriction of the freedom) of those who have been convicted of a criminal violation. Typically, misdemeanants are incapacitated in jail with sentences of less than one year, while felons are incapacitated in prison with sentences of more than one year. This rationale emphasizes public safety in that incarcerated offenders, during their period of punishment, are virtually without access to committing further crimes in the free world. Two kinds of incapacitation are currently practiced in the United States: collective and selective. Collective incapacitation refers to sanctions applied to offenders without regard to their personal characteristics. Belonging to the offending crime categories such as violent offender, drug dealer, or child molester would qualify one for a lengthy prison sentence regardless of the circumstances involved in the offense. Selective incapacitation refers to efforts to identify high-risk offenders based on their criminal histories, drug use, schooling, employment records, etc., and to set them apart from other offenders of the same group.

The newest rationale of punishment, restoration, refers both to restoring or making victims of crime whole through various forms of victim compensation programs and to successfully reintegrating offenders with their communities. Unlike the other forms of punishment, which focus almost exclusively on offenders and their punishments, *restorative justice* seeks to restore or repair the health of the community, meet the needs of victims, and to involve the offender in the processes of restoration. Restitution and community service are two common forms of restorative practice by which convicted offenders, as part of their sentences, are required to pay money or provide services to their victims, their survivors, or their community.

In 2010, all of these punishment rationales are currently in use, although more than thirty years of "tough on crime" rhetoric and practice indicate retribution plays a primary role. During this period, legislation advanced as being tough on crime, as well as "sentencing reform" that had the same aim, including: mandatory sentences, truth in sentencing (mandating federal offenders serve a minimum of 85 percent of their sentence), "habitual offender" laws (requiring enhanced prison terms for repeat felony offenders, in some cases regardless of the pettiness of the offense), "three strikes and you're out" (mandatory lifetime sentences after repeat convictions), and then moves to increase the number of offenses that count as strikes (see the opening narrative of chapter 8 about Leandro Andrade.) Further, even while the rest of the world moved away from the death penalty, the United States has expanded the number of offenses that can potentially result in execution.

As a result of more people going to prison *and* those going to prison serving longer sentences, incarceration rates have increased dramatically. Figure 10.1 clearly shows the escalation in the rate per 100,000 of those incarcerated in state and federal prison from 1925 to 2004. These trajectories would be increased further if it included jail populations as well as those under control of the criminal justice system by way of parole or probation. In 2008, over 7.3 million people were on probation, in jail or prison, or on parole at year-end, up from a "total correctional" population of 6.1 million ten years earlier (BJS 2009d). This represented 3.2 percent of all U.S. adult residents or one in every thirty-one adults. At year-end 2008, slightly more than 2.3 million people were incarcerated in state and federal prisons and local jails, which translated to an overall incarceration rate of 754 inmates per 100,000 people (BJS 2009f, table 8). After sharp increases throughout the 1980s and the 1990s, the recent growth in the incarceration rate is at a slower pace (see figure 10.2), due also to the growing number of inmates, currently some 650,000 per year, being released back into society (Clear 2008).

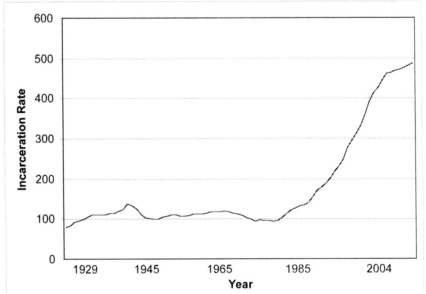

Figure 10.1.   U.S. Incarceration Rates in State and Federal Prisons (Per 100,000 Population), 1925–2004

Source: *Sourcebook 2003*, table 6.26, 500 and BJS *Prisoners in 2004*, 2.

Incarceration rate, 1980-2007
Number of offenders per 100,000 population

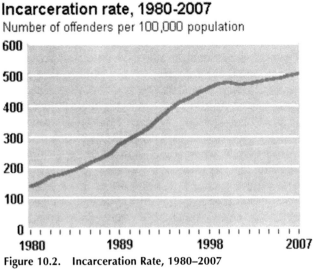

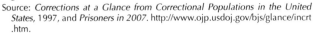

Figure 10.2.   Incarceration Rate, 1980–2007

Source: *Corrections at a Glance* from *Correctional Populations in the United States*, 1997, and *Prisoners in 2007*. http://www.ojp.usdoj.gov/bjs/glance/incrt .htm.

While incarceration rates from other countries are not always perfectly comparable, the picture still emerges that the United States leads the world with the highest incarceration rates, including developed and developing nations. The latest available figures from the International Centre for Prison Studies (2009) show the following incarceration rates:

- United States of America, 760 (2007)
- Russian Federation, 628 (2008)
- South Africa, 335 (2008)
- Brazil, 227 (2007)
- Mexico, 207 (2008)
- United Kingdom: England and Wales, 151 (2008)
- Australia, 129 (2007)
- China, 119 (2005)
- Canada, 116 (2007)
- Denmark, 63 (2007)
- Japan, 63 (2006)
- India, 33 (2006)

With the exception of Denmark, the rates for all the other countries rose a little from 2004. Going back to the 1990s, the U.S. rate was around 590 while other developed Western European countries had the following rates: Austria 85; France 90; Germany 90; Greece 55; Iceland 40; Italy 85; and Spain 110 (Christie 2000, 27). In terms of a decade ago or now, the rate of U.S. incarceration compared to other developed democracies in Europe ranged from a low of at least five times as great to more than fourteen times.

Importantly, criminologists have never been able to draw a connection between increases in incarceration and fluctuating crime rates (Platt and Takagi 1980; Currie 1998). As DiMascio (1998, 237) affirms: "Putting offenders behind bars may keep them from committing more crimes while they are there, but no significant overall deterrent effect has yet been proven." While many point to the decline in crime rates over the last ten years as "proof" that incarceration is effective at lowering the crime rate, this short-term analysis overlooks how incarceration rates have been increasing for more than three decades, and during much of that time crime was also increasing. Further, states and other countries that have not been as aggressive about "getting tough" have seen similar declines in crime rates.

While most criminologists do not deny the increased incarceration rate has had some impact on crime, overall estimates tend to be low. Blumstein, based on his research for the book *The Crime Drop in America*, suggests 25 percent of the reduction in crime is attributable to incarceration (Blumstein and Wallman 2000; see also Blumstein 2002, 22). Although his estimate is in the upper range, Conklin agrees in his book, *Why Crime Rates Fell,* but he also notes "the expansion of the inmate population certainly incurred exorbitant costs, both in terms of its disastrous impact on the lives of offenders and their families and in terms of the huge expenditure of tax revenue" (2003, 200). For 2006, the latest year for which expenditure data is available, all governments spent about $69 billion on corrections out of a total $215 billion spent on criminal justice (BJS 2008c, table 6.28). The corrections number is based on current operations only and thus substantially underestimates corrections spending because it does not include new prison construction—a high expense that frequently comes out of capital budgets or is supported by issuing bonds.

At about $24,000 per inmate per year plus construction costs for new prisons, money spent on corrections is an inefficient way to try to prevent crime. It also comes with what economists call an opportunity cost: money spent here cannot fund other programs. Some trade-offs are inevitable, but increasingly states are cutting budgets for schools, education, drug and alcohol treatment, and crime prevention programs that seek to create law-abiding citizens rather than simply punish them after a criminal act. One criminologist likens this tactic to "mopping the water off the floor while we let the tub overflow. Mopping harder may make some difference in the level of the flood. It does not, however, do anything about the open faucet" (Currie 1985, 85).

America's incarceration binge has been not only expensive and ineffective but it has also been a source of injustice. Normally, sentencing and incarceration are the culmination of the criminal justice system, where criminals get what they deserve. But as the sections below explain, incarceration is almost exclusively for poor criminals. It is disproportionate for minorities—so much so that the movement of black men into prison and back into the community is creating disorganization and eroding informal social controls that help prevent crime. And, though women represent a small portion of the incarcerated population, their sentences raise questions about gender and "equal justice."

CLASS AND THE PUNISHMENT OF OFFENDERS

Critics of the variability or disparity in sentencing have documented historical patterns of institutionalized discrimination against people of color and the poor (Lynch et al. 2008; Mann and Zatz 1998; Platt and Takagi 1980; Reiman and Leighton 2010). Significant inequalities are also described in the two previous chapters—that favor the rich through legislation defining what is a criminal violation and secondarily through prosecutorial discretion that dismisses multiple charges, in effect nullifying the possibility of severe punishments even before conviction and sentencing take place. The legislative and court processes taken together have consistently failed to criminalize the *analogous social harms* of the rich and powerful or have "decriminalized" them through nonenforcement or with "slaps on the wrist." During the same period, these same legal institutions have consistently ratcheted upward the severity of pain and punishment for the poor and/or powerless.

Even though the intention or motive of those who harm from the office suite is different from that of a street criminal who assaults a woman in an alley, their conduct may still fall within the statutory definition of the criminal law. For example, the people responsible for selling quantities of contaminated food to the public do not have the same desire to injure as the mugger in the park does. Nevertheless, the criminal law does recognize that harms committed with other states of mind are also criminal. An intentional and premeditated murder is the most serious, followed by murders that happen knowingly, recklessly, or negligently (Reiman and Leighton 2010a).

As criminologist Nancy Frank (1988, 18) has noted, the Model Penal Code from which many states borrow their statutory language "includes within the definition of murder any death caused by 'extreme indifference to human life.'" This language, of course, could include a number of scenarios where employers are commonly indifferent to the lives of their employees, such as when the former intentionally violates health and safety regulations or when miners die because they are made to work under unsupported roofs in places where the levels of explosive gasses have been falsely reported for months on end (Reiman and Leighton 2010a).

In 2005, an oil refinery in Texas City belonging to BP exploded, killing 15 and injuring 170. Several investigations, including one by the U.S. Chemical Safety and Hazard Board, traced maintenance problems to budget cuts (to increase profit) and noted that many ignored safety measures could have prevented the explosion. Carolyn Merritt, appointed by President Bush to be chair of the U.S. Chemical Safety Hazard Board, noted, "the problems that existed at BP Texas City were neither momentary nor superficial. They ran deep through that operation of a risk denial and a risk blindness that was not being addressed anywhere in the organization" (in Whiteside 2006). When asked on CBS's *60 Minutes* "if she thinks this accident could have been easily prevented, Merritt says, 'Absolutely'" (Whiteside 2006).

BP had to settle civil wrongful death suits and injury suits, and they had to pay fines levied by the Occupational Safety and Health Administration. But as far as the criminal law went, BP pleaded guilty to one violation of the federal Clean Air Act; it agreed to a $50 million dollar fine, made safety upgrades to the plant, and was on probation for three years (Fowler 2009).

Many victims protested the fine in light of BP's profits, which were more than $22 billion in 2006—about $50 million a day. In a challenge to the plea bargain, BP stated that the penalty was sufficiently "harsh" and the felony criminal prosecution is an "extraordinary outcome to a workplace accident, even an accident that results in multiple fatalities" (in Collette 2008). The company reviewed 3,000 records involving three or more fatalities and found only four criminal prosecutions. Obviously the fine did not do much to deter BP, because in 2009, OSHA alleged that BP had failed in 270 cases to comply with the terms of agreements and they found 439 new "willful" safety violations at the plant. The problems include failures to review, upgrade, and inspect critical systems that resulted in the earlier refinery explosion.

Holding corporations and/or their executives accountable can be difficult because their financial resources or "deep pockets" give them numerous advantages, which can be seen in the outbreak of Enron-style corporate fraud that included Health South, Adelphia, WorldCom, Global Crossing, Xerox, Waste Management, and others. In commenting on these corporate frauds, William Greider (2005, 4) captures the spirit of this contradictory approach to "getting tough" on crime when he writes: "In the deregulated realm of U.S. banking and finance, crime does occasionally pay for its foul deeds, not in prison time but by making modest rebates to the victims." For example, the WorldCom and Enron swindles could not have been accomplished without the ingenious balance sheet deceptions that required the active participation of financiers at Citigroup, JPMorgan Chase, and other leading banks. A *Wall Street Journal* editorial called the banks "Enron Enablers" (in Leighton and Reiman 2002), and a cover of the mainstream business publication *Fortune* magazine included the title: "Partners in Crime: The Untold Story of How Citi, JPMorgan Chase and Merrill Lynch Helped Enron Pull Off One of the Greatest Scams Ever" (quoted in Leighton and Reiman 2004). An earlier *Fortune* story commented, "They appear to have behaved in a guileful way and helped their corporate clients undertake unsavory practices. And they appear to have had an entire division that, among other things, helped corporations avoid taxes and manipulate their balance sheets through something called structured finance, which is a huge profit center for each bank" (in Leighton and Reiman 2002).

For its role in the WorldCom fraud, Citigroup, the biggest and most blatant of Wall Street offenders at the turn of the twenty-first century, paid $2.65 billion in fines to cheated investors as a result of civil—not criminal—suits. Similarly, for their roles in the Enron conning of thousands of investors and pensioners, Citigroup and JPMorgan Chase settled their lawsuits with the Securities and Exchange Commission (SEC) in June 2005 by agreeing to provide $2 billion and $2.2 billion, respectively, to some of the injured parties. These fines sound like a lot of money; however, considering that shareholders and pension funds lost more than $60 billion on Enron alone, such punishments are actually petty. (As noted in table 8.1, Citigroup is the fifty-eighth largest economy in the world and slightly smaller than the Gross Domestic Product of Egypt; JPMorgan Chase is the sixty-sixth largest economy and slightly bigger than Kuwait.)

As spelled out in the opening narrative of chapter 8, habitual offender laws apply to street crimes but not suite crimes. In the case of Citigroup, this global behemoth in international banking continued to engage in questionable banking practices and to grow despite its numerous fraudulent collaborations with other corporate giants such as Global Crossing, Dynegy, and Adelphia. Rather than face incarceration for executives or a breakup of the company, in 2008 the Federal Reserve declared that Citigroup was too big to fail. As of the summer of 2009, Citigroup had already "received $45 billion in taxpayers' money, along with guarantees on $300 billion in toxic assets, to mitigate its reckless risk-taking during the reign of such obscenely rewarded (and now departed) executives as Charles Prince and Robert Rubin" (Rich 2009b, wk. 8). Even though taxpayers now own some 34 percent of Citi, in order to get around Washington's new restrictions to reign in corporate abuse and greed, the bank that is too big to fail was busy not only increasing credit card interest rates (to nearly 30 percent in some cases) on the taxpayers whose money bailed them out but it also raised its own base salaries by 50 percent. As the boys on Wall Street are fond of saying, "New rules may come and go, but loopholes remain eternal" (Rich 2009b, wk. 8).

In short, when it comes to crimes of the powerful there are few apologies or penitence required. After all, neither the U.S. Congress, the SEC, nor any adjudicative tribunal is prepared to seriously challenge these and other large financial institutions that have plenty of money for campaign donations, high-powered lobbyists, and some potentially sweet job offers. In other words, the offending corporate giants simply pay out some money and get on with the business of making more money:

We might at least pause to marvel at what the modern bankerly imagination has created: a huge, all-service, guilt-free money machine. Criminal behavior is defined downward into a manageable cost of doing business. For its part in numerous reckless scandals, Citigroup has set aside (or already expended) an astonishing total of $9.8 billion. But since its quarterly earnings run around $5 billion, these costs are easily spread over years (and reduced by one-third after tax deductions) (Greider 2005, 4).

Sentences for some of those caught up in the corporate frauds have been long, certainly in comparison to previous sentences for white-collar crime

(Leighton and Reiman 2004). For example, Bernard Ebbers received twenty-five years for his role as CEO of Worldcom, which filed for bankruptcy just after Enron and displaced it as the largest corporate bankruptcy in American history. The sentence is worth investigating, as it is one that has made people question whether we have gone "too far" in punishing corporate crime. In upholding the sentence, the U.S. Court of Appeals states, "The securities fraud here was not puffery or cheerleading or even a misguided effort to protect the company." Rather, "the methods used were specifically intended to create a false picture of profitability even for professional analysts that, in Ebbers' case, was motivated by his personal financial circumstances" (in Reiman and Leighton, 2010b, 96). While Ebbers had no criminal history, the sentence length was determined by the severity of the crime. The court described the calculation:

> The pre-sentence report ("PSR") recommended a base offense level of six, plus sentencing enhancements of 26 levels for a loss over $100 million, of four levels for involving more than 50 victims, of two levels for receiving more than $1 million from financial institutions as a result of the offense, of four levels for leading a criminal activity involving five or more participants, and of two levels for abusing a position of public trust, bringing the total offense level to 44 levels. The government also sought a two-level enhancement for obstruction of justice on the basis of Ebbers' having testified contrary to the jury's verdict. With Ebbers' criminal history category of I, the Guidelines range calculated in the PSR was life imprisonment. The Probation Department recommended a 30-year sentence. Judge Jones declined to apply the enhancements for deriving more than $1 million from financial institutions or for obstruction of justice. She also denied Ebbers' motions for downward departures based on the claims that, inter alia, the loss overstated the seriousness of the offense, his medical condition was poor, and he had performed many beneficial community services and good works. She determined that his total offense level was 42 and that the advisory Guidelines range would be 30 years to life. She then sentenced Ebbers to 25 years' imprisonment and three years' supervised release, and imposed a $900 special assessment but no fines (in Reiman and Leighton 2010b, 96–97).

One question that comes up is whether Ebbers deserved a sentence longer than some people get for murder. But it is not inherently outrageous to say that causing $100 million in losses to more than fifty victims, while leading a criminal activity involving others and a breach of public trust, can be worse than taking one life. It is also true that his sentence was less than what Andrade received for two residential burglaries and two shoplifting charges over the course of decades (see chapter 8).

Perhaps such a sentence would not have been reasonable in the past, but the scale of financial crimes was also smaller then. The S&L losses were significantly smaller than the losses from WorldCom or Enron. Companies are now bigger, more powerful, and fraud—especially when it leads to a company's collapse—leaves a much larger financial crater. More people get hurt, and the losses are much more severe; there are more powerful ripple effects (including unemployment) through associated businesses and the economy in general (Reiman and Leighton 2010b, 99). While the sentence is long, note that the judge declined to apply several other enhancements. The court's opinion also notes that the sentence is based on a $100 million loss estimate, when "a loss calculation of $1 billion is therefore almost certainly too low" (in Reiman and Leighton 2010b, 100).

Further, attention has focused disproportionately on a relatively small number of sentences that are in the range of fifteen to thirty years. These were not run-of-the-mill white-collar crimes but systemic and widespread frauds that undermined the public's faith in the financial system and caused extensive harm to employees, communities, and shareholders. For example, the judge sentencing Enron's Skilling noted that he had "imposed on hundreds if not thousands of people a life sentence of poverty" (Johnson 2006). Focusing on the extreme cases gives a distorted sense of the overall picture of sentencing. An article in the *Federal Sentencing Reporter* tracked 440 of the highest profile cases of corporate fraud from the Enron era and found that 5 percent of cases resulted in acquittals and another 6 percent in dismissals. Eighteen percent were guilty verdicts, although 12 percent of these were overturned on appeal. By and large, the harsh sentences were reserved for those who went to trial and lost, although "the largest concentration of white-collar criminals convicted at trial received five-to-ten-year sentences." Guilty pleas accounted for 57 percent of the cases, and only two of those defendants received sentences of more than fifteen years: "The vast majority of those who plead received sentences of fewer than five years—the beneficiaries of sentencing guidelines that reward cooperation" (Barker, Baxter, Frankel, and Raymond 2008). So, a substantial number of those involved in the biggest financial scandal up to that point in time ended up with less than five years in prison, which is equivalent to the mandatory sentence triggered by possession of five grams of crack cocaine. Those who were found guilty at trial did receive longer sentences, although a final assessment needs to wait until we see how much actual time they serve because of reductions for good time and participation in rehabilitation programs.

Of course the Enron era fraud is dwarfed by the more than $2.5 trillion that American taxpayers paid to bail out Wall Street during the financial crisis of 2007–2008. AIG alone, among the world's largest insurance companies, received $180 billion because it too was "too big to fail." Another bailout recipient, Goldman Sachs, who was accused in a *Rolling Stone* article by Matt Taibbi (2009) as engineering every major market manipulation since the Great Depression, was "on track to pay its employees an average of $700,000 each in 2009, which, incredibly, is a bit higher than its compensation average in the pre-crash year of 2007. In the words of Bob Dylan, sometimes 'nothing succeeds like failure. . . .'" Whether or not one agrees with journalist Taibbi, what is "uncontroversial and indisputable is that Goldman alumni have played key roles in both the Bush and Obama administrations' responses" to the Great Recession of 2007—"even though Goldman has a big stake in the outcome" (Rich 2009b, wk. 8). Chapter 9 discussed the idea of agency takeover—where regulators come from the industry and return to it—and in many ways the Treasury Department of the government and related government functions have been taken over by Wall Street in general and Goldman in particular.

While people in the developed world seem not to understand what is going on, Nobel-winning economist Stiglitz wrote that: "In the developing world, people look at Washington and see a system of government that allowed Wall Street to write self-serving rules which put at risk the world economy—and then, when the day of reckoning came, turned to Wall Street to manage the recovery. They see continued re-distributions of wealth to the top of the pyramid, transparently at the expense of ordinary citizens" (in Rich 2009b, wk. 8). As Alyssa Katz, a New York journalist and author, argues in *Our Lot: How Real Estate Came to Own Us* (2009), the real estate bubble, like the Wall Street bubble, was a crime scene. But unlike other crimes, there are few chargeable criminal offenses and little punishment.

More generally, the point seems to be lost that sentences should be larger because the size and scope of the frauds are significantly larger than anything the United States or the world had ever seen. However, the situation has gone from bad to worse, in the "old days" at least, Enron and WorldCom were allowed to fail and file for bankruptcy; under the current economic regime, some financial institutions are too big to fail. As for the future, without the proper regulatory rules in place, the financial executives and their government enablers will continue to loot the general taxpayer and consumer without any negative consequences for themselves. And although the criminal justice system has really come down hard on some recent cases here and there, the powers of crime control are still largely disengaged from addressing the structural problems of the economy and financial fraud. Similarly, whatever toughness may have prevailed on a relatively few corporate offenders, it has been limited to a narrow range of financial offenses and has not spread to other types of white-collar crimes like willful violations of health and safety laws that result in death; these are still punishable by six months in prison—half the penalty for harassing a wild burrow on federal land (see chapter 8).

While wealthy offenders for more serious offenses are often weeded out on the way to prison, poor offenders often for less serious offenses find themselves on the "fast track" to prison. A profile of jailed inmates (BJS

2004b) and an older survey of state inmates (BJS 1993) revealed that one-third were unemployed before their arrests and that of those employed, about 30 percent described the work as part time or "occasional"; nearly 50 percent had annual incomes of less than $7,200 per year. These legal realities are even more pronounced when it comes to the administration of the death penalty in the United States. As Sister Helen Préjean, author of *Dead Man Walking*, has pointed out: "The death penalty is a poor person's issue. Always remember that after all the rhetoric that goes on in the legislative assemblies, in the end, when the deck is cast out, it is the poor who are selected to die in this country" (1995). On this point, Robert Johnson (1998), death penalty researcher and author of *Death Work*, concurs: "In America, and indeed around the world, members of poor and other marginal groups have been selected for the gallows with disturbing regularity."

Although societies are "quick" to execute the poor, the ultimate punishment of death is not sought when the poor are killed. As Préjean (1995) contends, "when the victim is poor, when the victim is a nobody, when the victim is homeless or a person of color—not only is the ultimate punishment not sought to avenge the death, but the case is not even seriously prosecuted." This pattern tells the poor and minorities that not only are they expendable but also that their lives are not worth killing for. By contrast, wealthy individuals are more likely to "get away with murder" either literally or figuratively when they victimize the poor rather than someone closer to their own social class.

RACE AND THE PUNISHMENT OF OFFENDERS

The United States is the world leader for the rate at which it incarcerates its citizens, and minorities are overrepresented in the penal system so they bear the brunt of this statistical trend. Long before gaining this status as the leader in incarceration, the United States had significantly higher rates of punishment for minorities handed out by the criminal justice system. The disparities between whites and minorities, especially among blacks, Hispanics, and Native Americans, are glaring because they reflect the cumulative biases from all stages of criminal justice administration in addition to other contributing factors, as indicated in figure 10.3.

The cumulative effect of these biases is striking and growing more intense with time even though the black imprisonment rates for both males and females have decreased between 2000 and 2007, as have the rates for Hispanic/Latino males, while white rates have increased (BJS 2008a). Most striking is the rate of incarceration in state and federal prisons compared to the respective populations. For example, the incarceration rate in 2007

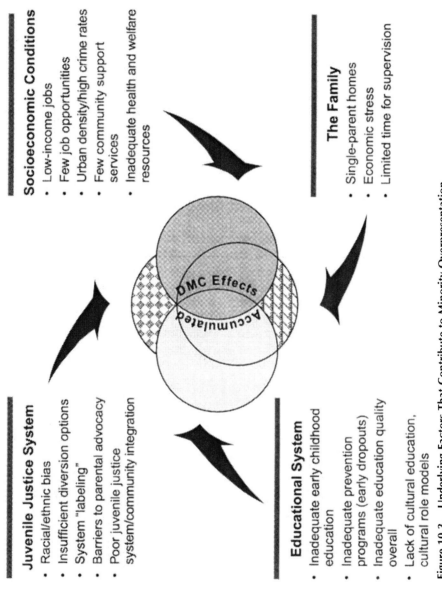

Socioeconomic Conditions
- Low-income jobs
- Few job opportunities
- Urban density/high crime rates
- Few community support services
- Inadequate health and welfare resources

The Family
- Single-parent homes
- Economic stress
- Limited time for supervision

Juvenile Justice System
- Racial/ethnic bias
- Insufficient diversion options
- System "labeling"
- Barriers to parental advocacy
- Poor juvenile justice system/community integration

Educational System
- Inadequate early childhood education
- Inadequate prevention programs (early dropouts)
- Inadequate education quality overall
- Lack of cultural education, cultural role models

DMC Effects
Accumulated

Figure 10.3.   Underlying Factors That Contribute to Minority Overpresentation

Table 10.1.   Imprisonment Rates for Sentenced Prisoners, 2007

Imprisonment Rate Per 100,000 U.S. Residents, on December 31	
Total (a)	506
Male (a)	955
White	481
Black	3,138
Hispanic or Latino	1,259
Female (a)	69
White (b)	50
Black (b)	150
Hispanic or Latino	79

Source: Bureau of Justice Statistics. 2008. *Prisoners in 2007* (December 2008, NCJ 224280).
(a) Includes American Indians, Alaska Natives, Asians, Native Hawaiians, other Pacific Islanders, and persons identifying two or more races.
(b) Excludes persons of Hispanic or Latino origins.

for white men is 481 per 100,000 population, compared to 3,138 for black men, with Hispanic or Latino men in between. Table 10.1 provides specific figures, which demonstrate a similar pattern for women.

While the intersections part of this chapter further explores the race and gender breakdown, table 10.2 provides a breakdown of the incarceration rate by race and ethnicity for jails and prisons. The third column hints at the cumulative impact incarceration policies have had on the current population by indicating the percentage of the current population that has been to prison. The final column provides the likelihood of incarceration in prison based on the current incarceration rate, which means that blacks are about five times more likely to go to prison in their lifetime and about one in five blacks will serve time in a state or federal prison.

Table 10.2.   People Under Control of the Criminal Justice System, by Race and Ethnicity

	Jail (Rate Per 100,000) 2004	Prison (Rate Per 100,000) 2001	% of Adult Population Ever Incarcerated in Prison 2001	% Ever Going to Prison during Lifetime If Born in 2001
White	160	366	1.4%	3.4%
Black	765	2209	8.9%	18.6%
Hispanic	262	759	4.3%	10%

Source: Bureau of Justice Statistics. *Prison and Jail Inmates Midyear, 2004* (NCJ 208801), 8; *Prison Policy Initiative, Racial Disparity in the United States,* available, www.prisonpolicy.org/graphs/US_incrates2001.shtml; Bureau of Justice Statistics. *Prevalence of Imprisonment in the U.S. Population, 1974–2001* (NCJ 197976), tables 5 and 9.

The analysis of cumulative likelihoods of incarceration is important because this population still suffers from the stigma of arrest records, which makes employment more difficult, and they carry the burden of a number of "invisible punishments" that reinforce social exclusion and marginalization (Travis 2002). Arrest and incarceration take people away from jobs and connections to the labor market while establishing a barrier to future employment because of the gap in employment history and the requirement of disclosing the conviction. Former National Institute of Justice director Jeremy Travis has also noted a number of punishments that continue after release, even though one has supposedly served the time for the crime. For example, those convicted of certain types of crimes lose their right to vote, hold certain professional licenses, and receive benefits like access to public housing, unemployment, food stamps, and student loans (Travis 2002). Although there is a rationale for these denials, they make it much more difficult for offenders to reenter society by denying access to affordable housing, denying them a source of legitimate income, and by erecting barriers to the education and professional credentials necessary to enter the workforce.

These effects attach most immediately; large numbers of formerly incarcerated people in a community can have negative effects on it as well. For example, incarceration "reduce[s] the marriageability of men and thereby reduce marriage formation. This, in turn, would increase the number of female-headed households in areas with high incarceration rates and, ultimately, increase crime rates due to an absence of supervision for young males in" areas of high incarceration (Lynch and Sabol 2000, 15). Criminologists also raise concerns about social disorganization from the removal ("coerced migration") of residents to prison and having them dumped back into the community with few resources—and, either not rehabilitated or ultimately worse off for their time in prison.

Todd Clear has summarized the point by stating that "very high concentrations of incarceration may well have a negative impact on public safety by leaving communities less capable of sustaining the informal social control that undergirds public safety" (2002, 181–82; see also 2008). This is not a general trend of incarceration per se but an analysis of how the effects of mass incarceration, when concentrated in areas with few resources like inner cities, can erode informal social controls like family, neighborhoods, and community groups. The results can mean the creation of criminogenic conditions, which are a potential exception to the general rule that incarceration adds to public safety by removing problem individuals from the community. If too many individuals are removed, especially for nonviolent offenses, the result could be different.

The increased rate of incarceration has fueled a prison construction boom in rural, and thus white, areas, with important racial consequences. Because of globalization and other economic trends, manufacturing and related jobs have disappeared from the United States. To make up for lost jobs, many communities actively lobby for a prison with unrealistic and exaggerated expectations about the economic development it will bring (Huling 2002). Having rural white guards oversee largely minority inner-city inmates creates some problems with racial harassment. But the larger issue is that for purposes of the Census, inmates are counted as residents where they are incarcerated, not their home. As a result, the population of largely white rural areas gets a boost, while cities show lower numbers of residents (Huling 2002, and see generally prisonersofthecensus.org). Then the Census figures used to allocate legislators to the state and U.S. Congress, as well as to distribute large amounts of aid, work against minority populations.

Collectively, higher rates of imprisonment for blacks and Hispanics also limit their abilities to participate in the political process and to affect changes in the system, criminal justice or otherwise. According to a report issued by The Sentencing Project, thirty-one states prohibit offenders from voting while they are on either probation or parole, and thirteen states disenfranchise most felons for life (Mauer 1997). The report estimated at the time that there were 4.2 million Americans currently or permanently disenfranchised from voting, including one in seven black males of voting age. Marc Mauer, the director of The Sentencing Project, has concluded, "The cumulative impact of such large numbers of persons being disenfranchised from the electoral process clearly dilutes the political power of the African American community" (1997, 12). When combined with population counts that affect legislators and financial aid, the sum total of these dynamics is to disadvantage racially diverse cities with large numbers of minority residents who have committed no crimes, while economically and politically privileging white areas.

A final significant issue with race and punishment is the death penalty, which is exercised less frequently each year although is of great symbolic importance because it represents one of the ultimate exercises of state power. Blacks made up 41.7 percent of the 3,207 prisoners under sentence of death at year-end 2008, and they were seventeen of the thirty-seven people executed that year (BJS 2009e, table 5, 4). But a forum sponsored by the American Bar Association on the death penalty reveals some of the deeper problems. For example, in capital cases, prosecutors routinely move to exclude all black jurors, on the grounds that such jurors would not only be sympathetic to black defendants but also to white defendants, because they are generally less supportive of the death penalty than whites are. As James Coleman argues:

> This can be traced to the legacy of our antebellum criminal justice system, in which slaves and free blacks were not considered equals and in which more severe punishment was accepted as normal. I think the country still believes

that black defendants deserve more severe punishment . . . especially when the victim of the crime is white. The criminal justice system will never be fair or nondiscriminatory until it is administered by both black and white citizens, until prosecutors and jurors are forced routinely to deal with the experiences of black people and to factor those experiences into their decisions. There is no such thing as a race-neutral decision in the criminal justice system, when it affects black people and when their voice is not part of the discussion leading to the decision (in Acker et al. 1998, 171).

While the overt discrimination has been reduced over time, disparity still remains. As David Baldus, one of the foremost authorities on the subject, has explained: "The risk of race effects was very low in the most aggravated capital cases; however, in the *mid-range* cases, where the "correct" sentence was less clear, and the room for exercise of discretion much broader, the race disparities are much stronger" (in Acker et al. 1998, 172). But even where the "correct" sentence was clear, the actual guilt of the convicted person can still be an issue along racial lines. That is, while exonerations of death-row inmates make headlines, the racial pattern of wrongful convictions has received less attention. But a study published in the American Bar Association's *Criminal Justice* magazine examined 107 cases of people on death row who were wrongfully convicted. Of these exonerated inmates, 58 percent were of minority defendants—45 percent were black and another 13 percent were other minorities (Parker, DeWees, and Radelet 2003).

Finally, Leigh Bienen points out the plight of blacks in a system where whites hold the power, although her words are a reminder about the mix of class and racial discrimination in the use of the death penalty:

> The criminal justice system is controlled and dominated by whites, although the recipients of punishment, including the death penalty, are disproportionately black. The death penalty is a symbol of state control and white control over blacks. Black males who present a threatening and defiant persona are the favorites of those administering the punishment, including the overwhelming middle-aged white, male prosecutors who—in running for election or re-election—find nothing gets them more votes than demonizing young black men. The reasons for this have more to do with the larger politics of the country than with the death penalty. I would also argue that the class and economic discrimination affecting the death penalty are "worse," in the sense of being more unjust, than the racial elements (in Acker et al. 1998, 171–72).

GENDER AND THE PUNISHMENT OF OFFENDERS

Although the environments of women's prisons are generally less oppressive than men's because there is less violence, conflict, interracial tension, and hostility toward staff, it has been suggested that women experience imprisonment more negatively than men (Pollock-Byrne 1990). Mostly, this has to do with women inmates' separation from their friends and family, especially children. Other contributing factors to this negativity are scarcity of resources, including a lack of work programs, vocational curriculum, and health services (compared to men's facilities); sexual harassment and abuse from prison staff; and fewer distinctions or classifications when it comes to custody and security levels (i.e., many states operate only one major prison for women).

At year-end 2008 women made up about 7 percent of the population in both state and federal prisons in the United States today, some 114,852 of the 1.6 million inmates in state and federal prison (BJS 2009f, Appendix table 1). However, for the past fifteen years incarceration rates for females have grown faster than incarceration rates for men. Between 1995 and 2003, for example, the total number of male inmates had grown 27 percent, while the number of female inmates had increased 42 percent. The pattern of faster growth in female incarceration rates has continued since 2003. Table 10.3 illustrates the recent rates, as well as the faster projected growth in the number of women who will spend time in prison. The absolute numbers are reported in table 10.4.

Because there are fewer women in prison does not mean the sentencing system is fair with respect to gender, as noted in the opening narrative. Indeed, compared to men, women are differently situated with respect to crime, most notably in that they typically commit less serious crimes than men do, engage in less violent crime, and are less likely to have a prior record. With women, "the most common pathways to crime are based on survival (of abuse and poverty) and substance abuse" (Bloom, Owen, and Covington 2003, 52). Thus, women are typically arrested for "survival" crimes, mostly property and drug-related crimes, including but not limited to bad checks, welfare fraud, and credit card abuse. Such crimes can be related to the gender inequality in the labor market (see chapter 5) and fewer well-paying jobs open to women, although criminal opportunities have a similar gender inequality; even with economic crimes women do not tend

Table 10.3. People under Control of the Criminal Justice System, by Gender

	Jail (Rate Per 100,000) 2006	Prison (Rate Per 100,000) 2006	% of Adult Population Ever Incarcerated in Prison 2001	% Ever Going to Prison during Lifetime If Born in 2001
Male	457	939	4.9%	11.3%
Female	66	67	0.5%	1.8%

Source: Bureau of Justice Statistics. *Prison and Jail Inmates at Midyear 2006* (NCJ 217675) tables 8 and 10; *Prevalence of Imprisonment in the U.S. Population, 1974–2001* (NCJ 197976). Table 5 and p. 1. BJS did not report the incarceration rate by gender in its 2007 and 2008 publications.

274 Chapter 10

Table 10.4. Number of Men and Women Prisoners, 1925–2007

Year	Total	Men	Women
1930	129,496	124,785	4,668
1940	173,706	167,345	6,361
1950	166,123	160,309	5,814
1960	212,953	205,265	7,688
1970	196,429	190,794	5,635
1980	303,974	303,643	12,331
1990	739,980	699,416	40,564
2000	1,331,278	1,244,454	84,913
2007	1,532,800	1,427,300	105,500

Source: *Sourcebook of Criminal Justice Statistics Online.* Table 6.28.2008.

to be drug kingpins or the ringleaders of retail theft organizations to nearly the extent men do.

Further, women are disproportionately represented among those incarcerated for public order violations, such as prostitution, begging, and driving under the influence (Warren 2005). Examining more specific crimes within each of these general categories of offenses reveals that women are nearly twice as likely as men to be jailed for larceny/theft and fraud, which probably reflects the greater likelihood of women being arrested for shoplifting and writing bad checks (Harlow 1998). While there are some violent women, reading the statistics about the increasing number of women in jail for assault requires caution because of the effect of mandatory arrest laws discussed in the previous chapter.

Characterizations of the "typical" male and female prisoners are useful for the purpose of appreciating why men typically receive harsher punishments than women and how the diverse needs of men and women call for overlapping, yet different, kinds of punitive responses. The typical male prisoner at the turn of the twenty-first century was black, twenty-five to twenty-nine years of age, convicted of a violent offense (Gilliard and Beck 1998), and probably the victim of physical and/or sexual abuse or neglect as a child. One study of adult male felons in New York, for example, found that 68 percent reported some form of victimization before age twelve, and that around one-third reported severe childhood physical abuse such as being kicked, bitten, burned or scalded, or threatened with a knife or gun (Weeks and Widom 1998). A typical woman prisoner was black, thirty to thirty-four years of age, convicted of a drug offense (Gilliard and Beck 1998), probably the victim of at least one sexual assault or rape (Warren 2005), and probably a mother of at least one child under the age of eighteen, with whom she lived before entering prison (Reed and Reed 1997).

Unlike male prison inmates who are usually incarcerated according to different levels of security (i.e., maximum, medium, minimum) and classification by type of offense, women prisoners are likely to be incarcerated at a facility with a diverse population of offenders. As measured on a per-inmate basis, expenditures for women for education, vocational, and other programs have been less than for men (Belknap 1996). The one notable exception has been for monies spent on health care, where women have received 60 percent more than men do. Reproductive issues are cited as one reason, but in a recent California investigation on the "state of female corrections," inmates told state legislators that they had not had a mammogram or Pap smear in years (Warren 2005). In fact, the greater expenditures are more likely related to the greater incidences of HIV and AIDS and with greater needs for mental health services.

In short, male facilities typically have more—and more diverse—programs than female facilities do, in part because of the occupational prevalence of stereotypical gender and sex roles and in part because of relatively more resources. Moreover, women's facilities tend to be smaller, fewer in number, and qualitatively different from men's prisons. For example, women's prisons are more likely than men's to have a cottage-style design and are less likely to have intimidating features such as gun towers, high concrete walls, and armed guards. This form of imprisoning inmates dates back to the early twentieth century when cottages were used to house small groups of women so they could "live with a motherly matron in a family setting" (Rierden 1997, 7). The legacy of this era has meant that women's prisons are still tending to infantilize and domesticize women while reinforcing gender stereotypes (Belknap 1996). Over time, there has been an increasing move toward the confinement model used in men's prisons, designed to hold hundreds of female inmates. This development, however, is another example of seeming gender neutrality that is actually based on a male standard (see chapter 5) rather than a genuine effort to address the actual needs of women.

The problem of seeming gender neutrality can be compounded when classification and risk assessment surveys designed with men are used with women, drug or alcohol programs designed for men are applied to women, and staff are not given training about the different needs and expectations of women (Bloom et al. 2003). Further, "national studies, research and national focus group interviews have all identified negative attitudes and cultural stereotypes about the female as major obstacles to supervising women and providing services for them" (24). Women can be seen as "more trouble" than men because of their different style of communication that emphasizes connection and their "expectation that agents will provide help, in terms of concrete assistance in navigating the system and providing other aid" (15).

Another important difference with female inmates is their relationship with children. While a large number of incarcerated men are fathers, 70 percent of female offenders have a child under eighteen and are likely to be the primary caretaker. While "there is significant evidence that the mother-child relationship may hold significant potential for community reintegration," women in prison tend to be isolated because of geography, transportation, economic resources, and the termination of parental rights (Bloom et al. 2003, 56–57). Further, programs do little to help women with job skills so that they are in a better economic position to support children or enhance their capacity in other ways to set up a life that would involve reunification with children.

Finally, although the Eighth Amendment does not mandate comfortable prisons, such sentences should not include *additional* punishments for women or men. Sexual and other abuses of inmates, particularly male inmates by other male inmates, female inmates by male staff, and juvenile inmates by both, continue to present serious problems in adult and juvenile institutions across America. Within women's prisons, inmates frequently form supportive "play family" or "prison family" arrangements, with substantially less inmate-on-inmate violence than in men's prisons. Victimization of female inmates has tended to come from male staff that uses the power differences between them to coerce or exploit inmates. An Amnesty International report noted that there is a "significant difference" between the law in the United States and international standards on the treatment of female inmates. The report, titled "Not Part of My Sentence," was based on a comment made by a female inmate that performing oral sex on male officers was not part of the judge's sentence. But deficits in cross-sex supervision coupled with inadequate procedures for reporting misconduct and fear of retaliation have lead to numerous problems (Amnesty International 1999b).

International standards provide that female prisoners should be supervised only by female guards, but sex discrimination laws in the United States mean that men can work in women's prisons and women can work in men's prisons. Thus, "under the laws of the USA, a male guard may watch over a woman, even when she is dressing or showering or using the toilet. He may touch every part of her body when he searches for contraband" (Amnesty International 1999b, 2). In popular culture, sex in women's prison is eroticized as evidenced by the "chicks in chains" film genre and the "jail babes" dating services that have sprung up to capitalize on the increasing number of women in prison. But the reality is very different, and "women prisoners with histories of abuse may be re-traumatized by sexual harassment and abuse in prison" (Bloom et al. 2003, 26). The result includes post-traumatic stress disorder, depression, "and decreased ability to participate in rehabilitative programs," which ultimately affect reintegration and recidivism (26).

In men's prisons, sexual violence tends to be inmate-on-inmate and rape functions as a violent rite of passage to convert "men" into "punks" to create hierarchies of power and control, to meet part of the demand for sexual partners, and establish claims to masculinity. Gresham Sykes (1958) noted that one of the pains of imprisonment was a deprivation of heterosexual contact. In this situation, men have to define "manhood" without women and do so by emphasizing the worst aspects of the male gender role—aggression, domination, and emotional coldness. The victims are symbolically transformed into women and even take on the "womanly" functions of the relationship. Punks will often do household chores that mimic those of the traditional female such as the laundry, making the bunk, making coffee, or cleaning the cell. Prisoner subculture dictates that aggressive-penetrative activity is not homosexual, while receptive-penetrated activity is considered homosexual. While in prison, "the guys are not as concerned about whom you are in bed with so much as who is in charge, that is, who is doing the (expletive), the penetrating, who is the Man, who is 'normal'" (Tucker 1981). The phrase "homosexual rape" is thus misleading since the overwhelming majority of prisoner rape victims and perpetrators are heterosexual and resume heterosexual behavior when they are released from incarceration.

One strategy some men use to avoid sexual victimization is to "hook up" with another inmate. In exchange for sexual favors, men who fear victimization can pair off with a "Man" or predatory "Wolf" for protection from gang rapes or repeated threats of rape. The resulting relationships do not reflect consensual homosexuality as much as survival-driven behavior. Men who wish to avoid being turned out, or who desire to undo its effect, must often use violence. Sometimes, they must even take on the characteristics of the perpetrator themselves. One Texas inmate explained: "It's fixed where if you're raped, the only way you [can stop the abuse is if] you rape someone else. Yes I know that's fully screwed, but that's how your head is twisted. After it's over you may be disgusted with yourself, but you realize you're not powerless and that you can deliver as well as receive pain. Then it's up to you to decide whether you enjoy it or not" (Human Rights Watch 2001).

INTERSECTIONS AND THE PUNISHMENT OF OFFENDERS

One classic illustration of corporate crime involved the manufacture and distribution of the Dalkon Shield, a birth control device, by the A. H. Robins Company. In 1971, the company started selling the intrauterine device (IUD) as a safe, modern, and effective product. Although A. H. Robins had performed few tests on the device, marketing and promotion went ahead quickly, and by 1975 some 4.5 million IUDs had been distributed. Early reports indicated many problems, including that the tail string from the device hung outside the vagina and wicked bacteria up into the woman's body, and the device was not especially effective at preventing pregnancy, either. Even worse, women suffered from a variety of crippling and life-threatening infections, some of which required emergency hysterectomies; others had unwanted pregnancies that resulted in miscarriages or sponta-neous abortions; or, because of infections, they gave birth to children with severe birth defects. Conservative estimates indicated that some 200,000 women were injured (Clinard 1990).

Two court-appointed examiners in 1985 found that Robins had engaged "in ongoing fraud by knowingly misrepresenting the nature, quality, safety and efficacy" of its IUD. The fraud also "involved the destruction and with-holding of relevant evidence" (in Clinard 1990, 104). In spite of these facts, no prosecutor brought criminal charges against the company or its execu-tives. Women were left on their own to file a variety of civil product liability suits. In response, Robins tried to file for bankruptcy in order to avoid li-ability. However, a judge required the company to establish a trust fund to compensate victims, and he had to reprimand Robins for giving substantial bonuses to its top executives in violation of the bankruptcy laws.

Judge Miles Lord, who heard some 400 civil law cases, in a famous plea for corporate conscience, pointed out the class bias of the judicial process workings:

> If some poor young man was, by some act of his—without authority or con-sent—to inflict such damage on one woman, he would be jailed for a good portion of the rest of his life. And yet your company, without warning to women, invaded their bodies by the millions and caused them injury by the thousands. And when the time came for these women to make claims against your company, you attacked their characters. You inquired into sexual practices and into the identity of their sex partners. You exposed these women—and ruined families and reputation and careers—in order to intimidate those who would raise their voice against you. You introduced issues that had no rela-tionship whatsoever to the fact that you planted in the bodies of these women instruments of death, of mutilation, of disease (in Hills 1987, 42).

Judge Lord also noted that the underlying harm—inflicting harm without consent—is expressed in the street crime of assault and punishable with imprisonment, but there is no analogous crime for corporations. Indeed, A. H. Robins may have been more harshly punished if the victims of its birth control device had included more wealthy women. Or, the consequences might have been harsher had the injured parties been men rather than women, who Judge Lord noted "seem through some strange quirk in our society's mores to be expected to suffer pain, shame and humiliation" (in Hills 1987, 42). The executives from Robins ultimately had to listen to a lecture and return some bonus pay as punishment, whereas offenders who engage in other assaults face prison time.

The previous sections discussed the disproportionate number of blacks and Hispanics in prison and the largely male nature of incarceration, with white rates of incarceration growing faster than black and brown ones between 2000 and 2007. The reality of the statistics does not necessarily capture how the experience of being incarcerated breeds feelings of despair and hopelessness, and often anger and rage, for those individuals imprisoned, thus impacting their lives. These disparities in sentencing or differential applications of the criminal law related to socioeconomic status or to class, race, and gender also collectively impact members of the affected categories or groups. For example, these feelings in combination with the stigma of having been incarcerated often make it difficult to find little else than minimum-wage employment, if that, upon release. Moreover, businesses are less likely to locate in areas with large numbers of poor people, especially those with high concentrations of black men, because of concerns about the pool of labor, so these communities find it difficult, if not impossible, to build any type of economically viable base.

Higher rates of black incarceration for men and women weaken both the economic and familiar stability of black and other poor communities (Johnson, Farrell, and Stoloff 1998). Specifically, these correctional practices that disproportionately affect African Americans and other poor minorities have an impact on noncriminal impoverished women and their children (Danner 1998). In other words, as corrections budgets have increased nationwide, state funds to support poor and low-income families have been slashed along with other social services and social service positions disproportionately staffed by women. These connections show problems with conventional discussions of punishment that tend to treat corrections as if it was a discrete and independent social institution. Far from being an entity separate unto itself, the entire criminal justice system, especially the correctional system, has become inextricably intertwined with the welfare system, the political system, and—with the increasing privatization of corrections—the economic system. For example, the impact of having one in three black men under the control of the criminal justice system cannot be separated from the welfare system's Temporary Assistance to Needy Families (TANF) program or to the high percentage of single-female black households. Similarly, the secondary impact of incarceration of poor women on their children cannot be underestimated with respect to the increased likelihood of the latter's delinquency.

Further, TANF, created by the Personal Responsibility and Work Opportunity Reconciliation Act of 1996 that replaced the Aid to Families with Dependent Children (AFDC), prohibits individuals who violate probation or parole orders and their families from receiving TANF or food stamps. The act does not distinguish between minor technical violations such as missing an appointment with a probation or parole officer and committing a new crime. Another provision bans persons convicted of drug felonies from receiving TANF or food stamps for the rest of their lives. Consequently, critics of the act were quick to express concern that children would feel the repercussions of provisions intended to punish their mothers and promote "personal responsibility." Hence, children of a poor woman suffer consequences for their mother's behavior in a way that middle-class children would not, should either of their parents get busted for using drugs.

Another important addition to the understanding of intersections comes from examining private prisons. While chapter 2 examined privatization in more detail, what is of interest here is that the dramatic growth in incarceration has attracted the interest of numerous business owners who see prison as a "growth industry" that they can cash in on. The most visible of these industries are for-profit companies, some of which have shares traded on the stock market, which build and run prisons (see box 10.1). A full review of the pros and cons is beyond the scope of this section (Dyer 2000; Killingbeck 2005), however, the important point is that those who are incarcerated are largely poor white, black, and Hispanic-Latino men, while those who benefit economically from private prisons are wealthy white men. The latter tend to own most shares of publicly traded stock as well as businesses, and the economic links also tend to benefit other white men who are in financial services (which underwrite loans) or corporate law.

More generally, privatization of correctional services can end up harming many in prison while enriching business owners. Take, for example, the story of Prison Health Services, Inc. The cover story of the *New York Times* for February 27, 2005, read: "As Health Care in Jails Goes Private, 10 Days Can Be a Death Sentence." The expose of Prison Health revealed that as governments try to reduce the burden of soaring medical costs—due to the expanding and aging prison populations, exacerbated by the exploding problems of AIDS and mental illness among inmates—this new for-profit field has become a multibillion-a-year industry.

The yearlong examination of Prison Health Services (the leader in the field) by the *New York Times* revealed repeated instances of medical care that had been flawed and sometimes lethal. "The company's performance around the nation has provoked criticism from judges and sheriffs, lawsuits from inmates' families and whistle-blowers, and condemnations by federal, state, and local authorities. The company has paid millions of dollars in fines and settlements" (von Zielbauer 2005, A1). Despite the

Box 10.1.   Punishment for Sale: Private Prison, Big Business, and the Incarceration Binge

Chapter 2 identified privatization as one of the major trends that would continue to exert an influence on the criminal justice enterprise. Privatization refers to the practice of outsourcing government functions and services to private, for-profit business under a contract with the government. Punishment and incarceration may seem like odd functions to privatize, but private prisons are a multibillion dollar a year business and the two largest firms—Corrections Corporation of America (CCA) and GEO Group—are multinational businesses that are traded on Wall Street.

In a recent groundbreaking examination of prison privatization, criminologists Donna Selman and Paul Leighton argue in *Punishment for Sale* (2010) that understanding the nature of the contemporary criminal justice system requires understanding privatization, including the business model and financial dynamics of these firms. It's not just a multibillion dollar business, but CCA has a billion dollar credit line with various powerful Wall Street investment banks. They—and all the shareholders—ensure that the private prison firms are managing the business risk factors that they must disclose in filings with the SEC. Risk factors include not getting enough inmates from government to be profitable, sentencing reform (like the repeal of certain mandatory minimum sentences), steps toward the legalization of drugs, and immigration reform. While these are controversial topics, the debate over justice policy needs to be on the merits of reform—not based on the financial interests of wealthy shareholders and Wall Street. Indeed, research demonstrates that private prison firms have already influenced public policy to their own benefit through campaign donations, and they have rejected a shareholder proposal to fully disclose donations and lobbying money. (They have also voted down proposals to make the performance incentive piece of executives include criteria related to the absence of human rights or labor violations.)

Selman and Leighton (2010) argue that privatization was born from two trends. First, the relentless war on crime and war on drugs caused massive prison overcrowding. Extremely costly prison expansion and renovation were the inevitable results of "getting tough," but it ran into conflict with politicans' other favorite lines about lower taxes and less government. Second, President Ronald Reagan declared in his first inaugural address that "government is the problem," and he set the stage for antigovernment politicians to privatize a range of services. The historical moment was ripe for several politically well-connected individuals, backed by the same venture capital that facilitated the expansion of Kentucky Fried Chicken, to use private funds to build their own prison and collect money from government to house inmates from overcrowded facilities.

As briefly noted in this chapter, the incarceration binge has been costly and ineffective—and has contributed to social injustice (especially racial). Selman and Leighton (2010), after developing these points more fully, argue that private

(*continued*)

Box 10.1. (*continued*)

of their business depends on the continuation of those dynamics. Companies traded on the stock exchange owe a basic duty to shareholders to grow and become more profitable, regardless of the impact on others or on justice.

Privatization has several important implications for understanding the intersections of class, race, gender, and crime. First, in a variation of *The Rich Get Richer and the Poor Get Prison* (Reiman and Leighton 2010a), with prison privatization *the rich whites get richer because the poor minorities go to prison.* As noted in chapter 3, stock ownership is concentrated in the hand of relatively few wealthy families who are mostly white. As noted in this chapter, those going to prison are disproportionately minority—and private prisons have a substantial number of contracts to house immigrants (including detained families). Racial fear means business and profits for private prison companies.

Second, chapter 2 noted that private prison firms pay substantially less than their government counterparts for prison staff, a point that generates opposition to privatization from unions. (Median earnings for all correctional officers and jailers were $35,760, but private prisons paid $25,050.) But private prison firms also pay their executives substantially more than the head of a Department of Corrections who manages substantially more inmates. For example, the cash pay (excluding stock awards and options) of the CEO for the GEO Group was almost $3 million in 2007 for having 54,000 beds under supervision. The Director of Corrections for Michigan was paid just over $200,000 that year for having almost 52,000 inmates under supervision *and* a parole and probation caseload of another 200,000 people (Selman and Leighton 2010).

Paying those at the top substantially more while paying those at the bottom substantially less directly contributes to income and class inequality. This process is exacerbated by additional fees at the top to the Board of Directors, who make $50,000 a year at CCA and $60,000 a year at GEO, plus fees for attending various meetings (including a compensation committee that decides how much the executive gets paid). In comparison, the median household income in 2007 was $50,230, so the pay for the part-time director position of a private prison was more than what half of all U.S. households earned from all their employment responsibilities (Selman and Leighton 2010). Overhead costs for the directors, SEC lawyers, consultants, mergers and acquisitions, "customer acquisition" (advertising and lobbying), shareholder lawsuits, and shareholder relations mean a wide variety of criminal justice workers will have lower wages and less economic security than if they had a government job.

similar patterns of abuse found across the nation, like the ones described in New York below, Prison Health has been an ongoing concern:

> In the two deaths, and eight others across upstate New York, state investigators say they kept discovering the same failings: medical staffs trimmed to the

bone, doctors underqualified or out of reach, nurses doing tasks beyond their training, prescription drugs withheld, patient records unread and employee misconduct unpunished. Not surprisingly, Prison Health, which is based outside of Nashville, is no longer working in most of those upstate jails. But it is hardly out of work. Despite a tarnished record [from coast to coast], Prison Health has sold its promise of lower costs and better care, and become the biggest for-profit company providing medical care in jails and prisons. It has amassed 86 contracts in 28 states, and now cares for 237,000 inmates, or about 1 in every 10 people behind bars (von Zielbauer 2005, A26).

IMPLICATIONS

Crime control policies constantly reward financial white-collar criminals, especially those corporate giants found on Main, Wall, and global streets alike, that line their pockets millions of times over at the expense of the general public and well-being of the world. At the same time, crime control policies overwhelmingly penalize the poor and people of color, especially black and Hispanic or Latino persons, for relatively harmless acts and numerous "crimes without victims." For the latter groups of people, who become inhabitants of U.S. penal institutions, the behind-bars abuse, violence, and victimization come in a variety of forms, shapes, and practices. Penal violence, however, is pretty much hidden or invisible from public scrutiny, much like the disproportionate numbers of minority citizens contained in prisons. For example, as Sykes and Piquero (2009, 214) have found with respect to contracting HIV inside and outside of prison as well as with other health testing in general that "the penal institution is an active agent in structuring and re-creating health inequalities within prisons, thereby exacerbating existing community health inequities when inmates are released."

Recent changes in state laws have been in the process of overturning a century-old juvenile justice system whose very reason for existence was to protect children from contact with adult prisoners. Despite the fact that whites commit most juvenile crimes, three out of four youths admitted to adult courts, jails, and prisons are children of color. In spite of the fact that penologists and criminologists almost all agree that these children are more likely to be physically and sexually abused in these institutions than in juvenile institutions and that they are more likely to continue committing crimes after their release, more and more prosecutors are moving young offenders into the adult system with little, if any, regard for the child's age or circumstances.

Ultimately, the institutionalization of penal violence cannot be divorced or separated from the structural conditions residing inside and outside the confining walls. As Angela Davis (1998, 2) has reflected, the "prison industrial system materially and morally impoverishes its inhabitants and devours the social wealth needed to address the very problems that have led to spiraling numbers of prisons." The focus should thus not be only on a criminal justice system in need of reform but also on the "Perpetual Prisoner Machine" (Dyer 2000) that has been increasing its size and proportion of state and federal fiscal budgets relative to the declining dollars spent on education and social services since the late 1990s. In turn, these relationships cannot be separated from the structural changes of a postindustrial service economy caught within the contemporary epoch of globalization.

REVIEW AND DISCUSSION QUESTIONS

1. When it comes to disparities in punishment, sentencing, and imprisonment in the United States, which is more important—class, race, or gender—and why?
2. Historically, there have been five major rationales or justifications for punishment. First, identify and briefly discuss each of these. Second, make a case for the support or rejection of each. Third, based on current trends in punishment in the United States, do you believe that any one of these is the dominant one?
3. Given that the United States is more punitive than any of the other developed nations and has the highest incarceration rates in the world, how can anybody make a case for mandatory sentencing laws?
4. What are some of the differences between men and women with respect to the crimes they commit, the punishments they receive, and the conditions of their imprisonment?
5. Though most critics of disparity in sentences point to the more obvious patterns in discrimination against certain minorities and the poor, what are some of the less obvious or more subtle forms of inequity or disadvantageousness experienced by the lower and middle classes in relation to the analogous harms and crimes committed by both the powerful and the megacorporations of America?

Conclusion

Crime, Justice, and Policy

This book has considered a variety of ways in which the independent and interdependent experiences of class, race, and gender help to shape both crime and crime control in the United States. In multiple chapters, we have described and examined male and female patterns of crime, victimization, and interactions with systems of criminal justice. In the late 1980s and early 1990s these unequal patterns of law enforcement and punishment were viewed in many jurisdictions as accounting for disproportionate minority confinement. Today, these institutionalized relations of inequality in the management of young persons caught up in the criminal justice apparatus are labeled by the Office of Juvenile Justice and Delinquency Prevention as "disproportionate minority contact" (OJJDP 2006).

A recent ethnographic study of the experiences of marginalized blacks and Latinos in the "criminal justice pipeline" provides an analysis of how the direct consequences of the enhanced policing, surveillance, and punitive treatment of these youths has resulted in the development of a specific set of gendered (masculine) practices that obstruct both criminal desistance and social mobility (Rios 2009). Moreover, the "cumulative disadvantage" has unintended negative effects not only for those individuals caught up in the system but also for those families and communities that they have left behind and will most likely return to.

More generally, our review and analysis of the latest crime control data demonstrate that four sets of relations continue to exist in the social realities of the administration of criminal law in the United States:

- Inequalities in class, race, and gender relations produce different lived experiences in society and in crime and crime control;

- Criminal law emphasizes the harms commonly perpetrated among the marginal members of society while it leaves the socially analogous harms committed by the more powerful well beyond incrimination;
- Discriminations based on class, race, and gender produce more prosecutions and harsher punishments for the "petty" offenses of the powerless and fewer prosecutions and softer punishments for the major offenses of the powerful; and
- Mass-mediated representations of class, race, and gender help to reproduce both the structural relations of oppression associated with crime and of repression associated with crime control.

In short, harms that are defined as crimes and the differential applications of criminal law enforcement, adjudication, and punishment are selective reflections and products of the social, political, and economic relations of class, race, and gender. We do not argue that the social realities of criminal justice in America are merely an expression of the inequalities and privileges of the larger society. On the contrary, the administration of justice is subject to many other factors and complex relationships, including bureaucratic needs of efficiency, economy, and effectiveness, and contradictory tensions between the rule of law (due process) and the rule of order (crime control). In addition, there are also the politics of crime control in the context of a globalizing process, which surrounds the criminal justice enterprise as a whole.

Finally, by incorporating legalistic analyses of crime and crime control with sociological analyses of inequality and privilege, we have conceptually broadened the traditional ("equal protection") framework for evaluating justice in the United States. In this regard, we have revealed those relationships not only between crime and class, race, and gender control but also as explicitly recapitulated below between the criminal justice system and the systems of political, economic, and ethical justice. By doing so, we have tried to demonstrate the need for the United States both to diversify its responses to crime and to expand its practices of justice.

The rest of this concluding chapter is divided up between summary discussions of the social construction of crime and criminality, of crime control and various types of justice, a critique of "equal justice" for all, and recommended policies and reforms aimed at alleviating the patterns of crime and inequality in the United States.

MEDIA, CRIME, AND JUSTICE

What constitutes crime and crime control is not constant. As the National Institute of Justice (NIJ) (2005, 1) declared of "crime" in its 2004 annual report: "The primary challenge for criminal justice professionals today is not from the number of crimes . . . but from the changing nature of the crime landscape. Although traditional criminal activities such as juvenile delinquency, gangs, burglary, and violent crimes remain problems for many communities, law enforcement agencies now face such new threats as the evolving globalization of crime, possible terrorism, and cybercrime." Omitted from the NIJ report, of course, was any mention of the traditional or new threats posed by corporate or governmental criminality. At the same time, in reference to changes in "crime control," the Justice Department underscored advances in technology "such as lower costs for the analysis of DNA samples" that "are changing how evidence is collected and crimes are investigated, as well as how judges and attorneys handle court cases" (NIJ 2005, 1).

Similarly, subtle transformations are occurring in who constitutes the criminal classes. The traditional stereotypes of dangerous criminals as poor, marginal, and nonwhite and as emanating from the streets remain. However, the images of threatening persons now include young people with backpacks, especially if they are (or look as if they are) of Middle Eastern origins. Once again, the threatening or dangerous persons do not include images (or texts) about greedy executives perpetrating corporate fraud or violence, or government bureaucrats deregulating industries and committing "nonfeasance" (willful failure to perform a required duty).

Take the "crime" of hiring illegal workers. Everyday, illegal aliens or undocumented workers are arrested, charged, and deported for breaking the law. However, those who employed them and broke the law have been given a virtual "free pass" to engage in this crime. In 2000, when the Bush administration took over, there was little law enforcement or prosecution by the previous Clinton administration. This policy of nonenforcement was escalated during the Bush presidency, and employers were rarely, if ever, charged with a criminal offense; if they were charged with "knowingly" hiring workers without papers, the first offense was a fine of $225. And, despite thousands of arrests of Mexican nationals, for example, from 2000 to 2008, not one employer had gone to jail. It remains to be seen whether or not enforcement policies under the Obama administration will change.

In the cases above, and more generally, the three Cs of mass society— culture, consumption, and communication—mediate the social realities of crime and justice. Together, these help not only to shape the fundamental attitudes, values, and behaviors of Americans but also non-Americans, too, through empire and globalization. In the processes of making and consuming ideas and things, our consciousness about life in general—and about crime and justice, perpetrators and victims, and cops and robbers in particular—are constantly forming and being reshaped. This constructing consciousness about "crime" expresses itself in our fears, discussions, and understandings about "crime control" and, more importantly, in what or who needs to be controlled. Ultimately, over and over vis-à-vis mass-mediated reconstructions, this consciousness (or sensitivity or perspective) on crime and justice spreads through our families, communities, nation-states, and beyond; in the process, our public and private policies on crime and crime control are developed both domestically and internationally.

The Internet, blogs, cell phones, and twittering, represent democratization in media as anyone can set up a webpage, blog, and "broadcast" their thoughts. But entertainment and news are still largely a mass-produced corporate phenomenon, relying for its very sustenance on advertisement as well as on the mass consumption of goods and services, ideas, and images. Even aspects of so-called independent media and alternative venues often consist of corporations playing on the rebellion against mass media and big corporations to appeal to consumers. Mass communication is quite expensive—bought and paid for by commercial advertising as well as by the owners and investors of private capital. For these reasons, what is aired, piped, or videoed into our consciousness are images and messages that are not value-free, objective, or neutral; rather, they reflect specific interests, and they are about selling, motivating, and reinforcing particular lifestyles and ideological points of view, not the least of which constitutes "crime and justice" in local, national, and international arenas.

Remember that corporations monopolize the ownership and distribution of newspapers, books, magazines, films, radio, video, television, and software. For example, General Electric (see chapter 8) has business interests in motors, transportation, turbines, electric equipment, communications, plastics, lighting, appliances, retail, medical services, music, financing, insurance, and software. Moreover, GE owns cable and network television stations, including NBC, MSNBC, CNBC, and USA. USA's series *White Collar* is an apolitical drama about white-collar crime; GE owns USA and does not want to bring attention to corporate crime, environmental pollution, or many other acts they—and the corporate advertisers who pay the bills—have done (Leighton 2010). Similarly, Westinghouse, in addition to its interests in communications and information, insurance, financing, banking, managing, electricity, nuclear power, and refrigeration, owns radio, cable, and television stations, including CBS.

The absorption of major media outlets by mega capital has merged, if not subverted, the interests of the "free press" with those of big business. So, virtually all news and most entertainment, whether politically "left"- (GE-owned MSNBC) or right- (FOX) oriented have fallen captive to the dominant ideologies of corporate-style free and unregulated enterprise. While there are more websites and blogs, corporate sites and news outlets still get the vast majority of the audience. As a result, there has become a greater uniformity in narrative discourses about most subjects, including crime and justice, especially considering media conglomerates can own radio, TV, and newspapers in the same city.

Our argument is not a media conspiracy theory. Ultimately, the consumer is part of the equation. That is to say, our approach to mediated crime and justice recognizes superficially that "being profit-driven, the media respond to the actual demands of their audience rather than to the idealized 'thirst for knowledge' demand posited by public intellectuals and deans of journalism schools. They serve up what the consumer wants, and the more intense the competitive pressure, the better they do it" (Posner 2005, 9). But, what does the average consumer of news and opinion want? What are audiences looking for? At the most general level, audiences want reinforcement of what they already believe. That is to say, "people don't like being in a state of doubt, so they look for information that will support rather than undermine their existing beliefs. They're also uncomfortable seeing their beliefs challenged on issues that are bound up with their economic welfare, physical safety or religious and moral views" (Posner 2005, 9). Accordingly, the news media, liberal or conservative, are careful not to step on the toes of their respective viewers, in the process polarizing further their respective deliveries (or "spins") on topical subjects. Each, in effect, defers to their loyal followings or audiences, selecting, slanting, and presenting their news accordingly. Further, the local presentations cannot be separated from the national or global portrayals that are constitutive of the "collective imaginations" pertaining to crime, law, and justice.

We suggest there is an interactive relationship between the so-called passive audience and the so-called active distributor of news, entertainment, and advertising. Generally, audiences consume crime news, for example, to learn of facts or trends that bear directly and immediately on their lives—hence the greater attention paid to local rather than to national or international crime news. They also listen and watch mass media to be entertained. In this context, distributors do not, for example, see the complexities of price-fixing or corporate fraud—with limited exceptions—to be "newsworthy" beyond its entertainment value because of an agreed-upon national narrative that precludes delving into the workings of the "higher order" criminality found on Wall Street or in Washington, D.C. In effect, journalistic opinion or commentary of print, radio, and television supply pretty much what their respective audiences think they want or demand, but they do so within the groupthink of a mainstream media and mass culture that, for the most part, shapes a "local" demand that is invulnerable to the realities of crime and justice in America.

The relationship between the producers and the receivers of mediated crime and justice, or anything else for that matter, is symbiotic, and serves more often than not to reinforce rather than to challenge the status quo. In terms of the "who," "what," "where," and "when" (if not "why") of the stories they report, news media typically strive for all the accuracy they can muster so long as they do not "step on the toes" of their advertisers and bosses or the relevant politicians or pundits. Investigative reporting does not have a high profit margin, and reporters represent high overhead costs that interfere with profit, so mainstream media reporters have become overly dependent on a short supply of news sources (including corporate press releases). Hence, when it comes to stories of crime and justice, the perspectives, biases, and distorted or slanted views of those in official positions of authority typically dominate the media. In short, the media whose beat is "law and order" rely almost exclusively on criminal justice professionals and their official statements or press releases about crime and crime control. As a result, there is a tendency to reproduce hegemonic or top-down views of crime and justice (Ericson, Baranek, and Chan 1987; Kasinsky 1994). In this regard, Mark Fishman (1978) has referred to the news gathering and reporting on crime and violence as involving "procedures not to know."

As a market-driven enterprise, mainstream media do not want to bite the financial hands that feed them, nor do they want to bite the informational sources that provide the news and authority for their stories any more than they want to disappoint their audiences. Thus, it is in their journalistic interests not to ordinarily challenge areas of social and political consensus, no matter how fictional, stupid, vicious, or harmful that consensus may be. Consequently, both before and after the Bush administration left office, their administration's lies to the American people and their acts of state-organized torture in violation of national and international law, for example, were primarily downplayed when not ignored altogether because confronting the normative beliefs and values that the United States does not engage in these types of crimes wins no friends and often alienates or turns off traditional audiences and mainstream sources. In the end, the narrative themes of crime and justice that are regularly reproduced by the mass media are highly reflective of selected and framed versions of social reality.

Take, for example, Sister Préjean's death-penalty book, *Dead Man Walking* (1993), and the Hollywood movie of the same title based on the book. In the book, Préjean notes that she became involved with prisons because she works with the poor, and part of her anti-death-penalty stance is out of concern about the effect of race and class inequalities. She is explicitly committed to a social justice perspective and notes her mission is unsettling "because taking on the struggles of the poor invariably means challenging the wealthy and those who serve their interests. 'Comfort the afflicted and afflict the comfortable'—that's what Dorothy Day, a Catholic social activist said is the heart of the Christian gospel" (Préjean 1993, 5). Further, being kind to the oppressed in an unjust system is not enough, she says, and "to claim to be apolitical or neutral in the face of such injustices would be, in actuality, to uphold the status quo—a very political position to take, and on the side of the oppressors" (Préjean 1993, 5–6).

She notes explicitly that she "cannot believe in a God who metes out hurt for hurt, pain for pain, torture for torture." And she's skeptical about executions by the government, "which can't be trusted to control its own bureaucrats or collect taxes equitably or fill a pothole, much less decide which of its citizens to kill" (Préjean 1993, 21). The book approvingly quotes Camus, who wonders about the followers of Christ "who have set at the center of their faith the staggering victim of a judicial error ought at least to hesitate before committing legal murder" (Préjean 1993, 89). And she asks the warden overseeing executions, "If Christ lived on Earth today, would he supervise this process?" (Préjean 1993, 103)

Interestingly, none of this critical content is included in the movie, which won praise for showing "both sides"—yet ultimately it presented no information or larger context from which to have further consideration about the death penalty. Given that most people in the United States are Christian, generally supportive of the death penalty, and do not want to be challenged about class or race inequality, the movie strips out anything that might offend them and combines the worst of both condemned men Préjean works with in the book into one character for the movie. The movie is about an individual bad guy who may or may not deserve to be executed; the book is an articulate critique using two men as examples of systemic inequalities that Christian gospel should challenge.

In addition, because issues of crime and crime control are too numerous, uncertain, and intricate, and because the benefits of being a well-informed audience member of crime and punishment are too small, viewers (and to a lesser extent listeners and readers) do not constitute audiences who are thriving for disinterested and sustained analyses of deviance. Instead, the average consumer wants to be entertained; she/he finds scandals, violence, crime, the foibles of celebrities, and some moral failings of the powerful too pleasurable to tune out.

Contemporary coverage of wrongful convictions in the United States is another example. Are we talking an occasional aberration or a statewide epidemic in the administration of criminal justice? While there is no definitive research revealing the magnitude of the problem, it is beyond question that we are not just talking about a few, but rather many, innocent people who have been sent to prison, sometimes for decades. As freelance magazine writer, book author, and part-time journalism instructor at the University of Missouri, Steve Weinberg (2008, 59), points out: "In each of those cases, the justice system failed. But so did journalism." More generally, the lack of serious journalistic reporting of crime and justice has serious consequences rarely discussed by the media, criminologists, or the general public. As Weinberg (2008, 56) argues, "Unless journalists get better at covering the justice system, many criminals will continue to go unpunished, free to murder or rape or rob again. So investigating wrongful convictions is not—as perceived by too many police, prosecutors and judges—an assault by soft-on-crime bleeding hearts." The lack of investigative journalism of white-collar crime, its deficient control, and questionable justice also has deleterious effects across society.

Turning briefly to entertainment, the dramatic crime narratives found in books, on television, or at the movies are usually more accurate and less distorted than are either the news stories of prime time or the so-called reality shows like *COPS* (Barak 1994, 1996). The pictures of criminals are reflective of the multiracial and ethnic distributions of index and occupational crime (although equal time, once again, is not given to the crimes of the powerful and to corporate misbehavior). Conversely, when it comes to crime control, the greater distortion is with the entertainment media because of their tendency, for example, to overrepresent women and persons of color in positions of criminal justice leadership compared to their actual distributions. In either venue, however, underrepresentation of corporate deviance or of the crimes of the powerful is the norm. Unless the violations involve powerful celebrities or blatantly outrageous behavior as exemplified by Enron or Bernard Madoff, they are typically glossed over. Even when there is coverage, corporate abuse, harm, and criminality is left unexamined in terms of the institutional or structural relations of crime control and its functionality to the upper echelons of power and influence in America. The reports leave the impression the problem is a "few bad apples" rather than a systemic problem.

Finally, what the mass media as a whole accomplish, consciously and unconsciously, is to separate the "criminals" from the "noncriminals" serving to reinforce the belief that "real" criminals are different from the rest of us. Therefore, they may be subject to severe and draconian forms of crime control and criminal justice administration both for their good and ours. If persons can be portrayed as belonging to a strange and dangerous breed driven to crime not because of inequality or injustice, but rather because they suffer from some kind of biological or psychological flaws, it becomes easier to sell "the idea of an increasingly punitive criminal justice system with fewer constitutional restraints to keep neighborhoods safe from the demonic 'Other'" that society has constructed as criminal (Kooistra, Mahoney, and Westervelt 2000, 147). And, if inequality, poverty, or injustice cannot be the culprits in the scenarios of crime and crime control, then neither can privilege, wealth, or deregulation. Hence, for all practical purposes, mediated crime and crime control have been stripped of their social context while criminals and criminality are reduced to the idiosyncratic behavior of isolated and free-willed, if not rational, individuals.

In sum, even though our criminal justice system revolves around the rule of law, rational intent, and retributive justice, the cultural productions of crime and justice nevertheless conveys the message that street criminals are fundamentally irrational or disturbed. As such, not only are they not entitled to, but also we are not obligated to, treat them rationally. Conveniently, however, when it comes to "suite" crimes the message is quite different: these offenders are fundamentally decent and rational people whose potentially bad acts are not evidence of bad character. Complex circumstances beyond their individual control created some kind of aberration or deviation, but not a serious breach worth fixing, even when such behavior is habitually practiced and may have brought the economy to its knees as with the recession of 2008–2010. On the other hand, on the rare occasions when stories about upper-class and/or corporate criminality are broached by mass media, these narratives and representations fail to challenge the larger economic system and do not communicate the real danger or threat of these crimes because their perpetrators are not only paragons of our socioeconomically stratified communities but also leaders of some of the most profitable corporations or financial institutions in the world. These paragons of market society, in the final analysis, must appear above all else to be rational and normative, and therefore, beyond serious incrimination.

THE ENDURING STRUGGLE FOR JUSTICE: EQUAL, RESTORATIVE, AND SOCIAL

Three systems of justice—equal, restorative, and social—cannot be separated from the modern evolution in the conceptualization of justice. Each of these justice systems or models represents a generation in the three-tier revolution of the rights of human beings to ultimately share in common the exact same formal rights as everybody else regardless of their class, race/ethnic, gender, religious, national, or sexual affiliation (Ishay 2004). The first generation of rights represented the struggle for *equal justice*, or the struggle for "negative rights," in that they called for restraint from the state and/or monarchy. These rights were derived from the American and French revolutions and the struggle to gain freedom from arbitrary rule; they are also articulated in the Civil and Political Rights of the International Bill of Rights. Collectively, these rights have helped shape what we usually refer to as governmental control by "rule of law" rather than by "rule of man." A product of this struggle has been an emphasis on the impartial and fair enforcement of the procedural and substantive criminal law.

The second generation of rights represented the struggle for *restorative justice*, or the struggle for "positive rights," in that they called for "affirmative actions" on the part of the state. These rights are articulated in the Economic, Social, and Cultural Rights of the International Bill of Rights. Collectively, these rights have helped shape what we refer to as the minimal duties or social obligations of the state to facilitate the "self-realization" of the individual. A product of this struggle has been an emphasis on community social welfare, penitence/redemption, and victim-offender reconciliation.

The third generation of rights represents the contemporary struggle for *social justice* worldwide, also identified as the struggle for universal "human rights." Evolving out of the emerging conditions of global interdependence, these rights call for international cooperation between all nation-states, such as the establishment in 1999, in The Hague, of the first International Criminal Court. Collectively, these rights recognize that the delivery of human rights for all cannot be satisfied within the body of individual states acting alone. A product of this international struggle for human rights or social justice include the global emphases on ending world hunger, forgiving the debt to underdeveloped Third World nations, and treating all the victims of AIDS/HIV and other life-threatening diseases, famines, and tsunamis worldwide.

Historically, the evolution of justice and the struggle for universal human rights has not followed a linear path forward. On the contrary, every generation of rights has not only met with resistance but also each major stride on the pathway to human rights has been trailed by severe setbacks:

> The universalism of human rights brandished during the French Revolution was slowly superseded by a nationalist reaction incubated during Napoleon's conquests, just as the internationalist hopes of socialist human rights advocates were drowned in a tidal wave of nationalism at the approach of World War I. The human rights aspirations of the Bolshevik Revolution and of two liberal sister institutions, the League of Nations and the International Labor Organization (ILO), were crushed by the rise of Stalinism and fascism during the interwar period; the establishment of the United Nations (UN) and adoption of the Universal Declaration of Human Rights were eclipsed by intensifying nationalism in the emerging Third World and global competition between two nuclear-armed superpowers. Finally, the triumphant claims made after 1989 that human rights would blossom in an unfettered global market economy were soon drowned out by rising nationalism in the former Soviet Union, Africa, the Balkans, and beyond (Ishay 2004, 4).

To be sure, reactionary forces have not totally nullified each chapter of progress in human rights. In fact, the record informs us otherwise: "History preserves the human rights record as each generation builds on the hopes and achievements of its predecessors while struggling to free itself from authoritarianism and improve its social conditions" (Ishay 2004, 4). Over time, the evolution of "human rights" has reflected the historical continuity and change that helped form the Universal Declaration of Human Rights (UDHR) adopted by the General Assembly of the United Nations in 1948. Drawing on the battle cry of the French Revolution, "dignity, liberty, equality, and brotherhood," on the demands of the Industrial Revolution for political, social, and economic equity, and on the communal and national solidarity movements associated with the postcolonial era, the articles of the UDHR brought together in one document the universal meanings of human rights. In 2010, issues of how to obtain human rights for all and of what constitutes equal human rights still remain, as legally and socially people disagree, for example, as in the case of Darfur as whether or not to have prosecuted for genocide or for gross human rights violations.

In the everyday practices of crime and social control, these three models or approaches to justice are central—equal, restorative, and social. Inside and outside the United States, the ideals and realities of equal justice are older than the ideals and realities of restorative or social justice. The ideas and practices of equal justice compared to those of restorative and social justice are more individually and less collectively oriented approaches to justice.

In the modern evolution of justice, history has moved from individual to collective notions of justice, and there has been a widening of fundamental rights (Crawford 1988). These expanding ideas initially found expression in small philosophical or political circles, gradually finding acceptance, if not consensus, in a significant portion of the body politic and, ultimately, finding incorporation in the procedural as well as the substantive sides of the law. In terms of the contemporary period dating back to the end of World War II, the United States has more slowly than other developed nations experienced a transition away from the relative limits or constraints of legal rights and toward the blossoming or escalating possibilities of human rights such as civil unions and same sex marriages. Politically, the USA is a signatory to or has ratified a number of United Nations conventions, and while the Supreme Court's decision striking down the death penalty for juveniles acknowledged "the overwhelming weight of international opinion against the juvenile death penalty," it pointed out that such opinion "is not controlling here, but provides respected and significant confirmation for the Court's determination that the penalty is a disproportionate punishment for offenders under 18" (*Roper v. Simmons* 2005, 543 U.S. 551 [2005]).

Equal Justice

In the United States, equal justice assumes the rationality of the prevailing political, economic, and social arrangements in general and of the administration of criminal justice in particular. Within this system of justice, whether criminals are viewed as "bad" or "mad," they are disconnected from their socioeconomic conditions as well as from their class, racial, and gendered backgrounds, and they are held equally accountable for the harm they inflict regardless of context or situation. Whether defendants come from profoundly vulnerable or at-risk social environments or from privileged and advantaged elite milieus are not relevant to blind or equal justice.

The current model of equal justice practiced in the United States has its root in the mid-eighteenth century, when the European age of reason or enlightenment was busy reforming the more arbitrary and barbaric justice practices from the medieval period. Although not driven by revenge or vengeance, these present-day models of equal justice are repressive in that they downplay flexible sentencing, community alternatives, and restitution. They also ignore the social structures, environmental milieus, and ecologies of crime. In addition, these models of justice have traditionally not considered the interests of either the injured parties or their communities, nor of the perpetrators themselves. In short, the adjudicative practices of equal justice serve to reinforce a repressive system of individualized justice that helps to sustain as well as institutionalize a permanent underclass of marginally threatening offenders.

In the final analysis, policies of equal justice do not take into account the concept of equal treatment of nonequal offenders or victims by class, race, gender, sexual orientation, and so on. Or put differently, the unequal treatment of analogous social injuries or harms by the powerful and the powerless, respectively, serve to reproduce the status quo of crime, victimization, and discriminatory justice.

Restorative Justice

Whereas equal justice systems are more legalistically oriented and punitive-repressive, and social justice systems are more structural and transformative in orientation, restorative justice systems may be thought of as located somewhere on a continuum between the other two systems. Globally speaking, restorative justice has been used more typically at the microlevel, when the approach is used to bring individuals and offenders together. But it has all been used at the macrolevel as a means of dealing with collective injury and guilty involving, for example, "the crimes of genocide in Rwanda, war crimes in Bosnia Herzegovina, and even war zones in Israel" (Hanser 2009, 193). Fundamentally, restorative justice is about "de-centering punishment in regulatory institutions while acknowledging the significant place that punishment will always have within them" as a source of communicating the actual "shamefulness" of the act in question (Braithwaite, Braithwaite, and Ahmed 2005, 287).

Unlike equal justice policies that strive to isolate and exclude offenders from the rest of society based on the alleged differences between "criminals" and "noncriminals," restorative justice policies assume that most offenders and nonoffenders, whether perpetrators or victims, or both, share an intrinsic humanity in common. Zehr and Mika (1998, 54–55) have maintained that restorative justice is being pursued when citizens:

- focus on the harms of wrongdoing more than the rules that have been broken;
- show equal concern and commitment to victims and offenders, involving both in the process of justice;
- work toward the restoration of victims, empowering them and responding to their needs as they see them;
- support offenders while encouraging them to understand, accept, and carry out their obligations;
- recognize that while obligations may be difficult for offenders, they should not be intended as harms and they must be achievable;
- provide opportunities for dialogue, direct or indirect, between victims and offenders as appropriate;
- involve and empower the affected community through the justice process, and increase its capacity to recognize and respond to community bases of crime;
- encourage collaboration and reintegration rather than coercion and isolation;
- give attention to the unintended consequences of [their] actions and programs [on particular communities]; and
- show respect to all parties, including victims, offenders, and justice colleagues.

Modern practices of restorative justice have their legal roots in the ancient patterns of such diverse cultures as the Sumerian Code of Ur-Nammu (2050 BC), the Hebrew Scriptures and the Code of Hammurabi (1700 BC), the Roman Law of the Twelve Tables (449 BC), and the earliest collection of the Germanic tribal laws, the Lex Salica (AD 496). Each of the legal systems of justice required that offenders and their families settle accounts with victims and their families, not simply to ensure that injured persons received restitution or compensation but also to restore or reestablish community peace. In many precolonial African and Native American societies, punitive sanctions were compensatory rather than retributive, intended primarily to make victims whole or to restore them to their previous position.

Today, the contemporary system of Japanese justice, emphasizing as it does "confession, repentance and absolution," is also about compensating the victim and restoring community peace (Haley 1989). Similarly, "indigenous populations in North America, New Zealand, Australia and elsewhere are experimenting with ways in which their traditional approaches to crime, which [were] restorative in intent, may exist in the context of the dominant Western legal systems" of colonization (Van Ness and Heetderks Strong 1997, 9). Moreover, since the 1980s, restorative justice has been represented both outside and inside the United States by a wide diversity of programs that may or may not contain the same "essential" elements or practices as ideally conceptualized.

In other words, the idea of restorative justice has come to have many different meanings and practices. It has come to be associated with innovations in community mediation, problem-solving justice, victim-offender reconciliation, alternative sentencing, and community service. As Daly and Immarigeon (1998, 21–22) point out:

> The concept may refer to an alternative process for resolving disputes, to alternative sanctioning options, or to a distinctively different, "new" mode of criminal justice organized around principles of restoration to victims, offenders, and the communities in which they live. It may refer to diversion from formal court process, to actions taken in parallel with court decisions, and to meetings between offenders and victims at any stage of the criminal process (from arrest, presentencing, and prison release). It is a process used in juvenile justice, criminal justice, and family welfare/child protection cases.

Regardless of the myriad of practices that seem to be part of a larger movement to incorporate restorative justice programs throughout the criminal justice system and local communities, what they all share in common is a view of crime and criminals that moves beyond defining some behavior as illegal to include at least some of the basic needs of human respect and dignity and the relevant sources of conflict and dispute resolution. Unlike equal justice systems that revolve around how much pain and suffering has been inflicted by the actions of the wrongdoer, restorative justice systems revolve around how much harm has been repaired or prevented. Hence, restorative justice sees criminality not only as involving the needs of offenders and victims as well as the mutual obligations and liabilities between offenders and victims but it also recognizes the different and often related harms that perpetrators and victims of street crimes experience in common.

In this way, restorative justice significantly views both the offenders and the victims as responding more or less rationally to their perceived needs, interests, and options. Unlike equal justice systems that view crime control as primarily a matter of individual perpetrators versus the state, restorative justice systems are preoccupied with the interpersonal (and larger mutualistic) relationships involving offenders, victims, family members, and their communities from which they are spawned. In short, restorative justice emphasizes the recovery of the victim through redress, vindication, and healing, on the one hand, and of the offender through fair treatment, recompense of the victim, and rehabilitation (or primary habilitation), on the other hand.

For example, reparation, restitution, and compensation programs are more concerned with healing injuries than they are with inflicting harm and pain. They are not about payback per say or about inflicting additional suffering, but they are about "getting even." While one concern is obviously public safety, their primary concerns are about seeing that victims are made whole and that offenders are involved in the process of mutual healing. The objectives of restorative justice are less about the narrow goal of diverting inmates from prison than they are about advancing the recovery of both the victims and the perpetrators, enabling or empowering both to "self-actualize" and to establish themselves as participating rather than marginal members of society.

In the final analysis, restorative justice relies on both the formal and informal mechanisms of social control in that it supports the role of government as responsible for preserving law and order and the community as responsible for establishing peace and justice. For example, victim-offender reconciliation programs offer a context in which the two parties to the crime have an opportunity to face each other in a nonadversarial setting. This encounter affords victims and offenders rather than the state prosecutors the chance to decide what they consider relevant to the crime. The encounter also tends "to humanize each of them to one another and permits them substantial creativity in constructing a response that deals not only with the injustice that occurred but with the futures of both parties as well" (Van Ness and Heetderks Strong 1987, 89).

Social Justice

While equal justice models reduce "conflicts" between offenders and victims to legally relevant material evidence, restorative justice models try to converge some of the formal and informal aspects of social control and conflict resolution through victim-offender conciliation and community peacemaking (Hanser 2009). While equal justice systems revolve primarily around retribution between the offender and the state and restorative justice systems revolve primarily around reparation and healing between the offender and the victim, social justice systems venture beyond the immediate conflicts between particular offenders and their victims. Neither the retributive equal justice models nor the reparative restorative justice models have paid attention to the "big picture" or to the "patterns of social inequality or disadvantage, which make both victims and offenders, and indeed their communities, more prone to the experiences of criminal harm and to the processes of criminalization" in the first place (White 1998, 17). The visions of social justice are broader and the policies more ambitious than the visions and policies of equal and restorative justice. Social justice models expand the notions of conflict and injury beyond what the law recognizes to include those harms identified as part of an evolving set of human rights, some established in treaties and covenants, some in international resolutions or tribunals. The violations of any of these fundamental rights constitute what are known in the world community as "crimes against humanity." These crimes generally, but not always, are committed by the authorities or agents of the state, such as the violation of a person and/or a group's inalienable rights to be free, for example, from exploitation, sexual slavery, hatred, impoverishment, discrimination, or genocide.

Social justice models also view "crime" as something more than an interpersonal violation between people and a particular nation-state's legal order. Moreover, these models see crime control as something more than the reparation, reconciliation, and reassurance of victims and offenders alike. Crimes are not merely personal expressions, but they are also institutional and structural expressions of fundamental political and economic arrangements. For example, rich folks, regardless of race and gender, do not ordinarily hold up fast-food markets, gas stations, or banking establishments. Likewise, poor folks, regardless of race and gender, do not violate insider trading rules, falsify corporate accounting statements, price-fix, or monopolize the sale, distribution, and production of goods and services. In other words, these are all crimes of structural opportunity and it is no accidental convenience that the legal orders and their administration disadvantage the perpetrators of the street crimes while they advantage the perpetrators of the suite crimes.

More generally, social justice models recognize the indivisible relations between, for example, the "crime" of homelessness in an affluent society and the crimes by and against the homeless as rooted in the violence of poverty and inequality and in the creation of dependent classes of marginalized people. To address these structural inequities or injustices, social justice stresses the importance of public policies of crime control that go beyond the confines of the criminal justice system and the crimes of the poor and powerless. Attention and care are also given, for example, not only to the crimes of the rich and powerful but also more generally to the economic and social harms of corporate deregulation, to the formation of social and human capital, and to the oppression and exploitation of a multiethnic underclass. Thus, domestic policies of crime control in the United States also focus affordable and accessible programs on family development, health care, subsidized housing, public education, community efficacy, and political empowerment. To the extent that social factors create crime and make crime control repressive for the purposes of securing a legal order that supports or reinforces inequality and privilege, the social justice model advocates intervening to prevent those social factors.

Historically, advocates of social justice in the United States have in the nineteenth century included members of various religious groups and others from organized labor. Its roots go as far back as the Quakers and their involvement with the development of the first penitentiary, the Walnut Street Jail, in Philadelphia in the early 1800s. More recently, the prisoner's movement of the 1960s, the second wave of feminism in the 1970s, the environmental movement of the 1980s, and the movement for universal human rights in the 1990s have nurtured and propelled forward models of social justice to this day.

Proponents of social justice, such as the late Michael Harrington (1989), talk in terms of the merits of "visionary gradualism" and "free-market socialism." Grounded in the global principles of feminist, antiracist, and ecologist communitarianism, this view of social justice ascribes to the capitalism structure, but it also believes in the eradication of social subjugation, oppression, and exploitation of people and the establishment of fundamental human rights for all. Often referred to as "democratic socialism," this vision of social justice does not seek to do away with all forms of privilege and inequality, but it does rest upon the capacity of people to choose and implement democratic forms of socialization and public policymaking in "the face of 'irresponsible,' 'unthinking' and 'unsocial' versions of corporate socialization" and private policymaking (West 1990, 59).

BEYOND "EQUAL JUSTICE" FOR ALL: A CRITIQUE

Persons who come before the various tribunals of justice have never been, nor are they now, equal before the law. Legalistic fairness, due process, and equal protection in actual practice is not synonymous with equal justice or the rule of law, in a court of law, or in the larger court of public opinion. As Anatole France (1844–1924), the French poet, journalist, and best-selling novelist wrote in *The Red Lily* (1894): "The law, in its majestic equality, forbids the rich as well as the poor to sleep under bridges, to beg in the streets, and to steal bread" (chapter 7). Of course, such laws then and now are only relevant to the marginal, to the destitute, to the homeless, to the mentally ill, and so on. Like this class illustration matters, race and gender also matter, both at law and in society, as this book has depicted throughout.

When evaluators of justice—criminal, civil, or corporate—falsely treat different or unequal persons of socioeconomic status, race, or ethnicity, and of gender or sexual orientation, as though they were the same or legally equal based on some kind of formal or abstract equality of all people, these evaluators ignore the very concrete inequalities that cut across the dynamic relations of class, race, gender, crime, justice, and society. Similarly, because of the common or ideological overemphasis on notions of individual or equal justice, most critiques of the administration of criminal justice focus on the procedural irregularities in the application of due process or the rule of law. Although recognition is often given to the selective enforcement and differential applications of the law in the facts of individual cases, less likely is there much discussion of the systemic-discriminatory outcomes, let alone any mention or critique of the substantive "irregularities" in the labeling of "crime" or in the unequal definitions of harm or analogous injuries in the first place.

The point is that there is a long list of harms and injuries that could be legally prohibited but have not been. They have not been labeled or criminalized as constituting "crimes worth pursuing" because of the advantages they accrue for powerful interests in society. In other words, the pursuit of equal justice within a legally biased system against the marginally impoverished is not only a narrow or limited goal but also, more importantly, it is one that obscures a multitude of oppressive dynamics that are of concern to social justice models because these would alleviate many of the roots of antisocial behavior in society.

The consequences of these omissions of equal justice are that crime control is stacked against the powerless rather than the powerful, as we have underscored with respect to the unequal war on drugs and its adverse affects on minority communities of African and Latin backgrounds. For example, the large-scale removal of young black males from their communities contributes to the depletion of the supply of potential marriage partners for young black females and to the accumulation of generational impoverishment. Some commentators have argued that these social relations of crime, victimization, and punishment have encouraged young female-headed households, creating precisely the types of family formations that have been linked with higher rates of street crime and domestic abuse when not given adequate social support (Currie 1985; Messner and Rosenfeld 1994; Foster and Hagan 2009). In short, these trends in racial and gender punishment are countereffective as they exacerbate the problems of absentee parents, convict reentry, and the lack of community efficacy.

Similarly, the increased processing of less serious marginal offenders throughout the criminal justice system has not only created a state of megawarehouses of nonviolent offenders but it has also undermined the capacity of formal systems of crime control to deliver on their promises of due process and equal protection during a period when the rates of crimes against the person, such as murders, and crimes against property, such as burglary, remain at multidecade lows in the United States. Nevertheless, assembly-line, plea-bargained "equal justice" pertains not only to defendants but to the convicted as well, as each of these groups become subject to the practices of actuarial justice or to the forecasting of the costs and risks associated with managing populations considered dangerous (Feeley and Simon 1992, 1994; Barak 2009). In the end, this type of bureaucratized equal justice for all helps to secure and reinforce stereotypic images of both crime and criminals through sophisticated systems of profiling and classification.

Working hand-in-hand with mediated images of crime and justice, bureaucratized justice helps to reinforce images of the "typical" criminal that do not include high-powered corporate executives, emphasizing the low-life predators who murder, rob, assault, kidnap, and do drugs rather than acts of inside trades, no-bid contractors, financial fraudsters, and so forth. Crimes are acts identified with poor and racial minorities, not with rich and powerful white folks. Crime control is represented by what the police, courts, and prisons do with the "dangerous classes," rarely providing background or context for the behavior in question. The images associated with these culprits and with the responses to their crimes only serve to inflame public fears and anxieties associated with crime and its control, while reproducing scenarios of retributive and repressive justice that reifies class, racial, and gendered patterns of disparity, exclusion, and isolation.

The implication of this critique is not to argue for an end to equal justice for all. On the contrary, equal justice is certainly a good place to begin, but it is only a beginning. Indeed, all agents or workers of the criminal justice system should aspire to act impartially or neutrally, according to both the letter and the spirit of due process and equal protection under the law. In addition, however, equal justice must be assisted by the goals and objectives of both restorative justice and social justice. These alternative approaches to equal justice offer substantial ways to improve the quality of justice inside and outside the criminal justice system, serving better to curb and reduce all forms of criminality—personal, institutional, and structural. These models of justice engage in more humanistic and inclusive approaches to crime control and in more holistic or integrated approaches to crime and justice than does the model of equal justice by itself. Both restorative and social justice models actively encourage and support the participation of offenders, victims, and communities of interest in the processes of local democratic crime prevention. Social justice models also promote and advocate the institutionalization of human rights across society. From the vantage point of policy development, restorative and social justice aspires toward an evolution in justice based on healing, recovery, reconciliation, and the ongoing struggle for diversity, equity, and inclusiveness. Once again, these approaches do not abandon the legalistic models of the rule of law; rather, they play down the wars on crime as they struggle for peace and justice.

RECOMMENDED POLICIES AND REFORMS FOR
ALLEVIATING HARM AND REDUCING CRIME

Based on a consensus of knowledge that a great deal of interpersonal crime and violence comes from the fault lines around economic and racial inequality and the absence of hope and opportunity in rural towns and inner cities alike, social control and crime control must be responsive to the life histories of offenders, victims, and communities. Furthermore, policy recommendations for reducing criminal behavior and improving the quality of crime control and justice not only calls for a readdressing of our structural ills but also for a healthy recognition of another criminological consensus; namely, that we cannot punish our way out of these structural conditions of crime and injustice.

Currie (2005, 303) has written: "If crime is heavily rooted in social structures and social policies that are created by human agency, then on its present level it is not an inevitable fact of modern life but is alterable through social action." In other words, if a market society establishes a nation with high rates of crime and violence because its competitive and consumptive lifestyles create a "toxic brew" of predatory social behavior, then domestic (and international) policies are required to ameliorate structural poverty and widening inequality in general and to avoid destroyed livelihoods, stressed-out families, dilapidated neighborhoods, and fragmented communities in particular. However, focusing on the production of crime has to be balanced by focusing on the infrastructure and groupthink that has dominated crime control in the United States. We are referring specifically to the war on crime mentality that for the past three decades has distorted our nation's approach to alleviating harm and reducing crime. As the editors of *After the War on Crime* (2008) maintain:

> It emerged as a slogan more than thirty-five years ago, but, from the first, the "war on crime" was much more than rhetoric. As in the case of the "cold war" and, more recently, the "war on terror," the war on crime produced significant and enduring effects on the entire American population in social, political, economic, constitutional, and, far from least, racial terms. . . . This campaign mobilized tens of thousands in law enforcement agencies and prison systems and tens of thousands more in the related war industries stimulated by our society's commitment of billions of dollars to this effort. In a nod toward total war, every member of the population has contributed, federal and state taxes, general revenues, and bond issues, to the most rapid, most thoroughgoing, most extensive buildup in carceral and police systems this country has ever undertaken. More than merely paying taxes . . . millions of Americans have adopted war thinking in how they perceive and respond to crime risk as citizens, parents, and economic actors (Simon, López, and Frampton 2008, 2–3).

Simon, López, and Frampton (2008, 3) argue further that the war on crime remade our society: "it reshaped our cities; transformed our social imagination about the nature of ourselves, our neighbors, and strangers; shifted the distribution of population between urban and rural areas; and ultimately changed the way motor vehicles, housing developments, shopping and office complexes look and operate." Optimistically, however, they argue more generally that the war on crime, if it is not over, it has at least peaked. They also point out that "the issues that increasingly come to the fore are those emerging from the consequences of the war on crime itself; its effects are suddenly visible across almost every institution of importance to civic life, including family, schools, the labor market, the political field, and race relations" (Simon et al. 2008, 3).

That is to say, now it is time to deal with the damage inflicted by the war on crime—to rescue those communities caught up in the grip of zero tolerance and aggressive policing as well as those young persons who have been extracted from them, for example. Now is the time to develop plans and policies to reintegrate into society more than 650,000 persons a year expected to return to the free world. Now is the time, as Obama's new drug czar, Gil Kerlikowske, has done, to call off the "war on drugs" (Fields 2009). Now is the time to reframe the problem of drug use and abuse as a public health issue, not a criminal one, as has been done in Vancouver, British Columbia, with positive results (Beiser 2008). Similarly, it is now time that the United States adopt those strategies of "harm reduction" that are more realistically geared to minimizing the damage inflicted on or by those folks, for example, who are abusing licit and illicit drugs or who are engaging in other destructive behaviors associated with the industries of vice.

Simon, López, and Frampton also argue that if we are to imagine a postwar on crime in America, moving in a different direction, it is important that people are made to reject the prohibitively expensive war on crime and to understand the viability of rehabilitative and reentry programs. They recognize, however, that these programs alone are not likely to fundamentally shake things up enough to end the war on crime. Nevertheless, they contend that:

There is some rhetorical value in simply declaring the war over. Maybe saying so will not, by itself, make it so. But saying so, loudly and often and in the context of an extended conversation regarding where we should go from here, can only help (Simon et al. 2008, 10).

Before we turn to our general recommendations, we concur with Simon, López, and Frampton about the importance of reframing the discourse on harm and crime reduction in a context of how the war on crime has actually been self-defeating and counterproductive, in at least three ways. First, the war on crime "represented a nationalizing project that promoted a highly artificial image of a crime problem that was more or less the same everywhere. Not only was this image highly misleading about the actual incidence and prevalence of different kinds of crime problems in different communities, but also it almost certainly created more fear and more readiness to respond harshly" (Simon et al. 2008, 11). Second, the war on crime was a double-edged sword that "simultaneously made race less visible as a set of public problems while having an enormous impact on the construction of race in the United States" (Simon et al. 2008, 12). In the same vein, Obama as a multiracial president or not (he's still regarded as black even though his mother was white) at a point in history when the fastest-growing census category is biracial, our country is not presently moving beyond racial hierarchies anymore than it is moving beyond class or gender hierarchies. Third, in replacing the repressive older discourse of the war on crime, the new discourse needs to be more democratic or conversational in its orientation and more willing to apply principles of crime and social control that look well beyond systems of criminal justice to those other societal systems that address the whole range of human needs and services, both at home and abroad.

Lawmaking

In the area of lawmaking at least two types of basic policy developments are called for as a means of curbing the emphasis on punitive retribution and of de-escalating the wars on crime in general and on drugs in particular. These policy alternatives include social capital investments and harm reduction strategies on intervention. Both of these types of legislation are aimed at structurally preventing crime and violence before they occur. Armed with the knowledge that many predatory criminals, adolescent or adult, have been victims of abuse and/or neglect before they become perpetrators, social capital anticrime bills are needed to tackle these early risks or symptoms of delinquency and criminality through community advocacy, efficacy, and development. In addition, socially realistic or responsible harm reduction bills are needed not only to decriminalize those personal choice activities of individual morality that are better left as private rather than public matters but also to criminalize those structural or deregulated activities of corporate malfeasance and misbehavior that adversely affect the well-being of millions of peoples.

Furthermore, those interested in justice for injured crime victims should join forces with the emerging movement for socially responsible corporations that have been struggling to rescind corporate "personhood" through model local ordinances that eliminate those constitutional privileges benefiting corporations doing business within a township, city, or county at the expense of ordinary citizens. By resisting the corporate hegemony within the United States and abroad, these relatively recent laws are attempts by average people to remove themselves from the strangleholds of big corporations and to democratize their local governments (Hartmann 2002). These efforts, more specifically, are helping to rein in corporations that are doing away with worker rights and/or are contributing to the deterioration of the general welfare of society (Derber 1998). Of course, the key to the security and well-being of all rather than just the relatively affluent involves the balanced growth of dynamic and sustainable economies in tandem with domestic and international policies that promote more equitable and just social orders worldwide. A tall order, we know!

Investing in Harm Reduction

Policies of harm reduction are typically associated first and foremost with substance abuse, but the philosophy or strategy of "first, reduce harm," also applies to other demographic hot spots that cause avoidable pain and suffering, not to mention unnecessary financial costs to the victims, to law enforcement, and to the taxpayers. In terms of drug abuse, dependency, and/or mental illness, policies of harm reduction make available on request drug, alcohol, and mental health treatment for all. These policies also provide syringes for shooting heroin, mouthpieces for crack pipes, and prescriptions of methadone for addicts at taxpayers' expense.

In the area of illicit drugs and/or substance abuse and in the spirit of de-escalating the war on drugs, there are those who philosophically call for decriminalization and others who call for legalization, regulation, and/or taxation. For examples of related legal changes, more than a dozen states have already decriminalized or legalized medical marijuana. Our position regardless of the preferred alternative is to recommend the wholesale shifting of the "drug problem" away from law enforcement and into the medical arena. The use and abuse of drugs becomes a matter of law enforcement and police concern when other violations of the criminal law are also involved, but otherwise the use and abuse of drugs should be treated as a public health concern. Age requirements, restrictions on driving while impaired, and similar necessary regulations remain in place. This kind of wholesale scaling back on the war on drugs would not only significantly reduce the number of persons jailed or imprisoned and lower the costs of incarceration but it would also free up hundreds of millions of dollars or more annually for community-based treatment programs. With this type of decriminalization policy in place, many fewer families, especially poor and minority, would find themselves needlessly ripped apart by the war on drugs.

De-escalating other public-order violations or crimes of morality such as those involving prostitution or gambling, decriminalizing, deregulating and so on, respects freedom, privacy, and individual autonomy. It also seems to be a fairer policy in light of the very unequal enforcement and application of current law.

Finally, there is the need to roll back a host of what have been collectively referred to as the new urban social-control techniques. These recently established measures of urban social regulation "have dispersed the logic and operations of spatial control beyond prison walls" and have broadened the range of behaviors and statuses subject to criminal justice intervention while they have diminished the rights of those people who have been targeted for exclusion (Beckett and Herbert 2008, 107) These acts include the establishment from coast to coast of off-limits orders, trespass laws, and park exclusion laws. What these ordinances have in common is that they combine elements of criminal, civil, and administrative law to define the mere presence in urban space as a crime that promises to "cleanse" those areas of disorder caused by the mere presence of the socially marginal, increasing the state's abilities to search, detain, regulate, and monitor those subject to these new misdemeanor offenses without having to necessarily make an arrest or place someone in jail. In effect, these rules criminalize such statuses as homeless or mentally ill in a public space and, at least initially, only require a person's disappearance from the area (Barak 1991a). Attached to the discredited "broken windows" theory and "zero tolerance" policies of the 1990s, these new techniques of surveillance and social control are leading to skyrocketing violations, and eventually, to the arresting and jailing of mostly poor people for the crime of poverty. This type of criminalization, of course, expands the net of formal social control, becomes criminogenic, and needs to be stopped before it spreads as a law enforcement rather than a social problem.

Other demographic "hot spots" that cause more pain and injury than the mere presence of debilitated and unsightly people are often under the radar, invisible, and/or ignored by public and private policy alike. Harm reduction, for example, of high-powered, white-collar offenders and corporate abusers move in the other direction. Since these behaviors are undercriminalized or lack the responsible enforcement and/or regulation needed, they call for the expansion of the law to regulate and/or criminalize. To put it simply, the United Stated needs more laws and socially appropriate penalties for harms perpetrated by the powerful players and institutions that damage the public, workers, and consumers. When acts such as toxic pollution, waste elimination, or environmental destruction adversely affect communities—that is,

inflict disproportionate pain and suffering, especially on marginal communities—then some type of compensation and social restitution should be in order for those victims. Further, funds should be allocated to set up investigating and prosecuting teams against those perpetrators for their "impersonal"
crimes and public disregard.

When it comes to penalizing corporate lawbreakers, sanctions should do
away with the slap-on-the-wrist fines, all too often passed on to the consumers and taxpayers. For example, the use of debarment sanctions would
prohibit habitually lawbreaking corporations from receiving any fraction
of the $300 billion worth of government contracts given out annually. In
addition, creative sanctions should be pursued that involve equity fines,
behavioral restrictions, dechartering of corporations, and probationary
treatment of corporations. For instance, the criminal justice apparatus now
charges probationers and parolees for monitoring these persons where it
can and often requires from them some form of restitution. There is no
reason that corporations, which have far greater abilities to pay than most
offenders, should not contribute to the costs of ensuring their compliance
with the law. In other words, as irresponsible members of the community
these offenders should also have to pay back their debts to society with siz-
able social investments as their penalties.

By instituting polices that regulate in the public interest rather than in
the corporate interest, two things become crucial. The ability, first, to ensure
enough oversight and regulation of the major industries like energy, banking, and accounting, and second, to scale back the corporate harms that
have been taking a toll on the health, lives, and pocketbooks of average
citizens for decades. It is well past time for government to put hundreds of
federal cops on the corporate beats of Wall Street and Main Street. Much
more in the way of resources for corporate law enforcement is required.
The Justice Department, the Internal Revenue Service, the Securities and
Exchange Commission, the Food and Drug Administration, and the Consumer Products Safety Commission, to name the most prominent, remain
seriously underfunded, understaffed, and undermotivated. Beyond funding
and morale, there needs to be established across these departments an in-
teragency corporate crime division or the development of something like a
Tactical Corporate Crime Team (TCCT).

More specifically, the U.S. Department of Justice should provide for
the collection and dissemination of comprehensive information about
the nature and extent of corporate abuse and damage. The Justice Department should also help law enforcement officials identify emerging trends
or patterns of corporate harm and direct resources appropriately. In terms
of the creation of a permanent, well-funded corporate crime division with
specially trained technical personnel, including those from the fields of law,

accounting, and information sciences, the TCCT needs to develop strategies to handle such problems as major fraud, corruption, and safety violations as well as the legal-technical means to pursue and prosecute the complexities of corporate-state crime.

Investing in Social Capital

Since domestic and cross-cultural studies alike reveal that there are strong associations between the production of marginal criminality and relative deprivation, economic frustration, social aggression, and family violence, policies of social maintenance are needed to reduce these sources of behavioral conflict. Policies designed to reduce poverty and inequality should be at the front of the agenda. One place to begin is to follow the lead of those communities, usually midsize cities with relatively secure economies, in the United States that have passed ordinances to establish a system of living wages rather than minimum wages. More broadly, legislation is called for that increases economic support and social services, inclusive of jobs programs, education and technical training, and the deployment of universal health care. Such policies, if they materialize, should not be limited to when the economy has tanked and is in need of a stimulus package to save it from another Great Depression; these policies should be deployed as a basic domestic strategy to prevent marginal criminality in good times and bad times alike.

For example, the reduced relative spending on children, families, and education in the United States that has occurred over the past several decades needs to be reversed, and even expanded, if the nation is to remain globally competitive over the next fifty years. Just as fundamentally, if not more so, monies need to be "earmarked" or redeployed from private-public sources and invested in those urban communities, like Detroit, for the twin purposes of economic and human development. Holistically designed domestic policies of inclusion should be aimed at providing prenatal care and early childhood development for all. Likewise, to prevent childhood abuse and neglect and to enhance children's intellectual and social growth, social skills and counseling programs are needed in all impoverished communities. Policies are also needed that make programs available to vulnerable or at-risk youth in general as well as more intensive programs of intervention to serve habitual juvenile offenders in particular and to make available on request drug, alcohol, and mental health treatment for all.

Law Enforcement

In the areas of police behavior there are at least five policy-related concerns that need attention. These include continuing to upgrade the profession of law enforcement, reaffirming due process and equal protection, de-escalating the wars on crime and terrorism, controlling the abuse of power and corruption, and enriching community-based input, control, and participation.

Collectively, these policy recommendations are aimed at curbing aggressive policing, enhancing respect for the rule of law, intensifying police-community empathy, and amending the police mission.

Professionalizing the Police

Many would argue that the police have already obtained professional status, given their hundreds of hours of instruction at statewide academy programs, degrees in law enforcement, and police agency accreditation requirements. Nevertheless, continued education and training should become the norm wherever possible. Academy training devotes little time to domestic violence issues, and a number of other important topics could be the subject of required ongoing training. Continuing education improves one's law enforcement skills and technical knowledge and it also helps to discourage police abuse of force and the condoning of racist and brutal tactics against marginal others.

Removing from the profession those officers who would, for example, participate in or overlook such beatings as those inflicted on Rodney King by the LAPD or on Abner Louima by the NYPD is absolutely essential if any significant progress is to be made in lessening racial antagonism and raising the perception of law enforcement as a profession worthy of trust and admiration. Many urban cops, in other words, bring to their jobs a negative attitude toward certain community members, undoubtedly a product of the stresses and frustrations of their job. Nevertheless, through educational awareness of human behavior and cultural differences, police officers can be taught to view their on-duty time as a "professional performance" geared toward providing the best service possible to all citizens regardless of class, race, and gender. Most police go into the profession to help make a difference in people's lives, and the training we have in mind will reconnect them with that spirit and provide tools to help them achieve that goal.

Curbing and/or eliminating overtime and moonlighting would probably go a long way toward improving the quality of police performance. For example, the National Institute of Justice (NIJ) (2005) pointed out that about one-third of police officers work twenty or more hours of overtime per month and more than half moonlight at other jobs. Although research has yet to determine how, exactly, fatigue affects police work, there is no doubt that "law enforcement suffers when officers are fatigued due to overtime, shift work, court appearances, and the emotional and physical demands of the job" (NIJ 2005, 13). While police salary may need to be raised to compensate for the lost salary, such a move would make police work more consistent with many other occupations affecting or involving public safety, such as airline pilots, truck drivers, and nurses—all of whom must abide by working-hours standards and restrictions designed to prevent excess fatigue. Such standards should certainly apply to law enforcement officials who have been delegated the only legitimate monopoly over the deadly use of force.

Reaffirming Due Process and Equal Protection

The erosion of due process and equal protection rights over the past decades in the United States gained momentum with the passage of the hurriedly passed antiterrorism law—the USA PATRIOT Act—in the weeks after 9/11. The original act had sixteen provisions that were scheduled to expire at the end of 2005 unless renewed by Congress. In the fall of that year, the 109th Congress made fourteen of those provisions permanent as part of the USA PATRIOT Improvement and Reauthorization Act that became law in 2006. The other two were passed with sunset clauses subjecting them to future congressional renewal. One of these provisions was on "roving wiretaps" and the other on "searches" of library records, business records, medical files, and other documents. These administrative (rather than judicially approved) subpoenas are not totally new to federal investigators, for the FBI had already been employing these surveillance and investigative procedures in drug and health care fraud cases. The second revision of the PATRIOT Act occurred in July 2008. It included the controversial immunity for the phone companies that cooperated in the National Security Agency (NSA) wiretapping program authorized by the Bush administration. Compared to the laws before and after 9/11, the most recent measure "gives the executive branch broader latitude in eavesdropping on people abroad and at home who it believes are tied to terrorism, and it reduced the role of a secret intelligence court in overseeing some operations" (Lichtblau 2008, 1), in spite of the very low rate of successfully prosecuting these cases, as shown in chapter 9.

Reinforcing the rule of law becomes all the more important not only in the context of homeland security and the increasing militarization of the police, especially in the light of terrorism, but also in light of the United States' denial of these rights to those suspected terrorists or "enemy combatants" incarcerated in prisons like Abu Graib in Iraq or Guantanomo in Cuba. For example, at a minimum, reinstating various legal safeguards that had previously been watered down, such as the "good faith" exemptions in having probable cause when obtaining reasonable search warrants or respecting the fundamental principle that no person should be deprived of his liberty without the right to habeas corpus, most notably being charged and tried for a crime in a court of law or set free. We also recommend the suppression of supersurveillance activities that indiscriminately invade every person's rights to privacy by way of the "interception of wire, telephone, and computer communications, the searching of businesses and residences, the seizing of business and library records, or other similar items of evidence" (Logan 2007, 287).

Finally, we recommend the creation of independent oversight boards of law enforcement practices in general as well as the mandatory videotaping of interrogations and use-of-force incidents in particular.

De-escalating the Wars on Crime and Terrorism

Once again, in the context of the recent conflation of the "war on crime" and the "war on terrorism," we need to de-escalate our language and our practices, keeping the actions and the roles of the police and the military as separate and as unique as "real politics" will allow. For example, even the Bush administration in the summer of 2005 toned down its metaphor from a "war on terror" to the "global struggle against violent extremism." The Obama administration has also pledged wherever they can to use criminal courts rather than military tribunals to combat terrorists. Similarly, rather than a war metaphor for combating illicit drugs and drug abusers, policy should be guided by a medical metaphor that seeks not to punish but to assist those who have become drug-dependent victims to heal and recover. More generally, as law enforcement knows that most of the answers to crime lie elsewhere than within the administration of criminal justice, efforts of social control should involve institutions other than law enforcement, whenever possible.

Two policy changes that would help to facilitate a de-escalation of the wars on crime, even during an era of heightened sensitivity to violent extremism, would include scaling back some paramilitary trends in law enforcement and curbing the use of zero tolerance policies as discussed above and below. In the case of paramilitary approaches to war on crime, for example, the use of SWAT teams has been extended from its original purposes of dealing with hostage negotiation situations to raiding public housing projects and college dormitories seeking out marijuana dealers. Such practices, especially in those marginal communities already disenchanted with the police, only serve to further alienate these groups of citizens. More selective and narrower uses of these tactics in law enforcement are called for.

Law enforcement must distinguish between battling murderers or terrorists, on the one hand, and confronting petty criminals or social nonconformists, on the other hand. Zero tolerance policies that disable police or judicial discretion are seldom good ideas, but where enacted they should distinguish between behaviors that pose serious risks of injury and harm and those nonviolent and unthreatening behaviors that pose no security risks or tangible harm. In other words, homeless addicts or veterans and the mentally ill should be referred by law enforcement to human services and/or voluntary agencies, thus "filtering" out from the criminal justice system all but the hardcore or serious offenders.

Controlling Police Abuse of Power and Corruption

Since the creation of formal policing in the nineteenth century, police abuse of power and/or corruption have always been to varying degrees a fact of local law enforcement. From the very beginning, police officers were known for selling protection and administering "curbside justice," buying their positions and promotions, and ignoring violations of the law for money or other favors. Historically, the use and abuse of the police force has always been a controversial issue, especially in those communities of color where a disproportionate use of this behavior, including deadly force, has occurred. Over the years, several policies have been used to reduce both necessary and unnecessary use of force by police officers. We support the use of all of these policies and encourage more extensive use of them. These include the instituting of tougher and clearer departmental guidelines, monitoring the levels of aggression and the use-of-force incidents with dashboard-mounted cameras and investigation, employing anger- and stress-management techniques, psychological counseling for officers who request such services, and the administering of psychological tests as prescreening efforts to identify individuals prone to abuse power or who are vulnerable to handling stress badly.

Ellwyn Stoddard (1968, 204) in a classic article on police corruption, identified ten types of corruption that he described as constituting the "blue-coat code":

1. Bribery—accepting cash or gifts in exchange for nonenforcement of the law.
2. Chiseling—demanding discounts, free admission, and free food.
3. Extortion—the threat of enforcement and arrest if a bribe is not given.
4. Favoritism—giving breaks on law enforcement, such as for traffic violations committed by families and friends of the police.
5. Mooching—accepting food, drinks, and admission to entertainment.
6. Perjury—lying for other officers apprehended in illegal activity.

7. Prejudice—unequal enforcement of the law with respect to racial and ethnic minorities.
8. Premeditated theft—planned burglaries and thefts.
9. Shakedown—taking items from the scene of a theft or a burglary [or a drug deal] the officer is investigating.
10. Shopping—taking small, inexpensive items from a crime scene or an unsecured business or home.

Policy recommendations here simply encourage all police departments to incorporate into their organizational frameworks some of the more successful efforts to control and reduce corrupt activities, which naturally contribute to the erosion of public confidence and trust in law enforcement. Beyond setting high moral standards, training in ethical issues, and selecting the most qualified officers, departments should establish rigid policies of discipline and prosecution in response to violating customary policies, procedures, and laws. Departments should, of course, also strive for the uniform enforcement of the law, neither favoring the affiliations of some groups nor penalizing the affiliations of other groups. Where possible, internal affairs units of law enforcement departments should become proactive in ferreting out illegal and unethical activity, and supervisors, as a rule, should be held responsible or answerable for the actions of their subordinates. When and where corruption becomes too widespread and "out of control," then these departments should become subject to outside commissions, task forces, special prosecutors, and court oversight if necessary.

Enriching Community Control of the Police

In those marginal communities like the ghetto and the barrio, where both overzealous policing and underenforcement occur simultaneously, disadvantaged blacks and Latinos believe that "they are always under terror without protection from the authorities" (Wilkinson, Beaty, and Lurry 2009, 36). Without dependable legal protection, self- or crew-protection exemplifies Black's theory of self-help where crime by these youth becomes a means of social control (Black 1983, 1993). Accordingly, it is little wonder that in these marginal communities, the history of police-community relations and efforts aimed at improving them have received mixed reviews at best, including a variety of activities that have fallen under the rubric of "community policing." Moreover, the widespread skepticism and mistrust from many inner-city urban residents leads them to often view these efforts as little more than public relations gimmicks. To go beyond those social interactions that are seen primarily as image boosters for the police or as citizens becoming extensions of local law enforcement as police "informants," reforms and programs are called for that empower the police.

This means above all else that the police need to take the frameworks, norms, and grievances of these marginalized groups seriously or risk the consequences of more crime as self-help and self-protection. In other words, the state is subject to losing its moral authority when it fails to recognize the moral imperatives of self-defense; for example, when people are defending themselves or their families from violence. Also, the racial and ethnic profiling often in Latino or Afro-Caribbean communities, for example, buttressed by the uncertainty of immigrant status, aggravates the disrespectful treatment experienced by the residents (Solis, Portillos, and Brunson 2009; Lopez 2008). In response, what are called for are not only police strategies with youth in mind but also the involvement of those groups, young and old, in discussions of proposed police strategies, such outcomes allowing for the coproduction of local strategies of harm reduction.

Other related strategies of police-community reform include the implementation of a community ombudsman or the creation of marginally represented citizen review boards with reasonable authority and power to serve or guard against overzealous and/or abusive police practices in "high crime" areas. When police must answer for their behavior and are accountable to the citizens from those communities that they serve, much can be done to improve police-community interaction and to build the public trust with regard to local law enforcement. The police may also identify and train their officers to lead workshops on conflict and dispute resolution and on human dignity and multiculturalism. In a different but related vein of raising the public confidence in these communities, the inclusion of all representative groups (e.g., minorities, women, gays) in neighborhood patrols, for example, should be highly visible as a means of sensitizing the police and the community to each other's needs.

Adjudication

The middle stage of the administration of criminal justice involving prosecutors, defense attorneys, and judges who are acting as legal agents of adjudication for the state and the accused, engaged in the processes of negotiated plea bargains or adversarial trials, is often thought of as the fulcrum of the system since ultimately who is and who is not guilty of a crime is determined here. Historically, until the decline of the indeterminate and the rise of the determinate sentencing systems beginning in the late 1970s, judges used to wield a great deal of influence vis-à-vis their discretion during the sentencing phase to decide on the type and length of punishment. A consequence of these changes in the sentencing law was to transfer this power of sentencing discretion to prosecutors. Recently, there has been a resurrection in the discretionary authority as well as in the social activism of the judiciary. One product of this activism has been the development of problem-solving courts.

As part of the movement in restorative justice, the appearance of problem-solving courts has blossomed throughout the United States. Today, every state has at least one problem-solving court and all total there are more than 2,000 of these courts. Of the eleven different kinds of problem-solving courts, the three most common are drug courts, domestic violence courts, and community courts. Originally designed for low-level criminal cases, mostly misdemeanors (involving such crimes as drug possession, prostitution, and vandalism), now there is an array of other courts addressing the less serious and more serious felony offenses. These include: mental health courts, reentry courts, DWI courts, gun courts, family treatment courts, juvenile drug courts, homeless courts, and youth courts (Berman and Feinblatt 2005).

These courts are the products of judges and attorneys who have turned the traditional adversary system of case processing and adjudication into a caring and problem-solving community tribunal. The goal here is to move away from treating criminal cases as part of an undifferentiated mass of assembly-line equal justice and toward a restorative model of case-by-case individualized justice. Using a tailored approach to justice, these problem-solving courts invite the community, victims, offenders, social service providers, and so on to participate in the adjudicative process and to come up with some kind of community-based alternative to jail or prison, usually involving social services and/or community restitution projects. The product of this nonadversarial and nonbureaucratic approach to personalized justice has been to change the behavioral patterns of habitual offenders, enhance the safety of victims, and improve the quality of community life. These problem-solving courts are in the spirit of harm reduction.

There are also prosecutors in this country that have modified their roles and use of prosecutorial discretion to become advocates for those who are vulnerable and/or cannot defend themselves, such as the prosecutors in Alameda and San Francisco, California, who instituted changes in the labeling and treatment of sexual molesters as well as of adolescent sex workers. In the case of teenage prostitutes, these adolescent girls were legally transformed from delinquent criminals to victims of exploitation and molestation. In these and other progressive offices of prosecution, these officers of the court are redefining crime and public safety, moving away from incarceration and throwing-away-the-key only approaches to ones that also involve the prevention of crime and violence. These prosecutors, like many of the problem-solving judges, are adopting a public-health approach to crime and violence, where policies and strategies are employed to treat the victims and to assault the problems with heavy dosages of early child intervention and preventions for those at high risk.

Improving Representation and Technology for Indigent Defendant

With respect to equal protection and other rights of due process for the indigent accused and convicted, there is a need to improve the criminal law competency and remuneration of legal counsel, especially those defense attorneys affiliated with court-appointed systems or in cases involving capital crimes and the death penalty. Wherever appropriate, defendants and their attorneys should also have access to the latest technological developments. For example, all persons accused or convicted of a crime where DNA tests would be relevant to proving or disproving the guilt or innocence should have access to that technology. We agree with those forty-seven states that have passed laws providing convicted felons access to DNA evidence and not with the Supreme Court's 5–4 ruling in 2009 that convicted criminals do not have a constitutional right to obtain access to a state's biological evidence in order to conduct DNA testing pursuant to their claims of innocence.

Finally, in light of some three decades of contracting legal rights, it makes sense to reexamine, expand, or reinstate the rights of those convicted to appeal their verdicts, sentences, and living and working conditions. Such policies both resist the human rights violations of correctional workers and locked-up inmates alike, and they improve the morale and human dignity of all concerned and responsible parties.

Corrections

Prison growth has (1) had only a limited impact on the amount of crime, (2) been the product of intentional policy, not natural forces, (3) decreased social justice, and (4) damaged the well-being of poor communities (Clear 2008). Changes are called for that curb excessively long sentences (i.e., more than 100 years), reverse the trends of increasing lengths of imprisonment for minor and nonviolent crimes, and create alternatives to incarceration for as many convicted offenders as possible. The types of policies include the abandonment of mandatory sentencing, increased judicial discretion in sentencing, the expansion of intermediate or community sanctions that go beyond slapping a tracking device on an offender, and the delivery of related human and social services. We also recommend abolishing the practices of treating adolescents as adult defendants and of housing juvenile or youthful offenders with adult offenders under any circumstances.

Most importantly, we recommend the repeal of the 1996 Prison Litigation Reform Act. This act has effectively barred inmate complaints from federal court and, in effect, has hidden prison operations from public view. Without the repeal of this act, subjecting correctional authorities once again to the rule of law, inmates are left unfree from the arbitrary and cruel practices associated with the incarceration binge in America.

In terms of professionalizing the field of corrections, educational and training requirements should be upgraded across the board, with a bachelor's degree in some behavioral or social science required as a minimum for gaining entrance into the field. Corrections is an occupation that can certainly benefit from workshops, experimentation, and research into institutionalized behavior and control. Finally, programs that promote the development of self-actualization and social integration for inmates or parolees are also advocated as essential for reintegrating offenders back into the community as full participating citizens. Former NIJ director Jeremy Travis noted some 5 years ago that 630,000 people leave prison each year and reenter society, so "reentry is not an option. Reentry reflects the iron law of imprisonment: they all come back" (2005, xxi). In short, prison must do a better job preparing inmates for their inevitable release and local communities should do a better job assisting those returning to society.

Abandoning Mandatory Sentences and Abolishing Capital Punishment

Current mandatory sentencing laws such as three strikes, even if uniformly applied, would still have adverse, accumulatively negative affects on African and Latin male Americans in particular, as these groups of the marginal classes are disproportionately overrepresented in prison. Accordingly, we recommend a sentencing system that does away with the minimum aspect of the sentencing guidelines but keeps a "maximum-time served" and allows for a fuller reinstitutionalization of "good time" reductions in sentences as an incentive for early release.

We also recommend abolishing the death penalty in the United States. First, its past and present use does not reflect equal justice for all. It is too selective and arbitrary in all but the most heinous crimes, and it is applied disproportionately to marginal offenders and majority victims. Second, the time is well past due for this nation, as one of only a few in the democratic nation-states worldwide to continue to violate the most basic of human rights—the right to life, to desist from this practice, as it briefly abolished it for a few years in the 1970s, and more recently, as several states instituted temporary if, unfortunately, not permanent, moratoriums on state executions.

A Moratorium on Prison Construction and the Privatization of Prisons

The United States has the largest per capita prison population in the world, at a time when rates of street criminality are generally as low or lower than they have been in some forty years. Put simply, we do not need additional prisons that will be filled with minor offenders at high costs to taxpayers and communities. Politicians are not as eager to talk tough on crime as they once were and are more likely now than perhaps ever before to talk about runaway prison expenses because they are raiding state budgets everywhere, draining money from already tight and contracting budgets in education, social services, and in other basic areas of crime prevention. Ultimately, this nation does not need more than 2.2 million cells, and a moratorium on building any more new facilities still leaves plenty of room for those who need to be there.

Private prisons, more so than public prisons, create vested interests in increasing the amount of punishment by involving big business and Wall Street in crime control for profits (Selman and Leighton 2010). Whether we are talking about the privatization of prisons or the privatization of prison services such as the delivery of health care, wherever possible, corners are cut to the bare minimums to support high salaries of the executives and a return on shareholders' investments. As corporate and not state bodies, privately owned prisons are exempt from many disclosure requirements because the Freedom of Information Act does not apply, so transparency and accountability are much more difficult to secure.

In a similar vein, private prisons do not, for example, provide lists of racial breakdowns of prisoners or other information considered vital in the public sector. They may also conceal some of their practices as these may be protected by "corporate policy" or "trade secrets." Finally, the movement for privatization inside and outside of the correctional apparatus provides one of the more obvious or conspicuous parts of what has become over the past couple of decades a growing criminal justice-industrial complex where interests other than those of the public in general and of crime-control in particular are subject to the vagaries of the marketplace.

Intermediate Sanctions and Community-Based Alternatives

We strongly recommend the development, elaboration, and diversification of intermediate sanctions, including but not limited to: intensive-supervision probation and parole, day reporting centers, halfway houses, fines, and home confinement and electronic monitoring. These community-based alternatives to prison have mostly abandoned the "rehabilitative ideal," emphasizing instead the retributive, deterrence, and punitive objectives of corrections. We recommend that policies reaffirm rehabilitation and prisoner reentry programs. These forms of reintegration, as the primary goal of corrections, working in tandem with the developing practices of restorative justice, are not only more economical but they are also preferred scientifically speaking as alternatives to jail and prison. Furthermore, expanding the use of intermediate sanctions in lieu of the more expensive and harsh methods of incarceration is more humane and constructive for offenders, victims, and communities alike.

Prisoner Reentry and Human Service Delivery

With the billions of dollars saved from expensive new prison construction and potentially from the lowered operating costs of serving hundreds of thousands of fewer inmates each year by way of intermediate sanctions and reduced sentencing structures, criminal justice could develop a whole range of human services inside and outside of prisons. In the spirit of both restorative and social justice and in the context of reintegration and community efficacy, victims and offenders both need access to programs in transition, employment, counseling, education, job training, and other types of reentry programs. Toward these ends, we strongly recommend a significant expansion of the $150 million dollars allocated per year for the Second Chance Act signed into law by Bush in April 2008.

Considering that there are at least 650,000 prisoners currently returning to the "free world" annually and that the United States currently spends more than $68 billion yearly on corrections, we think a more viable figure for reentry programs would be at least $2 billion dollars per annum. This figure would represent only 1/34th of the current total correctional budget, amounting to $300 per returning parolee/prisoner rather than the current $25 per year (less the expenses for operating transition programs). As a preventive measure against the existing high rates of recidivism in this country as well as the prohibitive costs of incarcerating inmates averaging about $30,000 per annum, these additional dollars for prisoner reentry programs represent common sense, not rocket science.

With respect to the more than 650,000 released inmates each year for the foreseeable future, there are various steps that local communities may take to facilitate reentry. These include banning the boxes on application forms that ask whether or not one has ever been convicted of a felony, city ordinances and laws prohibiting discrimination against former prisoners, and resolutions and other incentives for willing employers to assist ex-offenders.

In addition, support should be made available for families of inmates and for "criminal anonymous" groups.

Finally, related policy measures such as the denial or restriction of welfare benefits, public assistance, educational grants, and the loss of the right to vote for persons convicted of crimes need to be seriously reconsidered and overhauled. For the most part, these types of justice policies and practices of disenfranchisement tend to worsen situations of deprivation and to stoke the flames of more, not less, criminality. These punitive approaches also serve to reinforce the social exclusion rather than the social inclusion of ex-offenders.

References

Several common sources of data are referenced rather than through multiple similar entries for different years of the same publication:

BJS (Bureau of Justice Statistics), publishes annual data on prisoners, jail inmates, capital punishment, and victimization, to name a few. The Bureau of Justice Statistics is an agency of the U.S. Department of Justice. Most of the publications are listed below, although some text references to BJS that include the name of the publication are not. The Bureau of Justice Statistics can be accessed online at http://www.ojp.usdoj.gov/bjs.

FBI or UCR (followed by year): U.S. Department of Justice, Federal Bureau of Investigation, *Crime in America* (Washington, DC: U.S. Government Printing Office). The Federal Bureau of Investigation can be accessed online at http://www.fbi .gov.

Sourcebook or *Sourcebook of Criminal Justice Statistics (followed by the year)*: Kathleen Maguire and Ann L. Pastore, eds., *Sourcebook of Criminal Justice Statistics*. U.S. Department of Justice, Bureau of Justice Statistics (Washington, DC: U.S. Government Printing Office, 2003). The *Sourcebook* can be accessed online at http://www .albany.edu/sourcebook/.

Statistical Abstract of the United States (Stat Abs [followed by year]): U.S. Census Bureau annually punishes this reference volume. Current and historical volumes are available through http://www.census.gov/prod/www/abs/statab.html.

Acker, James et al. 1998. "The Death Penalty: A Scholarly Forum." In *Selected Readings in Criminal Justice*, edited by Philip L. Reichel, pp. 166–78. San Diego, CA: Greenhaven Press.

Agozino, Biko. 1997. *Black Women and the Criminal Justice System*. Aldershot, England: Ashgate Publishing Limited.

American Civil Liberties Union of Michigan. 2005. "Court Rules Every Michigan Citizen Is Entitled to Legal Representation." *Civil Liberties Newsletter* 4(10):1.

American Correctional Association. 2003. *Corrections Compendium.* January. Alexandria, VA: American Correctional Association.

American Society for Aesthetic Plastic Surgery. 2004. "Cosmetic Surgery Quick Facts." Available, http://www.surgery.org/press/procedurefacts-asqf.php.

Amnesty International. 2000. *Amnesty International: Annual Report 2000.* Available, http://www.amnesty.org/en/library/info/POL10/001/2000/en.

——. 1999a. *United States of America: Race, Rights, and Police Brutality* (January 9) (AI index AMR 51/147/1999). New York: Author. Available, http://www.amnesty.org/en/library/info/AMR51/147/1999.

——. 1999b. "'Not Part of My Sentence': Violations of the Human Rights of Women in Custody." Available, http://www.amnesty.org/ailib/aipub/1999/AMR/25100199.htm.

Andersen, Margaret. 1988. "Moving Our Minds: Studying Women and Reconstructing Sociology." *Teaching Sociology* 16:123–32.

Andersen, Margaret L., and Patricia Hill Collins. 1998. *Race, Class and Gender: An Anthology,* 3rd ed. Belmont, CA: Wadsworth Publishing.

Anderson, Charles H. 1974. *The Political Economy of Social Class.* Englewood Cliffs, NJ: Prentice-Hall.

Anderson, S. E. 1995. *The Black Holocaust: For Beginners.* New York: Writers and Readers, Inc.

Armstrong, David and Peter Newcomb. 2004. "The Forbes 400." *Forbes,* October 11, 2004, p. 103.

Armstrong, Karen. 2005. "Ghosts of Our Past." In *Violence and Terrorism,* edited by Thomas Badey, pp. 14–17. Dubuque, IA: McGraw-Hill/Dushkin.

Aronowitz, Stanley, and William DiFazio. 1994. *The Jobless Future: Sci-Tech and the Dogma of Work.* Minneapolis: University of Minnesota Press.

Auerbach, Jerold S. 1976. *Unequal Justice: Lawyers and Social Change in Modern America.* New York: Oxford University Press.

Austin, Regina, and Michael Schill. 1991. "Black, Brown, Poor & Poisoned: Minority Grassroots Environmentalism and the Quest for Eco-Justice." *Kansas Journal of Law and Public Policy* (Summer):69.

Baca Zinn, Maxine, Pierrette Hondagneu-Sotelo, and Michael Messner. 2005. *Gender through the Prism of Difference,* 3rd ed. New York: Oxford University Press.

Bakan, Joel. 2004. *The Corporation: The Pathological Pursuit of Profit and Power.* New York: Free Press.

Barak, Gregg. 2009. *Criminology: An Integrated Approach.* Lanham, MD: Rowman and Littlefield.

——. 2008. "Homeland Security Failed to Protect U.S. from Financial Harm." *Ann Arbor News* (December 12):A10.

—— (ed.). 2007. *Violence, Conflict, and World Order: Critical Conversations on State Sanctioned Justice.* Lanham, MD: Rowman and Littlefield.

——. 2005. "A Reciprocal Approach to Peacemaking Criminology: Between Adversarialism and Mutualism." *Theoretical Criminology* 9(2):131–52.

———. 2004a. "A Reciprocal Approach to Terrorism and Terrorist-Like Behavior." In *Terrorism and Counter-Terrorism: Criminological Perspectives*, edited by Mathieu Deflem, pp. 33–49. Amsterdam: Elsevier.

———. 2004b. "Class, Race, and Gender in Criminology and Criminal Justice: Ways of Seeing Difference." *Race, Gender, and Class: An Interdisciplinary and Multicultural Journal* 11(4):80–97.

———. 2003. *Violence and Nonviolence: Pathways to Understanding*. Thousand Oaks, CA: Sage.

———. 2001. "Crime and Crime Control in an Age of Globalization: A Theoretical Dissection." *Critical Criminology: An International Journal* 10(1):57–72.

———. 2000. "Repressive Versus Restorative and Social Justice: A Case for Integrative Praxis." *Contemporary Justice Review* 3(1):39–44.

———. 1998. *Integrating Criminologies*. Boston: Allyn and Bacon.

——— (ed.). 1996. *Representing O. J.: Murder, Criminal Justice and Mass Culture*. Albany, NY: Harrow and Heston.

——— (ed.). 1994. *Media, Process, and the Social Construction of Crime: Studies in Newsmaking Criminology*. New York: Routledge.

——— (ed.). 1991a. *Crimes by the Capitalist State: An Introduction to State Criminality*. Albany: SUNY Press.

———. 1991b. *Gimme Shelter: A Social History of Homelessness in Contemporary America*. New York: Praeger.

———. 1980. *In Defense of Whom? A Critique of Criminal Justice Reform*. Cincinnati, OH: Anderson Publishing.

Barak, Gregg, and Stuart Henry. 1999. "An Integrative-Constitutive Theory of Crime, Law, and Social Justice." In *Social Justice/Criminal Justice: The Maturation of Critical Theory in Law, Crime, and Deviance*. Edited by Bruce A. Arrigo. Belmont, CA: West/ Wadsworth, 1998.

Barker, Emily, Brian Baxter, Alison Frankel, and Nate Raymond. 2008. "Progress Report." *Federal Sentencing Reporter* 20(3) (February):206–10.

Barlow, Melissa. 1998. "Race and the Problem of Crime in *Time* and *Newsweek* Cover Stories, 1946–1995." *Social Justice* 25(2):149–83.

Barstow, David. 2003. "When Workers Die: U.S. Rarely Seeks Charges for Deaths in Workplace." Originally published December, 22, 2003, in the *New York Times*. Available, http://reclaimdemocracy.org/weekly_2003/when_workers_die.html.

Beckett, Katherine, and Steve Herbert. 2008. "The Punitive City Revisited: The Transformation of Urban Social Control." In *After the War on Crime: Race, Democracy, and a New Reconstruction*, edited by M. L. Frampton, I. H. López, and J. Simon, pp. 106–22. New York: New York University Press.

Beckett, Katherine, and Theodore Sasson. 2000. *The Politics of Injustice: Crime and Punishment in America*. Thousand Oaks, CA: Pine Forge Press.

Beirne, Piers, and James Messerschmidt. 2000. *Criminology*, 3rd ed. Boulder, CO: Westview.

———. 1991. *Criminology*. San Diego: Harcourt Brace Jovanovich.

Beiser, Vince. 2008. "First, Reduce Harm." *Miller-McCune* (Nov/Dec):60–71.

Belknap, Joanne. 1996. *The Invisible Woman: Gender, Crime, and Justice*. Belmont, CA: Wadsworth.

———. 1995. "Women in Conflict: An Analysis of Women Correctional Officers." In *The Criminal Justice System and Women*, edited by Barbara Raffel Price and Natalie J. Sokoloff, pp. 404–20. New York: McGraw-Hill.

Bell, Derrick. 1998. "Foreward." In *Images of Color, Images of Crime: Readings*, edited by Coramae Richey Mann and Marjorie S. Zatz. Los Angeles: Roxbury.

———. 1990. "Chronicle of the Space Traders." *Rutgers Law Review* 42:1; revised and expanded version in *St. Louis Law Review* 34 (1990):3.

Benjamin, Daniel, and Steven Simon. 2002. *The Age of Sacred Terror*. New York: Random House.

Berman, Greg, and John Feinblatt. 2005. *Good Courts: The Case for Problem-Solving Justice*. New York: New Press.

Best, Joel. 1990. *Threatened Children: Rhetoric and Concern about Child-Victims*. Chicago: University of Chicago Press.

Binstein, Michael, and Charles Bowden. 1993. *Trust Me: Charles Keating and the Missing Billions*. New York: Random House.

Black, Donald. 1993. *The Social Structure of Right and Wrong*. New York: Cambridge University Press.

———. 1983. "Crime as Social Control." *American Sociological Review* 48:34–45.

———. 1976. *The Behavior of Law*. New York: Academic Press.

Blast, Carol. 1997. "Driving While Black: Stopping Motorists on a Subterfuge." *Criminal Law Bulletin* 33:457.

Blau, Judith, and Peter Blau. 1982. "The Cost of Inequality: Metropolitan Structure and Violent Crime." *American Sociological Review* 47(1):114–29.

Blitstein, Ryan. 2009. "Racism's Hidden Toll." *Miller-McCune* (July-August):48–57.

Bloom, Barbara, Barbara Owen, and Stephanie Covington. 2003. "Gender-Responsive Strategies: Research, Practice, and Guiding Principles for Women Offenders." Washington, DC: National Institute of Corrections/U.S. Department of Justice. Available, http://www.nicic.org/pubs/2003/018017.pdf.

Blum, Deborah. 2005. "Solving for XX: What Science Can (and Can't) Tell Larry Summers about the Difference between Men and Women." *Boston Globe* (online edition) (January 23). Available, http://www.boston.com/news/globe/ideas/articles/2005/01/23/solving_for_xx/.

Blumstein, Alfred. 2002. "Why Is Crime Falling—Or Is It?" *Perspectives on Crime and Justice: 2000–2001 Lecture Series*, National Institute of Justice. Available, http://www.ncjrs.gov/pdffiles1/nij/187100.pdf.

———. 1995. "Interview with Professor Alfred Blumstein of Carnegie Mellon University." *Law Enforcement News* 422:10.

Blumstein, Alfred, and J. Wallman. 2000. *The Crime Drop in America*. New York: Cambridge University Press.

Body-Gendrot, Sophie. 2000. *The Social Control of Cities? A Comparative Perspective*. Oxford, UK: Blackwell Publishers.

Bohm, Robert. 1998. "Understanding Crime and Social Control in Market Economies: Looking Back and Moving Forward." In *Cutting the Edge: Current Perspectives in Radical/Critical Criminology and Criminal Justice*, edited by Jeffrey Ross, pp. 18–33. Westport, CN: Praeger.

Bohm, Robert M., and Keith N. Haley. 2005. *Introduction to Criminal Justice*, 4th ed. Boston: McGraw-Hill.

———. 2004. *Introduction to Criminal Justice*, 3rd ed. Boston: McGraw-Hill.
Bombardieri, Marcella. 2005. "Harvard Women's Group Rips Summers." *Boston Globe* (online edition) (January 19). Available, http://www.boston.com/news/education/higher/articles/2005/01/19/harvard_womens_group_rips_summers/.
Bonilla-Silva, Eduardo. 1997. "Rethinking Racism: Toward a Structural Interpretation." *American Sociological Review* 62:465–80.
Borg, Anita (institute). 2005. Letter in response to Summers. Available, http://anita borg.org/news/archive/chronicle-of-a-controversy/.
Braithwaite, John. 1992. "Poverty, Power and White-collar Crime." In *White Collar Crime Reconsidered*, edited by Kip Schlegel and David Weisburd. Boston: Northeastern.
———. 1989. *Crime, Shame, and Reintegration*. Cambridge: Cambridge University Press.
Braithwaite, John, Valerie Braithwaite, and Eliza Ahmed. 2005. "Reintegrative Shaming." In *The Essential Criminology Reader*, edited by Stuart Henry and Mark Lanier. Boulder, CO: Westview.
Britton, Dana M. 1997. "Gendered Organizational Logic: Policy and Practice in Men's and Women's Prisons." *Gender and Society* 11(6):796–818.
Brouwer, Steve. 1998. *Sharing the Pie: A Citizen's Guide to Wealth and Power in America*. New York: Henry Holt and Company.
Brown, Robert McAfee. 1987. *Religion and Violence*, 2nd ed. Philadelphia: Westminster Press.
Brune, Tom. 1999. "Census Will for First Time Count Those of Mixed Race." *Seattle Times* (online edition) (August 17).
Buhrke, Robin A. 1996. *A Matter of Justice: Lesbians and Gay Men in Law Enforcement*. New York: Routledge.
Bullard, Robert. 1994. *Unequal Protection: Environmental Justice and Communities of Color*. San Francisco: Sierra Club Books.
———. 1990. *Dumping in Dixie: Race, Class and Environmental Quality*. Boulder, CO: Westview.
Bureau of Justice Statistics. 2009a. "Jail Incarceration Rates by Race and Ethnicity, 1990–2008." Office of Justice Programs. Retrieved July 6, 2009, from http://www.ojp.usdoj.gov/bjs/glance/tables/jailrairtab.htm.
———. 2009b. *Asian, Native Hawaiian, and Pacific Islander Victims of Crime*. March, NCJ 225037.
———. 2009c. *Stalking Victimization in the United States*. January, NCJ 224527.
———. 2009d. Key Facts at a Glance. Available, http://bjs.ojp.usdoj.gov/content/glance/tables/corr2tab.cfm.
———. 2009e. *Capital Punishment, 2008—Statistical Tables*. December, NCJ 228662.
———. 2009f. *Prisoners in 2008*. December, NCJ 228417.
———. 2008a. "Corrections Statistics." Office of Justice Programs. Retrieved July 6, 2009, from http://www.ojp.usdoj.gov/bjs/correct.htm.
———. 2008b. *Probation and Parole in the United States, 2007—Statistical Tables*. NCJ 224707.
———. 2008c. *Justice Expenditure and Employment Extracts, 2006*. NCJ 224394.

———. 2006a. "Criminal Cases and Convictions." *National Survey of Prosecutors: Prosecutors in State Courts, 2005.*

———. 2006b. *Federal Law Enforcement Officers, 2004.* NCJ 212750.

———. 2006c. *Local Police Departments, 2003.* NCJ 210118.

———. 2005a. "Contacts between Police and the Public: Findings from the 2002 National Survey." NCJ 207845.

———. 2005b. *Family Violence Statistics.* NCJ 207846.

———. 2005c. *Probation and Parole in the United States, 2004.* NCJ 210676.

———. 2004a. *Criminal Victimization, 2003.* NCJ 205455.

———. 2004b. *Profile of Jail Inmates, 2002.* NCJ 201932.

———. 2004c. *American Indians and Crime, 1992–2002.* NCJ 203097.

———. 2001. *Federal Drug Offenders, 1999 with Trends 1984–1999.* NCJ 187285.

———. 2000. *The Sexual Victimization of College Women.* NCJ 182369.

———. 1999. *American Indians and Crime.* NCJ 173386.

———. 1998a. *Profile of Jail Inmates, 1996.* NCJ 164620.

———. 1998b. *Changes in Criminal Victimization, 1994–1995.*

———. 1998c. *Violence by Intimates.*

———. 1998d. *Stalking in America.* NCJ 169592.

———. 1997a. *HIV in Prisons and Jails, 1995.* Washington, DC: U.S. Department of Justice.

———. 1997b. *Lifetime Likelihood of Going to State or Federal Prison.* NCJ 160092.

———. 1993. "Survey of State Prison Inmates, 1991." NCJ 136949.

———. 1992. *Drugs, Crime and the Justice System.* NCJ 133652.

Bureau of Labor Statistics. 2008–2009. *Occupational Outlook Handbook.* Available, http://www.bls.gov/oco/.

———. 2004–2005. *Occupational Outlook Handbook,* pp. 9–10 of 12. U.S. Department of Labor.

———. 2004a. "November 2004 National Occupational Employment and Wage Estimates: Legal Occupations." Washington, DC: U.S. Department of Labor.

———. 1999a. *Highlights of Women's Earnings in 1998, Report 928.* Washington, DC: U.S. Department of Labor.

———. 1999b. *Employment and Earnings* (monthly). (January): Table 10. Available, ftp://ftp.bls.gov/pub/special.requests/lf/aat10.txt.

———. 1999c. "National Employment and Wage Data from the Occupational Employment Statistics Survey by Occupation, 1998." *Occupational Employment Statistics* (December): Table 1, Table A-1.

Burnley, Jane, Christine Edmunds, Mario T. Gaboury, and Anne Seymour. 1998. *1998 National Victim Assistance Academy.* Washington, DC: Office of Justice Programs, U.S. Department of Justice.

Business Week. 2005. "Death, Taxes, & Sarbanes-Oxley?" (January 17). Available, http://www.businessweek.com/magazine/content/05_03/b3916031_mz011.htm.

Butler, Anne. 1997. *Gendered Justice in the American West: Women Prisoners in Men's Penitentiaries.* Urbana: University of Illinois Press.

Calavita, Kitty, Henry Pontell, and Robert Tillman. 1997. *Big Money Crime.* Berkeley: University of California Press.

Camp, Camille Graham, and George Camp. 2002. *The Corrections Yearbook 2001: Adult Systems,* pp. 150–76. Middletown, CT: Criminal Justice Institute.

Cannon, Louis. 2000. "One Bad Cop." *New York Times* Section 6 (October 1):32. Retrieved September 24, 2002, from http://www.nytimes.com.

Cantor, Nathaniel E. 1932. *Crime: Criminals and Criminal Justice*. New York: Henry Holt and Company.

Carceral, K. C. 2005. *Prison, Inc.* New York: New York University Press.

Carmichael, Stokely, and Charles Hamilton. 1967. *Black Power: The Politics of Liberation in America*. New York: Vintage.

Catalyst. 2004. *Women in Business: A Snapshot*. New York: Catalyst.

Census Bureau. 2009. *Income, Poverty, and Health Insurance Coverage in the United States: 2008*, by C. DeNavas-Walt, D. Proctor, and J. C. Smith. Washington, DC: U.S. Government Printing Office.

———. 2008. "Current Population Reports," Table 1. "Income and Earnings Summary. Measures by Selected Characteristics: 2006 and 2007," Table 3. "People and Families in Poverty by Selected Characteristics: 2006 and 2007," Table B-1. "Poverty Status of People by Family Relationship, Race, and Hispanic Origin: 1959 to 2007," in *Income, Poverty, and Health Insurance Coverage in the United States: 2007*, by C. DeNavas-Walt, D. Proctor, and J. C. Smith. Washington, DC: U.S. Government Printing Office.

———. 2005a. *Income, Poverty and Health Insurance Coverage in the United States: 2004*. Washington, DC: U.S. Department of Commerce. Available, http://www.census.gov/hhes/www/income/income.html.

———. 2005b. *Voting and Registration in the Election of November 2004*. Available, http://www.census.gov/population/www/socdemo/voting/cps2004.html.

Center for Public Integrity. 2007. "EPA Document Lists Firms Tied to Superfund Sites." Available, http://projects.publicintegrity.org/superfund/report.aspx?aid=849.

Center for Research on Criminal Justice. 1975. *The Iron Fist and Velvet Glove*. Berkeley, CA: CRCJ.

Center for Responsive Politics. 2009a. "Top All-Time Donors, 1989–2010." Available, http://www.opensecrets.org/orgs/list.php?order=A.

———. 2009b. "Lobbying: Top Spenders." Available, http://www.opensecrets.org/lobby/top.php?indexType=s.

Center for the American Woman and Politics (CAWP). 2005. "Women in Elected Office 2005." Available, http://www.cawp.rutgers.edu/.

Chalk, Frank, and Kurt Jonassohn. 1990. *The History and Sociology of Genocide*. New Haven, CT: Yale University Press.

Chambliss, William. 1988. *Exploring Criminology*. New York: Macmillan.

Chambliss, William, and Milton Mankoff. 1976. *Whose Law? What Order?* New York: John Wiley.

Chambliss, William, and R. B. Seidman. 1982. *Law, Order and Power*, 2nd ed. Reading, MA: Addison Wesley.

ChattahBox.com. 2009. "Pentagon to Create New Cyber-Command: Turf War with NSA Looming." (May 29). Available, http://chattahbox.com/.

Chesney-Lind, Meda. 2006. "Patriarchy, Crime, and Justice: Feminist Criminology in an Era of Backlash." *Feminist Criminology* 1(1):6–26.

———. 1998. "Foreword." In *Crime Control and Women*, edited by Susan L. Miller. Thousand Oaks, CA: Sage.

———. 1996. "Sentencing Women to Prison: Equality without Justice." In *Race, Gender, and Class in Criminology: The Intersections*, edited by Martin D. Schwartz and Dragan Milovanovic. New York: Garland Publishing.

Chesney-Lind, Meda, and Jocelyn M. Pollock. 1995. "Women's Prisons: Equality with a Vengeance." In *Women, Law, and Social Control*, edited by Alida V. Merlo and Joycelyn M. Pollack, pp. 155–75. Needham Heights, MA: Allyn and Bacon.

Christianson, Scott. 1998. *With Liberty for Some*. Boston: Northeastern University Press.

Christie, Nils. 2000. *Crime Control as Industry: Towards Gulags, Western Style?* 3rd ed. London: Routledge.

Churchill, Ward, and Jim Vander Wall. 1990a. *Agents of Repression: The FBI's Secret Wars against the Black Panther Party and the American Indian Movement*. Boston: South End Press.

———. 1990b. *The COINTELPRO Papers: Documents from the FBI's Secret Wars against Dissent in the United States*. Boston: South End Press.

Clear, Todd. 2008. "The Great Penal Experiment: Lesson for Social Justice." In *After the War on Crime: Race, Democracy, and a New Reconstruction*, edited by M. L. Frampton, I. H. López, and J. Simon, pp. 61–72. New York: New York University Press.

———. 2002. "The Problem with 'Addition by Subtraction.'" In *Invisible Punishment: The Collateral Consequences of Mass Imprisonment*, edited by Meda Chesney-Lind and Marc Mauer. New York: New Press.

Clinard, Marshall. 1990. *Corporate Corruption: The Abuse of Power*. New York: Praeger.

Cockburn, Alexander. 2009a. "Twittergasms." *Nation* (July 13):9.

———. 2009b. "Derail the 'Hate Crimes' Bandwagon!" *Nation* (June 15):9.

Cole, David. 1999. *No Equal Justice: Race and Class in the American Criminal Justice System*. New York: New Press.

Coleman, James. 1985. "Law and Power: The Sherman Antitrust Act and Its Enforcement in the Petroleum Industry." *Social Problems* 32.

Collette, Mark. 2008. "BP: Fine Is Sufficiently 'Harsh.'" *Galveston Daily News* (January 23). Available, http://galvestondailynews.com/story.lasso?ewcd=411b93ca9e93157f.

Collins, Patricia Hill. 1998. *Fighting Words: Black Women and the Search for Justice*. Minneapolis: University of Minnesota Press.

———. 1990. *Black Feminist Thought: Knowledge, Consciousness, and the Politics of Empowerment*. New York: Routledge.

Collins, William C., and Andrew W. Collins. 1996. *Women in Jail: Legal Issues*. Washington, DC: National Institute of Corrections.

Conklin, John. 2003. *Why Crime Rates Fell*. Boston: Allyn & Bacon.

Conley, John (ed.). 1994. *The 1967 President's Crime Commission Report: Its Impact 25 Years Later*. Cincinnati: Anderson Publishing.

Connell, R. W. 1995. *Masculinities*. Los Angeles: University of California Press.

———. 1987. *Gender and Power: Society, The Person, and Sexual Politics*. Stanford, CA: Stanford University Press.

Conover, Ted. 2000. "Guarding Sing Sing." *New Yorker* (April 3). Available, http://www.tedconover.com.

Corrections Corporation of America. 2009. Form DEF 14A, filed with the Securities and Exchange Commission April 7.

Costello, Cynthia, and Barbara Kivimae Krimgold (eds.). 1996. *The American Woman, 1996–1997: Where We Stand.* New York: W. W. Norton.

Crawford, James. 1988. *The Rights of Peoples.* Oxford: Oxford University Press.

Crenshaw, Kimberlé. 1991. "Mapping the Margins: Intersectionality, Identity Politics, and Violence against Women of Color." *Stanford Law Review* 43:1258–99.

Cullen, Francis T., and Robert Agnew (eds.). 1999. *Criminological Theory: Past to Present—Essential Readings.* Los Angeles: Roxbury.

Cuomo, Andrew. 2009. "No Rhyme or Reason: The 'Heads I Win, Tails You Lose' Bank Bonus Culture." New York Attorney General's Office. Available, http://www.oag.state.ny.us/media_center/2009/july/pdfs/Bonus%20Report%20Final%207.30.09.pdf.

Currie, Elliott. 2005. "Inequality, Community, and Crime." In *The Essential Criminology Reader,* edited by Stuart Henry and Mark Lanier, pp. 299–306. Boulder, CO: Westview Press.

——. 1998. *Crime and Punishment in America.* New York: Henry Holt.

——. 1985. *Confronting Crime: An American Challenge.* New York: Pantheon.

Dahrendorf, Ralf. 1959. *Class and Class Conflict in Industrial Society.* Stanford, CA: Stanford University Press.

Daly, Kathleen. 2006. "Feminist Thinking about Crime." In *The Essential Criminology Reader,* edited by S. Henry and M. Lanier, pp. 205–13. Boulder, CO: Westview.

——. 1995. "Looking Back, Looking Forward: The Promise of Feminist Transformation." In *The Criminal Justice System and Women,* 2nd ed., edited by Barbara Raffel Price and Natalie J. Sokoloff, pp. 443–57. New York: McGraw-Hill.

——. 1994. *Gender, Crime, and Punishment.* New Haven, CT: Yale University Press.

Daly, Kathleen, and Meda Chesney-Lind. 1988. "Feminism and Criminology." *Justice Quarterly* 5:497–538.

Daly, Kathleen, and Russ Immarigeon. 1998. "The Past, Present, and Future of Restorative Justice: Some Critical Reflections." *Contemporary Justice Review* 1(1):21–45.

Danner, Mona J. E. 1998. "Three Strikes and It's Women Who Are Out: The Hidden Consequences for Women of Criminal Justice Police Reforms." In *Crime Control and Women,* edited by Susan L. Miller, pp. 1–14. Thousand Oaks, CA: Sage Publications.

Davis, Angela. 1998. "What Is the Prison Industrial Complex? Why Does It Matter?" *Colorlines Magazine* 1(2):1–8.

Day, Kathleen. 1993. *S&L Hell: The People and the Politics behind the $1 Trillion Savings and Loan Scandal.* New York: Norton.

DeCarlo, Scott. 2009. "What the Boss Makes." *Forbes* (April 22). Available, http://www.forbes.com/2009/04/22/compensation-chief-executive-salary-leadership-best-boss-09-ceo-intro.html.

DeFrances, Carol. 2002. "Prosecutors in State Courts, 2001." U.S. Department of Justice, Bureau of Justice Statistics *Bulletin* (May). Washington, DC: GPO.

Dekeseredy, W. S., Rogness, M., and M. D. Schwartz. 2005. "Separation/Divorce and Sexual Assault: The Current State of Social Scientific Knowledge." *Aggression and Violent Behavior* (in press).

DeKeseredy, Walter S., and Martin D. Schwartz. 1996. *Contemporary Criminology*. Belmont, CA: Wadsworth.

Delgado, Richard (ed.). 1995a. *Critical Race Theory: The Cutting Edge*. Philadelphia: Temple University Press.

———. 1995b (1993). "Rodrigo's Sixth Chronicle: Intersections, Essences, and the Dilemma of Social Reform." In *Critical Race Theory*, edited by Richard Delgado, pp. 242–52. Philadelphia: Temple University Press.

Delgado, Richard, and Jean Stefancic. 1997. *Critical White Studies: Looking behind the Mirror*. Philadelphia: Temple University Press.

———. 1991. "Derrick Bell's Chronicle of the Space Traders: Would the U.S. Sacrifice People of Color If the Price Were Right?" *University of Colorado Law Review* 62:321.

Demos, Telis, Richard Morgan, and Christopher Tkaczyk. 2004. "America's 40 Richest under 40." *Fortune* (September 20).

Denver Business Journal. 2009. "Obama's Cyber Czar an 'Important 1st Step to Security, says Qwest CEO" (May 29). Available, http://www.bizjournals.com/denver/stories/2009/05/25/daily77.html.

Department of Labor. 2006. *All about OSHA*. Washington, DC: Department of Labor. Available, http://www.osha.gov/Publications/all_about_OSHA.pdf

Department of Justice. 1998. *The Challenge of Crime in a Free Society: Looking Back, Looking Forward*. Washington, DC: U.S. Department of Justice. NCJ 170029.

Derber, Charles. 1998. *Corporation Nation: How Corporations Are Taking over Our Lives and What We Can Do about It*. New York: St. Martin's.

DiMascio, William M. 1998. "Why Inmate Populations Are Up." In *Selected Readings in Criminal Justice*, edited by Philip L. Reichel, pp. 237–45. San Diego, CA: Greenhaven Press.

Dinkes, R., J. Kemp, and K. Baum. 2009. "Indicators of School Crime and Safety: 2008 (NCES 2009–022/NCJ 226343)." Washington, DC: National Center for Education Statistics, Institute of Education Sciences, U.S. Department of Education, Bureau of Justice Statistics, Office of Justice Programs, and U.S. Department of Justice.

Domhoff, G. William. 1998. *Who Rules America?* 3rd ed. Mountain View, CA: Mayfield Publishing.

Douglas, William O. 1954. *An Almanac of Liberty*. Garden City, NY: Doubleday.

Doyle, James. 1992. "'It's the Third World Down There!': The Colonialist Vocation and American Criminal Justice." *Harvard Civil Rights—Civil Liberties Law Review* 27:71.

DuBois, Ellen Carol, and Lynn Dumenil. 2005. *Through Women's Eyes: An American History*. Boston: Bedford/St. Martin's.

Duffee, David. 1980. *Explaining Criminal Justice: Community Theory and Criminal Justice Reform*. Prospects Heights, IL: Waveland Press.

Durkheim, Emile. 1964 (1893). *The Division of Labor in Society*. New York: Free Press.

Dyer, Joel. 2000. *The Perpetual Prisoner Machine: How America Profits from Crime*. Boulder, CO: Westview.

Dyer, Richard. 2005. "The Matter of Whiteness." In *White Privilege*, edited by Paula Rothenberg. New York: Worth.

Dyson, Michael Eric. 2005. *Is Bill Cosby Right? (or Has the Black Middle Class Lost Its Mind)?* New York: Basic Civitas/Perseus.

Edelstein, Charles D., and Robert J. Wicks. 1977. *An Introduction to Criminal Justice.* New York: McGraw-Hill.

Editorial. 2009a. "The Torturers' Manifesto." *New York Times* (April 9), wk. 9.

———. 2009b. "A Shift on Immigration." *New York Times* (May 3), wk. 9.

Edwards, Adam, and Peter Gill (eds.). 2003. *Transnational Organized Crime: Perspectives on Global Security.* New York: Routledge.

Eichstaedt, Peter. 1994. *If You Poison Us: Uranium and Native Americans.* Red Crane Books.

Eisenhower, Dwight. 1961. Farewell Address. Available, http://en.wikisource.org/wiki/Eisenhower%27s_farewell_address.

Elias, Robert. 1986. *The Politics of Victimization: Victims, Victimology and Human Rights.* New York: Oxford University Press.

Emmelman, Debra S. 2004. "Defending the Poor: Commonsense Class-ism in the Adjudication of Criminal Cases." In *For the Common Good: A Critical Examination of Law and Social Control,* edited by Robin Miller and Sandra Lee Browning, pp. 49–67. Durham, NC: Carolina Academic Press.

Engel, Robin Shepard, and Jennifer M. Calnon. 2004. "Examining the Influence of Drivers' Characteristics during Traffic Stops with Police: Results from a National Survey." *Justice Quarterly* 21(1):49–90.

Engen, Rodney. 2009. "Assessing Determinate and Presumptive Sentencing—Making Research Relevant." *Criminology & Public Policy* 8(2) (May):323–36.

Ericson, R., Baranek, P. and Chan, J. 1987. Visualizing deviance: A study of news organization. Toronto: University of Toronto Press.

Essed, P. 1991. *Understanding Everyday Racism: An Interdisciplinary Theory.* Newbury, CA: Sage.

———. 1990. *Everyday Racism: Reports from Women in Two Cultures.* Claremont, CA: Hunter House.

Etzioni, Amitai. 1990. "Going Soft on Corporate Crime." *Washington Post* (April 1).

Ezekiel, Raphael. 1995. *The Racist Mind: Portraits of American Neo-Nazis and Klansmen.* New York: Penguin.

Faith, Karlene. 1993. "Gendered Imaginations: Female Crime and Prison Movies." *Justice Professional* 8(1):53–70.

Fanon, Frantz. 1967. *A Dying Colonialism.* New York: Grove Press.

———. 1963. *The Wretched of the Earth.* New York: Prentice-Hall.

Farrell, Amy, Geoff Ward, and Danielle Rousseau. 2009. "Race Effects of Representation among Federal Court Workers: Does Black Workforce Representation Reduce Sentencing Disparities?" *Annals of the American Academy of Political and Social Science* 623 (May):121–33.

Fausto-Sterling, Anne. 2000. *Sexing the Body: Gender Politics and the Construction of Sexuality.* New York: Basic Books.

Faux, Jeff. 2006. *The Global Class War: How America's Bipartisan Elite Lost Our Future and What It Will Take to Win It Back.* Hoboken, NJ: Wiley.

Feagin, Joe, and Clairece Booher Feagin. 1996. *Racial and Ethnic Relations.* Upper Saddle River, NJ: Prentice-Hall.

Feagin, Joe, and Hernan Vera. 1995. *White Racism: The Basics.* New York: Routledge.

Feeley, Malcolm, and Jonathan Simon. 1994. "Actuarial Justice: The Emerging New Criminal Law." In *The Futures of Criminology*, edited by David Nelken. London: Sage.

———. 1992. "The New Penology: Notes on the Emerging Strategy of Corrections and Its Implications." *Criminology* 30(3):449–74.

Fields, Gary. 2009. "White House Czar Calls for End to 'War on Drugs.'" *Wall Street Journal* online (May 14). Available, http://online.wsj.com/article/SB124225891527617397.html.

Fishman, Laura T. 1998. "The Black Bogeyman and White Self-Righteousness." In *Images of Color, Images of Crime: Readings*, edited by Coramae Richey Mann and Marjorie Zatz, pp. 109–26. Los Angeles: Roxbury Publishing.

Fishman, Mark. 1978. "Crime Waves as Ideology." *Social Problems* 25(5):531–43.

Flavin, Jeanne. 2009. *Our Bodies, Our Crimes: The Policing of Women's Reproduction in America.* New York: New York University Press.

———. 2001. "Feminism for the Mainstream Criminologist: An Invitation." *Journal of Criminal Justice Education* 29(4).

Fletcher, Connie. 1995. *Breaking and Entering.* New York: HarperCollins.

Florian, Ellen. 2002. "Executive Pay: Don't Go Buying That Third House Just Yet." *Fortune* (November 18):30.

Foley, Neil. 2005. "Becoming Hispanic: Mexican Americans and Whiteness." In *White Privilege*, edited by Paula Rothenberg. New York: Worth.

Fontanarosa, Phil, Drummond Rennie, and Catherine DeAngelis. 2004. "Postmarketing Surveillance—Lack of Vigilance, Lack of Trust." *Journal of the American Medical Association* (December 1) 292(21).

Forbes. 2009. "The Celebrity 100." (June 3). Available, http://www.forbes.com/lists/2009/53/celebrity-09_The-Celebrity-100_EarningsPrevYear.html.

———. 2008. "The 400 Richest Americans." (September 17). Available, http://www.forbes.com/lists/2008/54/400list08_The-400-Richest-Americans_FinalWorth.html.

Forell, Caroline, and Donna Matthews. 2000. *A Law of Her Own.* New York: New York University Press.

Fortune. 2005. "The Largest U.S. Corporations." (April 18).

Foster, Holly, and John Hagan. 2009. "The Mass Incarceration of Parents in America: Issues of Race/Ethnicity, Collateral Damage to Children, and Prisoner Reentry." *Annals of the American Academy of Political and Social Science* 623 (May):179–94.

Foucault, Michel. 1980. *The History of Sexuality, Volume I: An Introduction.* New York: Vintage Books.

Fowler, Tom. 2009. "OSHA Punishes BP over Safety." *Houston Chronicle* (October 31). Available, http://www.chron.com/disp/story.mpl/business/energy/6695722.html.

Francis, David. 2005. "The American Dream Gains a Harder Edge." *Christian Science Monitor* (online) (May 23). Available, http://www.csmonitor.com/2005/0523/p17s01-cogn.html.

Frank, Jerome. 1963. *Courts on Trial: Myth and Reality in American Justice.* New York: Atheneum.

Frank, Nancy. 1988. "Unintended Murder and Corporate Risk-Taking: Defining the Concept of Justifiability." *Journal of Criminal Justice* 16:17–24.

Frank, Robert, and Amir Efrati. 2009a. "Madoff Plays Fate Like His Fraud." *Wall Street Journal* (Saturday/Sunday, June 27–28):B1 and B3.

——. 2009b. "'Evil' Madoff Gets 150 Years in Epic Fraud." *Wall Street Journal* (Tuesday, June 30):A1 and A12.

Frankenberg, Ruth. 1993. *White Women, Race Matters: The Social Construction of Whiteness*. Minneapolis: University of Minnesota Press.

Franklin, H. B. 1989. *Prison Literature in America*. New York: Oxford.

Friedrichs, David. 1996. *Trusted Criminals*. Belmont: Wadsworth.

Funnell, Ben. 2009. "Debt Is Capitalism's Dirty Little Secret." *Financial Times* (June 30). Available, http://www.ft.com/cms/s/0/e23c6d04-659d-11de-8e34-00144 feabdc0.html.

Fussell, Paul. 1983. *Class: A Guide through the American Status System*. New York: Summit Books.

Fyfe, James J. 1990. "Blind Justice: Police Shootings in Memphis." In *Violence: Patterns, Causes, and Public Policy*, edited by S. A. Weiner, M. A. Zahn, and R. J. Sagi. New York: Harcourt Brace College.

Gabbidon, Shaun, and Helen Taylor Greene. 2005. *Race & Crime*. Thousand Oaks, CA: Sage.

Gamble, Sarah (ed.). 1999. *The Routledge Critical Dictionary of Feminism and Postfeminism*. New York: Routledge.

Gandy, Oscar. 1993. *The Panoptic Sort: A Political Economy of Personal Information*. Boulder, CO: Westview.

Garland, David. 1999. "The Commonplace and the Catastrophic: Interpretations of Crime in Late Modernity." *Theoretical Criminology* 3(3):353–64.

——. 1990. *Punishment and Society: A Study in Social Theory*. Chicago: University of Chicago Press.

GEO Group. 2009. Form DEF 14A, filed with the Securities and Exchange Commission March 30.

Geronimus, Arline, Margaret Hicken, Danya Keene, and John Bound. 2006a. "Weathering and Age-Patterns of Allostatic Load Scores among Blacks and Whites in the United States." *American Journal of Public Health* 96:826–33.

Geronimus, Arline, Cynthia Colen, Tara Shochet, Lori Barer Ingber, and Sherman James. 2006b. "Urban-Rural Differences in Excess Mortality among High-Poverty Populations: Evidence from the Harlem Household Survey and the Pitt County, North Carolina Study of African American Health." *Journal of Health Care for the Poor and Underserved* 17(3):532–58.

Gerth, Jeff, and Brady Dennis. 2009. "How a Loophole Benefits GE in Bank Rescue." *Washington Post* (June 29). Available, http://www.washingtonpost.com/wp-dyn/ content/article/2009/06/28/AR2009062802955.html.

Gilbert, Dennis. 1998. *The American Class Structure*, 5th ed. Belmont, CA: Wadsworth.

Gilliard, Darrell K., and Allen J. Beck. 1998. *Prisoners in 1997*. Washington, DC: U.S. Department of Justice.

Gladwell, Malcolm. 2005. "The Moral Hazard Myth." *New Yorker* (August 29). Available, http://www.newyorker.com.

Glazer, Myron, and Penina Glazer. 1989. *The Whistle-Blowers.* New York: Basic Books.

Gonzales, Alberto. 2005. "Prepared Remarks of Attorney General Alberto Gonzales: Sentencing Guidelines Speech" (June 21, 2005). Available, http://www.justice.gov/archive/ag/speeches/2005/06212005victimsofcrime.htm.

Goodstein, Lynne. 1992. "Feminist Perspectives and the Criminal Justice Curriculum." *Journal of Criminal Justice Education* 3(2):165–81.

Gordon, Diana. 1990. *The Justice Juggernaut: Fighting Street Crime, Controlling Citizens.* New Brunswick, NJ: Rutgers University Press.

Gorman, Tessa. 1997. "Back on the Chain Gang: Why the 8th Amendment and the History of Slavery Proscribe the Resurgence of Chain Gangs." *California Law Review* 85(2):441–78.

Grabosky, P., J. Braithwaite, and P. Wilson. 1987. "The Myth of Community Tolerance toward White-collar Crime." *Australia & New Zealand Journal of Criminology,* 20:33–44.

Greene, Judith. 2002. "Entrepreneurial Corrections: Incarceration as a Business Opportunity." In *Invisible Punishment,* edited by Meda Chesney-Lind and Marc Mauer. New York: New Press.

Greenfeld, Lawrence A. 1997. *Sex Offenses and Offenders.* Washington, DC: U.S. Department of Justice.

Greenwood, Peter. 1995. "Juvenile Crime and Juvenile Justice." In Crime, edited by James Q. Wilson and Joan Petersilia, pp. 91–117. San Francisco: Institute for Contemporary Studies.

Greider, William. 2009. "Obama's False Reform." *Nation* (July 13):8–9.

———. 2005. "Sins & the Citi." *Nation* (July 4):4–6.

———. 1996. *Who Will Tell the People? The Betrayal of American Democracy.* New York: Simon and Schuster.

———. 1994. "Why the Mighty GE Can't Strike Out." *Rolling Stone* (April 21):36.

Guardian.co.uk. 2008. "Countrywide Financial Faces Unethical Business Practices Prosecution." Bay Ledger News Zone (January 28). Available, http://www.blnz.com/news/2008/06/25/Countrywide_Financial_faces_unethical_business_9812.html.

Hacker, Andrew. 1995. *Two Nations: Black and White, Separate, Hostile, Unequal.* New York: Ballantine.

Hagan, John. 1994. *Crime and Disrepute.* Thousand Oaks, CA: Pine Forge Press.

Hale, Donna C. 1998. "Keeping Women in Their Place: An Analysis of Policewomen in Videos, 1972 to 1996." In *Popular Culture, Crime and Justice,* edited by Frankie Bailey and Donna Hale, pp. 159–79. Belmont, CA: West/Wadsworth.

Haley, John. 1989. "Confession, Repentance and Absolution." In *Mediation and Criminal Justice,* edited by Martin Wright and Burt Galaway. Newbury Park, CA: Sage.

Hammond, R. W. 1999. "School-associated Violent Deaths: United States, 1994–1998." Paper presented at the annual meeting of the American Society of Criminology, Toronto, Canada, November.

Hanser, Richard. 2009. "Conflicts and Geographical Flashpoints around the World: The Effective Application of Restorative Justice and Peacemaking Perspectives." *Contemporary Justice Review* 12(2):191–206.

Haraway, Donna. 1991. "Situated Knowledges: The Science Question in Feminism and the Privilege of Partial Perspective." In *Simians, Cyborgs, and Women: The Reinvention of Nature*. New York: Routledge, chapter 9, 183–201.

Hare, R. M. 1990. "Public Policy in a Pluralist Society." In *Embryo Experimentation*, edited by Peter Singer, Helga Kuhse, et al. Cambridge: Cambridge University Press.

Harlow, Carolina Wolf. 1998. *Profile of Jail Inmates 1996*. Washington, DC: U.S. Department of Justice.

Harring, Sidney L. 1983. *Policing a Class Society: The Experience of American Cities, 1865–1915*. New Brunswick, NJ: Rutgers University Press.

Harrington, Michael. 1989. *Socialism: Past and Future*. Berkeley, CA: Arcade Publishing.

Harris, Angela P. 1997. "Race and Essentialism in Feminist Legal Theory." In *Critical Race Feminism: A Reader*, edited by Adrien K. Wing, pp. 11–18. New York: New York University Press.

———. 1990. "Race and Essentialism in Feminist Legal Theory." In *Critical Race Theory: The Cutting Edge*, edited by Richard Delgado, pp. 253–66. Philadelphia: Temple University Press.

Harris, David. 1999. "The Stories, the Statistics, and the Law: Why 'Driving While Black' Matters." *84 Minnesota Law Review*, 265–326. Available, http://academic.udayton.edu/race/03justice/dwb01.htm.

Harris, Kamala. 2008. "Smart on Crime." In *After the War on Crime: Race, Democracy, and a New Reconstruction*, edited by M. L. Frampton, I. H. López, and J. Simon, pp. 145–52. New York: New York University Press.

Hart, Lynda. 1994. *Fatal Women: Lesbian Sexuality and the Mark of Aggression*. Princeton, NJ: Princeton University Press.

Hartmann, Thom. 2002. *Unequal Protection: The Rise of Corporate Dominance and the Theft of Human Rights*. New York: Rodale.

Harvard Law Review. 1988. "Developments in the Law: Race and the Criminal Process." *Harvard Law Review* 101:1472.

Hatty, Suzanne. 2000. *Masculinities, Violence, and Culture*. Thousand Oaks, CA: Sage.

Hawkins, Darnell. 1995. *Ethnicity, Race and Crime*. Albany: State University of New York Press.

Hawkins, Richard, and Geoffrey Alpert. 1989. *American Prison Systems: Punishment and Justice*. Englewood Cliffs, NJ: Prentice-Hall.

Hayes, Christopher. 2009. "Bucking the Banks." *Nation* (July 13):7.

Headlee, Sue, and Margery Elfin. 1996. *The Cost of Being Female*. Westport, CN: Praeger.

Hearings. 1990. Hearings before the Subcommittee on Financial Institutions Supervision, Regulation and Insurance of the Committee on Banking, Finance, and Urban Affairs, U.S. House of Representatives, 101st Congress, 2nd Session. "When Are the Savings and Loan Crooks Going to Jail?" Washington, DC: U.S. Government Printing Office.

Heidensohn, Frances. 1995 (1985). *Women and Crime*, 2nd ed. New York: New York University Press.

Henry, Stuart, and William Hinkle. 2001. *Careers in Criminal Justice*, 2nd ed. Salem, WI: Sheffield.

Henry, Stuart, and Dragan Milovanovic. 1999. *Constitutive Criminology at Work*. Albany: State University of New York Press.

──. 1996. *Constitutive Criminology: Beyond Postmodernism.* London: Sage.

Hightower, Jim. 1998a. *There's Nothing in the Middle of the Road but Yellow Stripes and Dead Armadillos.* New York: HarperPerennial.

──. 1998b. "All the Free Speech Money Can Buy." *Detroit Metrotimes* (August 19–25).

Hill Collins, Patricia. 2004. *Black Sexual Politics: African Americans, Gender and the New Racism.* New York: Routledge.

──. 1990. *Black Feminist Thought.* Boston: Unwin Hyman.

Hills, Stuart (ed.). 1987. *Corporate Violence: Injury and Death for Profit.* Savage, MD: Rowman & Littlefield.

Hinkle, William G., and Stuart Henry (eds.). 2000. *School Violence.* Annals of the American Academy of Political and Social Science. Thousand Oaks, CA: Sage.

Hinojosa, Ricardo. 2008. Statement of Ricardo Hinojosa, Chair, United States Sentencing Commission, before the Senate Judiciary Committee, February 12, 2008. Available, http://www.ussc.gov/testimony/Hinososa_Testimony_021208.pdf.

Hitt, Jack. 2005. "The Newest Indians" *New York Times* online Sunday magazine (August 21). Available, http://www.nytimes.com/2005/08/21/magazine/21NATIVE.html.

Holmes, Malcolm D. "Minority Threat and Police Brutality: Determinants of Civil Rights Criminal Complaints in the U.S. Municipalities." *Criminology* 38(2):343–68.

Horton, Kerry F. 1996. "Images of Penality: Prison Films and the Construction of Discourse Regarding Punishment and Obligation." MA thesis. Ypsilanti: Eastern Michigan University.

Horton, Paul B., and Chester L. Hunt. 1976. *Sociology*, 4th ed. New York: McGraw-Hill.

Huisman, Kimberly, Jeri Martinez, and Cathleen Wilson. 2005. "Training Police Officers on Domestic Violence and Racism." *Violence against Women* 11(6).

Huling, Tracy. 2002. "Building a Prison Economy in Rural America." In *Invisible Punishment: The Collateral Consequences of Mass Imprisonment,* edited by Meda Chesney-Lind and Marc Mauer. New York: New Press.

Hull, Gloria T., Patricia Bell Scott, and Barbara Smith (eds.). 1982. *All the Women Are White; All the Blacks Are Men, But Some of Us Are Brave: Black Women's Studies.* New York: Feminist Press.

Human Rights Watch. 2001. "No Escape: Male Rape in U.S. Prisons." Available, http://www.hrw.org/reports/2001/prison/.

──. 1999. *Human Rights Watch World Report 1999: United States.* New York: Human Rights Watch.

──. 1996. *All Too Familiar Sexual Abuse of Women in U.S. State Prisons.* New York: Women's Rights Project.

Humm, Maggie. 1990. *The Dictionary of Feminist Theory.* Columbus: Ohio State University Press.

Humphries, Drew. 1999. *Crack Mothers: Pregnancy, Drugs, and the Media.* Columbus: Ohio University Press.

Hurtado, Aida. 1989. "Relating to Privilege: Seduction and Rejection in the Subordination of White Women and Women of Color." *Signs* 14(4):833–55.

International Centre for Prison Studies. 2009. World Prison Brief. King's College, London. Retrieved July 6, 2009, from http://www.kcl.ac.uk/depsta/law/research/icps/worldbrief/.

Irwin, John. 2005. *The Warehouse Prison*. Los Angeles: Roxbury.

Irwin, John, and James Austin. 1997. *It's About Time: America's Imprisonment Binge*. Belmont, CA: Wadsworth.

Irwin, Neil. 2006. "Our Financial Failings: Family Savings Look Scary across the Board." *Washington Post* (March 5):F01.

Ishay, Micheline. 2004. *The History of Human Rights: From Ancient Times to the Globalization Era*. Berkeley, CA: University of California Press.

Isikoff, Michael. 1990. "Justice Dept. Shifts on Corporate Sentencing." *Washington Post* (April 28).

Jacob, Herbert. 1980 (1973). *Urban Justice: Law and Order in American Cities*. Englewood Cliffs, NJ: Prentice-Hall.

Jenkins, Philip. 1994. *Using Murder: The Social Construction of Serial Homicide*. New York: Aldine de Gruyter.

Johnson, Carrie. 2006. "Skilling Gets 24 Years for Fraud at Enron." *Washington Post* (October 24):A1.

Johnson, Gene. 2005. "Utilities Win Forum against Enron." *Washington Post* (March 13):A14.

Johnson, James H. Jr., Walter C. Farrell Jr., and Jennifer A. Stoloff. 1998. "The Declining Social and Economic Fortunes of African American Males: a Critical Assessment of Four Perspectives." *Review of Black Political Economy* 25(4):17–40.

Johnson, Robert. 2002. *Hard Time*. Belmont: Wadsworth.

———. 2001. "Village Life." *American Weekly* (November). Available, http://stopviolence.com/9-11/arts/villagelife.htm.

———. 2000. "American Prisons and the African-American Experience: A History of Social Control and Racial Oppression." *Corrections Compendium* 25(9):6–30.

———. 1998. *Death Work: A Study of the Modern Execution Process*, 2nd ed. Belmont, CA: Wadsworth.

Johnson, Robert, and Paul Leighton. 1999. "American Genocide: The Destruction of the Black Underclass." In *Collective Violence: Harmful Behavior in Groups and Governments*, edited by Craig Summers and Eric Markusen. Lanham: Rowman & Littlefield. Available, http://paulsjusticepage.com.

Johnston, David. 2005. "Richest Are Leaving Even the Rich Far Behind" *New York Times*, June 5. http://www.nytimes.com/class

Jordan, Carol. 2004. "Intimate Partner Violence and the Justice System." *Journal of Interpersonal Violence* 19:312.

Jordan, Emma. 2009. "A Fair Deal for Taxpayer Investments." Harvard Law School Forum on Corporate Governance and Financial Regulation. Available, http://blogs.law.harvard.edu/corpgov/2009/09/24/a-fair-deal-for-taxpayer-investments/.

Kandal, Terry. 1988. *The Woman Question in Classical Sociological Theory*. Miami: Florida International University Press.

Kangas, Steve. 1996. "Myths about Affirmative Action." *Liberalism Resurgent*. Available, http://www.aliveness.com/kangaroo/LiberalFAQ.htm.

Kasinsky, Renee. 1994. "Patrolling the Facts: Cops, Media, and Crime." Gregg Barak (ed.), *Media, Process, and the Social Construction of Crime.* New York: Routledge.

Kaufman, J. S., Arline Geronimus, and Sherman James. 2007. "Faulty Interpretation of Observed Racial Disparity in Recurrent Preterm Birth." *American Journal of Obstetrics and Gynecology* 197(3):327–37.

Katz, Alyssa. 2009. *Our Lot: How Real Estate Came to Own Us.* New York: Bloomsbury (USA).

Katz, Jackson. 1999. *Tough Guise* (video). Media Education Foundation.

Kennedy, Marc C. 1970. "Beyond Incrimination: Some Neglected Facets of the Theory of Punishment." *Catalyst* 5 (Summer):1–30.

Kennedy, Randall. 1997. *Race, Crime, and the Law.* New York: Random House.

Kennickell, Arthur. 2006. "Currents and Undercurrents: Changes in the Distribution of Wealth, 1989–2004." Federal Reserve Board. Available, http://ideas.repec.org/p/fip/fedgfe/2006-13.html.

———. 2003. "A Rolling Tide: Changes in the Distribution of Wealth in the U.S., 1989–2001." Federal Reserve Board. Available, http://www.federalreserve.gov/pubs/oss/oss2/scfindex.html.

Kilbourne, Jean. 2000. *Can't Buy My Love: How Advertising Changes the Way We Think and Feel.* New York: Free Press.

Killingbeck, Donna. 2005. "A Sociological History of Prison Privatization in the Contemporary United States." Doctoral Dissertation. Kalamazoo: Western Michigan University.

Kim, Jane. 2009. "Hunt Goes on for Missing Madoff Money." *Wall Street Journal* (June 29):CI.

King, Jeanne. 1998. "Two NYPD Officers Charge Discrimination against Gays." Reuters wire service. (October 28).

Klein, Dorie. 1998. "An Agenda for Reading and Writing about Women, Crime, and Justice." *Social Pathology* 3(2) (Summer):81–91.

———. 1995 (1973). "The Etiology of Female Crime: A Review of the Literature." In *The Criminal Justice System and Women*, 2nd ed., edited by Barbara Raffel Price and Natalie J. Sokoloff, pp. 30–53. New York: McGraw-Hill.

Klein, Naomi. 2007. *The Shock Doctrine: The Rise of Disaster Capitalism.* New York: Picador.

Kochhar, Rakesh. 2004. "The Wealth of Hispanic Households: 1996 to 2002." Washington, DC: Pew Hispanic Center. Available, http://pewhispanic.org.

Kooistra, Paul. 1989. *Criminals as Heroes: Structure, Power and Identity.* Bowling Green, OH: Bowling Green State University Popular Press.

Kooistra, Paul G., John S. Mahoney, and Saundra D. Westervelt. 1998. "The World According to COPS." In *Entertaining Crime*, edited by M. Fishman and G. Cavender, pp. 141–58. New York: Aldine de Gruyter.

Korton, David. 1995. *When Corporations Rule the World.* Kumarian Press & Berrett-Koehler Publishers.

Kozol, Jonathan. 1991. *Savage Inequalities: Children in America's Schools.* New York: HarperCollins.

Kraska, Peter. 2007. "The Blurring of War and Law Enforcement." In *Violence, Conflict, and World Order: Critical Conversations on State-Sanctioned Justice*, by G. Barak, pp. 161–87. Lanham, MD: Rowman and Littlefield.

———. 2004. *Theorizing Criminal Justice: Eight Essential Orientations.* Long Grove, IL: Waveland Press.

———. 1999. "Militarizing Criminal Justice: Exploring Possibilities." *Journal of Political and Military Sociology* 27(2):205–16.

Krisberg, Barry. 1975. *Crime and Privilege: Towards a New Criminology.* Englewood Cliffs, NY: Prentice-Hall.

Krivo, Lauren, and Ruth Peterson. 2009. Introduction to the special issue, "Race, Crime, and Justice: Contexts and Complexities." *Annals of the American Academy of Political and Social Science* 623(May):7–10.

Kuper, Leo. 1985. *The Prevention of Genocide.* New Haven, CT: Yale University Press.

Kurtz, Karl, and Brian Weberg. 2009. "NCSL's Survey Finds That after Growth in the '70s and '80s the Number of Legislative Staff Has Leveled Off." National Conference of State Legislatures. Available, http://www.ncsl.org/default .aspx?tabid=17904.

Labaton, Stephen. 2002. "Now Who, Exactly Got Us Into This?: Enron? Arthur Andersen? Shocking Say Those Who Helped It Along." *New York Times* (February 3):C01.

Lamy, Philip. 1996. *Millennium Rage.* New York: Plenum Press.

Lanier, Mark M., and Stuart Henry. 2004. *Essential Criminology.* Boulder, CO: Westview Press.

Lasswell, Thomas E. 1965. *Class and Stratum.* Boston: Houghton Mifflin.

Lattman, Peter, and Annelena Lobb. 2009. "'Victims' Speeches in Court Influenced Judge's Ruling." *Wall Street Journal* (June 30):A12.

Lauritsen, Janet. 2004. "Searching for a Better Understanding of Race and Ethnic Differences in Violent Crime." *Criminal Justice Ethics* (Winter/Spring):68–73.

Layton, Lyndsey. 2009. "Peanut Processor Knowingly Sold Tainted Products." *Washington Post* (January 28). Available, http://www.washingtonpost.com/wp-dyn/ content/article/2009/01/27/AR2009012702992.html.

Lazarus, Edward. 1991. *Black Hills, White Justice: The Sioux Nation versus the United States, 1775 to the Present.* New York: HarperCollins.

Le, Cuong Nguyen. 2005. "Socioeconomic Statistics and Demographics." Available, http://www.asian-nation.org/demographics.shtml.

Leaf, Clifton. 2005. "Enough Is Enough: White-collar Criminals: They Lie They Cheat They Steal and They've Been Getting Away with It for Too Long." In *Annual Editions: Criminal Justice,* 29th ed., edited by Joseph L. Victor and Joanne Naughton, pp. 35–42. Dubuque, IA: McGraw-Hill/Dushkin. (Reprinted from the March 18, 2002, *Fortune,* pp. 62–65).

Lee, Charles. 1992. "Toxic Waste and Race in the United States." In *Race and the Incidence of Environmental Hazards: A Time for Discourse,* edited by Bunyan Bryant and Paul Mohai. Boulder, CO: Westview Press.

Lee, Jennifer. 2000. "The Salience of Race in Everyday Life: Black Customers' Shopping Experiences in Black and White Neighborhoods." *Work and Occupations* 27:353–76.

Leighton, Paul. 2010. A Professor of White Collar Crime Reviews USA's "White Collar" series. Available, http://www.paulsjusticeblog.com/2010/02/a_professor _of_white_collar_cr.php.

———. 2007. "Judge Removed from Indian Trust Case for Saying Interior Dept. Is Racist." *Critical Criminologist* 17(2). Available, http://paulsjusticepage.com.

———. 2006. "Demystifying Terrorism: Crazy Islamic Terrorists Who Hate Us Because We're Free?" In *Demystifying Crime and Criminal Justice*, edited by Robert M. Bohm and Jeffery T. Walker. Los Angeles: Roxbury.

———. 2005. "The Challenge of Terrorism to Free Societies in the Global Village." In *Terrorism and Counter-Terrorism: Criminological Perspectives*, edited by Mathieu Deflem. Elsevier Science.

———. 2002. "Should Sept. 11 Victims Be Counted in the Crime Reports?" *Newsday* (August 29). Expanded version available, http://stopviolence.com.

———. 1999. *Mopping the Floor While the Tub Overflows*. Monograph written for the Citizen's Alliance on Prisons and Public Safety. Available, http://www.paulsjusticepage.com.

Leighton, Paul, and Donna Killingbeck. 2001. "Professional Codes of Ethics." In *Criminal Justice Ethics*, edited by Paul Leighton and Jeffrey Reiman. Upper Saddle River, NJ: Prentice-Hall.

Leighton, Paul, and Jeffrey Reiman. 2004. "A Tale of Two Criminals: We're Tougher on Corporate Criminals, but They Still Don't Get What They Deserve." Boston, MA: Allyn & Bacon. Available, http://paulsjusticepage.com.

———. 2002. "Getting Tough on Corporate Crime? Enron & a Year of Corporate Financial Scandals." Boston, MA: Allyn & Bacon. Available, http://paulsjusticepage.com.

———. 2001. *Criminal Justice Ethics*. Upper Saddle River, NJ: Prentice-Hall.

Leinen, Stephen. 1993. *Gay Cops*. New Brunswick, NJ: Rutgers University Press.

Leonard, Eileen B. 1995. "Theoretical Criminology and Gender." In *The Criminal Justice System and Women*, 2nd ed., edited by Barbara Raffel Price and Natalie J. Sokoloff, pp. 54–70. New York: McGraw-Hill.

———. 1982. *Women, Crime, and Society: A Critique of Criminology Theory*. New York: Longman.

Levine, James. 1997. "The Impact of Racial Demography on Jury Verdicts in Routine Adjudication." *Criminal Law Bulletin* 33:523.

Levy, Barrie (ed.). 1998. *Dating Violence: Young Women in Danger*. Seattle, WA: Seal Press.

Lichtblau, Eric. 2008. "Senate Approves Bill to Broaden Wiretap Powers." *New York Times* (July 10). Email delivery from nytimes.com.

———. 2005. "Profiling Report Leads to a Demotion." *New York Times* (August 24). Available, http://www.nytimes.com/2005/08/24/politics/24profiling.html.

Lichtblau, Eric, David Johnston, and Ron Nixon. 2008. "FBI Struggles to Handle Financial Fraud Cases," *New York Times* (October 18). Available, http://www.nytimes.com/2008/10/19/washington/19fbi.html.

Lichter, Robert, and Daniel R. Amundson. 1997. "Distorted Reality: Hispanic Characters in TV Entertainment." In *Latin Looks*, edited by Clara E. Rodriguez, pp. 57–72. Boulder, CO: Westview.

Lipsitz, George. 2005. "The Possesive Investment in Whiteness." In *White Privilege*, 2nd edition, edited by Paula Rothberg. New York: Worth.

Little Rock. 1989. "The American Indian in the White Man's Prisons: A Story of Genocide." *Journal of Prisoners on Prisons* 1(1):41–56.

Loftus, Elizabeth, and K. Ketcham. 1991. *Witness for the Defense*. New York: St. Martin's.

Logan, Keith. 2007. "Foreign Intelligence Surveillance Act." In *Battlefield: Criminal Justice*, a two-volume encyclopedia edited by G. Barak, pp. 287–98. Westport, CT: Greenwood Press.

Lopez, Gerald. 2008. "Rebelling against the War on Low-Income, of Color, and Immigrant Communities." In *After the War on Crime: Race, Democracy, and a New Reconstruction*, edited by M. L. Frampton, I. H. López, and J. Simon, pp. 151–65. New York: New York University Press.

Lopez, Mark, and Paul Taylor. 2009. "Dissecting the 2008 Electorate: Most Diverse in U.S. History." *PewResearchCenterPublications* (April 30). Retrieved June 10, 2009, from http://pewresearch.org/pubs/1209/racial-ethnic-voters-presidential election#end1.

Lusane, Clarence. 1991. *Pipe Dream Blues: Racism and the War on Drugs*. Boston, MA: South End Press.

Lynch, James, and William Sabol. 2000. "Prison Use and Social Control. Policies, Processes, and Decisions of the Criminal Justice System: Criminal Justice 2000." NCJ 182410. Washington, DC: U.S. Department of Justice.

Lynch, Michael J. 1996. "Class, Race, Gender and Criminology: Structured Choices and the Life Course." In *Race, Gender, and Class in Criminology: The Intersection*, edited by Martin D. Schwartz and Dragan Milovanovic, pp. 3–28. New York: Garland.

Lynch, Michael J., and Nancy K. Frank. 1992. *Corporate Crime, Corporate Violence*. Albany: Harrow and Heston.

Lynch, Michael, and W. Byron Groves. 1989. *A Primer in Radical Criminology*, 2nd ed. Albany: Harrow and Heston.

Lynch, Michael, and E. Britt Patterson (eds.). 1991. *Race and Criminal Justice*. Albany: Harrow and Heston.

Lynch, Michael, and Paul Stretesky. 1998. "Uniting Class, Race and Criticism through the Study of Environmental Justice." *Critical Criminologist* 9(1):1.

Lynch, Michael, E. Britt Patterson, and Kristina K. Childs. 2008. "Racial Divide: The Context of Racial and Ethnic Bias in Criminal Justice Processes." In *Racial Divide: Racial and Ethnic Bias in the Criminal Justice System*, edited by M. Lynch, E. Patterson, and K. Childs, pp. 1–14. Monsey, NY: Criminal Justice Press.

MacKinnon, Catharine A. 1991 (1984). "Difference and Dominance: On Sex Discrimination." In *Feminist Legal Theory*, edited by Katharine T. Bartlett and Rosanne Kennedy, pp. 81–94. Boulder, CO: Westview Press.

Madriz, Esther. 1997. *Nothing Bad Happens to Good Girls: Fear of Crime in Women's Lives*. Berkeley: University of California Press.

Mandle, J. R. 1992. *Not Slave, Not Free: The African American Economic Experience since the Civil War*. Durham, NC: Duke University Press.

———. 1978. *The Roots of Black Poverty: The Southern Plantation Economy after the Civil War*. Durham, NC: Duke University Press.

Mann, Coramae Richey, and Marjorie S. Zatz (eds.). 1998. *Images of Color, Images of Crime: Readings*. Los Angeles: Roxbury Publishing.

Marable, Manning. 1983. *How Capitalism Underdeveloped Black America: Problems in Race, Political Economy, and Society*. Boston: South End Press.

Marshall, Eliot. 1998. "DNA Studies Challenge the Meaning of Race." *Science* 282:654.

Martin, Susan E. 1992. "The Interactive Effects of Race and Sex on Women Police Officers." *Justice Professional* 6(1):155–72.

———. 1990. *On the Move: The Status of Women in Policing*. Washington, DC: Police Foundation.

Martin, Susan E., and Nancy C. Jurik. 1996. *Doing Justice, Doing Gender*. Thousand Oaks, CA: Sage Publications.

Massey, Douglas, and Nancy Denton. 1993. *American Apartheid: Segregation and the Making of the Underclass*. Cambridge, MA: Harvard University Press.

Mauer, Marc. 1997. *Intended and Unintended Consequences: State Racial Disparities in Imprisonment*. Washington, DC: Sentencing Project.

Mauer, Marc, and Meda Chesney-Lind (eds.). 2002. *Invisible Punishment: The Collateral Consequences of Mass Imprisonment*. New York: New Press

Mazzetti, Mark, and Scott Shane. 2009. "Interrogation Memos Detail Harsh Tactics by the C.I.A." *NYTimes.com* (April 16):1–4.

McDonald, J. 2001. "Some Question Police Tactics at Biotech Protest." *San Diego Union-Tribune* (August 18):A1. Retrieved October 2002, from http://www.signon sandiego.com.

McGee, Susan. 1995 [2005]. "Why Battered Women Stay." Available, http://stop violence.com/domviol/whytheystay.htm.

McGrath, Charles. 2005. "In Fiction, a Long History of Fixation on the Social Gap." *New York Times* (June 8). Available, http://www.nytimes.com/class.

McIntosh, Peggy. 1997 (1988). "White Privilege and Male Privilege: A Personal Account of Coming to See Correspondences through Work in Women's Studies." In *Critical White Studies*, edited by Richard Delgado and Jean Stefancic, pp. 291–99. Philadelphia: Temple University Press.

———. 1984. "Interactive Phases of Curricular Revision." In *Toward a Balanced Curriculum*, edited by Bonnie Spanier, Alexander Bloom, and Darlene Boroviak, pp. 25–34. Cambridge, MA: Schenkman.

Meeks, Gregory W. 1999. "Q: Does the Supreme Court Need Affirmative Action for Its Own Staff?" *Insight on the News* 15(3):24–27.

Messerschmidt, James W. 2004. *Flesh and Blood: Adolescent Gender Diversity and Violence*. Lanham, MD: Rowman and Littlefield.

———. 1997. *Crime as Structured Action: Gender, Race, Class, and Crime in the Making*. Thousand Oaks, CA: Sage.

———. 1995. "From Patriarchy to Gender: Feminist Theory, Criminology, and the Challenge of Diversity." In *International Feminist Perspectives in Criminology*, edited by N. H. Rafter and F. Heidensohn, pp. 167–88. Philadelphia: Open University Press.

———. 1993. *Masculinities and Crime: Critique and Reconceptualization of Theory*. Lanham, MD: Rowman and Littlefield.

Messner, Steven F., and Richard Rosenfeld. 1994. *Crime and the American Dream*. Belmont, CA: Wadsworth.

Meyer, Josh. 2009. "FBI Planning a Bigger Role in Terrorism Fight." *Los Angeles Times* (May 28). Available, http://www.latimes.com/news/nationworld/washingtondc/ la-na-fbi28-2009may28,0,329005,print.story.

Meyers, Jim. 2009. "DHS Chief Napolitano: Illegal Immigration Is Not a Crime." (April 22). Available, http://newsmax.com/InsideCover/napolitano-illegals -crime/2009/04/22/id/329647.

Michalowski, Raymond. 1985. *Order, Law and Crime.* New York: Random House.

Michalowski, Raymond, and Susan Carlson. 1999. "Unemployment, Imprisonment, and Social Structures of Accumulation: Historical Contingency in the Rusche-Kirchheimer Hypothesis." *Criminology* 37(2).

Michalowski, Raymond, and Ronald Kramer (eds.). 2006. *State-Corporate Crime: Wrongdoing at the Intersection of Business and Government.* New Brunswick, NY: Rutgers University Press.

Miller, Jerome G. 1996. *Search and Destroy: African-American Males in the Criminal Justice System.* Cambridge: Cambridge University Press.

Miller, Jody. 2008. *Getting Played: African American Girls, Urban Inequality, and Gendered Violence.* New York: New York University Press.

———. 2002. "The Strengths and Limits of 'Doing Gender' for Understanding Street Crime." *Theoretical Criminology* 6(4):433–60.

———. 2001. *One of the Guys: Girls, Gangs, and Gender.* New York: Oxford University Press.

———. 1998. "Up It Up: Gender and the Accomplishment of Street Robbery." *Criminology* 36:(1):37–65.

Miller, Robin, and Sandra Lee Browning. 2004. "A Critical Examination of Law and Social Control: Introductory Remarks." In *For the Common Good: A Critical Examination of Law and Social Control,* edited by Miller and Browning, pp. 3–8. Durham, NC: Carolina Academic Press.

Miller, Susan L. 1999. *Gender and Community Policing: Walking the Talk.* Boston: Northeastern University Press.

———. 1998. "Introduction." In *Crime Control and Women,* edited by Susan L. Miller, pp. xv–xxiv. Thousand Oaks, CA: Sage.

Miller, Susan, and Michelle Meloy. 2006. "Women's Use of Force." *Violence against Women* 12(1).

Millett, Kate. 1970. *Sexual Politics.* New York: Doubleday.

Mills, C. Wright. 1956. *The Power Elite.* New York: Oxford University Press.

Morrison, Toni (ed.). 1992. *Race-ing Justice, En-gendering Power: Essays on Anita Hill, Clarence Thomas, and the Construction of Social Reality.* New York: Pantheon Books.

Moulds, Elizabeth F. 1980. "Chivalry and Paternalism: Disparities of Treatment in the Criminal Justice System," In *Women, Crime, and Justice,* edited by Susan Datesman and Frank Scarpitti, pp. 277–99. New York: Oxford University Press.

Mullings, Leith. 1994. "Images, Ideology, and Women of Color." In *Women of Color in U.S. Society,* edited by Maxine Baca Zinn and Bonnie Thornton Dill, pp. 265–89. Philadelphia: Temple University Press.

Murphy, Sheigla B., and Marsha Rosenbaum. 1997. "Two Women Who Used Cocaine Too Much: Class, Race, Gender, Crack, and Coke." In *Crack in America: Demon Drugs and Social Justice,* edited by Craig Reinarman and Harry G. Levine, pp. 98–112. Berkeley: University of California Press.

Myrdal, Gunnar. 1944. *An American Dilemma: The Negro Problem and Modern Democracy.* New York: Pantheon.

Nagel, Ilene H., and Barry L. Johnson. 1994. "The Role of Gender in a Structured Sentencing System." *Journal of Criminal Law and Criminology* 85(1):181–221.

Nation. 2009. "Noted." (July 13):5.

National Association of Criminal Defense Attorneys. 2004. "Getting What They Pay For: The Fallacy of Quality Indigent Defense." *Indigent Defense* (May/June). Available, http://www.nacdl.org/public.nsf/DefenseUpdates/Louisiana029.

National Center for Health Statistics. 2004. "Americans Slightly Taller, Much Heavier Than Four Decades Ago." Available, http://www.cdc.gov/nchs/pressroom/04news/americans.htm.

National Center for Woman in Policing. 2002. *Equality Denied: The Status of Women in Policing, 2001.* Washington, DC: National Center for Women in Policing.

National Council on Crime and Delinquency. 1995. "National Assessment of Structured Sentencing Final Report." (January).

National Institute of Justice. 2005. *2004 Annual Report.* Washington, DC: U.S. Government Printing Office, pp. 1–24.

National Narcotics Intelligence Consumers Committee. 1995. *The NNICC Report 1994: The Supply of Illegal Drugs to the United States.* Washington, DC: DEA. DEA-95051.

Nelson, J. (ed.). 2000. *Police Brutality: An Anthology.* New York: W. W. Norton.

Newman, Katherine S., Cybelle Fox, David J. Harding, Jal Mehta, and Wendy Roth. 2004. *Rampage: The Social Roots of School Shootings.* New York: Basic Books.

New Webster's Dictionary of the English Language. 1984. New York: Delair Publishing Company.

New York State Office of the Attorney General. 1999. "Results of Investigation into NYPD 'Stop and Frisk' Practice." New York: Office of the Attorney General.

New York Times. 2009. "The Torturers' Manifesto." *New York Times,* April 18. Available, http://www.nytimes.com/2009/04/19/opinion/19sun1.html?_r=1.

Norris, Floyd. 2008a. "Misleading Numbers at the SEC." *New York Times* (September 11). Available, http://norris.blogs.nytimes.com/2008/09/11/misleading-numbers-at-the-sec/.

———. 2008b. "Can Mary Schapiro Save the SEC?" *New York Times* (December 17). Available, http://norris.blogs.nytimes.com/2008/12/17/can-she-save-the-sec/.

Obama, Barack. 2009. "Remarks at NAACP Centennial." Available, http://www.politico.com/news/stories/0709/25053.html.

———. 2007. "Remarks at Howard University Convocation," September 28, 2007. Available, http://www.barackobama.com/2007/09/28/remarks_of_senator_barack_obam_26.php.

O'Connell, John P. 1995. "Throwing Away the Key (and State Money)." *Spectrum* (Winter).

Office of Juvenile Justice and Delinquency Prevention. 2006. *Disproportionate Minority Contact Technical Assistance Manual,* 3rd edition. Washington, DC: U.S. Department of Justice. Available, www.ojp.usdoj.gov/ojjdp.

———. 1998. *Disproportionate Minority Confinement.* Washington, DC: U.S. Department of Justice. NCJ 173420.

Ogawa, Brian, and Aurelia Sands Belle. 1999. "Respecting Diversity: Responding to Underserved Victims of Crime." In *1999 National Victim Assistance Academy,* edited by Grace Coleman, Mario Gaboury, Morna Murray, and Anne Seymour. Washington, DC: Office for Justice Programs. Available, http://www.ojp.usdoj.gov/ovc/assist/nvaa99.

Omi, Michael, and Howard Winant. 1994. *Racial Formation in the United States*, 2nd ed. New York: Routledge.

Ontiveros, Maria L. 1997 (1995). "Rosa Lopez, Christopher Darden, and Me: Issues of Gender, Ethnicity, and Class in Evaluating Witness Credibility." In *Critical Race Feminism: A Reader*, edited by Adrien Katherine Wing, pp. 269–77. New York: New York University Press.

———. 1997 (1993). "Three Perspectives on Workplace Harassment of Women of Color." In *Critical Race Feminism*, edited by Adrien Katherine Wing, pp. 188–91. New York: New York University Press.

Oshinsky, David. 1996. *Worse Than Slavery: Parchman Farm and the Ordeal of Jim Crow Justice.* New York: Free Press.

Owen, Barbara. 1985. "Race and Gender Relations among Prison Workers." *Crime and Delinquency* 31(2):147–59.

Packer, Herbert. 1964. "Two Models of the Criminal Process." *University of Pennsylvania Law Review* 113:1–23.

Padilla, Laura M. 1997. "Intersectionality and Positionality: Situating Women of Color in the Affirmative Action Dialogue." *Fordham Law Review* 66:843–929.

Painter, Matthew, and Jonathan Vespa. 2008. "Race/Ethnicity, Cohabitation, and Marital Wealth Accumulation." Paper posted September. Retrieved June 10, 2009, from http://paa2009.princeton.edu/download.aspx?submissionId=91404.

Paley, Amit, and David Hilzenrath. 2008. "SEC Chief Defends His Restraint." *Washington Post* (December 24):A1.

Parenti, Christian. 1999. *Lockdown America: Police and Prisons in the Age of Crisis.* New York: Verso.

Parker, Karen, Mari DeWees, and Michael Radelet. 2003. "Race, the Death Penalty and Wrongful Convictions." *Criminal Justice* 18(1). Available, http://www.abanet.org/crimjust/spring2003/death_penalty.html.

Pasztor, Andy. 1995. *When the Pentagon Was for Sale.* New York: Scribner.

Patterson, William (ed.). 1971. *The Man Who Charged Genocide: An Autobiography.* New York: International Publishers.

———. 1970. *We Charge Genocide: The Crime of Government against the Negro People.* New York: International Publishers (reprint of 1951 edition published by Civil Rights Congress).

Pepinsky, Harold E., and Richard Quinney (eds.). 1991. *Criminology as Peacemaking.* Bloomington: Indiana University Press.

Perkins, John. 2007. *The Secret History of the American Empire: The Truth about Economic Hit Men, Jackals, and How to Change the World.* New York: Plume.

Perry, S. 2006. *Prosecutors in State Courts, 2005.* Washington, DC: Bureau of Justice Statistics (July). NCJ 213799.

Pew Hispanic Center. 2005. "Hispanics: A People in Motion." Washington, DC: Pew Hispanic Center. Available, http://pewhispanic.org.

Pfohl, Stephen J. 1985. *Images of Deviance and Social Control.* New York: McGraw-Hill.

Pinkney, Alphonso. 1984. *The Myth of Black Progress.* Cambridge: Cambridge University Press.

Pizzo, Stephen, Mark Fricker, and Paul Muolo. 1991. *Inside Job: The Looting of America's Savings & Loans.* New York: HarperPerennial.

Pizzo, Stephen, and Paul Muolo. 1993. "Take the Money and Run: A Rogues Gallery of Some Lucky S & L Thieves." *New York Times Magazine* (May 9).

Platt, Anthony. 1974. "Prospects for a Radical Criminology." *Crime and Social Justice* 1(Fall):1–14.

———. 1969. *The Child Savers: The Invention of Delinquency.* Chicago: University of Chicago Press.

Platt, Anthony, and Randi Pollock. 1974. "Channeling Lawyers: The Careers of Public Defenders." *Issues in Criminology* 9(Spring).

Platt, Anthony, and Paul Takagi (eds.). 1980. *Punishment and Penal Discipline.* San Francisco: Crime and Social Justice Associates.

Pollak, Otto. 1950. *The Criminality of Women.* Philadelphia: University of Pennsylvania Press.

Pollock-Byrne, Joycelyn. 1990. *Women, Prison, and Crime.* Pacific Grove, CA: Brooks/Cole.

Population Reference Bureau (PRB). 2009. 2009 World Population Data Sheet. Available, http://www.prb.org/Publications/Datasheets/2009/2009wpds.aspx.

Porter, Eduardo. 2005. "How Long Can Workers Tread Water?" *New York Times* (online) (July 14).

Posner, Richard. 2005. "Bad News." *New York Times Book Review* (July 21):1, 8–11.

———. 1992. *Sex and Reason.* Cambridge, MA: Harvard University Press.

Potter, Gary W., and Victor E. Kappeler (eds.). 1998. *Constructing Crime: Perspectives on Making News and Social Problems.* Prospect Height, IL: Waveland Press.

Préjean, Helen. 1995. "Dead Man Walking" (transcript of speech). Available, Radical Catholic Page, http://web.archive.org/web/20020209203423/http://www.bway .net/~halsall/radcath/prejean1.html.

———. 1993. *Dead Man Walking.* New York: Vintage.

Quinney, Richard. 1977. *Class, State and Crime.* New York: Longmans.

———. 1975. *Criminology: An Analysis and Critique of Crime in America.* Boston: Little, Brown.

Radcliffe-Brown, A. R. 1965 (1933). *Structure and Function in Primitive Society: Essays and Addresses.* New York: Free Press.

Radelet, Michael. 1989. "Executions of Whites for Crimes against Blacks." *Sociological Quarterly* 30(4):529–44.

Raeder, Myrna S. 1993. "Gender and Sentencing: Single Moms, Battered Women, and Other Sex-based Anomalies in the Gender-Free World of the Federal Sentencing Guidelines." *Pepperdine Law Review* 20:905–90.

Rafter, Nicole Hahn. 1997. *Creating Born Criminals.* Urbana: University of Illinois Press.

———. 1994. "Eugenics, Class, and the Professionalization of Social Control." In *Inequality, Crime, and Social Control,* edited by George Bridges and Martha Myers, pp. 215–26. Boulder, CO: Westview Press.

———. 1990. *Partial Justice: Women, Prisons and Social Control.* New Brunswick, NJ: Transaction Books.

Rand, Michael. 2008. "Criminal Victimization." *Bureau of Justice Statistics Bulletin.* Washington, DC: U.S. Department of Justice (December):1–11.

Rasche, Christine E. 1995 (1988). "Minority Women and Domestic Violence: The Unique Dilemmas of Battered Women of Color." In *The Criminal Justice System and Women*, edited by Barbara Raffel Price and Natalie J. Sokoloff, pp. 246–61. New York: McGraw-Hill.

Redstockings, Inc. 1978. *Feminist Revolution*. New York: Random House.

Reed, Diane F., and Edward L. Reed. 1997. "Children of Incarcerated Parents." *Social Justice* 24:152–69.

Reeve, Simon. 1999. *The New Jackals: Ramzi Yousef, Osama bin Laden, and the Future of Terrorism*. Boston: Northeastern University Press.

Reiman, Jeffrey. 1998. "Against Police Discretion: Reply to John Kleinig." *Journal of Social Philosophy* 29(1):132–42.

———. 1990. *Justice and Modern Moral Philosophy*. New Haven, CT: Yale University Press.

Reiman, Jeffrey, and Paul Leighton. 2010a. *The Rich Get Richer and the Poor Get Prison*, 9th ed. Boston: Allyn & Bacon.

———. 2010b. *The Rich Get Richer: A Reader*. Boston: Allyn & Bacon.

Renzetti, Claire M. 1998. "Connecting the Dots: Women, Public Policy, and Social Control." In *Crime Control and Women*, edited by Susan L. Miller, pp. 181–89. Thousand Oaks, CA: Sage.

Revell, Janice. 2003. "Mo' Money, Fewer problems." *Fortune* (March 31).

Rice, Marcia. 1990. "Challenging Orthodoxies in Feminist Theory: A Black Feminist Critique." In *Feminist Perspectives in Criminology*, edited by Loraine Gelsthorpe and Allison Morris, pp. 57–69. Milton Keynes: Open University Press.

Rich, Frank. 2009a. "The Banality of Bush White House Evil." *New York Times* (April 26): wk. 14.

———. 2009b. "Bernie Madoff Is No John Dillinger." *New York Times*, (July 8): wk. 8.

Richie, Beth E. 1996. *Compelled to Crime: The Gender Entrapment of Battered Black Women*. New York: Routledge.

Ridgeway, James. 1995. *Blood in the Face*. New York: Thunder's Mouth Press.

Rierden, Andi. 1997. *The Farm: Life inside a Women's Prison*. Amherst: University of Massachusetts Press.

Rifkin, Jeremy. 1995. *The End of Work*. New York: G. P. Putnam's Sons.

Rios, Victor. 2009. "The Consequences of the Criminal Justice Pipeline on Black and Latino Masculinity." *Annals of the American Academy of Political and Social Science* 623(May):150–62.

Ripley, Amanda. 2000. "Unnecessary Force?" *Time* 145(4):34–37.

Ritholtz, Barry. 2009a. *Bailout Nation*. Hoboken, NJ: John Wiley & Sons.

———. 2009b. "Tactical Error." The Big Picture Blog. Available, http://www.ritholtz.com/blog/2009/09/finance-reform-vs-health-care-reform/.

———. 2009c. "Is Consumer Protection 'Too Big to Fail'?" The Big Picture Blog. Available, http://www.ritholtz.com/blog/2009/11/is-consumer-protection-regulation-too-big-to-fail/.

———. 2008a. "CEO Clawback Provisions in the Bailout?" The Big Picture Blog. Available, http://bigpicture.typepad.com/comments/2008/09/ceo-clawback-pr.html.

———. 2008b. "What Is 'Nonfeasance'?" Available, http://seekingalpha.com/article/91465-what-is-nonfeasance.

———. 2008c. "Where's the Ref?" *Forbes* (September 12, 2008). Available, http://www.forbes.com/home/2008/09/12/lehman-greenspan-regulation-opinions-cx_br_0912ritholtz.html.

———. 2008d. "A Memo Found in the Street: Uncle Sam the Enabler." In *The Rich Get Richer and the Poor Get Prison: A Reader*, edited by Jeffrey Reiman and Paul Leighton. 2010. Boston, MA: Allyn and Bacon/Pearson.

Ritzer, George. 2004. *The McDonaldization of Society*. Thousand Oaks, CA: Pine Forge Press.

Roach, Stephen. 2006. "Globalization's New Underclass." Morgan Stanley Global Economic Forum.

Roberts, Dorothy E. 1993. "Crime, Race, and Reproduction." *Tulane Law Review* 67(6):1945–77.

Robinson, Matt. 1998. "Tobacco: The Greatest Crime in World History?" *Critical Criminologist* 8(3).

Rodriguez, Clara E. 1997. "The Silver Screen: Stories and Stereotypes." In *Latin Looks: Images of Latinas and Latinos in the U.S. Media*, pp. 73–9. Boulder, CO: Westview Press.

Rosenbaum, Marsha, and Katherine Irwin. 1998. "Pregnancy, Drugs, and Harm Reduction." In *Drug Addiction Research and the Health of Women*, edited by Cora Lee Wetherington and Adele B. Roman, pp. 309–18. Rockville, MD: National Institute on Drug Abuse.

Rosenfeld, Richard. 2002. "Why Criminologists Should Study Terrorism." *The Criminologist: The Official Newsletter of the American Society of Criminology* 27(6) (November/December).

Ross, Sherwood. 2009. "Solitary Confinement in U.S. Prisons Making Thousands Psychotic." *Opednews.com*. (March 24):1–2. Retrieved June 20, 2009, from http://www.opednews.com/articles/Solitary-Confinement-In-U-by-Sherwood Ross-090324-708.html.

Rubenstein, R. L. 1987. "Afterword: Genocide and Civilization." In *Genocide and the Modern Age: Etiology and Case Studies of Mass Death*, edited by Isidor Wallimann and Michael Dobkowski. New York: Greenwood Press.

Rusche, Georg, and Otto Kirchheimer. 1968 (1939). *Punishment and Social Structure*. New York: Russell and Russell.

Russell, Katheryn K. 1998. *The Color of Crime: Racial Hoaxes, White Fear, Black Protectionism, Police Harrassment, and Other Macroaggressions*. New York: New York University Press.

Samborn, Hope Viner. 1999. "Profiled and Pulled Over." *ABA Journal* 85:18.

Sample, Albert. 1984. *Racehoss: Big Emma's Boy*. New York: Ballantine.

SAMHSA (Substance Abuse and Mental Health Administration). 2004. Results from the 2004 National Survey on Drug Use and Health: Detailed Tables. Available, http://www.oas.samhsa.gov.

Sampson, Robert, and W. J. Wilson. 1995. "Toward a Theory of Race, Crime, and Urban Inequality." In *Crime and Inequality*, edited by J. Hagan and R. Peterson, pp. 37–54. Stanford, CA: Stanford University Press.

Satter, Robert. 1990. *Doing Justice: A Trial Judge at Work*. New York: Simon and Schuster.

Schell, Jonathan. 2009. "Torture and Truth." *Nation* (June 15):15–18.

Schemo, Diana Jean. 2000. "Despite Options on Census, Many to Check 'Black' Only." *New York Times* (February 12):A1.

Schlabach, Mark. 2005. "From a Stool, Tyson Ends It." *Washington Post* (June 12).

Schlosser, Eric. 1998. "The Prison-Industrial Complex." *Atlantic.* December. Available, http://www.theatlantic.com/doc/199812/prisons.

Schmitt, Richard. 2008. "FBI Saw Threat of Loan Crisis." *Los Angeles Times* (August 25, 2008):A1.

Schwartz, Martin D., and Dragan Milovanovic (eds.). 1996. *Race, Gender, and Class in Criminology: The Intersections.* New York: Garland.

Schwendinger, Herman, and Julia Schwendinger. 1970. "Defenders of Order or Guardians of Human Rights?" *Issues in Criminology* 5:123–57.

Scott, Janny, and David Leonhardt. 2005. "Class in America: Shadowy Lines That Still Divide." *New York Times* (May 15).

Scully, Diana. 1990. *Understanding Sexual Violence: A Study of Convicted Rapists.* London: HarperCollins Academic.

Seagal, Debra. 2001. "Tales from the Cutting Room Floor." In *Criminal Justice Ethics,* edited by Paul Leighton and Jeffrey Reiman. Upper Saddle River, NJ: Prentice-Hall.

Sellers, Patricia. 2003. "Power: Do Women Really Want It?" *Fortune* (October 13).

Sellin, Thorsten. 1976. *Slavery and the Penal System.* New York: Elsevier.

———. 1928. "The Negro Criminal: A Statistical Note." *Annals of the American Academy of Political and Social Science* 140:52–64.

Selman, Donna, and Paul Leighton. 2010. *Punishment for Sale.* Lanham, MD: Rowman and Littlefield.

Selman-Killingbeck, Donna. 2005. "A Sociological History of Prison Privatization in the Contemporary United States." Doctoral Dissertation. Kalamazoo: Western Michigan University.

The Sentencing Project. 1994. "Why '3 Strikes and You're Out' Won't Reduce Crime." Washington, D.C.

Shaw, Clifford R., and Henry D. McKay. 1942. *Juvenile Delinquency and Urban Areas: A Study of Rates of Delinquents in Relation to Differential Characteristics of Local Communities in American Cities.* Chicago: University of Chicago Press.

Shelden, Randall. 2000. *Controlling the Dangerous Classes: A Critical Introduction to the History of Criminal Justice.* Boston, MA: Allyn & Bacon.

———. 1999. "The Prison Industrial Complex and the New American Apartheid." *Critical Criminologist* (10)1:1, 3–5.

Sheptycki, James, and Ali Wardak (eds.). 2005. *Transnational and Comparative Criminology.* Oxford: GlassHouse Press.

Shine, Cathy, and Marc Mauer. 1993. "Does the Punishment Fit the Crime? Drug Users and Drunk Drivers, Questions of Race and Class." Washington, DC: Sentencing Project.

Siegel, Steven. 2009. "The Public Interest and Private Gated Communities." Available, http://works.bepress.com/steven_siegel/1.

Simon, David. 1999. *Elite Deviance,* 6th ed. Boston, MA: Allyn & Bacon.

Simon, Jonathan, Ian Haney López, and Mary Louise Frampton. 2008. Introduction to *After the War on Crime: Race, Democracy, and a New Reconstruction,* edited by M.

L. Frampton, I. H. López, and J. Simon, pp. 1–20. New York: New York University Press.

Skolnick, Jerome. 1996 (1967). *Justice without Trial: Law Enforcement in a Democratic Society.* New York: Wiley.

Smith, Dorothy. 1990. *The Conceptual Practices of Power.* Boston, MA: Northeastern University Press.

Smothers, Ronald. 1995. "Wave of Prison Uprisings Provokes Debate on Crack." *New York Times* (October 24):A12.

Solis, Carmen, Edwardo Portillos, and Rod Brunson. 2009. "Youth Violence—Crime or Self-Help? Marginalized Urban Males' Perspectives on the Limited Efficacy of the Criminal Justice System to Stop Youth Violence." In *After the War on Crime: Race, Democracy, and a New Reconstruction,* edited by M. L. Frampton, I. H. López, and J. Simon, pp. 39–51. New York: New York University Press.

Spohn, Cassia. 1990. "Decision Making in Sexual Assault Cases: Do Black and Female Judges Make a Difference?" *Women and Criminal Justice* 2(1):83–105.

Spohn, Cassia, and David Holleran. 2000. "The Imprisonment Penalty Paid by Young Unemployed Black and Hispanic Male Offenders." *Criminology* 38(1):281–306.

Stark, Rodney. 1987. "Deviant Places: A Theory of the Ecology of Crime." *Criminology* 25:893–11.

Starkman, Dean. 2009. "The Most Important Financial Journalist of Her Generation: Gretchen Morgenson of the *New York Times*." *Nation* (July 6):11–18.

Starr, Douglas. 1998. *Blood: An Epic History of Medicine and Commerce.* New York: Quill (HarperCollins).

Staub, Ervin. 1989. *The Roots of Evil: The Origins of Genocide and Other Group Violence.* New York: Cambridge University Press.

Steffensmeier, Darrell. 1995. "Trends in Female Crime: It's Still a Man's World." In *The Criminal Justice System and Women,* 2nd ed., edited by Barbara Raffel Price and Natalie J. Sokoloff, pp. 89–104. New York: McGraw-Hill.

Stephenson, Neal. 1992. *Snow Crash.* New York: Bantam Books.

Stiglitz, Joseph E. 2009. "A Real Cure for the Global Economic Crackup." *Nation* (July 13):11–14.

Stoddard, Ellwyn. 1968. "The Informal 'Code' of Police Deviancy: A Group Approach to Blue-Coat Crime." *Journal of Criminal Law, Criminology, and Police Science* 59:191–12.

Stolzenberg, Lisa, David Eitle, and Steward D'Alessio. 2006. "Race, Economic Inequality, and Violent Crime." *Journal of Criminal Justice* 34(3):303–16.

Strauss, David. 2007. "Militarization of Policing." In *Battlefield: Criminal Justice,* a two-volume encyclopedia edited by G. Barak, pp. 254–59. Westport, CT: Greenwood Press.

Sum, Andrew, and Tess Forsell. 2009. "Wealth in America." Center for Labor Studies, Northeastern University. Available, http://www.clms.neu.edu/publication/documents/Wealth_in_America.pdf.

Summers, Lawrence. 2005a. "Remarks at NBER Conference on Diversifying the Science & Engineering Workforce." Available, http://www.president.harvard.edu/speeches/summers_2005/nber.php.

———. 2005b. "Letter from President Summers on Women and Science." Available, http://wiseli.engr.wisc.edu/archives/summers.php.

Sumter, Melvina. 2008. "The Correctional Work Force Faces Challenges in the 21st Century." Research Notes. *Corrections Today.*

Swift, Pat. 1997. "At the Intersection of Racial Politics and Domestic Abuse." *Buffalo News* (December 27):B7.

Sykes, Bryan, and Alex Piquero. 2009. "Structuring and Re-Creating Inequality: Health Testing Policies, Race, and the Criminal Justice System." *Annals of the American Academy of Political and Social Science* 623(May):214–29.

Sykes, Gresham. 1958. *The Society of Captives: A Study of a Maximum Security Prison.* Princeton, NJ: Princeton University Press.

Tafoya, Sonya. 2004. *Shades of Belonging.* Washington, DC: Pew Hispanic Center. Available, http://pewhispanic.org.

Taibbi, Matt. 2009. "Inside the Great American Bubble Machine." *Rolling Stone* Issue 1082–83. Posted July 2, 2009, and retrieved July 7, 2009, from http://www.rolling stone.com/politics/story/28816321/the_great_american_bubble_machine.

Talvi, Silja. 2004. "Could You Repeat the Question, Please?" Available, http://www.alternet.org/story/20101.

Tatum, B. 1996. "The Colonial Model as a Theoretical Explanation of Crime and Delinquency." In *African-American Perspectives on Crime Causation, Criminal Justice Administration, and Crime Prevention,* edited A. Sutton. Boston: Butterworth-Heinemann.

This American Life. 2008. Giant Pool of Money (April 9, program 355). Available, http://www.thisamericanlife.org/radio-archives/episode/355/The-Giant-Pool-of-Money

Tjaden, Patricia, and Nancy Thoennes. 1998. *Stalking in America: Findings from the National Violence against Women Survey.* Washington, DC: U.S. Department of Justice.

Tobias, Carl. 2009. "Diversifying California's Federal District Courts." Findlaw.com. Available, http://writ.news.findlaw.com/commentary/20090903_tobias.html.

Toch, Hans. 1990. "The Shape of Police Violence." In *Violence: Patterns, Causes, and Public Policy,* edited by N. A. Weiner, M. A. Zahn, and R. J. Sagi. New York: Harcourt Brace College.

Tolnay, S. E., and E. M. Beck. 1995. *A Festival of Violence: An Analysis of Southern Lynchings, 1882–1930.* Urbana: University of Illinois Press.

Tong, Rosemarie. 1989. *Feminist Thought: A More Comprehensive Introduction.* Boulder, CO: Westview Press.

Tonry, Michael. 1995. *Malign Neglect: Race, Crime, and Punishment in America.* New York: Oxford University Press.

Toth, Jennifer. 1995. *The Mole People: Life in the Tunnels beneath New York City.* Chicago: Chicago Review Press.

Totten, Mark D. 2000. *Guys, Gangs, and Girlfriend Abuse.* Petersborough, ON: Broadview Press.

Travis, Jeremy. 2005. *But They All Come Back.* Washington, DC: Urban Institute Press.

———. 2002. "Invisible Punishment: An Instrument of Social Exclusion." In *Invisible Punishment: The Collateral Consequences of Mass Imprisonment*, edited by Meda Chesney-Lind and Marc Mauer. New York: New Press.

———. 1999. *NIJ Request for Proposals for Comparative, Cross-National Crime Research Challenge Grants*. U.S. Department of Justice, National Institute of Justice, April.

Tucker, Donald. 1981. *A Punk's Song: View from the Inside*. Available, www.spr .org/.

Uscourts.gov. 2009. Summary of Judicial Vacancies. Available, http://www.uscourts .gov/judicialvac.cfm.

U.S. Department of Health and Human Services. 2004. Women's Health USA 2004. Available, http://mchb.hrsa.gov/whusa04/index.htm.

U.S. Department of Justice. 2009. *United States Attorneys' Annual Statistical Report: Fiscal Year 2008*, pp. 7, 42. Executive Office for the United States Attorneys.

———. 1994. "An Analysis of Non-Violent Drug Offenders with Minimal Criminal Histories." February 4.

U.S. Sentencing Commission. 1999. *Sourcebook of Federal Sentencing Statistics*. Washington, DC: U.S. Sentencing Commission.

———. 1992. *Sentencing Commission Guidelines Manual*. Washington, DC: U.S. Sentencing Commission.

———. 1991. *Mandatory Minimum Penalties in the Federal Criminal Justice System* (August). Washington, D.C.

Van Ness, Daniel, and Karen Heetderks Strong. 1997. *Restoring Justice*. Cincinnati, OH: Anderson Publishing.

Van Riper, Tom. 2009. "The Highest-Paid Coaches." *Forbes* (May 14). Available, http://www.forbes.com/2009/05/13/highest-paid-coaches-business-sports-nba .html?partner=contextstory.

Veblen, Thorstein. 1969 (1919). *The Vested Interests and the Common Man*. New York: Capricorn Books.

Visano, Livy A. 1998. *Crime and Culture: Refining the Traditions*. Toronto: Canadian Scholars' Press.

Vold, George, and Thomas Bernard. 1986. *Theoretical Criminology*, 3rd ed. New York: Oxford University Press.

von Zielbauer, Paul. 2005. "As Health Care in Jails Goes Private, 10 Days Can Be a Death Sentence." *New York Times* (February 27):A1, A26.

Walker, Samuel. 1992. "Origins of the Contemporary Criminal Justice Paradigm: The American Bar Foundation Survey, 1953–1969." *Justice Quarterly* (9)1.

———. 1980. *Popular Justice: A History of American Criminal Justice*. New York: Oxford University Press.

Walker, Samuel, Cassia Spohn, and Miriam DeLone. 1995. *The Color of Justice*. Belmont, CA: Wadsworth Publishing.

Warren, Jennifer. 2005. "Rethinking Treatment of Female Prisoners." *Los Angeles Times* (Sunday, June 19):A1.

Warren, Patricia, and Amy Farrell. 2009. "The Environmental Context of Racial Profiling." *Annals of the American Academy of Political and Social Science* 623 (May):7–10.

Warrick, Joby. 2006. "Safety Violations Have Piled Up at Coal Mine." *Washington Post* (January 6):A04.

Washington Post (staff writer). 2002. "Are CEOs Worth Their Salaries?" (October 2).

Weeks, Robin, and Cathy Spatz Widom. 1998. *Early Childhood Victimization among Incarcerated Adult Male Felons.* Washington, DC: U.S. Department of Justice.

Weinberg, Steve. 2008. "Innocent Until Reported Guilty." *Miller-McCune* 1(5):54–63.

Weinstein, Henry, and David Rosenzweig. 2005. "Sentence Ruling Not Clear." *Ann Arbor News* (January 13):1, 12.

Weiss, Eric. 2006. "At U.S. Urging, Court Throws Lamberth off Indian Case." *Washington Post* (July 12):A13.

Weitzman, Susan. 2000. *Not to People Like Us: Hidden Abuse in Upscale Marriages.* New York: Basic Books.

Welch, Michael. 2000. *Punishment in America.* Thousand Oaks, CA: Sage.

———. 1999. *Punishment in America: Social Control and the Ironies of Imprisonment.* Thousand Oaks, CA: Sage.

———. 1996a. *Corrections: A Critical Approach.* New York: McGraw-Hill.

———. 1996b. "The Immigration Crisis: Detention as an Emerging Mechanism of Social Control." *Social Justice* 23(3):169–84.

West, Candace, and Don H. Zimmerman. 1987. "Doing Gender." *Gender & Society* 1:125–51.

West, Cornel. 1990. "Michael Harrington, Socialist." *Nation* (January):8–15.

Weyler, Rex. 1992. *Blood of the Land: The Government and Corporate War against First Nations.* Philadelphia: New Society Publishers.

White, Jack. 1990. "Genocide Mumbo Jumbo." *Time* (January 22):20.

White, Nicole. 1999. "NYPD White." *Village Voice* 44(10):23.

White, Rob. 1998. "Social Justice, Community Building and Restorative Strategies." Paper presented at the International Conference on Restorative Justice for Juveniles, Fort Lauderdale.

Whiteside, John. 2006. "BP, Texas City, and the Nature of the Corporation." *Houston Chronicle Blog* (October 31). Available, http://blogs.chron.com/blue bayou/2006/10/bp_texas_city_and_the_nature_o_1.html.

Whitty, Stephen. 2005. "Racism, Raw, and Modern: Film Review of *Crash.*" *Ann Arbor News* (May 6):E1–2.

Wightman, Linda F. 1997. "The Threat to Diversity in Legal Education: An Empirical Analysis of the Consequences of Abandoning Race as a Factor in Law School Admission Decisions." *New York University Law Review* 72:50–51.

Wildman, Stephanie M. 1997 (1996). "Reflections on Whiteness: The Case of Latinos(as)." In *Critical White Studies: Looking behind the Mirror*, edited by Richard Delgado and Jean Stefancic, pp. 323–26. Philadelphia: Temple University Press.

Wildman, Stephanie M., and Adrienne D. Davis. 1997. "Making Systems of Privilege Visible." In *Critical White Studies: Looking behind the Mirror*, edited by Richard Delgado and Jean Stefancic, pp. 314–19. Philadelphia: Temple University Press.

Wilkinson, Deanna, Chauncey Beaty, and Regina Lurry. 2009. "Latino Youths' Experiences with Perceptions of Involuntary Police Encounters." In *After the War on Crime: Race, Democracy, and a New Reconstruction*, edited by M. L. Frampton, I. H. López, and J. Simon, pp. 25–38. New York: New York University Press.

Willhelm, Sidney. 1970. *Who Needs the Negro?* Cambridge: Schenkman Publishing.

Williams, Chancellor. 1987. *The Destruction of Black Civilization.* Chicago: Third World Press.

Williams, Wendy W. 1991 (1982). "The Equality Crisis: Some Reflections on Culture, Courts, and Feminism." In *Feminist Legal Theory*, edited by Katharine T. Bartlett and Rosanne Kennedy, pp. 15–34. Boulder, CO: Westview Press.

Wilson, James Q. 1972. *Varieties of Police Behavior: The Management of Law and Order in Eight Communities.* New York: Atheneum.

Wilson, William. J. 1996. *When Work Disappears: The World of the New Urban Poor.* New York: Knopf.

———. 1987. *The Truly Disadvantaged: The Inner City, the Underclass, and Public Policy.* Chicago: Chicago University Press.

Winerip, Michael. 2000. "Why Harlem Drug Cops Don't Discuss Race." *New York Times* (July 9):A1.

Wing, Adrien Katherine (ed.). 1997. *Critical Race Feminism: A Reader.* New York: New York University Press.

Winslow, George. 1999. *Capital Crimes.* New York: Monthly Review Press.

Withrow, Brian. 2006. *Racial Profiling: From Rhetoric to Reason.* Upper Saddle River, NJ: Prentice-Hall.

Wolfgang, Marvin, and Bernard Cohen. 1970. *Crime and Race: Conceptions and Misconceptions.* New York: Institute of Human Relations Press.

Wonders, Nancy. 1999. "Postmodern Feminist Criminology and Social Justice." In *Social Justice/Criminal Justice*, edited by Bruce A. Arrigo. Belmont, CA: West/Wadsworth.

Wooldredge, John. 2009. "Short- versus Long-term Effects of Ohio's Switch to More Structured Sentencing on Extralegal Disparities in Prison Sentences in an Urban Court." *Criminology & Public Policy* 8(2) (May):285–13.

World Health Organization. 2005. Gender and Reproductive Rights. Available, http://www.who.int/reproductive-health/gender/.

Wray, Matt, and Annalee Newitz (eds.). 1996. *White Trash Studies: Race and Class in America.* New York: Routledge.

Young, Vernetta D. 1986. "Gender Expectations and Their Impact on Black Female Offenders and Their Victims." *Justice Quarterly* 3:305–27.

Zehr, Howard, and Harry Mika. 1998. "Fundamental Concepts of Restorative Justice." *Contemporary Justice Review* 1(1):47–55.

CASES

Brown v. Topeka, Kansas, Board of Education 1954

Lockyer v. Andrade 538 U.S. 63

Loving v. Virginia 388 U.S. 1

Plessy v. Ferguson 163 U.S. 537 [1896]

R.A.V. v. St. Paul 507 U.S. 377 [1992]

Roe v. Wade

Roper v. Simmons 543 U.S. 551 [2005]

Rummel v. Estelle 445 U.S. 263 [1980]
State v. Mitchell 485 NW2d 807
Terry v. Ohio 392 U.S. 1, 1968
U.S. v. Booker 125 S. Ct. 738
United States v. Brandt 907 F2d 31 [1990]
U.S. v. Fanfan 125 S. Ct. 738
United States v. City of Chicago
University of California v. Bakke 438 U.S. 265 [1978]
Virginia v. Black 538 U.S. 343 [2003]
Whitney v. California 274 U.S. 357 [1927]
Whren v. U.S. (1996)
Wisconsin v. Mitchell 508 U.S. 476 [1993]
Yick Wo v. Hopkins 118 U.S. 356 [1886]

Name Index

Subject Index

About the Authors

Gregg Barak is professor of criminology and criminal justice at Eastern Michigan University and the former visiting distinguished professor in the College of Justice & Safety at Eastern Kentucky University. In 2003 he became the twenty-seventh Fellow of the Academy of Criminal Justice Sciences and in 2007, received the Lifetime Achievement Award from the Critical Division of the American Society of Criminology. Barak is author and/or editor of sixteen books on crime, justice, media, violence, criminal law, homelessness, human rights, and related topics. His latest books are *Criminology: An Integrated Approach* (2009) and *Violence, Conflict, and World Order* (2007). He is also the series editor for Issues in Crime & Justice published by both Rowman & Littlefield and Lexington Books.

Paul Leighton is a professor of criminology and criminal justice at Eastern Michigan University. He is the coauthor (with Jeffrey Reiman) of *The Rich Get Richer and the Poor Get Prison*, 9th ed. His most recent book, with Donna Selman, is *Punishment for Sale: Private Prisons, Big Business and the Incarceration Binge*. Leighton is webmaster for StopViolence.com, PaulsJusticePage.com and PaulsJusticeBlog.com. He is vice president of the Board of SafeHouse, the local shelter and advocacy center for victims of domestic violence and sexual assault.

Jeanne Flavin is an associate professor of sociology at Fordham University. Her papers have appeared in *Gender & Society*, *Justice Quarterly*, and the *Fordham University Urban Law Journal*. She coedited (with Mary Bosworth)

Race, Gender, and Punishment: From Colonialism to the War on Terror. She has just published *Our Bodies, Our Crimes* on the criminalization of women's reproduction. She proudly serves on the board of National Advocates for Pregnant Women and received a Fulbright Award for research at the University of Cape Town, South Africa.

Breinigsville, PA USA
27 July 2010
242574BV00003B/2/P